STEPHEN KING
DOLLAR BABY:
THE BOOK

STEPHEN KING
DOLLAR BABY:
THE BOOK

Anthony Northrup

with an introduction by Stephen Spignesi

BearManor Media

2021

Stephen King Dollar Baby: The Book

© 2021 by Anthony Northrup

All rights reserved.

No portion of this publication may be reproduced, stored, and/or copied electronically (except for academic use as a source), nor transmitted in any form or by any means without the prior written permission of the publisher and/or author.

Published in the United States of America by:

BearManor Media
1317 Edgewater Dr #110
Orlando FL 32804

bearmanormedia.com

Printed in the United States.

All photos used with permission.

Cover by Paul Michael Kane

ISBN—978-1-62933-668-8

This book is dedicated to my wife, Gena who has been my strength, my companion, my supporter, and my best friend.

Love you to the moon and back.

Table of Contents

Introduction: Stephen King Modern Day Medici 1
    by Stephen Spignesi

Foreword: Dollar Baby Dreamers 9
    by Richard Chizmar

Author's Note 11
    by Anthony Northrup

PART ONE

Crypticon Horror Con MN Memories 19
    by Anthony Northrup

Crypticon Horror Con MN Stephen King Dollar
Baby Film Fest: Fans Respond 29

"…That's What The Fans Said…" 31

A Dollar Well Spent 32
    by Billy Hanson

Thoughts On Stephen King Adaptations 35
    by Lee Gambin

My Secret Dollar Baby 36
    by Robin Furth

Stephen King Memories 41
    by Amber Pace

A King's Treasure 44
    by Paul Michael Kane

King And Kissing Books – How Stephen King's
Work Influenced A Romance Author 46
    by Brooklyn Ann

Stephen King Memories 49
    by Tina Rooker

Women In the Dollar Baby World 51
    by Nicole Jones-Dion

The Role Of The Short Film In a Filmmaker's Career 54
    by Jay Holben

Location, Location, Location!: How a Trio of
Historic Sites Made *The Doctor's Case* 58
    by James Douglas

Otto, Brian, and Me: Fond Memories of a Deep
Dive Into Madness During the Filming of *Uncle
Otto's Truck* 66
    by Peter Holland

Dollar Baby Memories 68
    by Tonya Ivey

How I Became A Fan Of Stephen King 69
    by Oscar Garrido

Here There Be Tygers: My Story 71
    by Bryan Higby

The Curse Of Stephen King's 'Sometimes They
Come Back' 76
    by Tom Mcloughlin

The Long Maybe Of Dollar Babies 81
    by Kevin Quigley

I'm Gonna Scare the Hell Out of You…
And That's a Promise! 86
    by David Tocher

"Blood In the Veins": The Spiritual Collaborations
of Stephen King and Frank Darabont................................90
    by Andrew J. Rausch

The Good and Bad of Film Adaptation 98
    by James Cole

A Conversation With Director Mick Garris 103
    by Anthony Northrup

My Journey With My Husband, T. Anthony
Northrup and the Writing of *Stephen King Dollar
Baby: The Book* 109
    by Gena Lawson-Northrup

"…That's What The Fans Said…" – Part Two 111

Dollar Baby Thoughts About Stephen King and
the Dollar Baby Program..114

"Just The Facts Ma'am!" 117

Part Two

Author's Note 121

Survivor Type – Billy Hanson..122

Grey Matter – James B. Cox..127

The Reaper's Image – Dean Werner...................................132

Beachworld – Maria Ivanova 137

Umney's Last Case – Rodney Altman................................141

In the Deathroom – Damon Vinyard 145

Paranoid: A Chant – Jay Holben 151

Cain Rose Up – Ranjeet S. Marwa 157

The Last Rung On the Ladder – James Cole 161

The Things They Left Behind – Pablo Macho
    Maysonet IV 169

Luckey Quarter – Robert Cochrane 175

Strawberry Spring – Doveed Linder 181

The Boogeyman – Jeff Schiro 186

All That You Love Will Be Carried Away –
    James Renner 191

Everything's Eventual – J.P. Scott 195

Night Surf – Tony Pomfret 209

Rest Stop – Patrick Abernethy 215

The Man Who Loved Flowers – Drew Newman 219

The Man Who Loved Flowers – Justin Zimmerman 225

Suffer the Little Children – Corey Norman 231

Everything's Eventual – Max Heesch 238

Maxwell Edison – Warren Ray 243

I Know What You Need – Shawn S. Lealos 250

Love Never Dies – Peter Szabo 265

One For the Road – Jacob Sanders 270

The Road Virus Heads North – Dave Brock 276

Rainy Season – Vanessa Ionta Wright 285

I Am the Doorway – Joe Kowalski 299

The Doctor's Case – James Douglas	305
Dedication – Selina Sondermann	323
Beachworld – Jackie Perez	331
A Very Tight Place – Stephen Tramontana	338
Here There Be Tygers – Brian Higby	347
Here There Be Tygers – Jennifer Trudrung	357
Cain Rose Up – A.J. Gribble	363
Popsy – Jon Mann	369
Uncle Otto's Truck – Dan Sellers	377
All That You Love Will Be Carried Away – Hendrik Harms	385
In the Deathroom – Nicole Jones-Dion	391
Rest Stop – Mark Zimmerman	399
Graduation Afternoon – Marie D. Jones	404
The Man Who Loved Flowers – Mark Hensley	412
The Jaunt – Nick Smith	419
My Pretty Pony – Maciej Barczewski	431
The Boogeyman – Mando Franco	439
The Lawnmower Man – James Gonis	446
Uncle Otto's Truck – Brian Johnson	455
Mute – Rob Darren Newberger	461
Gray Matter – Red Clark	465
Sneakers – Gino Alfonso	477
The Boogeyman – Jenny Januszewski	482

One For the Road – Joseph Horning 489

Morning Deliveries – Will Roberts 503

Rainy Season – Patrick Haischberger 511

That Feeling, You Can Only Say What It Is In French –
    Nathan Gathergood 515

The Woman In The Room: The First Dollar
    Baby…Or Is It? 521

PART THREE

"The Dollar Babies Have Left the Building!" 527

Where Are They Now? 529

Places Dollar Babies Filmed 549

Dollar Baby Films Available To Film 550

"Cut! That's a Wrap!": Dollar Babies Final
    Thoughts On The Dollar Baby Program and
    Stephen King 551

"Cut! That's A Wrap!" – Part Two: My Final Thoughts
    On the Dollar Babies and Stephen King 554

Dollar Baby Treasures 556

Acknowledgements 557

Special Dedications 561

'You can, you should, and if you're brave enough to start, you will.'

– Stephen King

'It is a testament to what one can accomplish with sheer determination.'

– James Cole, *Castle Rock Newsletter* September 1988 issue

"We are the music makers, and we are the dreamers of dreams."

– Willy Wonka

Introduction

Stephen King, Modern Day Medici

A Look at King's Groundbreaking Dollar Baby Student Film Program

Stephen Spignesi

Over the objections of my accountant... I established a policy which still holds today. I will grant any student filmmaker the right to make a movie out of any short story I have written (not the novels, that would be ridiculous), so long as the film rights are still mine to assign. I ask them to sign a paper promising that no resulting film will be exhibited commercially without approval, and that they send me a videotape of the finished work. For this one-time right I ask a dollar.

- – Stephen King

Stephen King is a Medici

One of the greatest TV shows of all time is *The West Wing*. I have often said that every incoming President, regardless of party, should be sent a complete set of all the seasons of the show and not allowed to be sworn in until he or she has watched them all.

Whether or not Stephen King is a *West Wing* fan, he espouses many of the principles and ideas put forth by the characters in the show. One particular quote came to mind while considering King's creation and support of the Dollar Baby Film program.

In the Season 3, Episode 5 episode "Gone Quiet," President Bartlet's Communications Director Toby Ziegler has a contentious debate with a venal

Republican named Tawny Cryer, the head of the Appropriations Committee. She wants to cut $105 million from the National Endowment for the Arts. She asserts that the government shouldn't support the arts. Toby makes the point that European countries and Japan are spending between $1.5 and $3 billion dollars annually in support of the arts, but Tawny doesn't care.

Toby then tells her the following:

There is a connection between progress of a society and progress in the arts. The age of Pericles was also the age of Phidias. The age of Lorenzo de Medici was also the age of Leonardo da Vinci. The age of Elizabeth was the age of Shakespeare.

It turns out that Tawny was just leveraging the NEA budget to persuade Toby to get rid of the NEA's current director, but Toby's point is 100 percent correct: advancement in society parallels increasingly brilliant and sophisticated advancement in the arts. Thus, a government that supports the arts is supporting the citizens in that society. (During the 2020 COVID-19 pandemic that shut down the world, memes began appearing on Facebook reminding people that books, TV shows, movies, music, virtual tours of museums, streamed Broadway musicals, online concerts, virtual book discussions, and so forth—in other words, the arts—were what got people through the isolation of quarantining. That, too, is 100 percent correct.)

I tell you the *West Wing* story to tell you this: Stephen King is a Medici.

And no, that does not mean he's of Italian heritage like me. (My 23andMe DNA profile says I'm 96.3% Italian, which left me wondering how 3.7% Balkan got in there.) It means King's creation and support of the Dollar Baby program is similar to what the Medicis did in Florence during the Renaissance. The Medicis were patrons and supporters of the arts, and Stephen King is, thus, very Medici-esque.

The Medicis supported all the biggies, the artists who are now household names—Michelangelo, Da Vinci, Raphael—but they also supported scientists, most notably Galileo. It's hard to imagine what the historical artistic and scientific (and modern, for that matter) landscapes would look like without the patronage of the Medicis.

For those coming to this book unaware of what the Dollar Baby program is, here's the recap: For the grand sum of one dollar (and, yes, he does cash the checks), Stephen King will sign a contract with a student filmmaker allowing them to make a short film based on one of his short stories.

Just like a Medici would do.

It's the Other Way Around

Stephen King believes in art.

In *On Writing*, he said, "Life isn't a support system for art. It's the other way around."

Stephen King's Dollar Baby program is unique in the world of the arts.

The most popular writer in the world "sells" adaptation rights to his short stories to student filmmakers, with no hope of profit, of course, and no guarantee the resultant short films will be any good.

On the other hand, when King licenses an adaptation of one of his novels, he is deliberate in assessing and approving the screenwriter, the director and, in some cases, the cast.

Not so with Dollar Babies.

And aside from the buck, all he asks is that the filmmaker send him a copy of the completed short film so he can see what they've done.

His writings, comments, and deeds over the years speak to a dedication to not just the written word, but also to cinematic art, music, and other manifestations and interpretations of the human condition.

There's a quote by the painter Edward Hopper—a favorite artist of King's— that speaks to the communication between the artist and their consciousness and sensibility: "If I could say it in words there would be no reason to paint." This can be interpreted within the context of Stephen King's open championing of student filmmakers. King *can* say it in words. His novels and stories are replete with the characters, images, dialogue, scenarios, concepts, dreams, and nightmares that bespeak the human condition. Yet, he allows fellow artists—the passionate Dollar Baby filmmakers—to take his stories to a different place, to visualize them, to interpret them.

And the only result of this beneficence? More art.

It is, indeed, the other way around.

The First Dollar Baby I Ever Saw

The first Dollar Baby I ever saw was James Cole's 1987 short, *The Last Rung on the Ladder*, based on the Stephen King *Night Shift* short story of the same name.

I was working on *The Complete Stephen King Encyclopedia* (which frankly, since it's now thirty years out of date, is no longer "complete," but, as Tony Soprano might say, "Whadda ya gonna do?"), and Jim had heard I was interviewing "Stephen King-adjacent" (so to speak) writers, directors, filmmakers, and other folk of the SK ilk for the book. He wrote me a letter telling me about *Last Rung* and we ended up doing a whole section in the *Encyclopedia* about it. "Last Rung" is one of King's most poignant, heartbreaking stories. Jim Cole's adaptation is sensitive and, considering it was created in the pre-digital age (y'know, eons ago, in the Eighties), it is remarkably well done. The young actors are terrific, and Jim's script does the story justice.

As my first, it continues to be one of my favorite Dollar Baby adaptations of the ones I've seen.

Jim continues to write, and in 2003, wrote the award-winning short film *The Night Before*, which was directed by the Dollar Baby film *Paranoid* director Jay Holben.

The second Dollar Baby I saw (which was made before Jim's but I didn't see it until after *Last Rung*) was Frank Darabont's 1983 directorial debut, *The Woman in the Room,* adapted from the *Night Shift* story of the same name. It also remains a favorite and is one of King's more personal stories, based on his own experiences living through his mother's death. From the future screenwriter and director of fan favorites *The Shawshank Redemption* and *The Green Mile*, *The Woman in the Room* is an early look at Darabont's gift for adapting Stephen King's work.

The Most Adapted Stories

21 Dollar Babies
- "The Man Who Loved Flowers" (from *Night Shift*)
- *Who doesn't love getting flowers? Heh, heh, heh.*

19 Dollar Babies
- "Mute" (from *Just After Sunset*)
- *Deaf people can't hear, right? Right?!*

18 Dollar Babies
- "Rest Stop" (from *Just After Sunset*)
- *We all have a dark half, right? Sometimes, one can come in handy.*

17 Dollar Babies
- "All That You Love Will Be Carried Away" (from *Everything's Eventual*)
- *Leaving your fate in the hands of fate? Maybe not such a good idea?*

There's one particular *All That You Love Will Be Carried Away* Dollar Baby I'd like to single out. It's the 2004 film written and directed by my friend James Renner. Why this one? Because of the cast. Usually, Dollar Babies feature actors and actresses who the director knows, and many are not officially in this business of show (to quote Dr. Tobias Fünke.) However, Jim Renner managed to get two fairly high-profile personalities for his film: Comics writer Harvey Pekar (*American Splendor, Our Cancer Year*) and actor, comic, and writer Joe Bob Briggs (real name John Bloom, *Casino, Face/Off, Joe Bob Briggs Drive-In Theater*).

The late great Harvey Pekar played the motel clerk from whom Joe Bob Briggs rents a room. Briggs plays the star of the story, Alfie Zimmer, the traveling food salesman and narrator whose fate is a question mark throughout the story. "All That You Love Will Be Carried Away" was one of the stories I taught in my Stephen King class and I also showed Jim Renner's film. He kindly wrote something to share with my students about the adaptation of the story to film, and to this day, I owe him special thanks for his kindness and generosity.

16 Dollar Babies
- "In the Deathroom" (from *Everything's Eventual*)
- *Sometimes epilepsy can come in handy...*
- "One for the Road" (from *Night Shift*)
- *That was some fire a couple of years ago in the 'Lot, wasn't it?*

15 Dollar Babies
- "Harvey's Dream" (from *Just After Sunset*)
- *Dreams don't come true...or do they?*

14 Dollar Babies

The terrific website stephenkingshortmovies.com keeps track of the Dollar Babies. According to a recent count, there are currently 343 official Dollar Baby films. These are the top ten most adapted stories as of April 2020:

- "I Am the Doorway" (from *Night Shift*)
- *Watch where you put that hand, okay?*

12 Dollar Babies
- "Gray Matter" (from *Skeleton Crew*)
- *Seems even beer can "go bad," so to speak. Who knew?*

10 Dollar Babies
- "Cain Rose Up" (from *Skeleton Crew*)
- *Peculiar students are everywhere in college…but once in a while…*

These short stories are really good—chilling and compelling (and irresistibly re-readable!). It makes sense they were the stories many ambitious filmmakers chose to adapt.

The Greatest Dollar Baby Ever Born?

I've not seen the overwhelming majority of the Dollar Baby films, primarily because they're not available for watching. That's part of the deal with Stephen King: no Internet or commercial distribution.

I have seen a few, though, and one is so remarkable, and so unique, that I'll go ahead and brashly declare it my personal choice for the *Greatest Dollar Baby Film Ever Made*. (And please remember, this proclamation should have the concluding parenthetical "Of the Ones That I've Seen.")

What is this epic? It is Jay Holben's *Paranoid*, a film that uses King's poem "Paranoid: A Chant" as its script.

Technically, then, it's not really an adaptation, but rather a visualization.

The poem is a look inside the mind and thinking of a paranoid schizophrenic. The delusions, the fears, the psychosis of someone suffering from the illness is graphically depicted in one hundred lines of surrealism and abject terror. Not the likeliest candidate for a movie adaptation, right?

Wrong. Director Jay Holben and star Tonya Ivey, using King's poem as the script, create an unforgettable cinematic nightmare. And editor Eric Tozzi and art director Jennine Dwyer do extraordinary work bringing "Paranoid: A Chant" to the screen.

Stephen King allowed Holben's film to be released on a DVD included in a special 2002 edition of *Total Movie Magazine* (an offshoot of *Total Film* magazine) and then on the Internet for a limited time that same year. High praise, and utterly warranted.

When I was teaching at the University of New Haven, I devoted a section of my Composition and Literature courses to reading King's poem, "Paranoid: A Chant"; "The Love Song of J. Alfred Prufrock" by T. S. Eliot; and watching Holben's film. We then discussed my theory that the narrator of "Paranoid: A Chant" is what J. Alfred Prufrock would have become if his alienation, paranoia, and depression were not treated (and of course, at the time the poem was published, 1915, they would not have been). It was a look at how well-depicted paranoid schizophrenia is in King's poem.

The adaptation—as mentioned, using the poem as the script—is an equally well-depicted imagining of what a paranoid schizophrenic sees, hears, and thinks.

It is disorienting, frightening, insightful, and rather amazing. It probably deserves a category of its own, such is its distinctiveness. And I would like to note that in a generous gesture of support for studying King's work, director Jay Holben and star Tonya Ivey both wrote letters to my students discussing the film, which enhanced their appreciation and understanding of both the underlying text and the cinematic rendering.

Closing Thoughts

This Introduction is not meant to completely cover the vast and fascinating world of Stephen King Dollar Baby films, but rather to introduce the reader to what that world is, why it is worth a visit if you're a Stephen King fan, and why you'll likely enjoy this book.

Coverage of the multitude of individual films I leave to the stalwart and knowledgeable author of this book and my friend, Anthony Northrup, along with the interviews and writings by the filmmakers themselves. (I myself have begun writing a screen adaptation of King's *Bazaar of Bad Dreams* story, "Afterlife," and perhaps will one day have the honor of showing it to some of the talented filmmakers featured in this book.)

King's ability to write cinematically is well known.

A recent edition of the *Guinness Book of World Records* noted that he was the most adapted writer in the world. Thus, it is not surprising that his short stories comprise a cornucopia of wonders for the reader and fan wanting to start their life as a filmmaker with a short film.

– Stephen Spignesi
New Haven, Connecticut
April 20, 2020

Stephen Spignesi is the author of six books about the work of Stephen King, including *The Complete Stephen King Encyclopedia*, *The Lost Work of Stephen King*, *The Essential Stephen King*, and his latest, *Stephen King, American Master*. At some point, if he lives long enough, he plans to write a book about the work of Stephen King's kin: Tabitha King, Joe Hill, Owen King, and Kelly Braffet. (The book will be called *Stephen King's Kin: The Writings of Tabitha King, Joe Hill, Owen King, and Kelly Braffet*. He hears Billie Eilish in his head: "Duh.") For now, though, he is completing a novel set in 1851 London called *Crystal Palace* that he is writing with Montgomery. His next book, scheduled for August 2020, is *Robin Williams, American Master*.

Foreword
Richard Chizmar

DOLLAR BABY DREAMERS

I love dreamers. Those folks with big ideas and even bigger hearts, as well as strong work ethics and fearless streaks that enable them to jump in over their heads. That's how I launched *Cemetery Dance* over thirty years ago, the only way I could have started. I was twenty-one years old at the time, still in college, had no real business plan or money in the bank, but I did have an idea—a big idea.

And I was willing to roll the dice and work long and hard to make it happen. So, yeah, I have a special place in my heart for dreamers, which provides me with a natural segue way to Dollar Baby filmmakers. Believe it or not, I've never met one in person, but there are a handful of attributes that immediately come to mind when someone mentions a Dollar Baby filmmaker to me—passion, dedication, doers (as opposed to talkers), and of course, dreamers. I'm fortunate enough to call Stephen King my friend.

I've known him for thirty years now and can tell you firsthand how great of a guy he is. Generous, talented, kind, smart, funny—it's a long list. And I think it's a very cool and admirable thing that he does—allowing filmmakers to make movies based on his stories for a one-dollar fee. But I'll tell you a secret: I think it's even cooler that there are such creative people out there willing to "walk the walk" and make these films with no hopes of profit or stardom. They simply fell in love with a good story and possess the passion and talent to translate that story from the printed page to the movie screen. I admire that so much.

Now, keep in mind, there are millions of Stephen King fans. They even have their own collective nickname, as you well know: Constant

Readers. Stephen King fans that want to make a movie based on one of his short stories are also members of a pretty large group, numbering in the thousands (I admit this is a guess, but I'm betting it's pretty accurate). But Stephen King fans that have actually done something about this desire and made a real true-blue movie based on his work are in much more rare company. They're members of an exclusive club, and this fine book—created by King fan extraordinaire Anthony Northrup—is a well-deserved celebration of these people and their accomplishments.

Dollar Baby films have won awards and led to bigger opportunities for many of these filmmakers. The films have brought such joy and entertainment to so many viewers, present company included. And I'll tell you someone else who absolutely adores these labors of love: the man himself, Stephen King.

Let me set the scene for you: I'm in Florida to attend the Sarasota Film Festival, where one of my own short movies is screening. Heroes, based on my story of the same name, is co-written and directed by my longtime friend, Johnathon Schaech. It's approximately twelve minutes long, self-funded by John and me, and aimed solely at the festival circuit. Sound familiar?

Anyway, during one of my slow days, Steve swings by my hotel and picks me up. We drive to his house on the Gulf—stopping at a used bookstore on the way—and after giving me the grand tour, Steve and I sit down to watch a DVD of *Heroes* that I brought along with me. To my relief, he loves the film and actually asks if he can keep the copy to show it to Tabby when she gets home. A short time later, before we head out to dinner, Steve asks if I'd like to watch one more short film, a Dollar Baby of his story *Rainy Season* that just showed up in the mail. The lights lower and the movie starts. After a brief set-up, killer frogs fall from the sky and start munching on people. I look over and Steve is smiling… and then he's cringing. A few minutes later, I take another peek and he's grinning like a ten-year-old sitting in the balcony at his local theater with a tub of buttered popcorn in his lap. When the movie's finished, we start it over and watch it again.

To this day, I have no idea who the director of *Rainy Season* is. Steve never told me the name, and I'm much too old and senile to recall from the credits. But I do know this: for a few minutes, during one spring afternoon, that Dollar Baby of *Rainy Season* brought an awful lot of happiness to Stephen King. And that, my friends, is priceless.

Author's Note

AS FAR BACK AS I CAN REMEMBER, I have always been a horror movie fan. In fact, I can remember the exact day when I became one. It was the summer of 1975, I was 4 years old and was at a Drive-In movie theater in Long Island, New York. The film I was watching: *Jaws*. I can remember every detail of that night even to this day. My love for horror films would grow over the years, but it wasn't until May of 1980 when I first discovered the writer that would change my life: Stephen King. In May of 1980, I was 8 years old and I went to the movie theater to see the Stanley Kubrick film, *The Shining*.

My parent took us to R-rated films because she didn't have a babysitter and because she felt if we're going to learn the good and the bad things in life, it might as well be at the movies.

When I saw *The Shining*, there were many things in the film that was scary, but it was two things in particular that scared me the most: the music and those Grady Twins! They still give me the creeps to this day. Even though Stephen King had a few books out before the film was released, I did not know he wrote *The Shining* (I was 8 years old). It would be in 1984 that I would really discover King's works via films. I was living in Hollywood, California at the time. My parent raised us on music and movies our whole lives. She told us to '… give everything a chance, and then decide what you like'. So, one Saturday afternoon at the other end of Hollywood boulevard, they were having a Stephen King Film Fest. For a small price, we got to see Stephen King films back-to-back. Imagine, spending the whole day watching nothing but Stephen King films! Remember, this was 1984, they didn't have film fests like this like they did later on. With a packed theater, smell of popcorn in the air, the stickiness of soda on the floors – I had one of the scariest times I've ever had at the movies. I watched *Cujo, Christine, The Dead Zone,* and *Children of the Corn* that day. When I got home, I knew right then and there I was a fan. I looked for King's name everywhere I could and I didn't have to look far. He was right there on our bookshelf in our little apartment. I would sit there looking at the hardback covers for hours, flipping through them, but I didn't read them then. That would come later. Movies were my thing growing up and I saw A LOT of them! Back then, HBO, Cinemax, and Showtime were all new and whenever I saw a Stephen King movie being played (especially very late at night), I made sure to watch it even if I had to creep into the living room with the volume very low to watch it.

We moved from Hollywood back to North Carolina where I lived for 10 years of my life. In the mid-80's, North Carolina was the hot spot for filmmaking, especially for Stephen King films. Dino de Laurentiis film studios were in Wilmington, the big city by the beaches. Films like *Firestarter, Cat's Eye, Silver Bullet,* and *Maximum Overdrive* were filmed there and around North Carolina. In 1985, my Stephen King fandom grew when I found out *Silver Bullet* was being filmed in Burgaw, the small town where my cousins lived. I spent my summers with them and all the scenes on main street, the courthouse, and the baseball field I have been to when I was young. When the film opened, the whole town of Burgaw was there, sold out! We got in and the actress who played Corey Haim's girlfriend in the film was there that night. It was a very big deal that a big movie was being filmed in that small part of the world. Then in 1986, another King film was being filmed there: *Maximum Overdrive.* Of course, I was excited. The bridge they show at the beginning of the film I have been across 1000 times which leads from the city to the beaches. These were all exciting things growing up in the 80's, but there was one film that truly changed not only my life, but began my Stephen King fandom to the point I bought my first King book: *Stand By Me.*

Stand By Me was released summer of 1986, I was 15 years old. It came out at a very important time in my life. I was changing, putting my childhood behind me and not quite ready for adulthood. All I cared about at that time was horror films, heavy metal music, MTV, and where do I fit in? When I saw the film, I had a huge lump in my throat. I related to the character, 'Gordie Lachance' like you wouldn't believe. I saw on the credits that the film was based on the short novella, 'The Body' by STEPHEN KING! What!? Stephen King, the horror master wrote this!? I immediately ran to the local bookstore and bought the paperback edition of *Different*

Seasons which the story appears in. I read the story right away... multiple times. And then I thought, Why not read the other three stories in it?" So, I did. Little did I know then another story in the book would become a film in 1994 and really change my life: *The Shawshank Redemption*.

It wasn't until 1989 that I would buy my next Stephen King book and not just any book, but the one and only book to scare the heck out of me more than any other book I've ever read: *Pet Sematary*. I saw the film in the theater and I loved it immediately. It was also my first introduction to the punk band, The Ramones as they sang the title song and other music in the film. Again, I ran out and bought the paperback book. When I was done reading it, I literally threw it across the room! No disrespect to books or Stephen King, I did it because it scared me beyond words. No other book has ever done that. As I was older by this time and working, I was able to buy books and the top of my list was Stephen King. He had "sold me", so to speak, and he certainly knew how to tell a story. Not only did my love and life as a Book Lover truly begin in the later 80's and early 90's, but my love of Stephen King's works as well. In 1993, I met my wonderful wife, Gena. On the night we first met, we covered every topic you could imagine and that included favorite books and authors. Sure enough, hers was Stephen King. The conversation lit up and I knew this was just another plus why I liked her so much that first night we met. Six months later we were married. Her father was a huge Stephen King fan and collector as well. Between the two of them, they taught me and recommended to me King's works I never read, let alone heard of before. In the early 90's, I worked at a Laser Disc Video store in the San Fernando Valley off of Ventura boulevard. Since it was the only store at the time to rent and sell films on laserdisc, a ton of celebrities shopped there and rented LaserDisc films including actors and directors who worked on Stephen King films such as Mick Garris, Frank Darabont, and John Carpenter. I have been friends with some of them ever since and to this day. I spent a lot of my time in the 90's reading as much of Stephen King as I could and buying the VHS movies that were adapted from those stories. This went on for many years and as we entered the 2000's, VHS was on the way out and being replaced with DVDs. Stephen King was writing stories like a machine and it was almost hard to keep up. My wife and I bought Stephen King books, the movies, collectibles, and went to the theater to see the latest adaptation on the big screen. My collection was growing and became impressive as time went on. But then another change would enter my life: the Internet.

The internet was a brave new world for all of us King fans. I made friends and joined a few Stephen King groups where I could go and talk with other fans about King's works. I realized that this was something I wanted to do myself. I had ideas of what I wanted to do and present to other fans like myself. After a few months, I decided to give it a try, if I didn't like it I'd close it. So, on August 19th, 2012, All Things King – A Stephen King fan page was born. Myself and Co Ads, would go to the page and post fun things about Stephen King. Posts such as, trivia, games, biographies, fun facts, behind-the-scenes, interviews, reviews, and many other fun posts including pictures of either our current Stephen King book one was reading at the time and/or pictures of ones King collections or latest purchase. As the creator and head writer of the page, it has been a really fun and interesting ride. I have met so many wonderful people there, brought people together, and made connections to others who have either worked on Stephen King films or written books about Stephen King and his works. The films were not all played in the movie theaters, but somewhere else: film fests. And my introduction to the Dollar Baby program was born.

In the early years of social media, I was writing film reviews and doing celebrity interviews for our local newspaper, the Tri County Sun and also for the Through the Black Hole web page based in Italy. Over 500 interviews, film reviews, book reviews, promoting and other articles of entertainment. In 2013, I saw a post on Facebook from a man named, Billy Hanson. The post was about his Stephen King Dollar Baby film, *Survivor Type* which was based on the King short story published in Stephen King's *Skeleton Crew*. My first thought was, 'What's a Dollar Baby?'. I became friends with Billy and asked if I could interview him and review his Dollar Baby film. I did. And it was published at the Through the Black Hole web page. He enjoyed my article so much and was so impressed that he introduced me to other Dollar Baby filmmakers. I did the same interviewing and film reviewing for them as well. And so the ball kept on rolling… .more interviews and more reviews kept coming, but also a friendship and trust was being built in the Dollar Baby circle. A trust which led to a Dollar Baby film fest that I would host.

In 2013, I went to the Crypticon Horror Con in Minnesota as a representative of our local newspaper to cover the 3-day horror convention event. A packed hotel full of celebrities, collectibles, Q/A sessions, and a lot of parties! Nick Kaufman, the head of Crypticon conventions, was impressed with my coverage and newspaper article covering the event, that I was invited back the next year. I had also won a writer's award for the article about the convention. I talked to Billy Hanson, who got my start in the Dollar Baby interview/film review circle, and asked him if we could put together a batch of Dollar Baby films to play at Crypticon as a film fest? After speaking with Nick who was very excited about the idea, agreed. So, in 2014, I hosted the First Annual Stephen King Dollar Baby Film Fest at Crypticon Horror Con in Minnesota. For three days, I played several selected picked Dollar Baby films for horror fans who had never seen, let alone heard of before – had the honor and privilege of seeing them for the first time. The response was overwhelming and exciting! I had a blast!

The film fest was such a hit, I was invited back for the third time, and a second Dollar Baby film fest was planned. This time, bigger, more films, posters around the convention showing what was being played, and the crowd was even bigger than the last time. It was one of the best times of my life and an honor. The years since have gone on with more interviews and film reviews and with the amount going way over 500 articles and the second place winner of a statewide newspaper writers award, I felt a book was the obvious choice as my next adventure. Along with published interviews and reviews, the ATK fan page growing over 5000 members, and being a contributor to two Stephen Spignesi's books (Stephen King American Master and Elton John: Fifty Years On). Stephen is known for writing more books about Stephen King than anyone and we have become very close friends over the years and he wrote the Introduction to this book you are about to read. When I first became friends with Stephen Spignesi, I made it a personal goal to read all of his books he had written about Stephen King. He has covered more about Stephen King's works than anyone. Reading his books made me want to study the works of Stephen King and go beyond the stories, the man, and the films. I owe Stephen Spignesi a life debt for writing all those books about Stephen King, especially the "holy grail" of Stephen King books: *The Stephen King Encyclopedia* which is the best book about King's works I've ever read. With all of these amazing things happening in my writing career, I still wasn't sure if I was ready to write my first book. After speaking with Stephen and a close friend, author Andrew J. Rausch (a contributor to this book as well), the idea of a Dollar Baby book was pitched to a publishing company. When I first heard I was being published for a book about Dollar Babies, I was beyond excited. My dream of 30 years of being the author of my first published book, has finally come true! There is another Dollar Baby book out there, but I wanted to give the Stephen King fans a little more. And so, my journey and fandom of Stephen King has led to this point. The point of the book in your hands you are about the read. *Stephen King Dollar Baby: The Book* is, not just a collection of 55 Dollar Baby interviews I've done and their films reviewed, but it is also full of essays from writers, directors, and fans who know Stephen King best. This book will take you behind-the-scenes, a peek behind the curtain of writers and their thoughts about Stephen King, and into the lives of fans and how Stephen King touched their lives on many levels. You will hear from the Dollar Babies themselves and how their visions of Stephen King's works were brought to the screen, the making of the films, and the sacrifices they've made to bring their visions to life. This book will tell you the highs and lows, the making of careers and the breaking of some. Some Dollar Babies have fairy tale endings and sadly, some don't. But in the end, when you turn that last page, you will have had the next best thing from seeing a Dollar Baby film for yourself. You will have the opportunity to walk through a door to a whole different side of Stephen King's world that awaits you! This book was written for fans by a fan as we are all one. Embrace your fandom and come along to the world… of … *Stephen King Dollar Baby: The Book!*

PART ONE

Crypticon Horror Con MN October 2014.

Crypticon Horror Con MN Memories

IN 2013, I WAS FAIRLY NEW to the Stephen King Dollar Baby world. I had connected with *Survivor Type* director, Billy Hanson, I was getting more and more Dollar Baby interviews than I could imagine, and my film reviews of those Dollar Babies made a lot of my readers of my work get excited and were interested in them. I was helping spread the word about these films and amazing filmmakers on my All Things King fan page and at Through the Black Hole web page on social media. However, by 2014, I felt that there should be more than just word of mouth. That there should be a way these films could be seen by fans. Dollar Baby film festivals have been around the world for years prior, but not in the Northern Plains area... not until 2014.

When I covered the Crypticon Horror Con in Minnesota in 2013, the head of Crypticon, Nick Kaufman, had enjoyed my covering of his 3-day event for the newspaper, saw I had won a writers award for my coverage of it, and asked me to return the next year to do it all over again. I was very happy and honored at the opportunity. As the Dollar Baby interviews built up and more connections were made, I told Billy about how I covered the Crypticon Minnesota in 2013 and was asked back in 2014. I then asked him, how he felt about having a Dollar Baby film festival at Crypticon? Of course, he loved the idea and after pitching the idea to Nick, it was a green light and time to pick which films would play at the event.

The Crypticon Conventions have been around for many years. There are three major events of these events around the country. One is in Kansas City, Missouri, another is in Seattle, Washington, and the other is in Bloomington, Minnesota. The Minnesota event is the only one I've been to a total of three times. When I covered the convention in 2013, I was extremely nervous. Not only was this the very first time covering a 3-day event, but it was my first time at a horror convention. For 3 days, the hotel the event took place in was full of celebrities, Q/A sessions, photo opportunities, collectibles to buy, contests, and a lot of parties! I learned a lot my first year of covering the event. What to do the next time and what not to do. I made sure that when I returned there in 2014, I was prepared. I had to be double prepared because I was hosting the "Crypticon First Annual Dollar Baby Film Fest"! I had all my research done, my notes ready, and weeks leading up to the event I practiced what it would be like speaking in front of a huge crowd of people.

Crypticon Minnesota was on September 27, 28, and 29, 2014. On the first night of the film fest, we played *The Boogeyman* by Mando Franco, *Umney's Last Case* by Rodney Altman, and *In The Deathroom* by Damon Vineyard. On the first night, the crowd was a little small, a lot of celebrity

Crypticon Horror Con Minnesota 2014 1st Annual Stephen King Dollar Baby Film Fest.

Crypticon Horror Con Minnesota 2014 1st Annual Stephen King Dollar Baby Film Fest.

Q/A sessions were scheduled the same time and some of the big parties had already begun. But for those who were there, we had a great time. I introduced myself, spoke about the history of the Dollar Baby Program, and talked about each film before it was played on a big screen behind me. On the second night, we played *Survivor Type* by Billy Hanson, *Paranoid: A Chant* by Jay Holden, and *Beachworld* by Maria Ivanova. The word had gotten around the convention because more people showed up the second night. And lastly, on the third and final day of the convention, the Dollar Baby Film fest played, *Grey Matter* by James B. Cox, *The Reaper's Image* by Dean Werner, and *The Boogeyman* by Jenny Januszewski.

The festival was during the day because some of the celebrities leave early to head back home and so do the fans, so by 3:00pm that Sunday

Crypticon Horror Con Minnesota 2014 1st Annual Stephen King Dollar Baby Film Fest.

Crypticon Horror Con Minnesota 2014 1st Annual Stephen King Dollar Baby Film Fest.

Crypticon Horror Con Minnesota 2015 1st Annual Stephen King Dollar Baby Film Fest.

it came to a close and time to go home. I had an amazing time that year. Meet a lot of celebrities and two of them were in Stephen King films: Tom Atkins (*Creepshow*) and Corey Feldman (*Stand By Me*) although that was my second time in my life I had met Corey. However, as much as I had a great time those 3-days, it would be hosting the First Annual Dollar Baby Film fest that was a major highlight that weekend and in my life.

When I was asked to return to cover the Crypticon Minnesota 3-day event again in 2015, I was excited and honored. The Dollar Baby Film fest in 2014 was a hit and we wanted to make the Second Annual Dollar Baby Film fest in 2015 bigger and better! Word had spread around the Dollar

Crypticon Horror Con Minnesota 2015 1st Annual Stephen King Dollar Baby Film Fest.

Crypticon Horror Con Minnesota 2015 1st Annual Stephen King Dollar Baby Film Fest.

Crypticon Horror Con Minnesota 2015 1st Annual Stephen King Dollar Baby Film Fest.

Baby circle around the globe and Dollar Babies wanted their films to play at this second annual event. Credit goes to Billy Hanson for helping spread that word to his fellow Dollar Baby filmmakers and to Nick Kaufman for letting us do it again. The Crypticon Minnesota convention was over 3 days once again. This time it was October 23rd, 24th, and 25th 2015. I was just as excited the second time around and prepared once again, but this time we had flyers, posters and more advertising all over the hotel and on

Crypticon Horror Con Minnesota 2015 1st Annual Stephen King Dollar Baby Film Fest.

Crypticon Horror Con Minnesota 2015 1st Annual Stephen King Dollar Baby Film Fest.

the Crypticon web page. This helped a lot and brought in a packed house! I even had contests with prizes to give away as well.

On Friday, the first night of the film fest, we played Delver *Glass* by Matthias Greving, *Suffer the Little Children* by Corey Norman, and *Strawberry Spring* by Doveed Linder. The crowd cheered and were very excited seeing these films that very few people have ever seen before unless you've been to a Dollar Baby film festival somewhere else in the world. On Saturday night, we played Beachworld by Chad Boiling, *Cain* by Lyubo Yonchev, and *The Man Who Loved Flowers* by Justin Zimmerman. The crowd was much larger, the excitement was huge, and the crowd really got into it. It was a party in itself. On Sunday, the final day of the convention, it would be the last Dollar Baby film festival event of the weekend. This final day we played, *Night Surf* by Tony Pomfret, *Love Never Dies* by Peter Szabo, and *Maxwell Edison* by Warren Ray. It was a much quieter and sparse crowd that last day and everyone was pretty tired and ready to go home. I, myself, was more than tired, plus we had a 5 hour drive ahead of us to get back home to North Dakota.

Lots of things changed after that year. "Life happens" as they say. A Third Annual Dollar Baby Film fest didn't happen in the years that followed. Not really sure as to why? But life moves forward and for two years I was able to bring a slice of the Stephen King world to Minnesota and many horror fans were able to see these amazing films that they normally would have never seen before. I had the best time hosting those film fests and I'd do it again in a second anywhere if I could. I will always be thankful to Nick Kaufman for giving me that opportunity and trusting me and to Billy Hanson and all of those Dollar Baby filmmakers whose films were played those two years. I thank you all so very much. You brought a lot of happiness to the good folks of Crypticon Minnesota. As for me, you never know… maybe I'll host another Dollar Baby Film fest somewhere and help share these wonderful films to another lucky batch of horror fans… you never know.

Crypticon Horror Con Minnesota 2015 2nd Annual Stephen King Dollar Baby Film Fest.

Crypticon Horror Con MN Stephen King Dollar Baby Film Fest – Fans Respond

Now that you have an idea of what a Stephen King Dollar Baby Film fest was like at Crypticon Minnesota, let's hear from some of those who were there and their thoughts about the film festivals.

Nick Kaufman from Coon Rapids, MN. – Head of Crypticon Minnesota
 'I thought you did a great job running the festivals, they were very professional. The only thing I could really share is that the movies were all high-quality better than most of the stuff that we were getting turned in for the festivals previously and since.'

Nathan Monsour from Shoreview, MN – a guest at the event
 'I don't remember the names of the films we watched specifically, but I remember the one was about a flower delivery and the other ended with a twist, but it's been a while so my memory is hazy, but I really enjoyed how well shot they were and also getting to see/experience them with Stephen King fans like you and your wife. I also loved that you gave me a tote and book mark and recommended to me the Pet Sematary book. I would absolutely love a Dollar Baby film festival at future Crypticons, and I'd do what I could to

Curt Destler – from Coon Rapids, MN – Crypticon Volunteer
 'From what I saw, the films were pretty entertaining. Anthony Northrup did a great job of hosting them. Crypticon was also a great location for

them as well. I was only able to pop in for short times, since I was pretty busy, so I'm unfortunately not able to remember which ones I had watched. I thought it was a pretty cool concept. I had not known about it until then, and was glad that it had returned the following year. Seeing adaptations from short stories does make me want to read those stories that the movies came from.'

Greg Buchner from Cottage Grove, MN – Crypticon projectionist

'They were generally well received. People liked them. A few liked that there was the same story done by two different groups. Got to see two perspectives on the story. I remember that for at least one of the stories used. Don't remember how many duplicates there were. People also asked if it was coming back ever.'

Tiffaine L. Lafrance from Minneapolis, MN – Crypticon Staff Member

'I will say that I looked to add a serious element to our films fest. We had many talented filmmakers but we were trying to grow our convention. It was an honor to host them. I feel like it ushered more talent and creative film to us not only that year but going forward. It added an extra element of the local film community. I love an opportunity to create a supportive environment for creative folks to put on a show.'

"...That's What The Fans Said..."

ESSAY'S FROM THE FILMMAKERS, fans, and friends who know about Stephen King, the Dollar Baby Universe, and what it's like to be a fan in front and behind the camera.

A Dollar Well Spent

By Billy Hanson

BACK IN 2012, I was a Los Angeles filmmaker trying to make my mark on the business. I'd made a few short films, a couple of webisodes, and I'd written lots of stuff that was far too expensive to make on my own. I needed to do something big, something that would get me the attention I needed to make a splash in the oversaturated Hollywood system. Having grown up in Maine and being a huge fan of horror, Stephen King's stories are in my DNA. So naturally, I looked to his work for inspiration. That's when I found out about the amazing Dollar Baby Deal and found my next project.

For the cost of one dollar, I was given the right to produce an adaptation of the short story, *Survivor Type*. If you're not familiar with that particular story, it's about a surgeon who survives a shipwreck and ends up on a tiny island in the middle of the ocean with only a few small supplies and the mass amounts of heroin he was smuggling. And without spoiling it, I'll just say that it doesn't go well for him. It's a story that's been traumatizing readers since the 80s, because of its gruesome scenario and unapologetic attention to detail. And King himself was offering the rights to little ol' me. For a dollar.

Now, that didn't mean I could go out and do whatever I wanted with his story. There were a few caveats. First, my film was not allowed to earn or generate any money. I could never sign a distribution deal, sell tickets, host a fundraiser, push DVD copies of it, etc. Second, the film could never be posted in full on the internet, which took away the possibility of racking up views on YouTube, Vimeo, Shudder, or any of the other streaming platforms that have popped up in the last few years. Even with those caveats, I was excited to tackle the project and see what I could do with such great source material. But the deal itself left a lot of people in the film world scratching their heads, asking, "Why would you put time, energy and money into a film that you can never profit from and never distribute to the world?"

It's a fair question, especially from a business standpoint. But the answer is simple. I had permission to adapt my hero's work. I was damn sure going to make it happen.

I shot *Survivor Type* over four days in Malibu, California. We had a small crew, but it was mainly me and our lead actor, Gideon Emery, out on a tiny rock on the water. The resulting film is some of the best work I've ever done. It's a visceral experience, one that leaves audiences reeling for a long time after it's over. Along with compliments from fans of the short story, the film received more than fifteen awards at nearly sixty festivals around the world. It played the festival circuit for three years and took on a life of its own. As far as short films go, it was a rousing success. Eight years later, I still receive messages from people just about every week who have heard about my adaptation and ask for a screening copy.

After *Survivor Type* was finished and released, I was going into pitch meetings with agents, producers, and production companies to pitch my own scripts on the regular. When I was asked the inevitable question, "Have you done anything we might have seen," I was able to say that I made an adaptation of a Stephen King story. It piqued their interest every single time and started each conversation on a high. That paved the way for some great meetings.

I've been a writer and filmmaker for as long as I can remember. I graduated from the Florida State Film School in 2006, then moved to Los Angeles in 2007 and dove right into industry work. I was lucky enough to know exactly what I wanted to do, so I became hyper-focused on writing and directing. But even with that laser-focus and willingness to put in the extra work, I struggled for years to get a foot in the door. Every writer does. It takes much longer than anyone would think to get projects off the ground. Oftentimes, you can't even get meetings because people don't know your name or your work. That's where the Dollar Baby Deal really helps young filmmakers, or at least that's where it helped me. It got attention, even for just a moment.

The one thing I've struggled to find after thirteen years in this town is somebody willing to put in the effort to help others get a leg up. But with the Dollar Baby deal, Stephen King has done just that. Not an easy cash handout, not a fleeting tweet of support, but a simple contract in black and white that gives an unknown filmmaker the opportunity to use his work and get some attention with it.

The gesture, though it may seem easy, was a brilliant way for young filmmakers to distinguish themselves in the indie film world, especially at film festivals. In a sea of forgettable films, people would always buzz about "that Stephen King film". A shared love of his work brings people together and keeps them talking about these films for years.

There have even been film festivals across the world that screen only Dollar Baby films. I've curated a few of them myself, including a great showing of films at 2013's Comikaze (now LA Comic Con), which was hosted by none other than Joe Bob Briggs. That event was a huge success, and the audience was treated to some amazing adaptations of stories they all knew.

Since the release of *Survivor Type*, I've done a huge number of projects, ranging from comic books to music videos, short films to web series, and I'm currently finishing my first feature as a writer/director, called *Bone Cold*. That film is a psychological horror, much like my 2012 Dollar Baby. Several people came on board the new film because they watched *Survivor Type*, and many of them watched *Survivor Type* because we all love Stephen King.

I owe a lot of my successes to that film, to the Dollar Baby deal, and to the King himself. It's no small favor he's done for people like me.

So, from this Constant Reader and grateful Dollar Baby…

Thank you, Sai King. That was the best dollar I've ever spent.

Thoughts On Stephen King Adaptations

By Lee Gambin

ONE THE GREATEST THINGS that Stephen King does as a writer is dissect American institutions and dive into the terror embedded in such concerns. The horrors of high school and the anxiety/thrill of the prom is turned into a hell on earth in *Carrie,* the love boys have for their first car is turned into something demented and perverse in *Christine,* and so forth. So when the novels are adapted into feature films, it is up to those adapting such works to capture these cultural trappings, and many work beautifully.

As far as my favorites go, there are many, but those that get recurring re-watches would have to be *Salem's Lot,* which I think features some of the greatest visuals in modern horror cinema (and yes, that includes TV stuff too) such as the Glick brothers at the window or Geoffrey Lewis rocking in the chair hissing like a feral beast, and *Cujo,* which is a perfect condensation of the novel with a superb performance from Dee Wallace, the aforementioned *Carrie* and *Christine,* which break my heart every time for different reasons, *Misery,* for its tautness and parlour room ghoulishness, *The Dead Zone,* once again allowing for such a beautifully nuanced performance from Christopher Walken…

I mean, there are many elements in most of the adaptations that I love: the score from *Children of the Corn,* the cast in *Firestarter*…it goes on. King has blessed us with some excellent works, and thankfully a lot of the filmic adaptations have lived up to expectations.

My Secret Dollar Baby

By Robin Furth

LIKE SO MANY CONSTANT READERS, I have a movie theater inside my head. It only has seating for one, but the shows it plays are terrific. I don't know about you, but I think I love my theater's reruns even more than its premieres. There is nothing like sitting down with a favorite book at the end of the day and watching that inner screen illuminate. Yes, I know what's coming. Yes, I've watched this particular film a dozen times or more, but I still love it.

Perhaps it is because of this inner movie theatre, the one that transforms every book I read into a film, that I've always daydreamed about making a Dollar Baby. The story I return to over and over is only tangentially related to *The Dark Tower* books, though it definitely intersects with Roland's universe. In fact, my Dollar Baby has its roots in my childhood, in those early years before I had found the magic door that opens with the words, *The man in black fled across the desert, and the gunslinger followed...*

As I wrote at the beginning of my reference book, *Stephen King's The Dark Tower: The Complete Concordance*, the first time I stepped foot in the King Universe I landed in the town of Jerusalem's Lot. Not surprisingly, this is where my Dollar Baby is set. It comes from *Night Shift*, and is (as you've probably guessed by now) "One for the Road".

Last night, eager to make my daydream into a reality, I took my old 1979 Signet paperback off the shelf and started to read. "It was quarter past ten and Herb Tooklander was thinking of closing for the night when the man in the fancy overcoat and the white, staring face burst into Tookey's bar..."

An hour later I sat in front of my computer screen, thinking about the beginnings of films. I knew I *could* open my tale with Tookey and the narrator, Booth, having a final drink at the bar during one of Maine's blinding northeasters. But my gut told me it might be better to open the tale with the story of the man in the fancy overcoat, the vaguely unpleasant Gerard Lumley, whose unfortunate accident in the town of Jerusalem's Lot sets the sequence of events in motion.

Once I'd decided to begin with the Lumley family, I realized something else. In my own personal version of "One for the Road", it's not just the thick snow on Jointer Avenue that makes Lumley swerve into a snowbank...

FADE IN:

EXT. HIGHWAY — NIGHT
A blizzard. Snow blows over the deserted intersection of FALMOUTH ROAD and JOINTER AVENUE. An inch of slush covers the Falmouth Road, but four inches of pristine white lie on top of Jointer Avenue.

A SNOWPLOW drives down Falmouth Road, lifting its blade to mark the intersection, but it does not turn onto the Jointer.

Following the snowplow is a MERCEDES. Despite the snowdrift, the Mercedes turn right onto Jointer Avenue.

INT. MERCEDES — NIGHT
Seven-year-old FRANCIE LUMLEY sits in her booster seat in the back of the car and plays with her Barbie doll while singing along with the radio. Her parents, JANEY and GERARD LUMLEY, sit in front.

JANEY
Are you sure this is the right way, Gerard?

GERARD
These are the directions your stupid sister gave us.

JANEY
But the road is covered in a snowdrift.

GERARD
I told you we should use the GPS.

EXT. HIGHWAY — NIGHT
The Mercedes drives past a town sign. Someone has taken potshots at it with a bebe gun and someone else has defaced it with red spray paint. It says:

> WELCOME TO JERUSALEM'S LOT
> INCORPORATED 1765
> POPULATION ~~1,219~~ 0

INT. MERCEDES — NIGHT

> JANEY
> What's wrong with this town? It's completely dark.

> GERARD
> Probably a power cut.

Something on two legs, but with red eyes, darts in front of the car.

> JANEY
> WATCH OUT!

Gerard spins the wheel to avoid a collision. The car skids on ice and Janey screams.

EXT. AERIAL SHOT OF MERCEDES — NIGHT
The Mercedes' hood is deep in a snowbank and the horn is blaring…

INT. SNOW PLOW — NIGHT

BILLY LARRIBEE is driving past TOOKEY'S BAR on the Falmouth Road.

The proprietor, HERB TOOKLANDER, runs out of the establishment. He is carrying a large can of Budweiser. Billy rolls down his window.

> TOOKEY
> Here's one for the road, Billy. I'm shutting the bar down.

> BILLY LARRIBEE
> Don't blame you, Herb. Forty mile an hour winds are comin.' Nothin's gonna move in this town until mornin.'
>
> TOOKEY
> The main roads clear?
>
> BILLY LARRIBEE
> Ayuh. Except Jointer. I'm sure as hell not clearing that bastard road…

At this point, my Dollar Baby returns to faithfully retell "One for the Road" in the order we know and love. Back in the warm building, Tookey and his old customer and drinking buddy, Booth, share a final drink. Tookey is just about to lock the door when Lumley stumbles into the bar and collapses, his three-hundred-dollar coat covered in snow. After a stiff shot of brandy, he tells Tookey and Booth what has happened. His car's stuck in a snowbank six miles back and now his wife and daughter are stranded.

Despite the fact that Lumley is a rich New Jersey fool, neither Tookey nor Booth can leave an innocent woman and child alone in the Lot. Secretly armed with a Bible and a crucifix, the two old timers brave the storm with Lumley. Setting out in Tookey's old four-wheel-drive Scout, they crawl through the blinding snow towards Jointer Avenue. The Mercedes is just where Lumley left it and it's still running. But Janey and Francie are gone.

Even before Lumley runs off in the snow, clutching his daughter's coat and screaming, *Francie! Janey! Where are youuuu?* we know that he is doomed. As his undead wife answers his call and takes him into her hungry embrace, Tookey and Booth run. Tookey has a heart attack, but Booth manages to half lead, half drag him into the Scout's passenger seat. But as Booth trots over to the driver's side, seven-year-old Francie is waiting for him.

The child wears nothing but her shoes and her thin yellow dress, and at first Booth fears she will freeze to death. "Honey," he says. "Honey, you'd better get in the truck…" Yet no sooner does he speak these words than he thinks he's going to swoon. You see, little Francie hovers on top of the snow and she has left no tracks in any direction. Her face is a ghastly corpse white and her eyes are an earthly red and silver glitter. Just below her jaw are two small puncture wounds like pinpricks, their edges horribly mangled.

Mesmerized and unable to stop himself, Booth leans over to pick the child up. Yet even as the little girl clasps her hands around his neck, her pink mouth drooling, Tookey throws his Bible at her and she disappears in a flash of light and a puff of strange-smelling smoke. A moment later she reappears again. This time she hisses and her face is a mask of rage and hate and pain. Yet this, too, dissipates. When the two men drive off, all that remains of Francie is a twisting, girl-shaped knot of snow that the wind tatters, frays, and finally blows over the distant snowy fields. My favorite part of *One for the Road* is actually the postscript. In this short section, Booth tells us that in the years following that awful night on Jointer Avenue, he suffered from nightmares. In these dreams, he's out in that blinding snowstorm again, and he's alone with Francie Lumley. Lifting her arms, little Francie begs Booth to pick her up. She's cold, she says, and she wants her mother. She's so cold and lonely that she wants to give Booth a kiss. A final, goodnight kiss.

It's with this kiss, or the promise of it, that I'd end my Dollar Baby. Little Francie hovers atop the snow, her hair in pigtails, her corpse-white body wearing nothing more than a little yellow dress. Smiling, she opens her arms to us. We long to lean forward and pick her up, despite her ghastly whiteness and the two pinpricks at her throat, which are horribly mangled. The seasons pass, another winter comes, and another, but little Francie is still there, never aging, never sated, the tiny fangs inside the pink ring of her mouth, sharp as needles.

As the screen fades to black, some words appear:

If you ever find yourself driving through Falmouth, Maine, don't take the Jointer Road after dark. A hungry little girl waits there, and she would like nothing better than to give you a final, good-night kiss.

Stephen King Memories

By Amber Pace

STEPHEN KING HAS BEEN a pervasive force in my life for as long as I can remember.

I grew up watching both of my parents read King, but my mom was a big fan of his in particular. My mom was an avid reader, but she predominantly was drawn to his books as she enjoyed his writing style, his development of characters, and great attention to detail. I remember spending a lot of time at the library with her as a kid and quite often her with a copy of one of his books as we checked out. I remember often seeing her with one of his books in her hand. As a kid, I had grown a fascination with the horror genre and would spend a lot of time looking at his books that she brought home reading the dust jackets and small sections of his stories. She thoroughly enjoyed *The Gunslinger* and had a fascination with Roland and would spend time sketching out images from the book on pieces of paper. His movies also dominated our viewing. Of course, this was back in the days of VHS tapes and VCR's. I remember our first time renting the VCR and VHS. We came home with several fun movies to watch; the top of that list was Kubrick's version of *The Shining*. My mom loved Jack Nicholson and Stanley Kubrick so she was particularly intrigued by watching this one. It was the first movie we watched out of the stack and that was truly the beginning for me. After watching my first Stephen King movie, I was completely hooked.

My mom not only gave me my love of reading, but also my love of Stephen King and his style of writing. My mom died when I was 20 but I always feel a connection to her through his writing. In particular, the story of *It*. One time in particular I remember her being incredibly excited to read one of King's new releases was when *It* came out. She was able to obtain a copy of the massive thousand-page book on a 7-day loan from our local library. I remember as she was cooking dinner, my dad coming home from work, picking up the copy, and reading it. Needless to say, he had a hard time relinquishing his hold of the book and my mom ended up not getting to read it while it was out on loan. Still guilt-ridden from his sneaky theft of the library loan, that Christmas, my dad and I went to our local bookstore and purchased a copy of the book for her since she didn't get the chance to read it when it was on loan. My mom loved the present and also demolished the book when she got it. I was 10 when It came out, so it was far beyond my capacity for reading. I do, however, remember my mom telling me about the book. Already captivated by the horror genre, I began to develop a minor fascination for the story as my mom would read me excerpts from the book and talk about the characters in detail. I thought Pennywise was a fascinating character from the little bit I knew of him.

I began reading King when I was 12 with *Carrie* being my first read of his. I had been collecting his books for years knowing that someday I would read them all. I demolished his books in junior high and high school reading through books like *Pet Sematary*, *Christine* (still my most read King book to this date), *The Shining* (we have also stayed at The Stanley Hotel where King got his inspiration for the story) and I finally read *It* when I was 15. Still, with the fascination of the story in the back of my mind, I remember clearly the summer I read that book. That book was truly the book that gave me my deep love and respect for King and his writing. I was in awe of his ability to deeply develop characters that are relatable, enjoyable and I truly felt like I knew in some profound way. His attention to detail is unsurpassed and his ability to create the setting and background for his books is second to none. I read *It* in 5 days. I lost many hours of sleep and dove deep into the lives of Bill, Ben, Bev, Mike, Ritchie, Eddie, Henry, and Pennywise. I felt an almost transformative experience when I read that book and knew that King would always hold a place in my heart as my favorite author.

One of the other reasons this book holds a special place in my heart is because that copy of It that my dad and I gifted to my mom was re-gifted to me as a teenager. I grew into my love for King. My mom saw the love I had for his writing and felt that the copy of his book belonged to me. I still have that book and it is the most treasured book in my collection. I feel a bond to my mom each and every time I read King, but in particular that scary story about a killer clown and an amazing group of friends fighting evil in the sewers of Derry, ME. I often feel sad she never knew how Roland's story ended or was able to see King's evolution of his own writing through the years. But I know that I will also be able to pass these books along to my own kids (also hopefully a lifelong love for reading) and they can know and understand the power of being able to instantly transport to another world through someone else's words.

I am still an avid reader of King's and purchase every new release of his as they come out and have an expansive collection of his books missing only a few of his more obscure releases. I have my obvious favorites (*It, The Stand, Christine, The Shining*), but nothing will ever compare to that feeling I had as I was discovering his writing. I enjoy the ability to connect with other readers of his via the Facebook group, All Things King and have thoroughly enjoyed the privilege and pleasure of being able to co-admin the group with some of the most amazing people on the planet. I will forever have a love for the horror genre, but King will always top my list of favorite authors.

A King's Treasure

By Paul Michael Kane

THINK BACK ON SOME of your favorite films. If you're like me, you might have a few treasure hunting movies on your list. Watching Harrison Ford comb the desert to find the Lost Ark; or Nicolas Cage reading a map written in invisible ink on the back of the Declaration of Independence. We can't help but get excited about the prospect of taking part in an actual treasure hunt – finding that one, truly rare item, sometimes hidden in plain sight; or more likely, needing some digging to unearth.

Collecting the works of Stephen King – particularly his U. S. first editions – is very much like a treasure hunt! There are codes, clues, false leads and unscrupulous and shady characters around every turn. The thrill of the hunt follows you into used bookstores; lessened ever so slightly if you're buying your books online.

Take, for instance, a first edition of King's masterpiece, *IT*. There are 5 states – or printings – considered to be first editions of the novel. However, there is only one distinct notation that allows for collectors to identify a first printing of the first state. What that clue is – well, I don't want to spoil it for you – you're going to have to figure that out on your own.

This presented me with a very unique opportunity – rather than being the hunter – I've designed the treasure map! I wrote *A Guide to the U.S. First Editions of Stephen King* for my novice, book collecting self. It's a treasure map I wish I had had when I first started collecting King's work. From *Carrie* to *The Institute*, the book lists every identifying mark of a title's first edition – from ISBN numbers to printing errors and dust jacket states.

Writing the book was a joy – designing the book was a blast – especially recreating each book's title treatment. I worked with some very knowledgeable collectors and getting to know the Stephen King community was the best part of putting the book together.

With the release of *If it Bleeds* just months away, the question becomes, would I ever consider updating the book – and the answer is: absolutely! I may let a few titles come out before then – or wait until King retires from writing, so that the next edition of the book could be the most definitive, but yes – the treasure map will be expanding at some point!

King and Kissing Books

How Stephen King's work influenced a romance author

By Brooklyn Ann

I'VE READ SO MANY WONDERFUL stories about authors' and other creators' first experience with Stephen King. They are always charming tales, telling which book they discovered first and how they fell in love with King's books. Some of those stories are likely in this book. I confess that I'm a little jealous because I can't remember which Stephen King novel was my first. My introduction with King started with the movies.

I was seven when I first saw *Pet Sematary* at my grandmother's house after she'd gone to bed. My mom was a huge horror movie fan and I first saw A Nightmare on Elm Street when I was two. I'd been peeking behind the couch, and when she caught me and saw that I wasn't afraid, she plopped me down next to her and we were horror movie buddies until she passed away when I was twenty-seven. Back to *Pet Sematary*. That was the very first film to ever scare me. And since it was the *only* one to scare me, I forced myself to re-watch it at least once a year, and still do. It was years before I grew brave enough to read the novel. Afraid or not, seven-year-old me was hooked on all things King. Thirty-seven-year-old me remains hooked. I watched every one that came on TV or that I could convince Mom to rent.

As for the books, I didn't get to those until middle school. I was still reading children's books like the *Bunnicula* series, *Redwall*, and *Mrs. Frisbee and the Rats of NIMH* (and the terrible sequels). My first adult novel was *Jurassic Park* at age ten. I was then hooked on Michael

Crichton. Then I went to school and got my first King recommendation from my sixth-grade teacher. She told me and two other bookworms in the class to read *IT*.

And though *IT* turned out to be my favorite Stephen King novel ever, I was sadly unable to get hold of a copy right away. The Hayden Library didn't have a copy, so I picked up whichever one they did have on hand. I think it was *Eyes of the Dragon*, but it may have been *The Shining*. Either way, I was in love.

Around the same time as my introduction to King, another interesting literary journey began. My mom introduced me to V.C. Andrews. And while I found those books riveting with their dark, deranged drama, I always felt sad when I finished them. There was a depressing pattern to all. A beautiful girl has hopes and dreams, but she's living in terrible circumstances. Then said circumstances improve (except for *Flowers in the Attic* or *My Sweet Audrina*) and she begins to fulfill those dreams. Often, our heroine falls in love. But then it all comes crashing down. If she had a lover, he either turns out to be her unknown brother, or he turns into an abusive controlling monster. More terrible things happen to her, the end.I quickly became dissatisfied with these novels. I wanted stories where the girl learns and grows on her journey to pursue her dreams, like most of King's protagonists have growth. I wanted stories where the girl achieves her goals and has a happy ending, like in many of King's books. Yes, a lot of King novels have happy endings. In a way, thanks to King, I discovered the joy of romance novels. A character pursues a dream, meets the love of their life on the way, they go through a journey together, and there is always a happily ever after.My reading routine then went as follows: a Stephen King novel, a romance novel, another Stephen King novel, and so on. In between, I also indulged in my loves of historical fiction and fantasy.

By the time I became a published romance author (using King's *On Writing* as my bible), Stephen King's influence fully imbued my writing. I give little homages to him in my works. In my heavy metal romance, *With Vengeance*, the hero lives in a fictional town called Dark Score, named after a lake in *Gerald's Game*. In *Kissing Vicious*, I gave a character the last name of McVries from *The Long Walk*. There's a Stebbings in *Unleashing Desire*. I have other details like that in other works, but my homages are full blown in my B Mine series. In *His Final Girl*, there's a scene where the characters haul the bodies of murder victims into a chapel, to pay tribute to the body sorting scene in The Stand. In *His Scream Queen*, there are many blatant references to *Carrie*, like when the hero wonders if he could be a Tommy Ross and Sue Snell to the outcast heroine. But hey, it's a prom-themed horror romance, so I can't leave out *Carrie*.

Aside from my little tributes and homages, Stephen King holds a more subtle, but larger influence on my work. My *Brides of Prophecy* series features portals to other worlds, with fated characters needing to meet and form a special *Ka-Tet* with the main endgame being that they must defeat a great evil being who seeks to destroy all worlds.

And like King, I also have my own interconnected universe shared between my book series. Many of my characters hail from Coeur d'Alene or other Idaho towns. King has Maine, and I have Idaho. And for my horror series, I've invented my own fictional small town called Amteep (Salish for Devil). Like Derry is a fictionalized version of Bangor, Amteep is a fictional Coeur d'Alene.

Aside from tributes and styles, another way King has influenced me is that he's never been afraid to write in multiple genres: Literary, Fantasy, Science Fiction, Literature, Contemporary Thriller, Action Adventure, Horror, and Mystery. I'm doing the same with romance subgenres. So far, I write historical, paranormal, fantasy, and horror romance. All under my own name because I want my name to sell the books, not the genre.

But the biggest influence King has had on my writing and my life in general is that I must be myself and write what I want to write and never be afraid to embrace my own weirdness. Like King says, "Write what you like, then imbue it by blending your own personal knowledge of life, friendship, relationships, sex, and work."

And that's exactly what I will continue to do.

Stephen King Memories

By Tina Rooker

'The man in black fled across the desert and the Gunslinger followed.'

THESE ARE THE WORDS that pulled me in, held me captivated and made me feel as though it was okay to be traveling through the world all alone. I first read the story in 1984 when I was just 13 years old and reread it many, many times over the years. I found Roland just as I was wondering how in the hell I was going to find my path through the world alone and found a kindred spirit doing the same. Both of us toughened from heartache, wary of strangers but open to the call of adventure we began the odyssey. Our paths seemed to always connect over time and through the ages. We both lost children we cared for deeply, his Jake was my Jesse. We both lost soulmates, his Susan was my Gary. Roland is the last of his kind, a gunslinger. I became a United States Marine, third and final generation for my family of gunslingers. We have both been wounded and severely ill, made and lost friends and so much more. For some reason, KA maybe, I cannot leave the beam the way he cannot. There have been numerous stories of Stephen King's over the years that have connected to me as well but none more clearly than The Dark Tower ever has. I began reading and collecting every King book I could get my hands on the day I read that first opening line and it has now been 36 years worth. I even have an entire back tattoo dedicated to the Dark Tower, mostly as a reminder of our expedition along the beam. It has been an incredibly hard fought journey across the desert but I will continue to strap on my six-shooters and go after the man in black for as long as I'm able.

The pull (or attraction if you will) of a Stephen King story is once you discover the rules don't apply to 'happily ever after' or 'the good guys always win' you'll be hooked! You don't know what's going to happen and who wants to? If we wanted that type of fluffy bunny story we could watch a Pixar movie. King writes characters so likable that sometimes you root for the bad guys to win. The way uncle John makes the family dinner suck at Thanksgiving but it would be dismally boring without him. Everyday life doesn't have a happy ending 9 out of 10 times and having a good story to curl up with that'll make your day suck a little less is quite pleasurable. We ALL slow down to check out the car accident up ahead, peek out the window at the neighbors fighting and enjoy watching karma unfold on someone we dislike. It's okay to admit it and its okay to admit we like the evil people in a King novel. These novels take our worst nightmares and bring them to life. They show us characteristics in the people around us that maybe we aren't seeing for ourselves, the good and the bad. Surely we have all known someone like Jack Torrance who drinks too much and beats his wife, a Carrie who has been sheltered and bullied in school. The list could just go on and on. For those who have read a King novel and have experienced the phenomenon of feeling that connection to a character or setting then you know what I'm talking about. For those that haven't taken the plunge, I dare you!

Women In the Dollar Baby World

By Nicole Jones-Dion

IN OCTOBER 2018, Jason Blum, founder of Blumhouse, was asked by Polygon's Matt Patches why none of the films he produced had been directed by women. His response was, "There are not a lot of female directors period and even less who are inclined to do horror." As the ensuing internet uproar was quick to point out, women DO direct horror. We're just not given the opportunity. Gender parity is an issue for all women in Hollywood but the imbalance can be felt acutely in the horror genre.Researcher Stephen Follows analyzed every feature film in American cinemas over the last thirty years and found that only 9.9% of the directors were women. Of those, just 5.9% of horror directors were women. This disconnect is especially ironic because the horror genre skews overwhelmingly female in on-screen representation. Horror films are more likely to have female protagonists than any other genre; in 2017, Google and the Geena Davis Institute on Gender in Media reported that horror is the only genre where women appear on screen more than men (53%) and in which they have the most speaking parts (47%).

The message from Hollywood is clear: Scream Queens and Final Girls are welcome but only if men tell those stories. Women need not apply. It's no wonder then that more and more women who want to work in the horror genre are taking advantage of Stephen King's Dollar Baby program. By turning a blind eye to gender, Dollar Babies fill a critical void by giving aspiring female filmmakers the same access as their male counterparts.

Jackie Perez, the writer, director, and producer of Dollar Baby film, *Beachworld* agrees. "Because normal Hollywood barriers to entry are removed, the numbers speak for themselves: there is a higher proportion of women making Dollar Babies than being hired for features." Looking back across Stephen King's expansive library of film adaptations, we can see that his feature-length movies have been dominated by male filmmakers.

Of over 55 features based on King's work, just two women have directed: Mary Lambert's *Pet Sematary* (1989) and *Pet Sematary II* (1992), and Katt Shea's *The Rage: Carrie 2* (1999); and only two women received screenwriting credit: Diane Johnson for The Shining (1980) and Barbara Turner for *Cujo* (1983). This is problematic. According to Follows, 51% of the top 2,000 films of the last 20 years were movie adaptations and the most common source for adaptations is literary fiction.

The Dollar Baby program allows women to access source material that wouldn't normally be available to them. Cinematographer Rachel Garcia-Dunn has worked behind the lens of two award-winning Dollar Babies, *Gotham Cafe* and *In the Deathroom*. "It is incredibly generous of Steven King to donate his high-caliber stories to these filmmakers," she says, "this ensures that the tales being told are of the highest quality." Every good film starts with a good script. Director Star Victoria shot her Dollar Baby *Dead Man's Hand* through Whitestone Motion Pictures production company as a directing protege. "They also had several screenwriting proteges so each screenwriter was tasked to adapt the story, *The Man Who Would Not Shake Hands,* and then submit it to me to choose which one best matched my vision. It was a great experience to see so many different takes on the same story."

One common thread that runs through all Dollar Baby productions is universal love and passion for Stephen King. "Because it was a Stephen King short story, everyone was excited to work on the production," says Victoria. "They enjoyed the idea of having their name on a film that was based on a Stephen King story." As a cinematographer who has collaborated with both male and female Dollar Baby directors, Garcia-Dunn hasn't noticed a distinguishable difference between the genders but she notes, "to a large degree, I usually get hired by female directors and producers. I would certainly welcome the opportunity to work with more men in those positions."

This underscores another concern with women creatives – they tend to be overlooked by the men who are responsible for the bulk of the hiring in film and television. Even when a woman is in a producing role, gender-related conflicts can still arise, as Peggy Lewis discovered while filming

The Man Who Loved Flowers. Certain male crew members caused "a lot of problems on the set. You know, that 'I am a man, no woman is going to tell me what to do.'" She was quick to add that in her experience, this type of behavior is the exception, not the norm. "It is really the only time I have run into that kind of sexist crap or blatant disrespect. I loved doing that short for the most part."

For writer-producer Marie D. Jones, her Dollar Baby *Graduation Afternoon* was her first on-set experience. "I was the only female member of the crew so I was a little worried about trying to fit in. I got incredibly lucky because the crew was not only friendly and respectful, but they made me a part of everything. All egos were checked in at the door. I don't assume all sets are so gender-friendly, as I've heard of many of my newfound female filmmaking colleagues having trouble getting considered or hired. I know it happens." There is a false perception that women aren't interested in directing horror which leads to a hiring gender gap in genre filmmaking.

With every film, Dollar Baby women are proving the gatekeepers wrong. The day after his Polygon interview was published, Jason Blum apologized on Twitter for his "dumb comments." He acknowledged, "we have not done a good enough job working with female directors and it is not because they don't exist. I heard from many today." Blum has since joined the ranks of a growing number of producers actively seeking to create more opportunities for underrepresented voices behind the camera.

One of the leading advocates for hiring women and minorities is Ryan Murphy, creator of *American Horror Story*. In 2016, Murphy launched his Half Initiative to make Hollywood more inclusive. Since the program launched, Ryan Murphy Television's director slate has hired 60% women as directors and 90% met at least one diversity target. As Star Victoria discovered, Dollar Babies make valuable calling cards. "I used *Dead Man's Hand* for my Half Initiative application which got me into the Inaugural year of the Ryan Murphy director shadowing program. I'm blessed that I was able to get that."

Hopefully, we'll see more talented female Dollar Baby filmmakers working on our favorite horror films and television shows in the not-so-distant future.

The Role of the Short Film In a Filmmaker's Career

By Jay Holben

I'VE BEEN A PROFESSIONAL in the motion picture industry for over three decades now. My career has evolved from an actor to writer to cinematographer to producer and director. During that evolution, it was common practice for an aspiring filmmaker—especially directors—to make a short film as a "calling card" or demo reel to illustrate their skills as an entry into the industry. So many filmmakers followed this mold with Neill Blomkamp, Tim Burton, Brian DePalma, George Lucas, David Lynch, Christopher Nolan, Martin Scorsese and Steven Spielberg among the countless numbers. If you wanted to get the attention of the industry, you had to show them what you could do. It is somewhat with this in mind, that Stephen so very generously started his Dollar Baby policy by which aspiring filmmakers could attain his permission to make a filmed adaptation of one of his short stories with, of course, one of the most notable being Frank Darabont's adaptation of *The Woman in the Room*.

It was also with this concept in mind that I dove into the world of Hollywood short film making with *Paranoid*, my 1999 8-minute 35mm adaptation of King's poem "Paranoid: A Chant" from *Skeleton Crew*. My motivation to make that short film was to establish my "calling card" as a film director. It served me well and opened several doors for me in the Hollywood community, but it's "experimental" nature ended up leaving Hollywood wanting to see more "traditional" work from me resulting in my making two more short films: *The Night Before*, an intimate drama written by fellow Dollar Baby James Cole (*The Last Rung on the Ladder*) and *Descent* a terse thriller. It was at that point that I had developed a solid directorial reel with the three shorts and I felt my career had "graduated" away from making short films and I concentrated on the feature filmmaking world.

I worked primarily as a cinematographer and a producer during these years in independent feature films, documentaries, music videos, etc. But, as Sai-King is wont to say, *the world moved on...* Between the time that I made *Paranoid* in 1999 and *The Night Before* in 2002 the digital revolution reared it's aggressive head and changed the world. As technology advanced and filmmaking became more democratized, equipment became more readily available and the YouTube generation entered puberty – the Hollywood establishment began to ignore short films. Shorts were no longer considered an achievement and now the onus on the young filmmaker was to make the elusive feature film. That's the end game anyway, isn't it?

So while I shot my third "significant" short film, *Descent* (there were lots of others that didn't make the public eye, necessarily), and released that in 2004, I knew that the time had come to move on and grow up as a film director.

Yet, something was tugging on my pant leg and whispering in my ear in the small hours of the morning. *Shorts are fun...*

(do it!)

In the years I spent developing feature films and producing and photographing movies for other people, my days as a director were fewer and fewer. I yearned to get back behind the camera as a director and tell stories. But I had graduated beyond shorts – so what was I to do? I directed documentaries; I directed web series – but the *narrative* world was calling and the years it takes to put together a feature were growing longer and longer.

Meanwhile, I remained a faithful Constant Reader. From the time that I made *Paranoid*, Stephen, the prolific genius that he is, released *The Girl Who Loved Tom Gordon, Dreamcatcher, Black House, From a Buick 8, The Dark Tower V, VI* and *VII, The Colorado Kid, Cell, Lisey's Story, Blaze, Duma Key, Under the Dome, 11/22/63, The Dark Tower: The Wind Through the Keyhole, Joyland, Doctor Sleep* and *Mr. Mercedes...* Some truly extraordinary works and some

(stinkers)

...not so extraordinary, but the Master continued to release novel after novel after novel. The literary equivalent of the feature film.

Yet, during this same decade and a half, Stephen also quietly released *Hearts in Atlantis, Everything's Eventual, Just After Sunset* and *Full Dark, No Stars.*

And I devoured them all.

Voraciously.

While I feel that his short work never quite lived up to the earlier collections of *Night Shift, Skeleton Crew* or *Nightmares & Dreamscapes*, the fact is that King – one of the world's most preeminent and successful novelists – *continued to write short stories.*

Why?

Why would some of his stature and prowess continue to dabble in the more juvenile form of prose?

Because it's fun.

Because the short story, much like the short film, is a different beast entirely. It's a late night snack as opposed to a six-course luxury meal. It's a stolen indulgence of refined sugar that you just *have to have.*

It occurred to me, taking a near-literal (if you'll allow me that stupid phrase) page from Stephen's book, that even a grown-up filmmaker could make a short film. It *is* a different art form; a different method of storytelling. They have different venues, different rules, different feels... There was, truly, no reason to wholly abandon the short film and relegate it to the student and tyro filmmakers! Why not create my own beignet deluged in powdered sugar; my own short film confection delight?

If Stephen could continue to dabble in short stories – why couldn't I play in short films and *not* be apologetic about it? Embrace it!

And so I did.

In 2014, a decade after *Descent*, I made *Alone* a short thriller about a woman home alone and tormented by the certainty that she is *not* alone.

And you know what?

It was a blast.

It was *wonderful* to dabble once again in the world of short films. In something that didn't take a half a decade of development and fundraising to produce. I followed this directing another short, *If...* an intimate drama dealing with loss, the same year and then found a new home for two of my previous shorts in commercially-released anthology films. Since, I've produced half a dozen other short films and I continue to look at them as a viable art form, not just relegated to the primordial years of a burgeoning filmmaker's career. Just like Stephen's short stories, a short film is a delicious morsel to enjoy between the larger meals – both as a filmmaker and as an audience.

So enjoy your nibbles, fellow filmmakers. Apologize not and go forth and make more shorts! Perhaps another Dollar Baby? We shall see…

Location, Location, Location!

How a Trio of Historic Sites Made the Doctor's Case

By James Douglas

GOOD LOCATIONS ARE A KEY to success when you're looking to squeeze a little spectacle out of a shoe-string budget. If there isn't enough time or resources to build fabulous sets from scratch (and really, when is there ever?) an indie filmmaker's next best option is finding a remarkable place that is already built, adapting scripted scenes to suit the space, and hoping whoever owns it is film friendly. Kick-ass locations can make $50K look like $5 million, if you play your cards right. It can also bring a truckload of problems along for the ride if you don't.

In my case location wasn't just key to the success of *The Doctor's Case*, it was a catalyst for the entire project. I have been professionally associated with Barkerville Historic Town & Park, western North America's largest "living history" museum, for more than 20 years now. Barkerville is an authentic 19th-century gold rush town in the central interior of British Columbia, Canada. More than a hundred of the heritage site's 140 restored wooden structures are original buildings dating back as early as 1869, and dozens of those buildings have been painstakingly dressed, inside and out, to look exactly as they would have during the late-Victorian era.

I had been dreaming about adapting *The Doctor's Case* since my senior year in high school, so when working for Barkerville became a regular thing in the late-1990s I quietly started scouting locations for a fantasy version of the movie I never expected to make. One could use interiors from my favourite buildings to represent the drawing rooms of Sherlock Holmes's London, I thought, and save the exterior shots for some

Behind-the-Scenes of Dollar Baby *The Doctor's Case* by James Douglas.

Behind-the-Scenes of Dollar Baby *The Doctor's Case* by James Douglas 2017.

yet-to-be-considered second location. This would be necessary because Barkerville is an old wooden town in the middle of a subalpine forest that looks nothing like the Baker Streets and Saville Rows of Stephen King's short story, but I never really considered anywhere else because I knew nothing about the Dollar Baby deal back then. I didn't think I'd ever actually make the movie, so why bother?

Flash forward to 2016: I learned about the Dollar Babies in April, and by November permission to adapt *The Doctor's Case* has been granted. Those "yet-to-be-considered" exteriors suddenly leapt to the forefront of my mind. Stock footage was a viable (albeit less than satisfactory) solution that was seriously considered in the early days of pre-production, but something kept telling me the film needed more. It needed authentic

Behind-the-Scenes of Dollar Baby *The Doctor's Case* by James Douglas 2017.

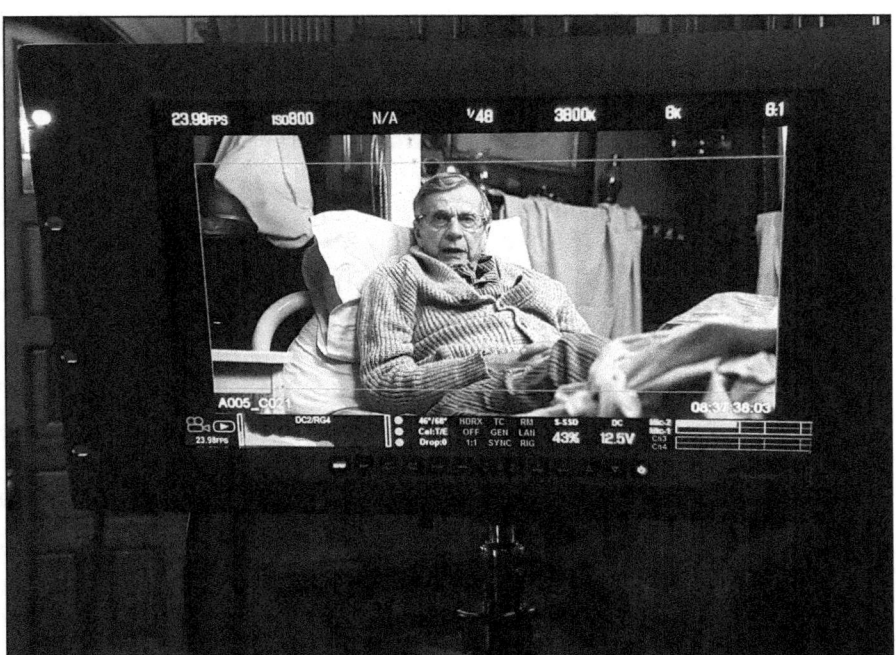

Behind-the-Scenes of Dollar Baby *The Doctor's Case* by James Douglas 2017.

exterior locations that would match or surpass the interiors I had been perusing for nearly two decades. It needed a miracle… and once again Barkerville provided. In a manner of speaking.

In December of 2016, while promoting Barkerville at a nearby tourism industry trade show, I went to dinner with an old friend from Victoria who was working as Visitor Experiences coordinator for Craigdarroch Castle National Historic Site. Built in 1889 by wealthy industrialist and federal politician Robert Dunsmuir, Craigdarroch is a 39-room, 25,000 square foot Scottish Baronial manor house on southern Vancouver Island constructed with locally-sourced granite and sandstone, tile from San Francisco, an elaborate oak staircase from Chicago, and an abundance of additional materials befitting a family of tremendous affluence. The "castle" later served as a military hospital, a college, government offices and a conservatory before it was eventually converted into a historical museum in 1979 and designated a National Historic Site in 1992.

Like Barkerville, Craigdarroch is a jewel in the crown of British Columbia's historic places, and large film companies pay more than five thousand dollars per day to film there. With no budget to even speak about at this point, I had never considered shooting at Craigdarroch – until that very evening. Before I knew what had happened, I found myself making the pitch of a lifetime right there in the restaurant (second only perhaps to the pitch I'd made for the Dollar Baby program a little more than a month earlier).

My friend the Visitor Experiences coordinator came from a theatre background so could totally understand the masochistic thrill of trying to make an officially sanctioned Stephen King movie about Sherlock Holmes with virtually no money. Added to the fact that it was a non-commercial venture that already had one BC-based NHS on board (Barkerville was declared a National Historic Site in 1924) my friend assured me that her board of directors would consider my plea, and she would get back to me as soon as she could. A week later, I got the call. If we agreed to shoot around the castle's operating hours, we could use Craigdarroch as a filming location for both exterior and interior scenes. All the historical society would charge us was the cost of them providing two museum staff members per day; staff whose sole job it was to ensure we didn't wreck the place (and they earned their wages, believe me).

Craigdarroch Castle made for an outstanding Hull House, the site of Sherlock Holmes's "perfect locked room mystery." It was much larger and more ornate than the Savile Row manor home originally described by King, but it was also more cinematic. It was monstrous, and every room came complete with better furniture and artwork and Victorian bric-a-brac than we could have ever provided ourselves. We couldn't touch any artifacts, of course: that's what the staff was for. But it made for great backdrops, and every day we were permitted to bring in (and required to bring back out) matching furniture and props that we could interact with.

The Dunsmuir's mansion became a wholly dynamic character in *The Doctor's Case*, and thanks to its very own history as a wartime field hospital the castle even had a direct influence on the "framing device" we had invented for our version of the story (an octogenarian Dr. Watson talks with an enigmatic military nurse during the London Blitz about events that occurred half a century before). These scenes could now take place in the same location as the murder investigation from fifty years earlier, which would save us a lot of time and effort on set while simultaneously providing new purpose to our creative license. Its suburban estate aesthetic allowed me to shift the in-story location of Hull House from uptown London to the historically-accurate borough of Crouch End, which thrilled both the Stephen King fan in me ("Crouch End" being the title and setting of another of my favourite stories from *Nightmares and Dreamscapes*) and the filmmaker in me (it's an appropriately long carriage ride from Baker Street to the real Crouch End). In short, Craigdarroch Castle was perfect.

The problem was, it was in Victoria. Nearly three hundred miles and one large body of water away. If we were going to accept this unbelievably generous offer to transform the castle into our Hull House, we would have to relocate the entire production from Barkerville to Vancouver Island. A budget-busting move unless we figured out a way to shoot not only the Hull House scenes in Victoria, but pretty much everything else there, too.

So, we did. We hauled everything to Victoria, and briefly bid adieu to Barkerville. The location that had got our ball rolling was no longer the most viable option, but we vowed to film at least one scene at our homespun heritage town as soon as we got back. We shot at Craigdarroch from 5:00 pm to 5:00 am every night for 12 nights in late-April and early-May of 2017. We then spent our days scouring Victoria for suitably London-esque exterior locations before crashing at our rented crew house for a couple of hours and doing it all over again.

Thankfully Victoria prides itself on being "more English than the English," and 19th-century Anglo-architecture abounds. We contacted City Hall about permits to shoot in Bastion Square (a delightfully cobblestoned and self-contained promenade at the heart of a modern city), spoke with some lovely people at a Bastion Square architecture firm about using their building's façade for the exterior of Holmes and Watson's Baker Street apartments, and drove our horse-drawn carriage around anywhere we could find that had a hint of British countryside.

The Baker Street location was our last shot at a heritage hat-trick. Emily Carr House National Historic Site is the early-Victorian home where Emily Carr (arguably Canada's most famous painter) was born and raised. The folks who ran Carr House at the time were good friends of mine through the heritage tourism industry, and they jumped at the chance to be the third in our collection of BC-based NHS shooting locations. For free. Their ground floor dining room became Holmes and Watson's sitting room and a scene shot on the central stairs helped present the illusion that said sitting room was a second-floor apartment. Our production designer and coordinators worked magic on that space, and Emily Carr House remains one of my absolute favourite memories from a memory-laden production.

Upon our return to Barkerville, a little road-weary and a hell of a lot wiser, we set about filming one last scene. We'd saved a flashback to the

Behind-the-Scenes of Dollar Baby *The Doctor's Case* by James Douglas 2017.

birth of one of Lord Hull's children for Dr. Watt's Office in the historic town where this all started, because the 1860s architecture of the gold rush serendipitously matched the "25 years earlier" design our flashback scene would need. The Barkerville shoot was, of course, the easiest on us. By then we were a well-oiled machine, we were back on home turf, and there was something really special about being able to go home to our own beds when production finally wrapped. *The Doctor's Case* started and stopped in Barkerville, made a few spectacular stops at equally inspiring heritage properties along the way, and we couldn't have been happier with the results onscreen. The movie looks and feels as good as it does because of the authenticity of its locations, and they elevated my own experiences as a first-time film director in ways I will never forget.

Otto, Brian, and Me

Fond memories of a deep dive into madness during the filming of *Uncle Otto's Truck*

By Peter Holland

GREAT FILM PARTS don't come along often. Take it from me, an old character actor who has mainly worked on stage his whole career. Otto is a great part. I'm thankful I had the opportunity to play him. I loved every grueling minute of making the film and working with Brian.

I was introduced to Brian Johnson a couple of years ago by Whitney Hodges, a former drama student of mine and my wife, Christina. Whitney thought I might be right for Otto (Thank you, Whitney!) and recommended that Brian read me for the part.

Whitney, Brian, and I then met in front of the Andy Griffith Playhouse in Mount Airy, NC and I had my first audition for Brian. Maybe I impressed him with my pantomime wood chopping or my willingness to scream "Come and get me, you son of a bitch!" at the top of my lungs in a public place.

Months later he asked for a second audition. We went up on the Blue Ridge Parkway and filmed a scene I had memorized in an old abandoned house. He gave me the part.

Then shooting was delayed because Brian and his wife, Tresha, lost their home from flooding caused by Hurricane Florence.

A less determined artist may have given up on making *Uncle Otto's Truck*. Not Brian. A few months after the hurricane he contacted me and said we were back on, that we would shoot the film this summer (2019). In the months that followed he sent me script revisions. We communicated regularly about Otto's motivations and guilt, his obsession with the truck, and the triggers for his insanity.

Was there a spark of good in this character, I wondered? Could he reach some level of remorse and take responsibility for his crime?

We shot most of my scenes in Levering's Orchard just off the Parkway. It's a beautiful place, but very rugged with rough roads and steep, rocky terrain.

I remember when filming the window scene where Otto sees the truck moving outside, that a Stephen King description from the story came to me. When the boy, Quinten, says to Otto that the truck isn't moving, Otto replies "with a wild and infinite contempt" according to Stephen King, "That's just what you see, boy! That's just what you see!"

During one of the takes I hit that contempt attitude just right on the first line and instantly, a wave of regret and remorse engulfed me. Then I repeated the line and could really feel Otto's agony. That's what you want as an actor. You want to know the character backwards and forwards, but always be open to new emotions and new directions for the character.

Brian gave me that artistic freedom to fully explore the character. We share a working class attitude and a silly sense of humor. God willing, we'll be doing more films together. He's just a great guy and an all-around superb filmmaker.

Dollar Baby Memories

By Tonya Ivey

SOON AFTER MOVING TO LOS ANGELES, Jay Holben approached me about making
"Paranoid: A Chant." Initially, I was nervous to take on a project penned by Stephen King, one of my creative heroes, but I trusted Jay and was excited to give it a go. I read the poem many times and in my first few passes I imagined the narrator as a man. I loved the idea of twisting my initial impression, but I wasn't quite sure where to begin. Jay was a great captain and together we created what this woman's world would look and feel like. He gave me journals, which I filled with conspiracies, observations and anecdotes.

I spent a lot of time alone and imagined what it would be like to live in her world. I fantasized about "the enemy" creeping around corners and peering through windows. I listened for code through the hum of my TV. I sought out secret compartments and hidden listening devices. I held my breath when dusty light particles filled the room. Fixation on these small details, helped ease me into her world of complete isolation with an understanding of what it must be like to be truly "Paranoid."

To this day, this project remains one of my favorite moments in filmmaking. I feel extremely lucky to have been a part of it.

How I Became a Fan of Stephen King

By Oscar Garrido

I WAS 12 YEARS OLD when I first read Stephen King. It was a hot summer. My mother was sleeping. My father worked in Switzerland for 8 months and came to Spain to spend four months on vacation. My older brother was four years older than me and had a lot of Stephen King novels in paperback. The two or three hours that the time nap lasted were eternal – it was very hot outside to go out to play – and we both had to play quietly, so as not to wake my mother and all our neighbors. My brother allowed me to read a short story from the *Night Shift* collection titled "*The Boogeyman*". When I finished reading it I was like "Wow! This is the best short story I have ever read." My brother asked me to read another story and recommended "*Quitters, Inc.*" Again I loved it. That's where my love for Stephen King's work began. In two or three years I read all the short stories and I start to reading the novels that my brother had in paperback: *Salem's Lot, The Dead Zone, Christine, The Stand, The Eyes of the Dragon, Four Past Midnight* and the only novel from King that I read after seeing the movie, *Pet Sematary*. In my town Library there were a lot of Stephen King novels, but because of my age, 15 or 16 at the time, I was afraid that they wouldn't lend me all those books. Fortunately, they never told me anything about it and so I managed to read more Stephen King novels: *Tommyknockers, Thinner, The Long Walk, Roadwork* and *It*, my favorite novel of all time. During that time I had saved some money and I became a Stephen King collector. I remember reading all of his novels when *Needful Things* was published. I was up to date. My passion continues (with some incident) Although I do not complain about how I have lived my life, luck turned its back on me when I was 29 years old. I had an accident at work and soon the aftermath appeared and I started to lose hearing in my right ear. It was a hard blow to accept it, but I got up stronger than ever. In those years I really liked going to concerts, but due to the accident I forced myself to quit. At 33 my hearing problem worsened and I started going to Literature conferences. I learned a lot there. They offered me to do book reviews for a website. And I did it for two years. At that time I was a contributor to Insomnia, the most widely read digital magazine on the work of Stephen King and had been the organizer of the first Dollar Baby Festival in Spain. Two years later I collaborated in the Argentine edition, called King On Screen. Currently I continue collaborating with my Argentine friends. I also collaborated on a podcast that received great reviews from the press and the public. The podcast was nominated for the Best Podcast in Spain. I collaborated on four programs. In these four shows I talked about the Dollar Babies that had been filmed and a comic special based on King's works, but soon after I had to quit. Again my hearing was getting worse. Despite everything, a new opportunity knocked on my door. I was offered to be the management

Here There Be Tygers: My Story

By Bryan Higby

How did I become a Stephen King Dollar Baby director? I guess we start with my first exposure to Mr. King's work. I was just a kid, a real little kid when I watched Tobe Hooper's terrifying version of *Salem's Lot* starring David Soul and James Mason. Yeah I started my King education in film and television long before I bought King's unabridged version of *The Stand* when I was fifteen. *Salem's Lot*, *The Dead Zone*, *Christine*, *The Shining, Cujo, Carrie, Creepshow*, and *Pet Sematary* were all movies and TV shows I watched before I bought *The Stand* in 1990. King was a legend in the Higby home. My parents, Raymond and Barbara, ran their own video store from the early 1990's through 2007, when tragically the place burned to the ground. In that time, I watched a lot of Horror films, other genres too, but Horror was my favorite and Stephen King was the master.

I was fifteen when I first read *The Stand*. My parents bought me a six month subscription to the Stephen King Library when I was a teenager. With that subscription I got six hardbacks, all King classics from *The Dark Half, Misery, Needful Things,* the *Stephen King Encyclopedia*, a hardback of *The Stand*, and *Nightmare and Dreamscapes*. I was hooked. King was my Horror drug of choice. I also read Clive Barker, but King spoke to me in a way that no other writer had spoken to me.

Speed ahead nearly thirty years. I continue to read King work, new and old. I watch film and television adaptations. Some good, some not so good. I started writing my first novel when I was seventeen. This would have been about six novels into King's cannon. That's what I wanted to do for a living, make stuff up. It wasn't until many years later that I would subscribe to King's philosophy of writing; that he pretty much just documents a higher calling. Something flushes through him. He taps into something greater than himself. I've written thirty novels, some on my own, some with my cousin Ricky Snyder. But all of them come from a similar creative source that King talks about. Sometimes I think all writers and creators tap into that same source. My connection to King didn't just start when I started writing novels, but it continues.

I'd known about the Dollar Baby deal for almost twenty years. I had heard that going back to the late 1970's when King started becoming a bestselling author that young filmmakers started contacting him for permission to adapt his short fiction into short films. Against his lawyer and agents best wishes Mr. King said yes. Joe Schiro I think was the first. Frank Darabont who is the most famous went on to become an Academy Award Nominated director of several of King's strongest works – *Shawshank Redemption*, *The Green Miles*, and His Dollar Baby was "*The Woman In The Room*". I think that all of us Dollar Babies have Darabont to thank for doing such a fantastic job with his Dollar Baby film, because if it had been a disaster who knows if the Dollar Deal would have continued for nearly forty years.

My personal experience with the Dollar Deal happened in 2018. At that point I had written nearly thirty novels. Many of which were published in print, eBook, and audiobook versions, but none had reached bestseller status. So, I started to take stock. How the heck could I get enough awareness of my fiction to hit the bestsellers list? This was not pure vanity. I'm married with three kids. I have a family to provide for. I reached out to Mr. King through his website. I went to his forums but there were like a million. I eventually got connected with Marsha DeFilippo King's personal assistant in the late 1980's. She encouraged me. Marsha allowed me to submit three of my Horror novels: *Pizza Man*, *Taco Bandits*, and *Chuck A Chik*, to Mr. King. When they arrived at his office in Bangor, she assured me that she placed them on his shelf (with a million others).

A few months later I got my Dollar Deal for "*Here There Be Tygers*". We filmed our short at Hudson Valley Community College in Troy NY on March 24, 2019. The film has since shown in the Netherlands, at the first ever Dollar Baby festival at the historic Town Hall Theater in Lowville NY, at the George Eastman Museum for Kodak in Rochester NY, (Our film opened on Halloween night, 2019), and at the Water NY Snowtown Film Festival in January 2020.

My experience hosting two Dollar Baby festivals was great. My first festival was at the historic Town Hall Theater in Lowville NY. With the help of Patrick O'Brien and his family we had ten dollar baby films from across the United States that played. I created my Dollar Baby list with the help from Shawn S. Lealos whose book: *Dollar Deal the Stephen King Dollar Baby Filmmakers*. Shawn was extremely helpful in sending me email addresses for many filmmakers. These filmmakers were incredible. They all sent me their films in either DVD format or links to protected sites. Jay Holben who produced and directed "Paranoid: A Chant", a King poem, who was the only Dollar Baby to date to be allowed to show his entire film in its entirety on-line with King's permission sent me a remastered version of *"Paranoid: A Chant"*. Pat O'Brien, owner of the Town Hall Theater, allowed our festival to play at no cost to me. The O'Brien family are huge supporters of independent filmmakers.

Funny story about the Town Hall festival. After I got permission to produce, *"Here There Be Tygers"*, I started to think about the exposure and having already shown my indie films at the Town Hall Theater in Lowville NY I knew Pat O'Brien. I reached out to Pat to ask if he might allow me to rent the theater for a couple of hours to have this Stephen King festival. He said no, I could have the theater space for free. LOL! Shortly after assembling the other ten filmmakers on my roster I reached out to King's assistant Marsha telling her about our festival and where it was. She surprised me by saying that she mentioned my film *"Here There Be Tygers"* and the festival to Steve. Steve was very interested in both my movie and the festival. He wanted me to keep him posted on the dates. I almost died with excitement. As the time approached for our festival hope was still alive that King would come. Marsha told me that Steve had relatives who lived in Lowville for a time and that Steve wrote about Lowville in *Firestarter* and *The Stand*. King was genuinely interested in attending but he wanted to slip in and slip out without any fan fair. I said that could be arranged. Unfortunately, as the time arrived for our festival King's streaming series *Lisey's Story* was greenlit by AT&T. He needed to be on set the weekend of our festival. So we missed out meeting King.

My second hosted festival was at Hudson Valley Community College. We were their centerpiece for their November 2019 Arts Festival. I was paid to speak about my Dollar Baby experience as well as my writing and movie directing experience. That festival was about half the length of the Lowville festival. But I do intend to continue hosting Stephen King

Dollar Baby Film Fest October 19, 2019 in Lowville, New York.

festivals. We had about a hundred guests in Lowville, population 3,600, not bad and about eighty at the Hudson Valley festival.

My experience with the Dollar Baby films has been nothing short of magical. I have Mr. King, Marsha and his team to thank for my opportunity to play in King's sandbox and piggy back on his name brand. I'm hoping that Mr. King will get a chance to read the novels I sent him: *Pizza Man, Taco Bandits,* and *Chuck A Chik.* I also hope that your readers, Anthony, will take the time to visit my Amazon author site here: https://www.amazon.com/-/e/B00CWEFNVS

I would also like to thank Anthony Northrup for inviting me to write this essay for his Dollar Baby book. It's been an honor and a pleasure.

The Curse of *Stephen King's Sometimes They Come Back*

By Tom McLoughlin

MY RELATIONSHIP WITH *Sometimes They Come Back* was cursed. Both in an actual and supernatural sense.

In all the films I have made over the years none have had the bizarre events that surrounded this one. It's prep, production and post were the biggest emotional roller coaster ride of my life. So many personal and professional situations all colliding at the same time. Yet somehow the mix of all of this created a film that is very personal to me and one I'm extremely proud of artistically.

Some movies you make. Some you survive. *Sometimes They Come Back* was a survival experience of the highest order.

The year 1990 was unlike any I had before or since. In my family life I was going through two major events. The birth of my daughter and the last days of my father. Knowing he was dying and doing everything possible to make my dad feel secure and loved was extremely emotional. During this same time my wife grew closer to having our baby, one of life's most joyful events. But it appeared both were going to occur simultaneously.

Meanwhile, my career never had so many jobs crisscrossing. I was prepping a pilot for Disney of *Steven Banks* Home Entertainment Center. I was not only the director of this four-camera comedy (something I had never done before), but Steven is also my longtime best friend (still is) and I wanted it to be great. I was also collaborating with my other good friend Mick Garris on two series with 20 episodes each for Universal Television *She-Wolf of London* and *They Came From Outer Space*. Then out of the blue producer Dino De Laurentiis called with an immediate green light for Stephen King's *Sometimes They Come Back*. All of these shows I had to creatively juggle.

Since this article is about making the Stephen King movie, I'll spare you all the details how things all managed to work themselves out and just say my father peacefully passed on and we brought our newborn daughter Hannah to Kansas for the movie shoot.

Anyone who has read King's short story knows we really took liberties with the script. So much had to be added, fleshed out, and still keep the essence of the core story. The first script I was shown was written by Lawrence Konner and Mark Rosenthal (*Jewel of the Nile, Superman; A Quest for Peace*). It was good but for me lacked the deeper family dynamic and a haunting and emotional tone that I felt was needed in a King tale.

Dino agreed and liked the ideas I proposed for the changes. But since we were already in prep with shooting dates locked in, I did not have the time to write it myself. We needed someone who got what we were after. Enter a talented, young, up and coming writer, Tim Kring. He had written a movie Bay Coven that I liked (he later created/produced the hugely popular series *Heroes*) and we hit it off instantly. His draft is the one we shot even though Konner/Rosenthal were credited.

With the casting I was truly blessed thanks to casting director David Cohn. Tim Matheson WAS Jim Norman to me in every aspect. A warm, loving husband/father and teacher who suppressed a secret from his childhood that caused emotional outbursts at previous schools. Tim is also an incredible person and we had a very strong bond working together. Brooke Adams was someone I always loved after first seeing her in *Days of Heaven*. She has such an unique cinematic quality. Robert Rusler, Nicholas Sadler, and Bentley Mitchum as the greasers from hell are unforgettable in their roles. They also gave me so many needed laughs on and off screen with their bad boy antics. And Chris Demetral's performance as Jim's older brother Wayne was the heart of the film to me.

I can go on and on with praise for all the others in the cast as well. There was certainly no curse in the acting dept of '*Sometimes*'.

Then what was cursed? Pretty much everything else had unexplainable problems and setbacks. Could it have been due to us unknowingly shooting the film's key scenes on the site of an ancient Native American burial ground?

What logically caused so much turmoil that production went eight days over schedule… unheard of in a low budget film.

Let's start with Day One. After much research of Kansas City's weather conditions at that time of year and the assurance of the Film Commission, we awoke at 4am to everything covered in two feet of snow! All our scenes were exterior and none of the interiors were ready to shoot yet. So, we shoveled off the porch of the Norman home and shot Jim Norman coming out of a nightmare and his wife finding him crying on the porch. That's all we could shoot. Day One we are behind a day.

It never snowed another day, but the air and wind chill were far below zero with everyone in pain from the bitter cold.

We continued to have serious issues that caused us to go further and further behind schedule. It seemed like every day an ambulance came to set because some extra or crew member got hurt. Never anything major, just injuries that delayed filming. Brooke twisted her ankle and couldn't do the scenes scheduled.

Another day something angered the transportation dept and they left all the trucks and vehicles at the previous location. There was an unusual number of crew walkouts during the show. Lighting set-ups took hours beyond normal due to weird miscommunication breakdowns. Firing and hiring new crew to be flown out.

Towards the end of the shoot the elderly actor who played the Old Cop had a massive heart attack back in Los Angeles. Since it was the first job in many years, he begged our producer Michael Murphy to not hire someone else. He desperately needed this job. The sweet man arrived weak and feeble and sadly couldn't remember any of his lines. We made huge cue cards that Tim Matheson held while they did the scene together.

Miraculously we got it done and sent the grateful actor back to L.A. happy he got to do the role.

Then we learned that the cameras shooting that day had been accidently using daylight exterior film stock that was being exposed for night interior. The scene was ruined with no chance of a reshoot. Fortunately, during post production the timer was able to get enough of an acceptable image so the scene, although washed out looking, is in the film.

But the most frightening incident occurred in the 'cursed' train tunnel. We did a lot of work in that location; the young Norman boys being bullied by the gang, the killing of Wayne, the death of all but one of the bullies, the adult Jim Norman confronting the dead gang members, and the redemptive ending with Wayne, the bullies, and the Norman family.

There was a moment near the final scene when Tim Matheson is down on the ground next to the train track. After I called 'Cut', Tim stood up. Literally the second he did a two-foot boulder dropped from the top of the rock tunnel and slammed down <u>exactly where Tim's head was</u>. A bolt of adrenaline shot through all of us terrified by what almost just occurred. This was too impossible to explain.

Or maybe not.

When we finished and were exiting the tunnel a local was standing and staring at us. As I passed him, he smiled, "Any other bad things happen to you folks"

I was surprised and a bit spooked by his attitude. I asked what he meant. He quite casually explained that what we are standing on, and the mountain that the train tunnel was dug through, was once all Indian burial ground. My immediate response was a laugh and a "You're kidding". He shrugged, "That's what they say. The river rose years ago and flooded everybody out of this area. That's why no trains come through here."

Now I was hooked. I had to share that this movie has had so many unexplainable problems. That ironic dark side of me wanted to be able to blame all our bad luck on something supernatural. Being innocent victims of an ancient curse is a far better story to tell why things went wrong. I asked him, "Do you believe in a curse?" He said, "Nope. I'm a born-again Christian."

I've always wanted to meet Stephen King and tell him this aspect of making this film that bears his name. I think he'd find it amusing.

As the years have gone by this movie that I survived has become deeper and more haunting to me. What is a somewhat traditional 'evil ghost from one's past return to torment them for being responsible for their deaths' has a lot more personal subtext then I was aware of at the time. The beautiful score by composer Terry Pulmeri, (that I am obsessed with), truly does capture the soul of the film. There's a strong feeling of love and humanity in it.

Yes, there are lots of classic Stephen King tropes in *Sometimes They Come Back*. But now for me I can sense the grief for the loss of my father and the hope for the future with the birth of my daughter. Also having my four-year-old son Shane on the set with me obviously bonded me to the father/son/brother aspects of the film in ways I was not conscious of when making it.

Maybe just working in the world of Stephen King and his characters you can't help but tap into the deeper aspects of life. And you get scared because you care about these characters.

Finally, despite the 'curse' we faced, getting the movie made I truly feel it did mysteriously capture who I was at that time in my life. I never thought I would ever say that about a horror film I made.

The Long Maybe of Dollar Babies

By Kevin Quigley

THE WHOLE DOLLAR BABY thing is so weird that I didn't get it at first.

I first heard about them in Stephen Spignesi's *The Shape Under the Sheet: The Stephen King Encyclopedia*. My local bookstore had to special order that book, and it was so massive and expensive I spent most of the next two months paying for it in increments with paper route money. My mom, in an uncharacteristic display of generosity, ended up paying off the balance for my fourteenth birthday. It was 1989 and I carted that five-pound sucker everywhere, absorbing so much Stephen King knowledge, lore, and ephemera that I could barely keep it all in my head.

Dollar Babies were just another aspect of the onslaught at first ... and they weren't called Dollar Babies then. The section in the *Encyclopedia* was simply called "Student Cinema Focuses on Stephen King," exploring two of the earliest DBs, "*The Last Rung on the Ladder*" (directed by James Cole and Dan Thron) and "*The Lawnmower Man*" (directed by Jim Gonis). As exciting as the article was for a kid just starting to understand the broader scope of the Stephen King thing, a lot of what we now understand as the basic tenets of Dollar Babies were simply left out of the piece. No mention of the dollar deal, or how you were supposed to send a copy to King himself, and nothing about keeping the whole production noncommercial. The whole genre was still so nascent that maybe it didn't even have a name yet.

Spignesi's article also quoted a *Castle Rock* essay written by "*Last Rung*" co-director Cole, but I was still new to everything. I only had the vaguest idea of what *Castle Rock* was. Flash-forward three years and

I'm in a used bookstore in Boston that just happens to have purchased a whole passel of old *Castle Rock* newsletters ... including the one with Cole's essay, "The Good and Bad of Film Adaptation." I read it. Studied it. At this point, I'm studying everything with even a tertiary connection to King. This was my GREAT INTEREST, if the allusion to *"Apt Pupil"* isn't too horrifying. It's a fantastic essay, but still no mention of the term "Dollar Babies," or the rules. And would I ever get to *see "The Last Rung on the Ladder"*? Maybe. A long maybe. But probably not.

What the essay *did* mention was another couple of student films that had already been made, ones that had eluded Spignesi's time: *"The Woman in the Room,"* directed by someone named Frank Darabont, and *"The Boogeyman,"* directed by Jeffrey C. Shiro. I looked up from my *Castle Rock*. "Wait a minute," I said to myself. "I *know* those."

You have to remember: this is in the pre-Internet days. Even the text-based version of the Web that would eventually come to my local library was still years off. The way I learned my Stephen King minutiae in those days was through research, reading, and random happenstance. I dug through my old video cassettes until I unearthed one I'd labeled *Stephen King's World of Horror* in the same barely legible scrawl I still employ today. Clicking on my ancient TV and VCR I fed the tape in and fast-forwarded until I got what I wanted. Long clips of both films, seemingly professional, interspersed among selections from other cinematic King fare like *Maximum Overdrive* and *Creepshow*. If anything, the student films almost looked *better* than the ones I'd seen on HBO and videocassette. How had I never heard of these before?

The problem, in those early-ish days of King fandom (and remember, this is circa 1989-1991, which felt to me like an awfully late time to become a fan ... but the reality was that King's first novel had only been birthed into the world a year or so before I was, and I caught up as quickly as I could), it was a lot harder to know everything, to have a universal knowledge of King. Especially for a kid growing up poor in deep suburbia, someone who had to save up paper route money in order to buy *Needful Things* in hardcover day one, the ready access to knowledge simply wasn't there. Picking up *The Stephen King Companion* by George Beahm broadened my knowledge considerably, and I read it to literal tatters. The short volume *Stephen King: The Art of Darkness* was a constant handbook. Beyond those lay nothing. I heard rumors about a whole set of Borgo Press books that tackled King from a more academic perspective, but I had no idea what a Borgo Press even *was*.

And thus, my trail to find Dollar Babies ran cold, and I forgot about them. After all, King movies were a dime a dozen, and I was in the phase of my fandom when I was willing to watch literally anything. Sometimes you get great, like with *Misery*. Sometimes you get pretty good, like with *It*. Sometimes you get a *Graveyard Shift*. We can't always win.

The Dollar Baby thing went public in 1996, when King published his essay discussing the phenomenon in his introduction to Frank Darabont's shooting script for *The Shawshank Redemption*. 1996 was also the year the Internet finally hit the suburbs. I was twenty-one, living on my own, and trekking to the Quincy Public Library every day to log in and talk to the Stephen King fan-friends I found on the computer. The group I gravitated toward most was called SKEMERs – short for Stephen King E-MailERs, because in our primitive computer world, we had to email the head of the club every day, and she would compile the emails into a newsletter and send it back out. The 90s, man. I can barely imagine doing anything like this today. I get freaked out if the waiting ellipses pulse for longer than 30 seconds after I send a text.

Interest in the subject of Dollar Babies rose to a frenzied pitch in my small bubble of King aficionados. There was such scant information on this whole new avenue of peripheral King material that no one really knew where to look. We were still calling the internet the "World Wide Web" and "The Information Superhighway" with no sense of irony, but the truth is, the vast stores of knowledge that were on the horizon hadn't really arrived yet. You had to know someone who had firsthand information for anything approaching clarity. Luckily, the SKEMERs knew someone.

Now, all these years later, I'm not entirely sure who got us that copy of "*The Last Rung on the Ladder*," but I know the first viewing happened during a SKEMERs convention. Oh yes. We had conventions. A year after the group began, we all piled into cars and planes and buses and headed up to Bangor, Maine for a little taste of the King's life. I know we didn't watch James Cole's short film that first year, because we were too busy crammed into Room 218 of the Days Inn to *MST3K* the Kubrick version of *The Shining* (217 was occupied). It was the first time I'd ever been drunk and the whole situation was hazily glorious. We guzzled whiskey coolers and wandered around the outskirts of Bangor talking about the implications of *The Dark Tower*. But the second convention, where we all got a little more organized and a little more invested ... I think that's when I saw my first Dollar Baby.

I liked it a lot. It was a student presentation, sure, but I'd seen how Hollywood could muck up short story adaptations more than once. *Children of the Corn* and *Maximum Overdrive* had a certain cheesy charm, but nothing could forgive *Graveyard Shift*. But "*The Last Rung on the Ladder*" was one of King's quiet, beautiful, tragic stories that don't get adapted into gory, big-budget splatterfests or TNT original movies. As a kid just getting his footing in the world of King, I'd read about this film, knowing it was an unfindable and unwatchable thing, always out of reach. And here it was in front of me, as well-acted and produced as Stephen Spignesi promised it was.

It was a special moment, made even more special years later when, on a trip to Los Angeles, I actually met James Cole, the film's co-writer and co-director. We re-watched "*Last Rung*." He showed me his other, more mature work, *The Night Before*. We talked about Stephen King and movies and Los Angeles; here I was, sitting on the couch with someone I'd read about and wondered about and admired for years and I was becoming friends with him. The fan world of Stephen King is a strange place.

What I didn't figure on was the resurgence.

One of my go-to website check-ins every day is Lilja's Library, who's had the leading Stephen King fan site since 1996 (at one time, I had the salutatorian fansite, but then, you know, *life*). When I first read there was going to be a Dollar Baby of the poem "*Paranoid*," my immediate reaction was, "That's not real. Lilja must have gotten some wrong information." Who could make a Dollar Baby out of a poem? One that wasn't even narrative, really?

Then in 2000, Jay Holben's masterful short film starring Tonya Ivey appeared online like magic, the same year that King's "*Riding the Bullet*" was released exclusively to the Internet. Lilja absolutely *hadn't* gotten it wrong; I had. It seemed to me that we were entering a brand-new era of Stephen King, one in which new Dollar Babies, once the domain of a few disconnected but passionate artists, could now come out from behind the shroud of mystery and into the light.

You know, there's a whole fan attitude, a lament, that things aren't as exciting or as pure as they were when they, the fan, got into their fandom. As the band Drive-By Truckers puts it: "Everyone claims that the times are a-changin' as theirs pass them by / and everyone's right." Was it thrilling to read about Dollar Babies in Spignesi's book and to be one of the few who had seen one, as opposed to just surfing over to Wikipedia and reading about it, or seeing one online? Absolutely, just as it was exciting to snag an illicit copy of "*The Glass Floor*" long before it appeared in *Cemetery Dance*. When getting your hands and eyes on hidden art is a maybe prospect, it can be intoxicating when that maybe turns into yes. That intoxication can turn to gatekeeping easily: new fans aren't real fans because they've never had to live in a world where *Blaze* was just a trunk novel and Cole's "*The Last Rung on the Ladder*" was just an item in an encyclopedia.

But if there's anything that my own journey as a Stephen King person has taught me, it's that stories are meant to be read, and movies are meant to be seen. Dollar Babies have touched on the fringes of my fan-life all these years, and at the start I could never have imagined there would be grand viewings and conventions tied to this art form that seemed so obscure. Not anymore, and I'm happy for it. The making of art is personal, but the enjoyment of art should be public. And after all these years, it still only costs a buck.

I'm Gonna Scare the Hell Out of You... And That's a Promise!

By David Tocher

SUMMERTIME. NINETEEN EIGHTY-SIX. My aunt's trailer in Cache Creek, British Columbia. I was eight years old, and this was the hallowed ground where I first encountered the works of Stephen King.

My aunt had rows of bookshelves running the length of her hallway—one section dedicated exclusively to King's hardcovers. To say I felt a magnetic attraction to them would not be exaggerating. Each one whispered in that beseeching voice that only the heart can hear: "Take me off the shelf, David, hold me, sniff my binding, flip through my pages, study my cover art, and, most importantly, read me."

Skeleton Crew's toy monkey, and the menacing Pet Sematary cat both seemed to call out. Come on, big guy. Let's go for a ride. Let's cruise.

At that moment, I abandoned childish hobbies and became fixated with a single-minded purpose—reading Stephen King novels.

These stories desired me; and I, them. It was love at first sight for us both. And true first love can be dangerous.

I tried to read Christine, but I was barely able to make it past the first paragraph. King's vocabulary and his compound sentences were too advanced for my eight-year-old mind to grasp.

After that summer, I returned home to East Vancouver, where I'd go to the library, and where, along with the Choose Your Own Adventure and Dark Forces series, I would sign out stacks of Stephen King novels from the Adult Fiction section. I didn't care if I couldn't read them yet. I craved their presence, flipping longingly through their pages, my desire to read them increasing every day.

One time, I'd gotten my hands on a copy of Cycle of the Werewolf. It was also difficult to read, but…it had illustrations! Bernie Wrightson's gruesome depictions of the werewolf attacking the townspeople absolutely, wickedly, enthralled me. I brought it to school to show my friends, but when my grade-four teacher saw it, she confiscated the book until my mom came in personally to get it. I hated that teacher with a raw and venomous loathing. How could I not? She had come between me and my first love.

Video stores wouldn't allow a kid my age to rent horror movies without parental consent, so, when I saw films like Cujo, Christine, or The Shining on their shelves, I could only gaze ardently at the VHS boxes in vain. It felt as if the entire world was conspiring to keep me away from Stephen King stories—whether in written or cinematic format.

After a couple years had passed, I was now the worldly-wise age of ten. Look out, world. One night, while I was watching TV after school, I saw the trailer for Maximum Overdrive. You know, the one where Stephen points his finger at you and says, "I'm gonna scare the hell out of you… and that's a promise!"

When the channel announced that the movie would air late the next Friday night, my heart swelled with joy. My mom had already taught me how to pre-record television programs for her, so I devised a plan. With the same stealth and determination of Marty Coslaw sneaking out of his house with his wonderful bag of fireworks, I secretly recorded Maximum Overdrive on a blank VHS, and hid it, then watched it when no one else was home.

I'll never forget the opening scene: Planet Earth, suspended in outer space, suddenly enwreathed in sickly green light, as words were superimposed onto the screen…

"On June 19th, 1987, at 9:47 A.M. EST, the Earth passed into the extraordinarily diffuse tail of Rhea-M, a rogue comet …"

A free-floating dread crept into my heart, along with the constraint to keep watching.

I followed the film until the driverless steamroller crashed its way into the baseball park. That scene filled the ten-year-old me with horror—a true, sinking horror that hit me way too close to home.

In other movies I'd watched, only adults died and maybe the teenagers if they were really bad. Little children? They were safe. It was as if being a kid granted you immunity from death. This was one of the many comforting, unspoken lies of Movie Land.

Not in Stephen King's universe. In his world, children could be crushed under steamrollers or have their heads bashed in with flying cans of cola.

All of this was too real because it spoke to me on a deep, instinctual level. Sure, the premise of machines coming to life was far fetched…but still, there was a truth underneath the fiction, and that's what gave the film its power.

Stephen King was communicating on a raw emotional level, and if one were to translate that visceral emotion into words the best one could, even at the risk of committing intentional fallacy, the message was this:

You're trapped on this planet, kid. You can't escape. Oh, and everything here is out to kill you…even the little children aren't safe.

As Angus Young played his dark and bluesy guitar riffs for the film's score, I saw a steamroller crush a little boy underneath it—a boy my own age! Fearfulness and trembling came upon me, and horror of great darkness took ahold of me; alone at home, I burst into tears and screamed. It took me a bit of time to collect myself, but after I did, I watched the movie all the way to the end.

"I'm gonna scare the hell out of you…and that's a promise!"

Well, Stephen, you kept that promise. You kept it real good.

It's no secret that Stephen King himself does not like the first and only movie he has ever written and directed (and I understand why he feels that way). I still love Maximum Overdrive, however, for all its cheesy '80s gloriousness. I'm a grown man now, in my early forties, and those death scenes don't frighten me anymore. But every now and again, I pop my Maximum Overdrive disk in the Blu-ray and watch it on the widescreen TV, and when I do, the hairs still raise on my arms and I still get the shivers. Why? Because it takes me back to the first time a film truly scared the hell out of me.

And, for a horror fan, going down that memory lane is the same as reminiscing about your first romantic kiss…in the dark.

Now, you're probably wondering, how did our little David finally get what he was longing for—to finally read those Stephen King novels that seized his attention all those years ago?

Here's how it happened.

When I was eleven, I had saved money from my paper route, and I used it to buy a copy of Night Shift. While flipping through the paperback at the bookstore, I noticed that it had a story in it called Trucks, and wondered if perhaps it could be the basis for the movie I'd watched. Turned out I was right.

By then, I was almost a teenager, and I had matured to the point where I was able to comprehend King's writing. Plus, they were short stories, which were more suited to my attention span at that time. All I needed was a little patience.

I remember the first three stories in Night Shift that I read—Quitters, Inc., The Mangler, and Trucks. I was proud of myself for being able to read a "Grown Up Book." That sense of accomplishment, however, did not come without a catch—The Mangler scared the crap out of me. I slept with my desk light on for an entire week after reading that.

Then, by the time I was twelve, I had read The Shining. That was my first King novel. The Room 217 scene came alive in my mind, making me scream and throw the book across the room.

"I'm gonna scare the hell out of you…and that's a promise!"

As I said before, Stephen King kept his promise. But he also did something else. He ignited a promise within me.

Looking back, I see that he stirred up my desire to read, to possess intellectual maturity, and to understand ways of communicating that were above my reach—and to ultimately become a writer myself.

And he did that for more than just me. I mean, look at you, reading this. You showed up to the party too. So did an entire generation of '80s kids who would go on to become writers and filmmakers. A generation dedicated to their own promise.

Thank you, Stephen King.

Blood In the Veins:
The Spiritual Collaborations of Stephen King and Frank Darabont

By Andrew J. Rausch

STEPHEN KING HAS HAD HIS WORK adapted into nearly 100 films, making him one of the most adapted authors in literary history. Despite this, less than 10 of those movies are actually what you might call "good." Several are downright great. But there is one screenwriter/director who has consistently fashioned quality King film adaptations, and that man is Frank Darabont. He is, in my humble but deadly accurate estimation, the single finest adapter of King's work (sorry, William Goldman). This essay will explore all of the King/Darabont collaborations to date. I know, I know, they aren't *technically* collaborations since King himself wasn't actually assisting Darabont with the script writing. But I assert that they absolutely should be recognized as collaborations, and I will get into that later in this piece.

The story of Darabont's most famous of all Stephen King "dollar babies" began in 1980. At that time, the 20-year-old would-be filmmaker was working as a theater usher. Darabont dreamed of being a Hollywood screenwriter and director. Since he hadn't attended film school, he believed the clearest path towards achieving that would be to create a quality short film that he could show as a calling card. He then read and enjoyed Stephen King's *Night Shift* short story "The Woman in the Room," about a man considering euthanizing his terminally ill mother. Finding the story "lovely and deeply moving," Darabont sought to adapt the story to screen. He then wrote King a letter asking for his permission, and King wrote back. Darabont recalls, "Because he is a great human being and believes in giving back his success, he said yes. Go ahead. See what happens." (*On Story*, episode 402.) King then explained to Darabont that he had established the Dollar Baby program in 1977, allowing film students and would-be filmmakers to purchase the rights to his available short stories for a single dollar. So, Darabont forked over his dollar and the process began.

Darabont would then spend the next three years making the 16mm short film. First he went to work on the script. In adapting the story, he realized he would have to alter it a bit. While Darabont once told me he believes most King adaptations fail due to the adapters' not being able to see past the horror elements of King's work, Darabont did this himself with *The Woman in the Room*. While the original story is a decidedly non-horror (in the traditional sense of horror) story, Darabont added a horrific dream sequence in which John, the protagonist, is chased and then confronted by his grotesquely-decayed dead mother. When I asked Darabont why he added this scene, he told me, "I think I wrote that scene because I wanted to keep the film from being a talking-head movie. I mean, that's mainly what it is: thirty minutes of those characters sitting and talking. I just felt like I needed something else there." In addition, he also added a new character, billed only as Prisoner.

While Darabont tinkered with the script, he landed a low-level film industry job as a production assistant (glorified go-fer) on the Linda Blair-starrer *Hell Night*.

When he eventually went to cast the film, Darabont was lucky enough to land experienced actors in Michael Cornelison, Dee Croxton, and Brian Libby. (It should be noted that Darabont later cast Croxton in *The Green Mile* and has used Libby in all of his subsequent films.)

The total budget for *The Woman in the Room* isn't known, but it wasn't much. Darabont raised the majority of the funds from a group of undisclosed investors from Iowa. In addition to this, Darabont put most of his yearly earnings into the project. He would later tell Hans Lilja of *Lilja's Library* that he earned $11,000 one year and put $7,000 of that into the film. "How I survived on $4,000 that year is something I still can't explain," Darabont said. "To this day I have no idea how I did it." (Darabont went on to say that the IRS did not believe he had lived on this paltry sum and wound up auditing him.) "All I can say is, my rent was cheap and I lived very frugally."

Darabont also figured out creative ways to cut costs. For instance, the decayed corpse prop for the dream sequence was one he had worked with (adjacently) on *Hell Night*. Remembering the prop, Darabont reached out to the film's makeup FX artists and asked if he could use it. They said yes, and, *voila*, Darabont had his decayed mother!

When the film was completed, Darabont sent it to King, who loved it. Darabont cringes at the thought of this now and says he can no longer watch the film because of its amateurish nature, but surely his complaints are just those of any artist seeing his own growth and comparing his earliest works unfavorably to his later more-polished efforts. Interestingly enough, King's favorite scene in the film was the one Darabont added. King also appreciated the addition of the prisoner character (played by Libby), but told Darabont that he found the character a bit cliched. But overall, King liked the film and dubbed it the finest of the dollar babies that had been produced at the time.

In fact, King liked the film so much that he later allowed Granite Entertainment Group to release it on video as part of their two-film *Stephen King's Nightshift Collection*. (The second film was another dollar baby, Jeffrey C. Schiro's *The Boogeyman*.) According to Darabont, neither he nor Schiro ever saw a dime from the release of these films. (Both films were later re-released by Simitar Entertainment.)

The Woman in the Room was ultimately submitted for Oscar consideration. Darabont says it was ranked in the top ten of the ninety short films submitted that year. Unfortunately, it did not make the cut as one of the four films nominated.

Darabont was later promoted to the big leagues when his screenplay (co-written with Chuck Russell) for *A Nightmare on Elm Street 3: Dream Warriors* was produced. After that, he approached King again, expressing his interest in adapting the author's *Different Seasons* novella *Rita Hayworth and the Shawshank Redemption*. (It should be noted that at some point, the filmmaker also expressed interest in adapting "*The Monkey*," but it has never come to pass.) King agreed to let him make the film based on the fact he'd loved *The Woman in the Room*. He then gave him a "handshake agreement" option. Darabont then held onto the rights for five years before he finally felt capable enough as a writer to sit down and adapt it.

Just as he did with *The Woman in the Room*, Darabont took liberties with King's story. Here he did it much better than he had with *The Woman in the Room*. While the short film is great, Darabont now believes he held back, playing it safe. Taking that one step further, it is likely that he was afraid of displeasing King. But now that he had the author's trust,

Darabont, realizing the differences between storytelling in the different mediums, made many important alterations and contributions. He added scenes, such as the one where Red listens to and reflects on an Italian operetta. That scene feels very much like it was written by King. In fact, not only does it feel as if it were written by King, but it feels like the very best of King's writing.

Darabont also changed and consolidated characters. Examples of these are his decision to make the character Red, who is an Irishman in the novella, black, and also his combining the multiple wardens who come and go in King's story into a single character. Darabont, like King, is an artist in the truest sense of the word. The changes he made actually improve the material in a way that no other King adapter has done. Their voices combine and become one, creating a beautiful harmony not unlike the opera singers in the aforementioned scene.

Darabont once told me he accomplished these things by *not* writing like Frank Darabont. Instead, he says he wrote as Stephen King. "I think when you're adapting something from a very good source, you have to sort of pretend to be that writer and to not let your own voice take over," he said. "With *Shawshank*, that's an example of me doing my Steve King impression, kind of like Rich Little doing Johnny Carson. ... I love it whenever someone tells me that *Shawshank Redemption* is the most faithful adaptation of a Stephen King story, because it's not really that faithful. It just *feels* faithful. ... I tried to maintain the essence of King's original story."

The reason I call Darabont's King adaptations "collaborations" is because their voices intertwine in a unique manner. It is hard to imagine them combining any more seamlessly or producing anything more qualitative had the two men sat together sharing a word processor. If they are not collaborations in the literal sense of the word, then they are surely spiritual collaborations. There have been many great King adaptations, but very few that actually capture the feeling and essence of King, and even fewer that actually contribute new elements that improve upon the material. King's original novella is good, but it isn't great. Not on the level that Darabont's film is. *Rita Hayworth and the Shawshank Redemption* isn't even the best novella in *Different Seasons*, yet Darabont's film is an undisputed masterpiece that rightfully received seven Academy Award nominations and has remained the number one film on the Internet Movie Database (Imdb) for nearly a decade. Stating that the film version is superior to the novella is in no way intended to slight the author; like all great collaborators, Darabont's writing complements (and heightens) King's.

King has stated that whenever strangers tell him they don't like his work, he asks them if they have ever watched *The Shawshank Redemption*. According to King, they are always shocked. The fact that King uses the film as a go-to cultural touchstone is a testament to its near universal popularity and also the love and pride the author feels for it.

The film ultimately became so popular and loomed so greatly over Darabont's career that he once remarked, "If the obituary is, Frank 'Shawshank Redemption' Darabont died today,' that would be awesome. Of course, I hope people check out the other films I've made, too." To date, there have only been three more feature film entries on the man's filmography, two of which are King adaptations.

Interestingly, Darabont's second King adaptation would be another prison tale, *The Green Mile*. (Darabont has joked about his being the master of the smallest genre on earth, the Stephen King prison movie.) The filmmaker told *Empire* magazine that King pitched him the idea for the movie adaptation before he'd even begun work on the six-part serial novel. He said, "Well, I've been kicking this story idea around, Frank. I think it would be a great movie for you but I think you probably don't want to do another prison movie." King then shared the story of jailhouse savior John Coffey and a mouse named Mr. Jingles to Darabont. Upon hearing this, Darabont said, "If you write this, please give me first crack at it because it sounds extraordinary." King later sent the first installment of the series to Darabont, who loved it so much that he committed to making the movie without having read the remaining volumes.

As Darabont began writing the screenplay, he learned that his cat had a tumor. Since the cat was not in pain, Darabont decided to keep the cat at home and continue caring for it rather than having it put down. As he cared for this cat in its final days, the cat sat with him at his desk while he wrote. Darabont would later refer to the cat as being his co-writer on the project. He likened the feline's situation to the film's death row theme, saying he felt as if the cat was walking the Mile. Darabont says he basically sequestered himself until the screenplay was finished. As he wrote, he listened to jazz music from the 1930s. He produced the screenplay in two months to the day. The cat died soon after.

This time Darabont did less inventing and many of the film's most powerful lines of dialogue come directly from the novel. Darabont told *Creative Screenwriting's* Erik Bauer that being true to an author's work in adaptation involves "a certain amount of texture and a certain amount of poetry. It's not just, 'Let's put the simplest version of the narrative on screen that we possibly can,' because often that winds up being unsatisfying. If an adapted story tells you the story but you feel it's not quite the same—well, we've all had that experience of seeing a book we loved turned into a so-so movie. It's the same story, but it's missing the soul; it's missing the blood in the veins somehow. And that's because oftentimes, writers who adapt are focused on narrative and they toss out a lot of that in-between-the-lines stuff, which is another thing that makes King such a compelling writer. There's a lot of between-the-lines stuff with his characters, and with his texture, that's important."

This isn't to say that Darabont didn't take any liberties with the story, but most of them were smaller this time. A framing story with Paul's companion Elaine was added, a menacing orderly appears in the novella but is absent in the film, and the year in which the movie takes place was changed from 1932 to 1935 so the film *Top Hat* could appear in it. But overall, the changes weren't significant. Darabont is a talented adapter who knows when to add to the material but also recognizes when it doesn't need tinkering. King would later call this film the most faithful adaptation of any of his works.

The project attracted top notch talent, including one of the finest and most popular actors in cinematic history, Tom Hanks, who played the protagonist, Paul Edgecomb. (The cast would ultimately include two Oscar winners and five Oscar nominees.) A handful of actors were considered to play John Coffey, including Shaquille O'Neal and Ving Rhames, but none seemed right. Then Bruce Willis suggested Michael Clarke Duncan, whom he had worked with on Armageddon. Darabont and casting director Mali Finn then agreed that Duncan was right for the role and he was cast.

The Green Mile ultimately became a huge hit, becoming the first Stephen King adaptation to top the $100 million mark. Both King and Darabont loved the film, and Darabont later called it the most satisfying movie of his career. Like Shawshank before it, the film was lauded by critics and was an awards season favorite. It received four Oscar nominations, including one for Best Picture, and ranks on many all-time favorite films lists.

Darabont had discussed a desire to adapt King's novella *The Mist* since the 1980's but had never gotten around to it. After his first non-King-related feature, *The Majestic*, was released in 2001 and failed both critically and financially, *The Mist* returned to the front burner. One thing (aside his longtime appreciation of the story) that made Darabont return to the material was a desire to stay fresh and work in a different genre. He would later explain (in a classic-horror.com interview), "I loved getting out of my comfort zone as a director, because you develop a certain skill set, and then you learn to depend on that skill set, and if you're not careful, you get stale doing that."

Where Darabont's previous features had been "elegant" (his word) films inspired by filmmakers like Stanley Kubrick, he sought to channel "down and dirty" (also his) directors like George A. Romero and David Cronenberg with *The Mist*. He shot the film with a short six-week schedule and, according to Darabont, he relied more on improvisational on-the-fly filmmaking than he had previously. "[I]n a lot of these scenes we had a dozen leads and 80 to 100 extras," he said. "But we're still cranking out pages like crazy bastards and it's not about elegance." Wanting to honor the spirit of low-budget horror films (the kinds that actually inspired the novella in the first place), he also made the film with the smallest budget he'd ever worked with and utilized the crew from the television show *The Shield*. (It was in that same classic B horror movie spirit that he would later convince Dimension Films to release a black-and-white version of the film.)

While *The Mist* isn't as universally praised or loved as *Shawshank* or *Green Mile*, it's an incredibly powerful film. Its cast, including Thomas Jane, Andre Braugher, and Marcia Gay Harden, is spot-on. Their performances, coupled with Darabont's deft direction and fine script (as well as King's story, obviously), do a fantastic job depicting a suspenseful under-siege-by-monsters scenario where the people inside are scarier than the monsters outside. In *The Mist*, Darabont made his most substantive alteration to a King story to date. He believed the ending to the film should be more conclusive than the open-ended close of the novella. When considering possible ways to accomplish this, he kept coming back to the almost oppressively dark ending that appears in the film. Ever the considerate adapter wishing to honor King's work, he did two key things here. First, his version actually found its cue in a line in the novella in which David Drayton considers the possibility of doing what he does at the end of the film. Because of this, Darabont believed this alteration would be true in spirit to King's work. Second, Darabont did not do this on his own, but rather, allowed King to make the decision himself. When King read Darabont's script, he *loved* the new ending.

King said he wished he'd thought of it. He also likened it to the ending of *Night of the Living Dead*, where the protagonist survives the zombies only to be shot by the would-be saviors. King also said that once-in-a-generation there must be a horror film that pisses everyone off. "And it felt okay to me," Darabont said. "On balance, it feels like, thematically, it's a pretty good companion piece to *Shawshank*, in a weird way. Because if *Shawshank* is the movie about the value of hope, then *The Mist* becomes a movie about the danger of hopelessness. And believe me, I knew that it was going to be one of those endings that people either dug, or really hated."

A lot of people hated it. (I loved it, for the record.) But the King loved it. And it's important to note that King's favorite scenes in the Darabont films have almost always been the scenes Darabont wrote himself or took great artistic liberties with. This is because King sees him as an equal in terms of artistry and the two share the same storytelling aesthetic. They are, as I have said, "spiritual collaborators" whose ideas and artistic sensibilities are so similar that they merge together in a way that would suggest that a single (extremely talented) writer was responsible for these works. Film may be a different medium, but King's and Darabont's voices combine as well, if not better, than King's voice with the voices of literary collaborators like Peter Straub, Richard Chizmar, and son Owen. Stephen King has always had a knack for collaborating with talented artists whose contributions complement his own writing, and Darabont is no exception.

And to think, none of these beautiful (or horrifying, in regards to *The Mist*) collaborations would have existed had it not been for Stephen King's "Dollar Baby" program and his desire to help young artists develop their craft. King established that program out of a sense of charity and for no benefit to himself. But in the end, this yielded several works of art that are a benefit to King's legacy, as well as viewers around the world.

The Good and Bad of Film Adaptation

By James Cole

"*THE LAST RUNG ON THE LADDER*" is by John D. MacDonald put it, "one of the most resonant and affecting (of Stephen King's stories)." However the content does not lend itself to the screen as easily as one might think. Hollywood, for the most part, has not made completely faithful adaptations of Mr. King's novels, so how can two students with no budget and no equipment do any better?

Money (money?) was not the issue. My partner Dan Thron and I believed anything was possible with enough enthusiasm, never mind non-existent funds and the technical limitations of Super-8. On top of that was the challenge of working with children. How does the old saying go? "Never work with kids, animals, or special effects." Tackling one of those three was enough. We were clearly in over our heads.

Yes seventeen months later and a couple thousand poorer, our interpretation of "*The Last Rung on the Ladder*" was complete. No masterpiece by any means, it still managed to exceed our expectations. But the real memories lie in the making.

July 1985. Dan Thron and I plan to adapt Stephen King's short story to film. Armed with my handwritten screenplay I slapped together during work hours, the minor questions involve things like actors, locations, and money. After a few days we find our leads, and obtain permission to film in the attic of the Methodist Church. (The old post and beam construction looks like a barn interior.)

The first day of filming went wonderfully despite the intense heat and cramped space. However, after viewing the results, which are good, Dan and I realize that the film is too complex for us at this time, and we must find a real barn as well. Project is abandoned.

April 1986. Browsing in a video store, I ran across The Night Shift Collection, two short films adapted from Stephen King stories. Nothing the films, "*The Woman in the Room*" and "*The Boogeyman*" are made by college students, I figure, "If they did it, why can't we?" I manage to write a new twelve-page screenplay in one evening. We're rolling.

June 10, 1986. After almost a month of searching, I found a genuine post and beam barn in Dennis, Mass. Permission to use the barn for filming is given by the owner, a 91 year-old lawyer from Boston, who mentions nothing about liability. Amazing!

June 19. As filming will naturally take up most of the summer, I must work out a schedule, and most importantly, get permission from our stars' parents. I spend a grueling hour with Adam Houhoulis' (the thirteen year-old who will play Larry) father, answering every question imaginable about the story, transportation, and safety. When I'm asked if the two hundred year-old barn has fire exits, I almost break into hysterical laughter. Adam sits by silently during the interview. During a break, however, he restores my faith when he whispers, "You're doing good." It's clear he wants to do this film as much as I.

June 21. Principal photography begins (again). My 1730 house is used for interior shots. Gathered on "the set" are co-director Dan Thron, 15, and the two leads, Adam (Larry), and Melisa Whelden (Kitty), a bubbly eleven year-old who so matches the story's description it's scary. Melisa's older brother Glen, star and composer of a previous film of mine, is also on hand. We're off to a good start when Adam starts choking at dinner from laughing. He's okay, but shaken up. Filming proceeds successfully, though Adam will suffer the whole summer in old fashioned-looking boots that are two sizes too small.

July 1. Our first day on location in Dennis. A crystal blue-sky day adds to the scenery as we film the leads in an open field behind the barn. Dan and I refer to the scene as "The Color White" due to the abundance of Queen Anne's Lace. In this first scene set in the past (circa 1960s), all the dialogue between brother and sister is original, and the kids pull it off beautifully. Dan and I are ecstatic.

July 8. Barn interior shots begin, and will continue from now on. To simulate the hay pile, two layers of empty boxes are positioned on the barn floor, with a mattress on top. Four bales of hay hide our safety devices, and work well. The true difficulties arise from our equipment, or lack thereof. With only two cameras and two hand-held lights, problems are numerous. Lighting is the worst. The dark, cavernous interior causes the internal light meters to not register, when light on the actors is actually often overexposed. A lot of guessing comes in handy.

July 15. It's a "more relaxed" day of shooting in the barn. Melisa is sick, so it's solo work with Adam. Dan and I take pains to get him to loosen up and understand the part. Using three different ladder segments, it seems we film him climbing up from a trillion angles. On one take, we didn't notice how high Adam had climbed, and yelled, "Stop!" just in time. Not nailed to the beam, the ladder was close to toppling backwards. The rest of the day Adam moves hay bales back and forth, just like in the story. I have a hard time getting him to move fast enough, to realize how perilous the situation is supposed to be.

July 21. A break from the hay, as we reshoot the bedroom scene in which Larry and Kitty talk after she has been saved. The original footage was stiff and talky. Visuals work just as well, and we condense nearly twelve lines of dialogue down to four. The kids' performances are a hundred times better. Now having done most of the "crisis" scenes in the barn together, they understand what they should be feeling. I've come to believe they really are brother and sister.

July 29. We only have this last day to use the barn, and have to get everything finished. The list of required shots is enormous, and I have to be serious with the kids and tell them that there's no time to goof around today. By the end of the afternoon, every shot on the list is crossed-off. Whether it will come out as usable, and whether or not we've thought of everything we need, is unknown, but we're finished. The kids are tired but excited. All potential accidents and mishaps with a creaky barn have been avoided, save the time Adam brushed against a hot light and burned his hand. Minor. We are not truly done with the barn until Dan and I return a week later to rake up and bag the hay. If I never smell hay again, it will be too soon.

August 4. Away for a weekend in the Berkshires, I film all the credits, as well as exterior shots of the farmhouse, fields, and the big red barn. When combined with other footage, no one will ever know that Larry was glancing at a barn 250 miles away, or that the mid-western farmhouse bedroom was five doors from the ocean! The magic of film.

August 9. The prologue and epilogue are shot. A grown-up Larry, played by a different Adam, contemplates the letter he has just received from his sister, and what it means. When Dan and I began this project we resisted using narration, as it can backfire so easily. To make Kitty's letter as readable as possible, the actual letter is two feet wide, with oversized handwriting. After reshooting this damn piece of paper three times, it's finally legible. The real credit for these scenes must go to Adam Howes, who conveys thoughts and emotion without a single word.

August 12 to November 22. The first stage of post-production begins. Putting together the rough cut from all the best takes and usable footage takes a mere three months. This is due to the fact that I'm a full-time college student, and must drive down to New York City to rent a Super-8 editor every third weekend or so. The process is tedious, but even at this stage I see the film is coming together.

January to April 1987. Between classes and studying I work to edit the final cut. All the shots we filmed were needed, with not a single to spare. The order and particular takes are switched back and forth until a sense of timing emerges. For such a primitive medium, the scenes flow and are the most professional looking in any film I've made.

April 23. After a month of collaboration, my composer Anne Livermore, a seventeen year-old prodigy, performs her original piano score in a University of Massachusetts music hall. With the assistance of a student sound engineer, we record the entire score in one frantic hour. Beautiful.

May. I premiered the film for some close friends and others in my dorm. The term bloodbath is an understatement. The critiques are needed (as the wraparound story of the prologue and epilogue is incomplete and not yet clear), but as the comments get nastier and less constructive, I cry "Uncle!" and crawl into a corner. A small group of supportive friends who loved the film despite evident problems keep me going.

June 1. After reshooting, re-editing, and insertion of some additional scenes, I try again. The second, bigger premiere at home on Cape Cod is seen by nearly 25 friends, including star Adam Houhoulis. The response is very much improved, and Adam, while a bit embarrassed to watch himself, is excited. Dan and I second that emotion.

October 2. Many improvements and a whole summer later, the film is transferred to professional ¾" video, then down to VHS in New York City. The quality is beautiful. Our true goal is achieved, for this Super-8 film looks as good on video as a bigger budget 16mm film. These two hours of transfer work cost a mere $280.

October 14. The VHS copy is sent off to Stephen King via his secretary, Stephanie Leonard. Though we hope for a response, this is not the sole reason for making the film. Nevertheless, we wait.

November 1987 to March 1988. Months pass, and after a few follow up letters, I receive an answer from Stephanie Leonard. After such an understanding letter I am content with what we set out to do, and what we accomplished. If Stephen actually saw our film, I hope he enjoyed it.

After all the work, I was pleased that "*Last Rung*" was well received by a few film teachers and executives. I will never forget the experience of making this little film. It's a testament to what one can accomplish with sheer determination.

A Conversation With Director Mick Garris

By Anthony Northrup

I HAVE HAD THE HONOR and privilege of knowing one of the biggest names in the horror genre and films and a friendship spanning almost 30 years. Mick Garris has made some of the biggest and best in film and television for decades, as well as, a very talented writer. He is known for adapting more Stephen King films than any other director in Hollywood. His Stephen King adaptations such as, *The Shining, Sleepwalkers, Desperation, Bag of Bones, Riding the Bullet*, and the biggest of all and fan favorite: *The Stand*. I have interviewed Mick several times over the years and what would a book about Stephen King adaptations be without a few words from the man who knows all about adaptations of King's works.

Here are some parts of several interviews I've had with Mick over the years, talking about his Stephen King adaptations, the film industry, and personal thoughts he was kind enough to share with us.

Anthony Northrup: Which films inspired you growing up?

Mick Garris: I watched a lot of television growing up as a kid, but originally I wanted to be a cartoonist, and make animated cartoons. My father had gone to art school, though he was never able to make a living at it. So I inherited his art abilities, but kind of gave it up when I started writing at age 12. But I watched cartoons, all the Universal horror movies, the horror and SF movies of the fifties and sixties, *Twilight Zone, Outer Limits, Abbott and Costello,* Hammer horrors, the Corman Poe stuff, Red Skelton, *The Avengers*. It was a pretty great time to be growing up.

AN: Who were your influences?

MG: Well, you can't help but being influenced by what you take in, so I'm sure all of those had an effect on me. But at 12, I started reading all of Ray Bradbury's books, as well as Richard Matheson and a bunch of others. But Bradbury inspired me more than anyone as a writer at that time. As a filmmaker, well, that runs the gamut from the Universal horror movies to Corman to Landis to Preston Sturges to Hitchcock to Cronenberg to Carpenter to Capra and to a lot of the oddball Euro stuff that would show up on Chiller Theater from time to time.

AN: You seem to do very well doing books-to-films, what's that like?

MG: Well, it's quite a tightrope-walk. You want to savor the things that make the book's story worth telling, but you have to realize at the same time that books and film are different media. Generally speaking, books are internal and films are external. A good book won't necessarily make a good movie. I've been lucky with the King material, as he writes so cinematically. But even so, you have to remap the build and release of suspense, convey a character from his actions and dialogue, rather from his thoughts, and build something that works on the screen, something that you can make unique and still accessible. It's not always easy. *The Stand* was surely the most difficult of all to pull off.

AN: In *Sleepwalkers*, there's a scene in a graveyard with King, Tobe Hooper, & many legendary directors: how did that come about & what was it like?

MG: Well, it was my first real meeting with King; we'd only talked by phone between LA and Maine. But I thought it would be great for the fans to put them all in the movie, all in one scene. Tobe and I have been friends since I did publicity on *Poltergeist,* and Clive and I had been working on a couple projects together at that time. King's quote on Clive's books—"I have seen the future of horror and its name is Clive Barker"—really made Clive's career in this country. So it was fun and exciting and nerve-wracking, because King was only going to be there for a couple hours. And then, early that morning at the craft service table, I broke a tooth on my morning granola… and had to rush down and get an emergency crown before King got there. So there was way too much to think of.

AN: What are your thoughts when you first learned you would tackle Stephen King's Masterpiece, *The Stand*?

MG: That it would be a tunnel with no light at the end. Incredible excitement, but also a great sense of the burden of responsibility. I loved that book so much and wanted to do it right. I knew that King and Romero had spent years trying to make it a movie, and now it was my responsibility. I knew how much it mattered to the fans, because I was one of them.

AN: With SO many remakes being the trend now, how did you feel remaking *The Shining*?

MG: We never really thought of it as a remake, believe it or not. It was a chance to do honor to the book in a film form with the author himself writing the screenplay and producing. Another task I didn't take lightly, as it was my favorite of King's novels.

AN: What attracted you to the Horror Genre?

MG: I think it's the whole outsider thing, being someone who came from a less than happy family childhood seeking refuge in the darker side of popular culture as an escape. Reading and watching stories about lives that were a lot worse than mine… many of which had happy endings.

AN: What scares you?

MG: Real life, not movies. The safety and health of the people I love being threatened is far more frightening than a guy with knives in his gloves.

AN: How do you feel about Horror films today as compared to 20-30 years ago?

MG: Well, most of those being made by the studios today are a lot less original, and all seemed aimed at teenagers, not discerning audiences (not that all the stuff from the 70s and 80s were great works of art, of course). There was a lot more invention, a lot more originality, a lot more fantastic new filmmakers with unique visions that exploded forth in those days than there are today. Of course, you still get some great independent stuff now and then, and a lot of wonderful stuff from Asia and Europe.

AN: You've worked with some very talented actors; Ron Perlman, Steven Weber, Henry Thomas, & the entire cast of *The Stand*… what was that like for you?

MG: One of the best parts of filmmaking is working with actors who care about their craft. I love working with actors, being of whatever help and guidance I can be to someone who really knows what he or she is doing. A great, confident actor is the highest possible production value you can have on a movie.

AN: What it was like working with the legendary Anthony Perkins?

MG: I'll just say that he was a very complicated man, a guy who wanted to test his directors to make sure that they were doing something for a better reason than that it would be a cool-looking shot. Tony had directed *Psycho III* and wanted to direct *Psycho IV,* but the previous film was not a success, so here I was thrust into that situation. I learned a lot from him, and enjoyed much of working with him, but there were some very trying times as well. He could get very caught up in minutiae.

AN: What was your first encounter with Stephen King like?

MG: It was really on the phone, so there was some distance and hesitancy involved. We met on that fateful day on the *Sleepwalkers* set, but really, our friendship began with the time I screened my cut for him and Tabitha at a screening room in New York. That was one of the great days of my life.

AN: You once said that working on *The Stand* was like nothing you've ever worked on before. What was it like & were you nervous that you wanted it to live up to the fan's expectations?

MG: Ulcer City. It was a huge story over a long shoot, and everything I had done before that was on a very small scale. But I had a great script, and then a great cast, and once you have a script that you feel is ready to shoot, you trust it. But I knew what a tremendous responsibility and opportunity it was. But it was a massive undertaking: 2 months of prep on location, 5 months of shooting six states, 125 speaking parts, a 460-page script. Really, really a tough but rewarding shoot.

AN: When you filmed, *Riding the Bullet,* you spent your birthday in a graveyard filming, was THAT your strangest birthday?

MG: It's surely one of them. But I always find myself somewhere strange when we're shooting on my birthday. I had forgotten about that, but you're right. And it was cold and wet, too, as is usually the case.

AN: Did you ACTUALLY ride The Bullet roller coaster?

MG: As often as I could!

AN: You've had to face some tough challenges(heat, kids, animals, long shoots, long hours, etc.), do those types of challenges make for a better director?

MG: That which doesn't kill you makes you stronger.

AN: You've seemed to have stayed away from the "Slasher" type of horror films & stayed with suspense & thriller. Do you feel more comfortable than doing "killers in masks" films?

MG: For me, story and character come first. Just a slate of "creative skills" gets boring really fast. There have been great ones, but it's not what I'm drawn to as a filmmaker.

AN: What was your favorite project? Toughest?

MG: The toughest was easily *The Stand*. But the one that is most personal to me was probably the least successful of all of them: *Riding the Bullet*.

AN: Your name has been said in the same company as John Landis, Joe Dante, Tobe Hooper, Wes Craven, Stephen King: how does it make you feel to be considered a legend?

MG: No, that's not a position I occupy. I've been lucky enough to work with all of those guys, and be friends with them and share time with all of them. But they changed the course of horror history; they are legends. I'm just a guy trying to do the best work he can in a genre that's tough to make a mark in. If anything, in creating MASTERS OF HORROR, I was able to set up a canvas for so many of the greats to do work they wanted to do without interference.

AN: What advice can you share with us for future writers & upcoming directors?

MG: Just do it. Write. Shoot. Create. And don't do it for the money, do it for the love of it. Break some boundaries!

AN: How much do you let the books, story, author, and fans of the book influence your film?

MG: First of all, I am a huge fan of the books. If you're adapting a book, there's a reason. That said, and King knows this better than anyone, books and movies are different media. A good book isn't necessarily a great blueprint for a movie. But I do believe if you have a beloved story, it deserves respect. And I've been lucky with the material I've had to adapt.

Yeah, it's really important and gratifying to have King happy with the material, and surely the fans for the source material, but mostly it has to be a movie that works on its own terms, and reach an audience that hasn't read the books. They all influence me, but as a fan myself, I have to feel that I've done the best I can to make the book into a movie.

AN: I want to thank Mick for taking the time to talk with us today and wish him the best in his future projects.

My Journey With My Husband, T. Anthony Northrup, and the Writing of *Stephen King Dollar Baby: The Book*

By Gena Lawson-Northrup

IN FEBRUARY OF 1993, while at a concert in Hollywood, I met my now husband of nearly 28 years, Anthony Northrup. I was not intending to meet anyone that particular evening, but it seems the powers that be had other plans for me. We immediately struck up a great conversation, and when he asked me if I knew the works of author Stephen King, my eyes lit up. Did I know who Stephen King was?

Well, we talked with one another for nearly 5 hours, first at a little after hours place, then moved it over to one of my favorite hangouts, Canter's Deli, in the Fairfax district. We talked about so much, however, we always came back around to the topic of what we both discovered about one another, our favorite author, King.

I went home that night hoping we would meet again, but was a bit concerned, as my husband is 16 years younger than I, and what could we possibly have in common? Well, obviously a lot, and we have sustained nearly 3 decades of common interests... including our love for our still favorite author.

When T. opened up his fan page, ATK (All Things King), I was eager to see how it would go. It was a hit, and we now have over 5,000 members, eight years later. Through the years, T. had met several people who are not only enthusiastic readers of Stephen King, but who are in the position to bring his written word to film, television mini-series, biographies, other publications, artwork, cons, and other means of expanding the great works of this author.

I was surprised when T. came in one day and told me about a program where anyone who wanted to make a film from one of the short stories published by Stephen King could do so, with his approval, and for ONE dollar. What! This seemed strange to me, but after he pursued looking into it further, it was true.

That's when I saw the wheels in motion. I knew he was happy to have the ATK page, and he was now writing a film review column biweekly in our local newspaper, but I couldn't imagine what he was thinking of with this Dollar Baby thing.

Now, about seven years later, here we are, and I have to say, I am so proud of him for his arduous task of taking on writing a book about the Dollar Baby films, and the great directive talent behind these short films. He has poured his heart and soul into this. Not only reviewing the films (of which all these wonderful people were so happy to send to him), but interviewing the directors, holding 2 film fests, one in 2014 and 2015, at a local con in Minneapolis, MN, where he showcased several of these fine short films. It was an honor for me to help him with these two events, and the people loved them!

Along the way, I have viewed these great short films, and they are all good. I do have a couple favorites (*Beachworld* by Maria Ivanova, *Maxwell Edison* by Warren Ray, and *The Doctor's Case* by James Douglas), however, I truly do enjoy the independent aspect of all fifty-five of these fine films.

I am proud to say that T. is able to share the official published version, (with the blessings of all involved), with all of you, the readers of, "*Stephen King Dollar Baby: The Book*". I love you my sweetie darling, and I know you have had a great time with this journey… wishing you much success. your, G.

"... That's What the Fans Said..."
Part 2

WHAT WOULD A BOOK BE without hearing from the fans themselves. The people who know him best. Stephen King fans (also known as "Constant Readers", as King likes to call us), are some of the most dedicated, supportive, and loving fans in the world. They are not afraid to show their fandom and here are just some Stephen King fans and their thoughts and memories about Stephen King.

Karen Steinley Beaudrie: The "how I discovered Stephen King" is easy --- I came across *Carrie i*n a box of hand-me-down books from my cousin. I first read it in 1982, and I've pretty much been a Constant Reader ever since. As for the Why I read Stephen King, I guess it's because King's writing speaks to me. He writes about people I care about, and makes the craziest things seem plausible. How can you not admire that?

Amy Baker: I started reading at four years old to escape a difficult life. I first really discovered King's works with *The Stand*. I had to sneak to read them due to growing up in a super religious home. King's works were, in many ways, relatable to my life and made me realize I could overcome. I still use his works with the troubled adolescents I treat today.

Terri Nielsen: A friend of mine gave me *Pet Sematary* when I was 12 or 13. (78-79) I read it in about 3 days, and got thirsty for more. Read every book by King they had in our little Library over that year. Collected *The Green Mile* book, by book. Counted the days til the next one like counting down Christmas. I still have them all, and the hardbound edition. As an Adult I started collecting all His works in Hardbound. When a new book comes out, I am on it! Like Amy Baker said, a wonderful escape from an awkward life, and oddly relatable to me. I love the way King seems to put you in the midst of the characters, and has you cheering them on from the sidelines. Hands down my favorite author!

Tina Navarro: When did I first start reading Stephen King? My mom was a huge Stephen king fan and had all his books. She would always try to get me to read them. Then one day when I was 16 I did. I have been a SK fan for about 40 years. Why do I read Stephen King? Because I love his writing style and story ideas.

Hans von Wirth (All Things King Co Ad): Why read Stephen King? Because even though I can't afford most of the books I would love to have by King (eventually to own a signed Copy is still a massive dream of mine) I enjoy talking about his works a lot, and love to be a helping hand for those who are at the beginning of that journey. Still remember my first walk on the road towards *The Dark Tower*. Oh, discovering those books… <3 I have a severe handicap, and reading books in general gave me a way of travelling without moving. Building those worlds in my mind was and still is magical. Oh all those miles I walked with Roland…

When did I first start reading Stephen King? It was in April 1998. My bro had surgery at a hospital. One time when I visited him, he had to go to an examination and I was bored while waiting for him, so I checked out the books the little kiosk had to offer. One caught my eye. It was a thick green/black paperback with the silhouette of a tall man on the cover and a little mouse in one corner The title sounded familiar and I remembered my classmate Didi had brought the first part of the novel to school. I was allowed to read it that day in school, but I could not finish it when school was over for the day, so I was glad when I found it there as the complete edition of all six volumes and finished it within 2,5 days.

Sara Kinney: Books were always my escape from reality and my most constant friends. I found King at 10 after watching *Pet Sematary* and read the book a little while after. From that point on I was obsessed with finding every book I could that he'd written, buying them at flea markets and second hand stores with Birthday and allowance money. When I got older, I began hunting down the first edition hardbacks, then later kept finding other things to add to my collection such as the CD limited editions, soundtracks, movies, posters, artwork, etc. King became an everyday part of my life that exists to this day. I enjoy getting others to read his books or even watch the movies based on them. I'm also very lucky to have a husband who's so supportive of my obsession!!

Frank Lewis: I was 13 in 1976 when *Carrie* (movie) and *Salem's Lot* (book) came out. I don't remember which came first but fans ever since.

LaWanda Odom: I am your Biggest fan!!! Lmao… I love Sai King's writing and My Brother and I shared this love!!been reading him since I was 11..35 years. Crap that a long time… I am indeed a constant reader!

Hans -Ake Lilja (creator of Lilja's Library Stephen King web page): Imagine being a young filmmaker and getting the chance to do a Stephen King movie!

Most of them are really bad but there are some that I really wish all of you would get the chance to see.

Who else gives young filmmakers a chance to do a movie based on something written by a bestselling author? And for just $1!

Monica Wooddall: Stephen King, or Sai King as I (ardent Tower Junkie), call him has influenced almost every aspect of my life. I discovered Sai King in 1984, when I was only 8. I discovered so much from King's book and films, I heard *'Don't Fear the Reaper'* from a King book and also blue chambray shirts (ha!). I guess I don't really have adequate words to describe what Sai King's works mean to me other than I am his number one fan!!!

Dollar Baby Thoughts About Stephen King & the Dollar Baby Program

J.P. Scott (*Everything's Eventual*) -
It is a really cool thing to be an A list writer and allow a program like this to exist that encourages young creatives to do what they love. I hope that King has made plans to keep this tradition alive even after he, to use his words, gets to the clearing at the end of the path. I hope that day is far ahead as I'm sure he does. I do hope that he knows that he has not only had a big impact on his readers but also a massive impact on every Dollar Baby filmmaker. He certainly has on me. Getting the opportunity to even attempt my dream and make my passion a profession is more than what many get a chance to do. I count myself lucky and will always remember *Everything's Eventual* and Stephen King's Dollar Babies. And, I think that is what King wanted. To encourage young and passionate creatives to do something that will drive them to bring to fruition their dreams and ambitions.

Nicole Jones-Dion (*In the Deathroom*) -
It's unprecedented for an author of Mr. King's stature to share his work with other artists. I love his "pay-it-forward" attitude to help the next generation of aspiring filmmakers. I plan to continue his spirit of giving by helping others who are coming up behind me to reach their goals as well.

Jon Mann (*Popsy*) -
Stephen King is my literary hero. I believe he will go down in history as the American writer with the most emotional range across his body of

work. It's unbelievable that stories like *The Girl Who Loved Tom Gordon* and *Shawshank* came from the same imagination that gave us *It* and *Carrie*. People always talk about how 'prolific' he is, which is a word that is thrown around a lot in art. He's an absolute workhorse. I've always looked up to Mr. King's work ethic. I am sure that he would probably bring that all back to his love for the craft and his passion for literature and the paranormal – which is equally as inspiring.

Jennifer Trudrung (*Here There Be Tygers*) -
I feel that the Dollar Baby program is such a gift. We creatives normally feel so disconnected from our heroes. It can feel like they live on another plane and to be able to have the freedom to mold and work with our hero's story and to have his name attached to our project is huge. Stephen King has so heavily influenced my imagination and world and I have great respect for him and his voice.

Joe Kowalski (*I Am the Doorway*) -
I think one reason we all love Stephen King so much is that he puts himself entirely out there. I can't tell you how many ideas I never flesh out into writing simply because I fear that I'm going to make something bad by the end of it. Yet Stephen King doesn't let that fear stop him. He seems so open to any idea and concept. Yes, sometimes the end result is mediocre. Other times it's a story that will last for generations. Either way, he moves on to the next story and the next story after that. It's fearlessly forward-thinking, and it's something I strive to learn from.

A.J. Gribble (*Cain Rose Up*) -
The Dollar Baby program is the best thing for any young filmmakers or just filmmakers in general! They have the chance to adapt a King story and possibly get a career started because of it. I believe that it is so nice of Stephen King to do that for us. And if I ever get the chance to meet him, I would just like to say thank you.

Vanessa Ionta-Wright (*Rainy Season*) –
I think one of the great aspects of this program is that it allows aspiring and student filmmakers who have not yet established themselves in the industry, to start their careers with an established piece of material to breath life into. Even though King, himself, isn't directly involved in the productions, just having his name on the film gives instant credit to the

project, which can really help elevate a new filmmaker's career. I had a lot of people from my community and the community we shot the film in, offering services and resources simply because they wanted to be attached to a King related film. For a first time filmmaker, this is invaluable. The fact that King releases his work to the general public to help aid in an artist's career, speaks volumes about hias character and the type of man he is. He is constantly giving back and creating opportunities, which is inspiring. I appreciate his work, as a constant reader, and I appreciate his place in this community and very grateful to him.

"Just the facts, ma'am!"

HERE ARE 10 FUN FACTS about Stephen King Dollar Babies.

1. *Umney's Last Case* had a budget of $60,000.

2. It took director Frank Darabont three years before he could make his Dollar Baby film, *Woman in the Room*. He asked Stephen King in 1980 and the film was made in 1982. Darabont was only twenty years old at the time he made the request.

3. The youngest Dollar Baby filmmaker was only sixteen years old. It was A. J. Gribble, the director of *Cain Rose Up*.

4. The first Dollar Baby was the 1982 film, *Boogeyman*, directed by Jeff Schiro.

5. Jay Holden's *Paranoid: A Chant*, starring Tonya Ivey, was the first Dollar Baby to play on the Internet in 2000 with Stephen King's permission. It was later approved to be on a DVD collection included in an issue of Total Movie Magazine.

6. In October 2009, J. P. Scott made the first full-length Dollar Baby film, *Everything's Eventual*. Stephen King was so impressed, he allowed it to have theatrical release.

7. In 2011, the first British Dollar Baby, *Mute*, was made. It was directed by Jacqueline Wright.

8. Woman in the Room and Boogeyman were the first two Dollar Baby films available for home viewing. They were released together on VHS called Stephen King's Night Shift Collection.

9. In 2018, *Dedication*, directed by Selina Sondermann, was the second Dollar Baby filmed in Germany.

10. In 2015, British director, Matthew Rowney won 41 international film awards for his Dollar Baby, *I Am the Doorway*.

PART TWO

Dollar Baby original art by artist Glenn Chadbourne ©2020

Author's Note

THE FOLLOWING SECTION of the book is all the Stephen King Dollar Baby interviews and my reviews of their Dollar Baby films. I began interviewing Dollar Babies in 2013 for publication. After many Dollar Baby interviews and reviews, I hosted the 1st Annual Stephen King Dollar Baby Film Fest at Crypticon Horror Con in MN in 2014. After word got around and it was a big success, I hosted the 2nd Annual Stephen King Dollar Baby Film Fest there in 2015. My opportunities for interviewing more Dollar Babies grew beyond my expectations. The following 55 interviews and reviews are the original text and the original date of that interview. I hope you enjoy this very in depth and personal view behind-the-scenes of what it is like being a Dollar Baby and what it took to make their films. So, sit back and relax and take a look behind the curtain to the *Stephen King Dollar Baby: The Book…* the interviews and reviews!

Survivor Type

Billy Hanson
May 19, 2013

IN A WORLD FULL OF BLOCKBUSTERS, big budget studio films, and franchises/reboots/remakes/ and sequels: it is always refreshing to take a break from the CGI invested blockbusters and settle for something a little quieter. I have a huge respect for films, but it is the world of Independent and Short films that I have the biggest respect for. Even more so, I have respect for the up-and-coming filmmaker. Such is the case with director, Billy Hanson. Billy was raised in the state of Maine and later went to college at Florida State University where he studied to become a filmmaker. Moving to California, Bill started out as an actor and then worked at Nickelodeon in 2008 and later began his filming. Billy directed the Short film, Silver, a black & white film about werewolves with a 1940's style. He also did other Short films such as *Revolver* in 2006 and *Apology Day* in 2009. However, it is his latest film, *Survivor Type* that has really put Billy on top of his game. Based on a short story by Stephen King in the book, *Skeleton Crew, Survivor Type* is a horror beyond your imagination.

Survivor Type has already won and been nominated for several awards such as, Best Actor in a Short Film and Best Horror Short film at the Bare Bones International Film Festival. Nominated for Best Horror Short Film at the 2012 Shriekfest and Won the first ever "Truly Disturbing Award" and the 2012 Everybody Dies Horror Fest. It is still on the Film Fest circuit collecting more nominations and wins. Billy was kind enough to take a few moments from his busy schedule to answer a few questions for us.

Here is my exclusive interview with Dollar Baby filmmaker, Billy Hanson.

Anthony Northrup: Out of all the Stephen King short stories, what attracted you most to this one?

Survivor Type by Billy Hanson

Billy Hanson: *Survivor Type* was a story that somehow slipped by me for a long time. I read a lot of Stephen King and I consider myself a huge fan, so when somebody gave me the basic summary for *Survivor Type*, I was surprised that I hadn't heard about it. Even the idea for it creeped me out, so I found the story and read it that day. I remember sitting up all night, not being able to sleep, just thinking about this poor guy on an island who finds a really smart way to use his skills and keep himself alive, but ultimately has to go through so much to do it that you start wondering if it was even worth it. It wasn't just the gory stuff (although that stuff is pretty great), it was all the questions the story was asking that really hooked me.

AN: While on location, what was the hardest obstacle to overcome?

BH: Two things come to mind; tourists and sand. We shot in Leo Carrillo State Park, which is in Malibu, California, so there were a lot of people there for the beach and for surfing. Even though we had permits to shoot there, we could legally only ask people to move for a few minutes, then we'd have to let them back out on the rock, since it was such a popular location. People were nice enough to move out of the way once they saw we were shooting, though. The sand, however, was unrelenting. Our base camp was right on the beach near the water, so within a couple hours, everything (and I mean EVERYTHING) was covered in sand and salt, no matter how much we shielded it. I think I spent two weeks cleaning out my camera and audio gear after the shoot.

AN: What was your main goal you wanted to achieve about this film?

BH: I think the Dollar Baby Deal is an amazingly generous opportunity for Stephen King to create, so I will never say a bad word about it, but it does have its limitations. We are not able to profit at all from this film and we're unable to publish it anywhere online. We went in knowing that, though, so our goal became festivals. As soon as the film was finished, we started submitting to a bunch of festivals and thankfully we've had a lot of luck with them. As of today, we've been accepted to 13 festivals, been nominated for 6 awards and won 4 of them. A second goal has always been to help get our names out there as filmmakers. The movie is a great calling card for everybody involved with the movie who are looking for their next projects.

AN: What is your greatest moment so far with the success of *Survivor Type?*

BH: There have been a lot of great moments for me, much more than I expected, honestly. If I had to choose a favorite, I'd say our screening at Shriekfest. That was the first festival screening that I was able to attend, the atmosphere was great, the theater was packed and a lot of the crew was in attendance and seeing the film for the first time. I remember being really nervous, because it was a crowd of horror fans that had been watching horror films for two days, so I was praying the effects would go over well. Nobody can spot camera tricks like horror fans. After the first big effect scene, arguably the most important scene in the movie, the audience actually burst out in applause. I had the biggest smile on my face and right then, I knew that we had something special. After the screening, I could hear everyone talking about it, which was fantastic all over again.

AN: What King story would you like to adapt on a large scale?

BH: I would've said 11-22-63 if I hadn't heard the recent news about Bad Robot buying it, but there are plenty of SK projects I'd love to do. It would be awesome to figure out how to make *Survivor Type* as a feature film, but that's a tough one. Another one that comes to mind is *Blaze*. It's one of his lesser talked about books, but I really loved that one. Just from a writing standpoint, that story would be really interesting to adapt.

AN: Lastly, What's next for Billy Hanson?

BH: Well, I'm always working on something, but I've got a couple of things happening now. One is a comedy web series called, *Total Ghostage*, which should be out later this year. The other is a feature project, a supernatural thriller (very Stephen King), called *Katahdin,* which is the tallest mountain in Maine. I'm a few drafts into the script now, and I'm hoping that the strength and success of *Survivor Type* will gain us an opportunity to get that film off the ground. It's a tall order, but I'm pushing to get that together within the next couple of years.

And now, here are my thought's and review of the Short film, *Survivor Type*!

Survivor Type is a Short film like I've never seen before. It is scary, suspenseful, and very graphic! All the ingredients for a great Stephen King adaptation. The story is about a surgeon, Richard Pine (played perfectly by Gideon Emery) who has crash landed on a deserted island after being on a cruise ship on a special trip. He is the only survivor, has no food, no phone, the only supplies he does have is from the lifeboat (which isn't much), a video camera to log his stay on the island, and two bricks of heroin. Richard logs every day of his stranded stay on the island and as the days turn to weeks, we not only see a man begin to starve, become frustrated, scared, and do everything he can to stay alive and not go crazy. When killing birds and fish fail, Richard must turn to a "different" form of eating and that's when the story really takes off! We soon find out that Richard isn't quite who we think he is and his form of survival is not of the norm. Without giving away any spoilers, I can tell you this is a mind-blowing adaptation of one of Stephen King's best Short stories. I highly recommend it!

I am a huge Stephen King fan and I know his work very well. Books, movies, TV mini-series, Short stories: it is all entertaining and scary, but one of the problems with King's stories is that they are hard to adapt. There have been hits and misses. However, in this case, it is a ball out of the park hit! I was drawn into the story, it was scary, entertaining, and very graphic even for me. It is truly one of the best adaptations I have seen from King's work. The lead actor, Gideon Emery, was perfect! Not only did he do a fine performance, but he nailed the variety of emotions one must go through in a situation like that. Billy Hanson did this adaptation perfectly. I can see why his film is winning awards and I look forward to his next project with anticipation. Stephen King himself said about the film, quote: 'As far as short stories are concerned, I like the grisly ones the best. However, the story 'Survivor Type' goes a little bit too far, even for me.' And that says it all right there! I highly recommend *Survivor Type* and see this film at your nearest film fest as quickly as possible.

I want to Thank Billy Hanson for taking the time to speak with us today and wish him the very best in all his future projects.

Grey Matter

James B. Cox
June 16, 2013

AS A FIRM BELIEVER in Short films and Independent films, I feel it is important to bring more of these types of films into the spotlight and be recognized as what they truly are; Art. Part of that is supporting your local Film Fests, Independent filmmakers, and supporting the Dollar Baby program. Dollar Baby is a special film program brought to you by the ultimate storyteller; Stephen King. It gives the chance for up-and-coming filmmakers to have their big break into the film business and at the same time, show the world how talented they are. We have another Dollar Baby film for you. The film is called; *"Grey Matter"*. It is a film based on the Stephen King short story, *"Grey Matter"* which is in the book *Night Shift*. Filmmaker James B. Cox has brought his vision of this very scary tale of suspense and horror to the big screen.

James B. Cox was born March 21, 1984 and is a California native originally from Menlo Park, CA. Growing up in the "movie capital of the world", it was fitting for James to go into that field he would grow to love. James went to Chapman University where he studied Media Service (2004-06), Film Production (2006), and Masters of Fine Arts, Film & TV Producing (2011). It was soon thereafter James worked at Disney as ABC TV Group and ABC Family at The Sublime & Beautiful. However, it was the love of movies that brought James his first major film and how lucky he was that it was based on a Stephen King story, *Grey Matter*.

Grey Matter by James B. Cox

The film has won many awards so far as it travels the Film Fest circuit. It has won at Big Bear Horror Film Fest for "Outstanding Performance", the cast of *Grey Matter*. At the Vail Film Fest for "Best Student Film". Hollywood Reel Independent Film Fest for "Best Horror Short". And Charlotte Horror Fest for "Best Student Film" and Nominated for "Best Actor: Tyler Chase. It has also been presented at Comic Conventions, Comicpalooza, and other film fests.

Here is my Exclusive interview with James B. Cox!

Anthony Northrup: Out of all the Stephen King short stories, what attracted you to this one?

James B. Cox: Creatively, I was attracted by the signature King themes of human frailty and normal people facing supernatural situations in *Grey Matter*. From a practical perspective, it had not yet been made into a Dollar Baby Film at the time. This offered the opportunity to not be compared to another filmmaker's vision of the story. Since we started making *Grey Matter*, other filmmakers have been approved to adapt the same story, although I have not seen any of their films yet.

AN: Your version differs from the original text a bit, what changes did you prefer over the original book?

JBC: The changes I made came out of translating the story from the written page to the projected screen. The original short story is told through Richie's son alerting the men at the local bar to his father's transformation. For the sake of the film, I wanted the action of the story to be playing out in front of the audience—- not as a "flashback." This decision led me and my co-writer, C. D. Tomlinson, toward finding a new way to tell the story and convey the son's perspective. We arrived at the "Boy Who Cried Wolf" parable as a dramatic structure to deliver the story with maximum emotional impact.

AN: What was your main goal you wanted to achieve about this film?

JBC: My first and foremost goal was to capture what has always compelled me about Stephen King's stories-- his depiction of the distortion of the human body, the dark side of our world and ourselves. All three of these are at play in the original short story and my film, although they appear in different ways. For instance, Richie's transformation is very different from David's. Richie becomes a completely inhuman monster, a type of fungus (what could be more unnerving?). David becomes a different kind of monster-- He never loses his humanity, but he's distorted by the ravages of war and corrupted by his addiction to alcohol. Both are exploring the same themes, but differ in their approach. The biggest difference between the original story and our film is that the film is more concerned with how this transformation affects his son.

AN: What is your greatest moment so with the success of *Grey Matter*?

JBC: Everyone knows that making a film is really difficult and it requires the concentrated effort of many people. Usually just finishing a film feels like a great accomplishment. So the opportunity to screen for audiences around the world and hear their reactions as they watch is really satisfying. I'm also very grateful for the special recognition and awards we've received from nearly every festival where we've been invited to screen. It's been a really fantastic run.

AN: What Stephen King story would you like to adapt on a larger scale?

JBC: *The Sun Dog* and *The Road Virus Heads North* are some of my favorites. I would love to take a crack at one of his novels that deal with portals into other dimensions like *From A Buick 8*. Those stories painted very vivid images in my mind.

AN: And our closing question: What is next for James B. Cox?

JBC: I'm currently finishing a feature screenplay for director Douglas Schulze's sequel to his original Mimesis released by Anchor Bay Entertainment. I'm also developing many exciting original projects to write and direct, which I'll be able to announce very soon.

> And now, here is my review of *Grey Matter!!!*

The story is told through the eyes of a little boy, Isaac (played by Tyler Chase) who gets into trouble at school, does what he pleases, and mostly lies. He lies to his father, his teachers, and anyone who will listen. He comes from a broken home without a mother. His father (played by Rob Patterson) is a war vet and alcoholic who doesn't really care about anything, not since his wife and Tyler's mom left. All Tyler's dad cares about is drinking and nothing else. However, all of that is about to change when suddenly his father begins to... change due to an unexplained substance that was in one of the beer bottles he drank out of. When Tyler tries to tell his vice principal (played by Allan Trautman) no one believes him because it's a bad case of "the boy who cried wolf" scenario. This creepy tale takes a turn for the worse when Tyler's dad can't stop this unfortunate horror known as...*Grey Matter*.

I enjoyed this tale of horror by Stephen King in the book *Night Shift*. However, it is told differently here in this adaptation. The core of the story is the same, but with this different take on it, it's sure to entertain. It reminded me a lot of the Jordy Verril story in *Creepshow* when he too was trapped in his own hell being turned into a human weed. In this tale, it's the same only grey, jelly, gross looking substance. Although I would have liked a little more of how he got infected, but also what happened to the father? It leaves it up to one's imagination and sometimes that's best. I recommend anyone who can get to a film fest near you to see this film and enjoy yet another Dollar Baby hit!

I wish to thank James for his time and wish him even more success and look for *Grey Matter* at a film fest near you!!!!!

Grey Matter is directed by James B. Cox & produced by Chapman University, University Dodge College of Film and Media Arts. Filmed on Location in Long Beach, CA. Screenplay by C.D. Tomlinson and James B. Cox

Starring: Tyler Chas, Rob Patterson, Allan Trautman
Released: May 21, 2011

The Reaper's Image

Dean Werner
August 12, 2013

SEEING THE BIG BLOCKBUSTERS at the movie theaters is fun and exciting, but it's the little films that are just as entertaining. Independent films are part of that and so are Short films. One form of Short films is the Stephen King film program, Dollar Baby program. It has been around for many years and it is a way for unknown or up-and-coming filmmakers to get their vision out there and be noticed. I am a full supporter of that program and here is another example of that. This time it is with filmmaker Dean Werner and his film, *The Reaper's Image*.

Dean Werner was born on January 15, 1980 and originally from San Bernardino, CA. Dean has been making films since he was 10 yrs. old. He went to San Bernardino High School in the movie capital of the world, California. He went to school to study law and learn about films on the side. He took a hiatus from school, but then went back to major in film production. He graduated from Valley College in San Bernadino in film production. In 2012, he went to the University of Redlands where he studied and majored in filmmaking. Magna Cum Laude with honors for both University and his department with a Bachelor's in Creative Writing. It was in 2003 that he made his first Short film, *The Hand*. He would later do other Short films such as, *The Girl You Never Kiss, You Kiss Forever* (2008), *The Little Duck* (2010), and *Tarantula Silhouettes* (2012) among others. Now, Dean brings us to his

The Reaper's Image by Dean Werner

latest film which so happens to be part of the Dollar Baby program. The story, *The Reaper's Image*, is based on the Stephen King short story of the same name and was first published in *Startling Mystery Stories* magazine in 1969. It would later be published again in the Stephen King short story collection, *Skeleton Crew* in 1985. Here is my review of the short film, *The Reaper's Image*.

The story takes place at the Samuel Claggett Museum where the possessions and antiques of Claggert are on display and in some cases for sale. At this museum, the antique DELVER'S MIRROR is waiting to be seen by an antique collector, Mr. Johnson Spangler(played by John-David Wiese) for a possible purchase. As he is lead through the museum by the curator, Mr. Carlin (played by Will English) who begins to tell Spangler all about the history of Claggert, the museum, it's antiques, and the most important of all; Delver's Mirror and the "possibility" that Delver's Glass is... cursed!

Once they reach the mirror, Mr. Carlin begins telling Spangler all about the history of the mirror and about a high school boy who once looked into the mirror, never to return. You see, once you look into it, it is said the Grim Reaper can be seen and when that happens... .but Spangler doesn't believe the legend and looks for himself. Mr. Carlin... .and you will have to see if the legend is true.

There are many Dollar Baby films made based on Stephen King's Short stories and this is one of the better ones. Werner has captured the feel of the story, the thrill and build-up of the legend of Delver's Glass, and added his own touch and style of filmmaking while keeping the core of the story intact. I thought the music by James Post added to the feel of the film and the actors did a fine job. An enjoyable and entertaining film that should be seen on the Short Film Fest circuit near you. I recommend *The Reaper's Image*.

THE REAPER'S IMAGE
Director: Dean Werner
Based on Short Story by Stephen King
Produced by: Nichole Aurora & Aurora Productions
Music by: James Post
Post Sound by: Noe Rivera
Cast:
John-David Wiese: Johnson Spangler
Will English: Mr. Carlin

Film time: 19 minutes
Shooting: 6 Days

Here is my exclusive interview with writer and director, Dean Werner.

Anthony Northrup: Out of all the Stephen King short stories, what attracted you most to this one?

Dean Werner: Stephen King does great monster stories and blood and guts tales, but he also writes compelling dramas and character driven suspense pieces, so to work on one of his more character based stories intrigued me. The opportunity to do an old style creepy house film also attracted me to *The Reaper's Image*. The challenge of what to do with the ending sealed the deal for me. I wanted to know what happens to the chosen ones, do they just disappear, and how? I came up with an answer and then decided between going in a Picture of Dorian Gray path for the ending or more special effects heavy, because the images of a scene from Something Wicked This Way Comes, where the old schoolteacher transforms to a little girl would be another solution of how to show the answer visually. I saw it as a kid and hadn't thought about it in years and then it came back to me as I worked on my adaptation. I knew I picked the right story if it could bring back a memory of watching an old movie with my brothers.

AN: So many Stephen King fans want adaptations to be as close to the book as possible, how do you handle the pressure to keep the fans happy?

DW: At the end of the day you have to make your film and not someone else's. I spent a year in pre-production, production, and post production, so with that much of my life invested; I wanted a movie I'd be proud of as a finished product. Some people realize that books and movies are two completely different mediums and can't do the same things and others don't. They fall in love with a ten page description of a tea room, in a film that's one or a handful of shots to see the room. The balance for an adaption comes from keeping the core values of what made the original work so well, but make it your own without changing so much that it may as well be called something else. The pressure is definitely there because no one wants to let down fans. My version delves more into the characters and leaves Carlin more damaged with decisions to make.

AN: What was your main goal you wanted to achieve about this film?

DW: The story has these moments of verbal sparring between the characters. It's like a chess match, each man thinks he knows more than the other. What do they know and is the reaper real? I tried to add another layer by making Carlin more voyeuristic in a way, maybe he's trying to see the mirror take someone to better understand what he's storing. The atmosphere from the story was another goal; I wanted it to feel like this tumble-down museum with a sense of impending doom. Some of that is done through the senses. Like the smells, it would be great to do a William Castle style tour with it and have smells come out when Spangler smells odors. Spangler, and the audience hopefully, can't get comfortable with the house or Carlin. The house adds the biggest element to the atmosphere and credit with that goes to my producer Nichole Aurora. I couldn't have done this film the same way without her. She found this great Queen Anne style home, decorated and furnished from pieces up until the 1940s. All of that great wallpaper and ceiling designs are all a part of that house. My favorite is the game room, the wallpaper looks like eyes are surrounding them. Then we worked on going from this gran manor to smaller and smaller rooms. It gets claustrophobic with the characters being pushed to the next room throughout, and the rooms grow darker. I wanted to shoot in a way so the viewer feels the way each character does at that moment. My other goal was to not make anything obvious. The audience has to get the breadcrumbs to fully realize the ending, which I like to do. I like when you have to pay attention. It's more cerebral. It's not a monster movie or slasher horror. I considered using this great monster costume we had and cloak it and make a great reaper, but that's not what makes the original work, so I decided against it and keep it in the vein of a thriller.

AN: What is your greatest moment so far with the success of *The Reaper's Image*?

DW: I'd like to say awards, but we are just now submitting to festivals and awaiting notification. Even with awards, a great success for this project would be the new people I worked with on it, and I'd liked to continue working with, including Nichole Aurora from Aurora Sinclair Productions. She's very much a director's producer and worried only about supporting my vision. Our first two days of shooting were tight because I worked all night and then got up early for school. Once for Honors convocation and then my graduation. Both days I left the ceremonies in Redlands and drove straight to our set in Colton. Nichole or my DP Nico would text with updates or questions, they helped steer the ship while I was gone. I was proud of the cast and crew that everything was ready for me when I showed up those days.

AN: What Stephen King story would you like to adapt on a large scale?

DW: I'd like to do Joyland, but hear that Tate Taylor from *The Help* is adapting it. The story has such great noir moments and layers, that a lot could be done with it. Going the Frank Darabont route and expanding a shorter story could work. *Rest Stop*, or *Mute*, offer some possibilities. With *Mute* being a great haunting and poetic possibility.

AN: Lastly, What's next for Dean Werner?

DW: I'm working on a series of short films now that would have the stories connect in a way I've never seen before in a film. Also going into production on a feature film that is more mid-apocalyptic than post, if that makes sense. Concentrating on festival submission deadlines for *The Reaper's Image,* and an audience award winning film from the 2012 48 Hour Film Project titled *Tarantula Silhouettes*. I also look forward to new challenges that will help me perfect my craft.

I'd like to take this moment to thank Dean Werner for taking the time from his schedule for this interview and wish him continued success. Look for *The Reaper's Image* at a film fest near you.

Beachworld

Maria Ivanova
November 19, 2013

THE DOLLAR BABY PROGRAM is a film program designed by Stephen King many years ago for up-and-coming filmmakers to get their work out there and show the world what they can do with his words. The latest comes from filmmaker, Maria Ivanova and her film, *Beachworld*.

Maria was born March 3rd, 1986, in St. Petersburg, Russia and still lives there to this day. She says she "loves that city with all my heart, can't imagine any other place as my home." Maria went to school there and later graduated with a degree in Law. She realized it wasn't her dream job or meant to be her future, so she studied everyday and learned Maya, Photoshop, After Effects, and other Animation & Designs programs. She studied all by herself, read books, watched tutorials. She got into the Stephen King Dollar Baby program because she loved Stephen King and his works very much. She knew of the program and one day stumbled upon the Dollar Baby webpage and the rest is history. She felt, "Why not!" And now she is the proud filmmaker of *Beachworld* and here is my review....

Stephen King's Short Story, *Beachworld*, was first published in *Weird Tales* magazine in 1984. A year later, it was published in his collection of Short Stories book called *Skeleton Crew* in 1985. *Beachworld* is about a story that takes place in a distant future that is not specified. A spacecraft crash lands on a deserted planet that is nothing but sand. The two remaining passenger's, Rand and Shapiro are the only ones who have survived. After Rand becomes a bit insane, another spacecraft arrives to rescue them. When Shapiro tries to take Rand onboard, he resists causing a hand of sand to prevent him from leaving. With Shapiro barely escaping onto the ship, leaving Rand behind only to be sucked up by the sand planet itself.

Beachworld by Maria Ivanova

This is a serious tale, yet unique in it's own way. What I enjoyed was the way Maria decided to film this King tale. She used nothing but animation, computer graphics, and NO DIALOGUE! None. It was told on pure visual, sound, and imagination. I found that very intriguing. What was even more so was, she also filmed it in black and white. No color of any kind was used. That gave the futuristic look of the spacecraft an even more unique appearance and it made the planet of sand even more eerie. It's very deep, artistic, and creative. Personally, I would like to see King's *The Dark Tower* series filmed this way, it was that unique. I enjoyed this take on *Beachworld* and found it very entertaining.

Here is my exclusive Interview with Maria Ivanova.

Anthony Northrup: Out of all the Stephen King short stories, what attracted you most to this one?

Maria Ivanova: I was into science fiction themes at that time. Also, I was interested in exploring and showing in film *Solitude, Loneliness, and Madness*. The interesting thing about this story is that the Sand (in my opinion) is also a character, even though its presence (as a character) is implicit.

AN: What made you decide to go with animation with this story as opposed to live-action and do you feel the "no dialogue" adds to the feel of the story as it was presented?

MI: For me: animation is the only way to tell stories. With animated films I can create everything from nothing, from scratch, from blank pages. And I'm not depending on the weather, actors, filming locations, etc. Basically you can create universes in animated films As for "no dialogue": it's just the way I used to create films. I rarely use any dialogues, when I feel that the story can be told without words.

AN: So many Stephen King fans want adaptations to be as close to the book as possible, how do you handle the pressure to keep the fans happy?

MI: I'm not sure how many fans are happy with my film. I didn't think about that when I was making the film. I just tried to be honest with myself and took a risk.

AN: What was your main goal you wanted to achieve about this film?

MI: I wanted to create a good film, a unique work, with memorable atmosphere and characters, and sound.

AN: What is your greatest moment so far with the success of *Beachworld*?

MI: I guess it's people's joy. I really enjoy when my films are watched, when the stories are told. Basically it's all I need: I want people to watch my films. It's like "Every actor needs an audience". Last week I got the People's Choice Award in "Dollar Baby Film Festival Russia 2013" (Krasnodar). I'm very happy because it's People's choice.

AN: What Stephen King story would you like to adapt on a large scale?

MI: I think it would be *Lisey's Story*, or *Crouch End*.

AN: Lastly, What's next for Maria Ivanova?

MI: Well, I've just completed my new animated short for *ABCs OF DEATH 2* contest, it's called *M is for Mactation*. And it's available online. I'm still working on several of my personal projects including stop-motion animated films. And all of them are in the horror\mystery\fantasy genre. Wish me luck.

I want to take this moment to Thank Maria for taking this time out of her schedule to do this interview and wish her the very best of luck in her future projects. Check your local Entertainment for the Dollar Baby Film Fest when it comes to your area.

Umney's Last Case

Rodney Altman
December 3, 2013

RODNEY ALTMAN IS A 32 YEARS OLD, originally from Pittsburgh, PA. When he was younger, he took filmmaking classes in High School at Pittsburgh Filmmakers. He loved it so much, he wanted to instantly pursue his filmmaking career and education. He applied at the New York University Tisch School of the Arts, but unfortunately didn't get in the first time around.

He then did a year and a half of college at the University of Pittsburgh and later transferred to NYU. Rodney graduated with a BA in Film & Television. While in college, he made lots of Short Films, but the most successful were *Echoes* based on the Short Story by Lawrence C. Connolly. *Umney's Last Case* based on the Stephen King Short Story from his book, *Nightmares and Dreamscapes* was Rodney's final project for the Advanced Film Production class.

His film, *Umney's Last Case* was nominated for Best Short Film of the Year at NYU's First Run Film Festival. He also won awards for editing, cinematography, and directing. After Rodney graduated, he moved to Los Angeles, CA. where he currently lives. He has currently been writing scripts and working on finding a good low-budget script to direct as his first feature film.

Here is my exclusive interview with Dollar Baby director, Rodney Altman...

Anthony Northrup: Out of all the Stephen King short stories, what attracted you most to this one?

Rodney Altman: Out of all the short stories, I liked *"Umney's Last Case"* because it was very different from most King stories. It wasn't horror.

Umney's Last Case by Rodney Altman

Everyone knows Stephen King for his horror stories, but not so much for the other things he writes. Also, I liked that it was set in the 1940s, and I thought it would be a fun challenge to try to recreate that period on film.

AN: There was another "Umney's Last Case" short film in the television series, Nightmares & Dreamscapes with William H. Macy. How did you want to approach your story that was different from that version?

RA: To be fair, my version of *"Umney's Last Case"* was finished before the one done with William H. Macy. I got the rights shortly before TNT picked them up. So really, my film had already been finished and screened for audiences when I saw the version with William H. Macy on TV.

AN: So many Stephen King fans want adaptations to be as close to the book as possible, how do you handle the pressure to keep the fans happy?

RA: Being a King fan myself, I know how annoying it is to see someone adapt a favorite story or novel and make too many changes. When I was adapting *"Umney's Last Case,"* I wanted to stick to the original story as much as possible. I really loved the story, so I wanted to make that as a film. A lot of the dialogue is lifted directly from the story. I even shot a lot of stuff that's in the story that had to be edited out for time, like the scene with Bill Tuggle, and later with the two painters in the hallway. We shot all that stuff, including longer scenes with Peoria Smith and Samuel Landry. However, the running time was like 28 minutes, and I needed to get it under 20, so that stuff had to go. It was hard, because I really loved a lot and wanted to be accurate to the story, but sometimes stuff just has to go. Another change I made was the addition of Candy Cain as a character. In the story, she just leaves a note for Umney, but I thought it would be more visual to see her leave. Plus the film badly needed a female presence. I also wanted to keep the little title cards that break the story up into segments. I tried to keep them as close as possible to the story, but after editing some things needed to change. I couldn't call the one section "Vernon's Cough" because we cut out all the coughing. And the "Of Painters and Pesos" had to go, because again, all that stuff got left on the editing room floor. Finally, in the book, Umney and Landry look the same. For budget reasons I just couldn't do that, so I used two separate actors.

AN: What was your main goal you wanted to achieve about this film?

RA: The mail goal I wanted to accomplish with the film was to make something professional. I wanted people to watch it and feel like it was a real film, something you'd see in a movie theater, just shorter. I wanted people who knew the story to like it, as well as people who had never heard of it. That's the real trick: entertaining the fans and non-fans at the same time.

AN: What is your greatest moment so far with the success of *"Umney's Last Case"*?

RA: Honestly, I've been honored by how many people get in touch and ask to screen it at their Dollar Baby festivals around the world. When I made it, I never would have believed that 7 years later people would still want to watch it. Also, I've had many people tell me that they prefer my version to the William H. Macy one. It's a huge honor to have a serious King fan tell me that they like my little student film over a big budget production like that.

AN: What Stephen King story would you like to adapt on a large scale?

RA: If I could adapt one King story on a large scale, it would be *The Dark Tower*. I would do it as a trilogy, and it would be the coolest thing you've ever seen. However, since Ron Howard is working on that, it seems unlikely at the moment. So my second choice would be "*The Jaunt.*"

AN: Lastly, What's next for Rodney Altman?

RA: What's next? Well, I have several projects I'm working on. I have a TV pilot that was recently a finalist at the Austin Film Festival, so I'm shopping that around. I have a couple features I'm developing, and hopefully I'll end up directing one as my first feature. I'm always on the lookout for a good script. So if anyone has something they think I'd be the right director for, they should get in touch. And if Ron Howard ever gives up the rights to *The Dark Tower*, I'm going to try for that!

To see this film or any of the Dollar Baby program films, please check out Dollar Baby Film Fest fan page on Facebook. I want to thank Rodney Altman for taking the time from his busy schedule for this interview and his time.

In the Deathroom

Damon Vinyard
December 7, 2013

IT'S TIME ONCE AGAIN to take a moment and recognize the art of the short film. One way of showing you is by the Stephen King Dollar Baby Film program. Started many years ago by King, it gives the Independent filmmaker a chance to get their work out there and show the world how talented they are with the adaption of a King short story. This time I bring you the film *In The Deathroom* adapted by talented filmmaker, Damon Vinyard.

Damon Vinyard is originally from Amarillo, Texas where he went to Tascosa High School until 1994. Right out of High School, Damon went to Oral Roberts Univ. on a Track Scholarship. He transferred to Oklahoma State Univ. his first year so that he could play football. Laughing back at it now, Damon felt he should have stuck with track because of Oklahoma Univ. the football players were 'HUGE!' He says looking back now, 'It was a lot of fun and I have no regrets.' Damon moved around a lot, but ever since he was a kid he knew he always wanted to be a filmmaker. After his many travels, Damon settled in Los Angeles where he became a Broadcast director before now becoming a filmmaker of a Stephen King Dollar Baby, *In The Deathroom*. And now, here is my review of *In The Deathroom*.

In The Deathroom is a short story that was first published in 1999 on an audiobook called, *Blood & Smoke* by Stephen King. A year later, it was published in *Secret Windows* and in 2002 it was published in King's collection of short stories called, *Everything's Eventual*. The story takes place in a room, a "deathroom".

It is about a New York Times reporter named Fletcher, who is captured by South American dictatorship. When their government kills a group of nuns, one of them is Fletcher's sister. He is brought in and

In The Deathroom by Damon Vinyard

questioned about other involvements, however, he knows he will never leave that room alive. He is tortured and interrogated repeatedly until he fakes a seizure and steals one of the guards guns, shooting everyone he can. When he escapes the "deathroom" and we are left with Fletcher standing at the top of the stairs, not knowing if other guards heard the gunshots or if he escapes the country. Those who've read the book know how it ends.

Without giving out any spoilers, I can tell you this was clearly an edge-of-your-seat thriller. What seems like just another war room plot, turns into a room of hell, blood, violence, and suspense. The actors were very convincing, the story of course kept my interest, and Damon's directing was clearly spot on. He truly made you feel for this poor man and what he had to go through to stay alive, yet kept your interest wondering just how he was going to get out of such a hellish situation. This is one of the better Dollar Baby adaptations I've seen and I enjoyed it very much. By the films end, when you're squirming in your seat from the torture scenes and the surprising ending… you KNOW you've got a winner!

Here is my Exclusive Interview with Dollar Baby filmmaker, Damon Vinyard!

Anthony Northup: Out of all the Stephen King short stories, what attracted you most to this one?

Damon Vinyard: This one appealed to me mainly because it was only one location and there were only 5 actors. I knew that I could spend my money on the production value of it, which was really important to me. That also made it tougher because it is hard to hold someone's attention when it is only one location, and the actors have to be good or I am in trouble. I feel like all the actors did a good job and I finished with a product that I am proud of. Don't get me wrong, I really liked the story, mainly the twist at the end when you find out why he is even in that country and in this position, but it just wasn't my favorite of Mr. King's, my favorite is *The Long Walk*.

AN: What changes did you make to make this your own as opposed to King's original text?

DV: I didn't change anything other than a short monologue that the lead actor says over black at the beginning. That was done because I felt that the viewer needed to know a little back story about who the lead is but yet still now know why he is in the predicament that he is in. Other than that I didn't change a thing, I mean who am I to edit Mr. King's work.

AN: So many Stephen King fans want adaptations to be as close to the book as possible, how do you handle the pressure to keep the fans happy?

DV: My biggest concern was honoring Mr. King's work, keeping it as close to what I thought his vision of it was when he was writing it, and making a product that King fans would be proud of. The only pressure I felt was getting all the shots I needed in the time that I had. Paying for it out of your own pocket insures that everything has to be done in a timely manner, and that is hard to do on set. On a movie set nothing ever goes as planned.

AN: What was your main goal you wanted to achieve about this film?

DV: Make something I was proud of, something that if Mr. King ever saw it he would be proud of, and make a product that all the actors involved would be proud to show others.

AN: What is your greatest moment so far with the success of *In The Deathroom*?

DV: I would say the greatest moments are when filmmakers from overseas contact me because they have seen it somewhere, or read about it online, and they talk to me about it. It is so neat to be part of a fraternity of filmmakers to do a Dollar Baby. It is a group that has a great admiration for Mr. King's work and has a special bond amongst each other for it. It was Stephen King that was the catalyst to get me to read. I was never interested in reading a book, there were sports outside I could be playing, but I read *The Thinner* and all of that changed. After I finished it I went to *The Stand*, then I started reading his collections of short stories and I was hooked. I knew I wanted to make one into a film one day, in fact I hope to do another one down the road.

AN: What Stephen King story would you like to adapt on a large scale?

DV: Well as I said *The Long Walk* is my favorite short of his, but I don't know if I would ever take that on. I get depressed when I see one of his books done as a movie and it doesn't translate, at least to me. There have been quite a few that I really enjoyed the book, but the movie let me down. I think if I could do any of them I would like to do *The Girl That Loved Tom Gordon*. I really enjoyed that one and it is my style and genre that I would like to direct.

AN: Lastly, What's next for Damon Vinyard?

DV: I have a short I am filming at the beginning of next year I am really excited about, after that I want to shoot one more short and get ready for a feature. I have a couple ideas for a feature that I really like, I am going to attempt to write basically a long treatment for them and get an accomplished writer to work with me on creating the dialogue, maybe I will ask Frank Darabont if he is interested in working with me, he is a fantastic writer and what's the worst he can do, say no?

I would like to take this moment and Thank filmmaker Damon Vinyard for his time and this wonderful opportunity to see his Dollar Baby film, *In The Deathroom* and for our interview together. It was certainly a pleasure. I want to wish Damon much success in his future and look forward to his future projects.

Paranoid: A Chant by Jay Holden

Paranoid: A Chant

Jay Holden
January 12, 2014

THE STEPHEN KING'S DOLLAR BABY film program is for up-and-coming filmmakers to show the world their work and at the same time adapt one of King's short stories to scare fans around the world. This TIME, our Dollar Baby is from filmmaker Jay Holben and he has adapted King's short story, *Paranoid: A Chant* from the book, *Skeleton Crew*. Before we begin, let's learn a little bit about director Jay Holden.

Jay has been a director since the early age of seven! Most kids were out playing at that age, but Jay played with a different type of toy: an 8mm camera. Running around his backyard filming everything and anything. He knew back then that making movies was not just his passion, but his destiny as well. Jay was born in Chicago, Ill., but moved to Scottsdale, AZ in 1977. Attending Horizon High School till 1990 and from there he went to Scottsdale Community College. He later moved to Los Angeles, CA where he has covered just about every job there is when it comes to making a film. Jay has studied and practiced the art and craft of Cinematography, worked in the theater community, and has done jobs on sets ranging from electrician to Gaffer to Director of Photography. Jay has done it all in his 20 plus years in the business including Short films, commercials, television, and music videos. He has worked with musicians such as; Korn, Brandy, Shaquille O'Neal, and Ice Cube. He has worked on films including *Free Enterprise* and Short Films like *Decent* as well as a documentary called, *Camgirls*.

Jay is also a well-known writer with contributions to such magazines as the Hollywood Reporter, Geek Magazine, American Cinematography Magazine, and Digital Video Magazine. He also has been on the faculty of Global Cinematography Institute as well. When asked about, How did you get the opportunity to do a Stephen King Dollar Baby film?, Jay said, '..I was working on a current film and there was a time factor involved and I knew the program was for film students which I was not. I sent a work in progress video of my film along with a letter to King. Three weeks later, it was a Saturday night and I was brushing my dog and my girlfriend, Jennine came in white as a ghost and said, 'It's Stephen King on the phone'. I went to the phone and said, 'Hello?' and King said, 'Hello Jay? This is Steve King.' He told me to get in contact with his assistant and the deal was signed." And as they say, 'The rest is history.' When Jay isn't making films, he enjoys sailboating, his wife Jennine, and their dog, Ripley and currently still lives in L.A. One thing that has been said about Jay and his dedication to the film industry is: 'Since the very beginning, Jay understood the importance of being a director by understanding ALL jobs on the set' and Jay has proven his dedication and love to the industry by studying, learning, and not being afraid of hard work to get the job done.

Here is my review of Jay's Dollar Baby film, *Paranoid: A Chant* .

This story is actually based on a 100 line poem that was published in King's 1985 short story collection, *Skeleton Crew*. It is a dark, eerie, and moody story about a young girl (played by Tonya Ivey), who is in a motel room deep in an unknown city, keeping herself from the outside world. She is, of course, "paranoid" by recalling all of the wrong doings that have happened to her throughout her life. Ranging everything from a waitress at a diner to faceless men standing on a corner… waiting for her (she thinks). She catalogues all of these wrong doings in 100's of notebooks and her walls in her motel room are covered with newspaper clippings of what she believes are government conspiracy theories. She is troubled, a schizophrenic, and on the edge of insanity.

Out of all the Dollar Babyfilms I have seen, without question, this is the darkest, creepiest, glued to the screen, eerie, most gothic filmed film I have seen. Jay truly makes you feel her "paranoia" while you look for a door to escape that horror she has built for herself. The actress (Tonya Ivey) did a wonderful job at covering every possible sense in the human psyche there is. I felt very disturbed after watching this film and agree that Jay Holden has learned his craft well. This Dollar Baby was shot on a 35mm color camera and in a week's time. Jay has said he had a challenge on his hands when trying to collect 100's of notebooks, shopping at every store he could find so he could have enough for the shoot. The newspaper clippings on the walls in the girls motel room were cut from The Globe,

The National Enquirer, and The Star which were stained with coffee and cooked in an oven to give it that "old" look. When asked what he wanted to achieve with *Paranoid: A Chant*, Jay replied, '..I wanted to get under people's skin a bit... .I wanted them to have a chance to look inside the mind of a woman who isn't particularly healthy and not really enjoying being there.' The film/story also has tie-in to Stephen King's *The Stand* ("a man with no face" which was described as Randall Flagg before) and also *The Dark Tower* (the can-toi).

PARANOID: A CHANT
Starring: Tonya Ivey: Woman in Motel Room
Cinematographer: Jay Holben
Original Story by: Stephen King
Produced by: Jay Holben
Directed by: Jay Holben
Adakin Productions
Running Time: 8 minutes

Here is my Exclusive Interview with Jay Holben.

Anthony Northrup: Out of all the Stephen King short stories, what attracted you most to this one?

Jay Holden: *Paranoid: A Chant* always stood out to me. It was one of the first poems I ever read that I truly loved. It was visceral, full of powerful images, and beautifully rhythmic. In high school, I competed in several forensic competitions with *Paranoid* and did very well. I used it as an audition piece for several years as an actor. Back in 1999, I was producing a series of intensive film tests and several short films and spec commercials and realized that I had a small window of time (a single day) in which to direct something myself. I needed something logistically simple, yet narratively powerful and *Paranoid* came to mind. A short poem that takes place, primarily, in one location with one character. It was a chance to bring this great small work to life and really show off some of my visual storytelling skills. Also, people said I shouldn't try to tackle a poem as a film: which just inspired me more to prove them wrong!

AN: What made you decide to go with this particular King story, especially since it's based on a poem?

JH: Oops. Pretty much answered that one already.

AN: So many Stephen King fans want adaptations to be as close to the book as possible, how do you handle the pressure to keep the fans happy?

JH: I am King fan, myself. There was no question that my adaptation would be as faithful to the original work as I could possibly make it. That's not to say that it's what everyone else envisions when they read the poem. It's MY faithful adaptation of what the poem means to me. There's also a significant difference in the medium of film versus the medium of literature: and certain alterations and concessions must be made (hence it being called an adaptation). I did, however, study the poem intensely. The pacing of the film comes strongly from the rhythm of King's writing. Where he breaks a line or where he adds a period or coma, where he makes a new paragraph: all of that inspired the rhythm of my adaptation. It was important to me that the entire poem: without alteration: be in the piece. So, was I worried about the fans demanding faithfulness? No. I was worried about getting it right in my own mind!

AN: What was your main goal you wanted to achieve about this film?

JH: *Paranoid* was a director's "calling card" piece for me. It was my first "serious" 35mm short film as a director: I had done several on 8mm, one on 16mm and several on video before this. At the time I was primarily working as a cinematographer, but my aspirations have always been to direct. I finished it right at what I felt was the peak for the excitement about short films online. It played on iFilm.com for a while: and was a #1 short. I took a couple meetings with fantastic production companies because of *Paranoid*: and it's still part of my director's reel to this day.

AN: What is your greatest moment so far with the success of *Paranoid*?

JH: By and far the night Stephen called me to give me his permission. It was a short, but really wonderful conversation. He was then, and continues to be, extraordinarily supportive of this film: and I could never express how honored and humbled I am by his generosity.

AN: What Stephen King story would you like to adapt on a large scale?

JH: That's actually one I'm keeping under my hat. Stephen and I have spoken about it, but he hasn't yet agreed to let the rights go. Yet.

AN: Lastly, What's next for Jay Holben ?

JH: I'm constantly working. I'm currently in production on a reality television series that I'm producing and directing. I have several projects in development including three feature films and a television series. I also continue to write for American Cinematographer, Digital Video and TV Technology, along with teaching at the Global Cinematography Institute and a monthly lecture series with Hollywood Shorts and Panavision. I have a couple shorts that are in post-production, including a new horror (original, not King). I stayed away from short films for a number of years, with the mistaken mentality that I had 'moved on' in my career: but I really find them a wonderful alternate medium to play in. If a prolific and extraordinary novelist like Stephen King can continue to write short stories along with his novels, I can certainly continue to make short films between the larger projects: so expect more of those from me in the coming years.

Well, there you have it! Yet another spotlight on another Dollar Baby short film that you will enjoy! I want to say Thank You to Jay Holben for taking the time out of his busy schedule for doing this interview and giving me the opportunity to watch and review his gripping film. I wish Jay the best of luck in his future projects.

Cain Rose Up by Ranjeet S. Marwa

Cain Rose Up

Ranjeet S. Marwa
March 2, 2014

TIME FOR ANOTHER LOOK behind-the-scenes of the Dollar Baby universe. This time, our Dollar Baby is from filmmaker Ranjeet S. Marwa and he have adapted King's short story, *Cain Rose Up*, from the book, *Skeleton Crew*. Before we begin, here is some background history on it's director, Ranjeet S. Marwa.

Ranjeet was born and raised in the UK and came from a very artistic family. At the young age of 11yrs., Ranjeet saw Stanley Kubrick's classic, *The Shining* and that is the film that inspired him enough to become a filmmaker. At that very age, he went out and wrote his very first script and at age 15 years old, he made his first film. His education began at James Watt Primary School and Lordswood Boys High School where he was greatly interested in art where he excelled highly. His first film experience came in 2010, when his cousin needed help with a film project for his college assignment. His cousin was so impressed he let Ranjeet direct the film itself! From then on, he never looked back. As a filmmaker, Ranjeet's films have won many awards and just as many nominations, showing the filmmaking community he does indeed have the talent and the makings of becoming a great filmmaker. His favorite types of films include subjects ranging from time, space, infinity, the human condition, altering and shifting of the mind. As well as the consciousness being moved from one place to another. His filmmaking inspirations range from Nicolas Winding Refn, Darren Aronofsky, David Fincher, Stanley Kubrick, Steven Spielberg, and Francis Ford Coppola. Since the young age of 15 years old. Ranjeet has made 48 Short films, 2 feature length films, with more in development now. He is an Official Member of the Directors Guild of Great Britain and part of the Stephen King Dollar Baby filmmakers with his first Dollar Baby in 2012 with *The Man Who Loved Flowers* and 2013's *Cain Rose Up*.

Ranjeet's choice for a Dollar Baby was *Cain Rose Up*, first published in the Spring issue of Urbis magazine in 1968 and was later part of Stephen King's Short Story collection, *Skeleton Crew*. It is the story of a young college student, Curt Garrish (played by Matthew Harris), who is inspired by Charles Manson and Beethoven and with the voices in his head decides to go on a murder rampage in his student house executing everyone.

In the original King story, the student is a "sniper" and knocks off students all over campus, but in this version it is just in one setting. This was a very dark, disturbing, and very violent film. It is known that in King's works, not all monsters are in the closet or under our beds, but within us as well. This film shows that at any given time that very innocent student could "snap" at any time. With the stresses of college pressures of young adult life, Curt takes the stress to the ultimate extreme. Ranjeet's vision shows that darkside and even though there's not too much in the explanation as to, 'Why' he did it, it's a violent story in the tradition of Tarantino, but from King's mind. For me personally, I would've liked a little more background and reasoning. Still, a well done adaptation and worth your time.

Here is my Exclusive Interview with Dollar Baby filmmaker, Ranjeet S. Marwa.

Anthony Northrup: Out of all the Stephen King short stories, what attracted you most to this one?

Ranjeet S. Marwa: What I love most about this story was the dehumanizing of the mind, how one slowly becomes insane. It's about how an ordinary everyday man becomes a killer. It's not just in this story, but a continuing theme throughout all of my films. Discovering how the true instincts of human behavior are settled by our own minds. When our species is born, we are given instruments of destruction, which are our hands but along the way as we evolved, as our minds expanded, we lost our true identities. We are born killers.

AN: What changes did you make to make this your own as opposed to King's original text?

RM: I had to change it drastically to fit our day and age that we live. King's original text is great for its time, but doesn't really make sense now. To copy a book and make it into film is a very hard task to undertake, however, to be faithful to the book you have betrayed. Copying it word for word doesn't work, I learned that from my first adaptations. The film is supposed to be an adaptation, meaning you adapt it to your needs and your style whilst keeping the core essential elements in place.

AN: So many Stephen King fans want adaptations to be as close to the book as possible, how do you handle the pressure to keep the fans happy?

RM: I don't. Ultimately you make the best film you can. I learned pretty quickly in my filmmaking career that you can't make films for other people, you can't try and make everyone happy because you will undoubtedly fail. You can't be true to the source material because what works on the page doesn't necessarily mean it'll work on the screen.

AN: What was your main goal you wanted to achieve about this film?

RM: I wanted to show through a series of events how a man becomes engulfed in fear, anxiety, and madness. How a man becomes insane throughout life until one day, like a rubber band he snaps. When you put tension on something for too long, if it's constantly under strain sooner or later it'll snap and that's what I wanted to show with Curt. We see him as an everyday kid, but we never see what lies beneath him and that's what I wanted to explore.

AN: With all the shootings at schools and colleges in our modern times on the rise, how did you handle the subject matter and was it something you felt you had to handle very carefully considering?

RM: I did consider it. I understand that families have lost loved ones due to these atrocious crimes. It's hard to bring these memories back into light. However, I see it like this, if it's not shown then more and more people will lose their lives. If it is shown through a medium which we are all familiar with then we can understand the situations that affect our society and we can protect our loved ones as well as the many other people who this could potentially happen to.

AN: The film is very disturbing and violent, is this the type of film making style you want to be known for such as fellow filmmakers such as Quinton Tarrantino, for example?

RM: How I approach films is like art. I come from a background as an illustrator and have drawn my whole life, film is a combination of all my talents rolled into one. I'm drawn to violence, like I said it's a human trait which we hide but are all capable of. I like to create an experience on the screen, like art, you look at it and you don't really understand it, but you continually look at it because it's intriguing, it draws you in, it's captivating.

AN: What is your greatest moment so far with the success of *Cain Rose Up*?

RM: The greatest thing for me, is the fact that I got to make the film that I wanted. I got to show what was in my mind and how I combined that with King's great story. The other greatest thing was that I got to redeem myself from my first attempt at a Dollar Baby.

AN: What Stephen King story would you like to adapt on a large scale?

RM: There are 2 that I'd like to make. The first being *Beachworld*, it's really a fascinating story, again it deals with the condition of the human mind. The other being *The Death of Jack Hamilton*, I love period films set in the depression era. However, if I could make another one of King's films, it would be *Christine*. I love the original, but I think I could make something great for this day and age.

AN: Lastly, What's next for Ranjeet S. Marwa?

RM: Well, I just finished my second feature film. The only thing I do day in day out is make films, that is my life and nothing more. What's next is also two more biblical horror films and another feature film. Then, hopefully I'll get to make my World War 1 film towards the end of the year at some point.

And there you have it, another exclusive Dollar Baby interview and review. I want to Thank Ranjeet for his time and patience to do this interview and wish him nothing but success in his future projects. I know that he will no doubt make film history with his talents and determination to bring the world stories to the big screen.

Last Rung On the Ladder

James Cole
March 24, 2014

TIME FOR ANOTHER behind-the-scenes look at the Dollar Baby universe. This time, our Dollar Baby is not from one of the current Dollar Baby filmmakers, but from one of the original Dollar Babies ever! We're honored to have filmmaker James Cole with us who directed *Last Rung On The Ladder* which was featured in Stephen King's short story collection, *Night Shift*, but before we begin, here is some background history on it's director, James Cole.

James Cole was born in Greenwich, Connecticut. His love of movies came at the age of 11 years old., but it was at the young age of 13 years old. that he discovered the love of horror and would begin his lifelong collection of Stephen King books. James studied and graduated from Chatham High School in 1985, from there he continued his education at the University of Massachusetts Amherst till 1989. However, it was in the summer of 1986 that James would make history, as he would soon be a part of what is known as: Stephen King's World. He would be part of this because he would become part of the Stephen King Dollar Baby Film Program. He began filming *Last Rung On The Ladder* in summer of 1986 in Cape Cod, Mass. Working in hot conditions, old barns, and with kids and with a low-budget of $1500—James had his work cut out for him, but with his partner, Dan Thron, they made the film and sent it off to Stephen King. James still has the canceled $1.00 check with Stephen King's signature on it. A treasure, indeed.

The Last Rung On The Ladder by James Cole

What's interesting about James Cole is that he was one of the original Dollar Babies. Back in the late 70's/early 80's, the Dollar Baby program was really not known only by word of mouth or King rep's. It was a different time then for the Dollar Baby program. There were 17 members in the beginning and no one could see these films but King himself and if you were lucky enough see some at Short Film Fests you were one of the lucky ones. Very unlike today where you can either go to Film Fests (which there are a lot of them than long ago), Horror Conventions, or on the Net itself, but not all are available. James had to depend on his talent and craft to get his film seen and it was at conventions around that time. With the success of his Dollar Baby under his belt and putting a name out there for himself, James moved to California in 1991 to pursue films. He worked as a temp, primarily at Walt Disney Imagineering. In 2003 James teamed with fellow Dollar Baby Jay Holben (*Paranoid: A Chant*) to make the short film *The Night Before,* a drama written by James based on his hospital experiences as a child and directed by Jay. However it was James' Dollar Baby that would stay with him during his career. James had write-up by himself and others about '*Last Rung*' in such books as, Castle Rock

Newsletter, Stephen King Encyclopedia, Lost Works of Stephen King, Scifi Universe, Video Watchdog, books about the Making of Shawshank Redemption and Making of The Green Mile. Two of these books are by Stephen Spignesi and the two films by Frank Darabont, both very well-known in the Stephen King world. Although James has covered almost every job in the entertainment business from director to writer to actor and beyond, he moved back to Massachusetts recently and currently writes for The Cape Cod Chronicle doing film reviews while writing new material for new book and film projects and we can look forward to his return back behind the camera once again.

Here is my review of *Last Rung On the Ladder.*

'*Last Rung*' is a Stephen King short story that was first published in King's short story collection, *Night Shift*. The story is about a brother and sister who are always there for each other. One day on a hot summer's day, they play a game in a barn where one jumps off the top of the inside of a barn and the other catches them at the bottom. When the sister is at the top, the ladder breaks and it is up to her brother to save her like he always has. He gathers hay quickly to save his sister. She falls hoping he catches her. This is all told in a flashback, in reality the brother and sister have lost contact with each other over the years and this is mostly due to the brothers busy lifestyle. What he doesn't know is, she needed him. Going through her own troubles and depressions she needed her brother like she needed him that day in the barn. He learns of her suicide and regrets that the time he should've spent with her he could've saved her once again. He realizes all of this by the last letter he just now gets around to reading. A sad, yet bittersweet tale by King.

This is indeed a very sad, yet human tale very unlike the work King is known for. Stories like *The Shawshank Redemption, The Green Mile, The Body,* and a few others are more real than any of King's stories about monsters and horror and I feel these types of stories truly show King's other side very clearly and are some of his better works. James Cole's version of this tale is well done, true to the story even with the connections of other King's works mentioned in the story like Hemmingford Home which is the home of Mother Abigail from Stephen King's *The Stand*. Books like "1922" from *Full Dark No Stars* and *IT* are also connected to '*Last Rung*'. Although one of the original Dollar Babies and a very low-budget, Cole himself he would like to remake this story on a much larger scale someday. However, he captured King's vision perfectly.

Credits: Cast: Adam Houhoulis (Larry) Melisa Whelden (Kitty) Directed by: James Cole and Dan Thron Written by: Stephen King Adapted for the Screen by: James Cole and Dan Thron Filmed on Super 8mm film Budget: $1,500 Running Time: 12 minutes Talisman Film

Here is my Exclusive Interview with filmmaker, James Cole.

Anthony Northrup: Out of all the King stories, What attracted you to this one?

James Cole: I just loved the story and characters and I wanted to see if I could adapt it to film faithfully enough to maintain that bittersweet tone. I hoped I could do King's story justice, both in terms of getting great performances out of our young actors and getting that 'King Flavor.' Of course a secondary goal – if the film turned out well – was to get it to King and hope he might like it.

AN: What was it like working with kids? Were they afraid of heights?

JC: When I was little, the adults I liked the most were ones who never talked down to me. I think that's the key to working with kids. Working with Adam and Melisa was fun but I was responsible for their safety in the barn: rusty nails, splinters, and heights. Though Dan was co-director he was only 14 at the time whereas I was almost 20 so if something went wrong it was on me.

Neither Adam nor Melisa were afraid of heights and the beam was only six feet off the ground. I created the illusion of them jumping from a great height with camera angles and editing. Still, it would have been easy for them to lose their balance so either Dan or myself were always just out of frame, ready to catch should either of them fall the wrong backwards. When they jumped forward they landed on a pile of hay with two mattresses hidden beneath!

AN: Considering this was filmed mostly in a barn, what were the conditions like, weather, and set-up?

JC: It was hot and humid, especially with our hand-held lights but we made sure to give the kids breaks outside when it got too hot or just sick of being inside. I don't remember anything unusual about the conditions – it was just an old barn. We shot over about 9 days during July and August 1986. In fact, we wrapped production with the kids about the time *Stand By Me* was released so there was a real feeling of fate and synchronicity.

AN: What would you have changed in the film looking back now, if any?

JC: It's easy to second-guess yourself – look at George Lucas and his "Special Editions" of *Star Wars* or Spielberg removing the guns from *E.T.* The biggest thing I would change would be to improve the sound quality. We shot Super 8 sound and the primitive magnetic stripe sound was very muddy. It's hard to understand some of the dialogue from the kids. If I could I'd sweeten the sound digitally. Also the insert shots of Kitty's letters are hard to read and a bit shaky. But in general I am happy with the film – it's the best I could do at that age with that equipment.

AN: Out of all the Stephen King short stories, what attracted you most to this one?

JC: I loved all the stories in *Night Shift* but I remember after finishing *Children of the Corn* I was surprised by the shift in tone with *The Last Rung on the Ladder*. I realized this was something special. It reminded me of *The Body* but somehow even sadder. I could just see the story in my head. When my friend Dan Thron – whom I met after moving to Cape Cod in early 1984 – read 'Last Rung', we decided to try to make a short film adaptation. It seemed possible because Dan had already helped on my original Super 8 film *Sponge!* and the fact that *'Last Rung'* had no monsters or complicated effects – just two kids in a barn and out in the countryside – made it feasible for two young filmmakers.

AN: You were one of the original Dollar Baby filmmakers, tell us how the early years compare to now & how hard or easy it is to get one approved today?

JC: From what I've heard there are more legal hoops to jump through today than back in the 1980s when I made *'Last Rung.'* I heard about the "Dollar Deal" from an article in the "Castle Rock" newsletter. I got King's office address in Maine and just sent him a letter asking to make a short film of his story, along with a check for $1. I never got any written or verbal reply from King, let alone a contract to sign. But when my check turned up in my bank statement cashed (with King's signature on the back!) I figured that meant it was OK to go ahead. The main requirement was to mail King a video copy of the finished film, which I did.

AN: You spent time on the set of Stephen King's film, *The Green Mile*, What was that like and looking back at it's success now did you know Frank Darabont had something special then?

JC: I actually wrote a long article about my time on the set of *The Green Mile* which I hope to publish on a friend's website soon, so I am going to hold off answering this question in detail. Suffice to say it was an incredible experience and it was obvious the film was going to be something special. The set alone captured the "King Flavor" and all the actors were gracious and were having a good time despite it being a grueling, six months shoot.

AN: What is it about Stephen King's work that made you become not only a fan, but a filmmaker of his works?

JC: King's writing is accessible and easy to read but at the same time very visual. King himself has said that his writing is like having a movie projector in his head. The stories and characters are just so "real" it's easy to imagine them as a movie. As to how I became a filmmaker/adaptor of his works – just fate and passion I guess.

AN: What is your greatest moment so far with '*Last Rung on the Ladder*'?

JC: There was no one moment or incident that stands out. I just had a wonderful time working with the kids and Dan and then all the post-production work on my own. There's something so great about physically cutting a piece of film as opposed to editing on a computer (which I have never done). It was a pivotal experience in my life – both in terms of my development as a filmmaker and storyteller – and it certainly got me some notice in the King community, which was wonderful.

AN: If you could adapt any of Stephen King's works, which ones would they be and why?

JC: Many people have wanted to adapt *The Long Walk* – my pal Jay Holben among them. I believe Frank Darabont still plans to do it someday. As for other short stories, I would love to make the *One for Road* but logistically it's a nightmare – simulating a blizzard and shooting on location. I have seen a couple Dollar Baby adaptations but don't think they've quite captured the terror of that story. The only other King project I'd love to do – or at least see done right – is *Firestarter*. It's one of my favorite novels but the 1984 film is really not good. Ironically the script is faithful to the novel but a strange combination of miscasting, poor direction, and lousy editing make it feel like a bad TV movie.

AN: Lastly, What's next for James Cole?

JC: For the time being I've moved away from film and focusing on books. I'm currently writing my memoirs and then I plan to 'reverse engineer' and adapt two screenplays to Young Adult novels, as YA is a huge industry and I think I'd have better luck getting these stories sold as books instead of movies.

I want to Thank James Cole for taking the time to speak with us today and wish him nothing but success in his future projects.

The Things They Left Behind by Pablo Macho Maysonet IV

The Things They Left Behind

Pablo Macho Maysonet IV
May 11, 2014

It's time to take another look behind-the-scenes of the Stephen King Dollar Baby universe. This time, our Dollar Baby comes from a young filmmaker who has been watching horror films since he was born (literally)! Director Pablo Macho Maysonet IV, brings us a more serious story based on Stephen King's works, but with all of King's writings even the serious ones can still be scary in their own way. Pablo brings us *The Things They Left Behind,* a story based around the most terrifying event in United States history: 9/11.

Pablo Macho Maysonet IV was born February 2, 1982 in Vineland, New Jersey. His mother took him to horror films even as an infant and is known to not even cry once during a movie, only to simply be amazed at the screen and the horrors it showed. From that moment on, he was captivated by the magic of movies and filmmaking, especially horror films. Pablo was born into an artistic family, he used art as a form of expression or as he calls it, "horrific art".

For the last 10 years, Pablo has been involved with films and filmmaking, however without any schooling he took a big risk. With the help of his friend Brian Rivera and an inspirational meet and greet with legendary indie filmmaker Roger Corman, his life was changed. Corman helped by giving them wisdom they needed that helped produce their first feature film *Deadhouse* which was picked up and distributed worldwide. In 2003, Pablo and Brian started Shattered Dreams Productions together only later in 2006 resigned and gave Pablo full run and ownership of the film company.

Pablo's love for Stephen King and his works began when he first saw the film, *Creepshow* and his journey truly began right then which would lead him years later as part of the Stephen King Dollar Baby family with his adaptation of *The Things They Left Behind* in 2011. Pablo has done many small independent films and even a comic book based on one of his films called, *Who's the Suicidal*. However, the best way to describe Pablo's love for horror and filmmaking is one of his quotes: 'Horror will be the best genre in film whether people like it or not, because fear is the world's oldest emotion.'

Here is my review of *The Things They Left Behind*.

This short story based on Stephen King's works, was first published in *Transgressions: Volume 2* and in 2008 added to the short story collection book, *Just After Sunset*. The film takes place on and days after the most terrifying event in America's history: bombings at the World Trade Center in New York on 9-11 2001. Jamie Eagleton worked in one of the Trade Towers, but didn't make it into work on the terrible day, he was at home. One could say "something" was looking out for him, so to speak. However, the stroke of luck comes with a price. Strange personal objects from his co-workers suddenly appear out of nowhere in his apartment. Strange things like farting cushions, fake sunglasses, a small statue, a baseball bat and other objects that once belonged to his colleagues at work who all died in the Trade Center bombings. He tries to get rid of them but they keep coming back! He has nightmares of them & his colleagues, so he decides to give the objects to his neighbor Paula, but even she starts having nightmares and returns them quickly to Jamie. There is only one solution to solving his nightmare problem: return them to the families of his colleagues. Will this solve his problem and end his nightmares forever? Like Stephen King said: 'survivor's are victims too.' See this film and find out!

I enjoyed this story very much. Some people think Stephen King is nothing but "horror" stories, but his stories like *The Shawshank Redemption, Stand By Me (The Body)* or *The Green Mile* are far from that. I believe this story is one of those that is more realistic and less horror and that's good because it's all about the story sometimes and not the scares. I think Pablo handled this very sensitive subject matter very professionally and carefully and I respected and enjoyed that. He respected the families of those victims by getting his story told, but with gentle care. His style of filmmaking is spot on and professional and moves the story along nicely.

It kept my interest and was one of the better Dollar Baby adaptations I've seen. This is worth your time for sure.

CREDITS:
Director: Pablo Macho Maysonet IV
Writer: Pablo Macho Maysonet IV and Stephen King
Released – 2011
Running Time: 44 minutes
Budget: $10,000

CAST:
Jamie Eagleton: Jamie Camarota
Waiter: Bryan Cheeseman
Paula: Caitlyn Fletcher
Scott: Chris Gozalez

Here is my Exclusive Interview with filmmaker Pablo Macho Maysonet IV.

Anthony Northrup: Out of all the Stephen King short stories, what attracted you most to this one?

Pablo Macho Maysonet IV: Being a Jersey native, I have had a sense of attachment to the story because of how near I was to the tragedy of 9/11. I had a feeling it was something that would intimidate filmmakers to produce so I naturally knew it would be on our plate.

AN: What changes did you make to make this your own as opposed to King's original text?

PM: Very little. We knew we wanted to be as close to the story as possible but wanted to add some of our own flavor to the mix. I felt some visual references were needed to portray what exactly the characters were going through. Also with some stylized elements, we were able to tell the same story but keep it visually entertaining.

AN: So many Stephen King fans want adaptations to be as close to the book as possible, how do you handle the pressure to keep the fans happy?

PM: Well first of all, I'm one of those types of fans. However, I'm a filmmaker as well. I understand that not everything can translate to film properly or respectably. I wouldn't say it was much pressure because the end product was always intended to be so close to the material.

AN: What was your main goal you wanted to achieve about this film?

PM: Of all the years being a filmmaker and fan of film, I have always seen adaptations that were horrible. I always see people say, "It's nothing like the book!". My team's goal was simple, can we put our money where our mouth is and successfully produce an adaption of someone else's material and stay true to it while adding our own style. From the responses we've received, we feel we were successful with that intention.

AN: The subject of 9/11 is a very sensitive topic, how did you handle this without causing any upset?

PM: The main thing that we always returned to was to remember that this was still a very sensitive topic. As a filmmaker my job is to entertain, but throughout the process I always keep that in mind. There were times that one of the producers would say, "hey wouldn't this be cool" and I would always say, is it respectable?

AN: The objects that were left behind, how did you decide on what would be used and what wouldn't and what were some that didn't make the cut?

PM: We always intended to use every object featured in the story. However, once shooting began, we knew we would go over our runtime so we had to cut back on some scenes. Specifically, we had to cut out the references to the punch doll and Mr. yow git down. Although, we had already shot scenes involving these objects, in the end we had to edit it all out or else it would've added an additional 5-10 mins in the story.

AN: What is your greatest moment so far with the success of *The Things They Left Behind*?

PM: One of the greatest moments I would say was when it was screened at a local horror film festival. The film screened early in the day and I was feeling really under the weather. However, while trying to keep my cool I started noticing audience members crying in reaction to the film. One of my producers looked to me and said "I guess it works", making a point that we originally feared people wouldn't get the emotion behind the story. After the film screened, I had several people come up to me and email us after the festival ended expressing how much they enjoyed the film and how it deserved more recognition. One person in particular wrote a very long email telling us that our film should've been the highlight of the festival because our film was the only one screened that felt like it was made from the heart. That made my day.

AN: What Stephen King story would you like to adapt on a large scale?

PM: If the rights weren't already taken, I would love to adapt a feature film version of *From a Buick 8*. I love the way Stephen King tells the story and I believe it really shows his ability to scare you with pure wonder. Besides "*Buick*", I would be head over heels to purchase the rights to the *Creepshow* franchise and continue them properly instead of the abomination that was *Creepshow III*.

AN: Lastly, What's next for Pablo Macho Maysonet IV?

PM: At this moment I am about to begin principal photography for my next feature horror film *The Red Suit*. It's something my team and I have been working on over the past year and are really excited to produce. Keep an eye out!

SYNOPSIS: Seeking a cure for her sister Ally's fatal illness, Star seeks help from two mysterious men who offer a very unconventional and dangerous remedy. Through the power of a mysterious red suit, they must pull the disease killing Ally into the physical world and destroy it. But when things go wrong, the disease is now on the loose to infect and devour everyone in its path back to its original host.

There you have it, another exclusive Interview with another talented Dollar Baby filmmaker. I want to thank Pablo for taking his time to do this interview and his patience.

Luckey Quarter by Robert Cochrane

Luckey Quarter

Robert Cochrane
June 11, 2014

OUR NEXT DOLLAR BABY FILM comes from a young filmmaker who went from Las Vegas card dealer to filmmaker, Robert Cochrane. His film, *Luckey Quarter* is quite fitting for him considering he went from behind the card table to behind the camera.

Robert Cochrane was born June 6, 1970 and originally from Walnut Creek, CA. His education went from Ygnacio Valley High School in Concord, CA to studying Radio/TV Journalism at San Diego State University. From there Robert went to study Directing/Screenwriting at UCLA and also attended The Art Institute. Although little is known about Robert's background, I can tell you from doing our interview he has the ambition of a dedicated filmmaker and the heart of a die hard Stephen King fan.

Here is my review of *Luckey Quarter* (2005).

This short story was originally published in the June 30/July 2 1995 issue of *USA Weekend*. It was later published in 1997 in the limited edition Stephen King book, *Six Stories*. In 2002, it was published along with many other short stories in the collection, *Everything's Eventual*. The story is a simple one; a single mom of two/hotel maid cleans one of the rooms like she does everyday and when she looks in the tip envelope she finds a single quarter. Of course, the first reaction is disappointment, but when she goes to the casino and begins playing she wins a small fortune. As her luck grows, so do the bets AND the winnings. Suddenly, she wakes up from her fantasy and thinks the quarter is just that… a coin and not lucky, so she gives it to her son. He puts it in the lobby slot machine and it turns out the quarter IS lucky after all!

Robert's version of this Dollar Baby was very well done. Shot on location in the gambling capital of the world, he captures the story perfectly. The actress who plays the mother did a very fine job and the story was simple, but pleasantly paced. We all wish for that lucky coin and this was a nice "fantasy" story from King adapted very well.

Here is my exclusive Interview with Dollar Baby filmmaker, Robert Cochrane.

Anthony Northrup: Out of all the Stephen King short stories, what attracted you most to this one?

Robert Cochrane: I love that it's one of his quiet stories, the kind of story people who only know him viscerally wouldn't believe he actually wrote. It's a story of hope, fear, acceptance and redemption. It's the same reason *Rita Hayworth and Shawshank Redemption* was one of my favorites even before it became one of my favorite movies. I used to enjoy asking people what they thought of *Shawshank Redemption* (almost all said they loved it) then reminding them it's based very faithfully on a King novella. The look of shock and surprise was as good as any plot twist. These days most people seem to know, so a lot of other Constant Readers were probably out there getting the same thrill I was bringing the masses up to speed.

AN: What changes did you make to make this your own as opposed to King's original text?

RC: I remained very faithful to the text as it was my intent to follow in Frank Darabont's footsteps as he did with *The Woman in the Room*. There were small changes, like how the dream within a dream sequence played out in the casino and one omission, in particular, that bothered me a lot: not getting the scene at the bus stop where she decides to ride with the quarter instead of the bus. We were set to shoot it but just ran out of time.

AN: So many Stephen King fans want adaptations to be as close to the book as possible, how do you handle the pressure to keep the fans happy?

RC: With all due respect to the other Constant Readers, being one myself, I wasn't concerned about them in making this film. I wanted to find the greatest truths in the story and express them via the medium of film.

AN: What was your main goal you wanted to achieve about this film?

RC: My main goal was to treat his work with respect and demonstrate my skill. It was a step forward in my Directing career because I hadn't directed something with this much heat on it. King's name will do that for you. This was also just before the flood gates seemed to open up for Dollar Babies. In 2003, making a Dollar Baby was not a well-known opportunity nor was the opportunity given out nearly as commonly as it is now. I wrote letters to Marsha DeFilippo for months, including silly personal trinkets like a picture of me performing as Caesar at Caesars Palace (my "regular" job at the time) or signing the letters "Andy Dufresne" in homage to Andy's efforts to get the library in the prison. Interestingly, not long after wrapping *Luckey Quarter,* Simon and Schuster ran the American Gunslinger contest for King's release of book number five in the *Dark Tower* series, *Wolves of the Calla.* The contest was to make a dramatic reading video of an excerpt from one of the first four books. I made a video from the first book called "Roland Meets Brown". You can see it here:https://www.youtube.com/watch?v=WDqFbiv3Mro. To my delight, I won the contest and got to meet King, in person, at the Simon and Schuster offices in Manhattan. Although the video is very poor quality, you can see a little bit about that meeting here:https://www.youtube.com/watch?v=zVZLdWMnBzQ&feature=youtu.be.

AN: The slot machine in the hotel lobby, How did you operate that to show she wins?

RC: We just pulled it until we got the winner we wanted. It was a prop, so the pulls were free, but you can't move the drums without damaging the machine – something we obviously didn't want to do. Once we had the winner we shot it, then reversed the film in post so it looks like they're landing on the right reels. We also composed the shot in thirds in post so you'd see the drums that were still when we wanted them still and the ones moving we wanted moving at the right time.

AN: Where were the hotel and casino locations filmed and were there any difficulties filming on location?

RC: We shot at a Super 8 motel in Boulder City, NV. It's a nice little community about 20 minutes southeast of Las Vegas. It has a small town feel and they were very friendly about allowing us to shoot there. The casino was the Joker's Wild, in Henderson, NV. Henderson and Las Vegas have grown into each other over the last 15 years, but Joker's Wild is still on the outskirts. It was the first casino I dealt 21 at – a break-in house, as they call them (I had a short, but fast rise in the dealing biz). They were friendly, too, but the shoot had to be from 9p to 9a on a Sunday in order to take advantage of the times they were least busy. We shot there last, the third day of a three day shoot. The unfortunate part about that was how tired everyone was by about 5a. That was when we missed the bus stop and some other visually interesting shots we had slated.

AN: What is your greatest moment so far with the success of Luckey Quarter?

RC: The greatest moment was either getting the email from Marsha that approved me for the Dollar Baby or having Steve hold the poster up at Simon and Schuster.

AN: What Stephen King story would you like to adapt on a large scale?

RC: My first desire was to do *The Long Walk*. I spoke to Steve about that when we were at Simon and Schuster. He gave me about 10 minutes of face time where we talked about all things baseball (we're both junkies for the game) and other projects. I asked, very awkwardly, about the rights to *The Long Walk*. I think my exact quote was "What's up with '*The Long Walk*'"? To which he replied, "What do you mean?" I asked what he wanted from it in terms of being made into a film. He said he wanted an independent to make it so it would be done right. I said, an independent like say, me? I told him how I'd like to adapt it and get his thoughts (again, like Darabont did with Shawshank). He said, I can't promise you anything, but send me the script when it's done. Four months later, I did just that. Marsha got right back to me with an apology saying Frank Darabont had recently optioned it. Son of an ironic bitch.

AN: Lastly, What's next for Robert Cochrane?

RC: I'm in production with my latest documentary, *Boys of Summer – Second Base*. It's a sequel to the original, which won several awards (you can see it here if you like :http://www.bosmovie.com). The original is the story of my dad, who has Parkinson's Disease, and me road-tripping 20,000 miles in two months to see a game at each of the 30 Major League Baseball parks. We were supposed to meet Steve at the Red Sox game we went to and interview him. He was kind enough to give me his hotel and contact info, but he was out of town the day we were there (another near miss). Ten years later, we're exploring Parkinson's Disease differently. My dad is undergoing some interesting, somewhat controversial treatments this summer. We're tying baseball in to all we do, but, like the original, baseball is a vehicle.

I want to thank Robert for his time and patience for doing this interview and wish him the best for future projects.

Strawberry Spring by Doveed Linder

Strawberry Spring

Doveed Linder
June 1, 2014

OUR NEXT DOLLAR BABY comes from a young filmmaker who is a boxer and trainer, but when he's not in the ring he's behind the film camera making his stories come to life. His contribution to the Dollar Baby film program is Stephen King's short story, *Strawberry Spring* and his name is Doveed Linder.

Doveed Linder was born on September 7th and from the great state of Missouri. He graduated from Ladue Horton Watkins High School before going off to college. He later got into the world of boxing. He started his career literally walking off the street into a gym and got right into the ring. Learning on his own, he later agreed to teach young kids how to box and by doing so a few times a week had his gym fees waived in exchange. Six days a week, he practically lived at that gym he was so dedicated. Three years later, he moved from St. Louis to Los Angeles. He started teaching a TAO class two times a day. He is very dedicated to his clients and believes in them if they believe in themselves. He gives 110% as long as his clients do the same. He truly cares about people, very dedicated, and passionate about his work. In between all of this, he got into the film world. Making short films since 2001, Doveed directed films such as; *The Tall Tale Heart, The Ice Cream Man, The Basement Room, Defiance,* and a Stephen King Dollar Baby, *Strawberry Spring*. He writes, directs, produces, and occasionally acts. He currently is working on *The Box*, a "Twilight Zone"-type film about four stories revolving around a mysterious box.

Here is my review of *Strawberry Spring*.

This Stephen King short story was first published in *Urbis* magazine in 1968 and in 1978 added to the short story collection, *Night Shift*. The story is about a narrator thinking back over a horrible event that took place at New Sharon College over a Strawberry Spring. A Strawberry Spring is a "false Spring", when you think Winter is over, everything is melted, and warm temps make it look and feel like Spring finally has come, but in reality it is a tease and it means a real Winter storm is coming and hard! During this Strawberry Spring comes heavy, thick fog. Fog that covers up clues from a killer that kills students at a college 8 years before. When a serial killer by the name of "Spring-heeled Jack" goes on a killing spree, he gets away with it and is not seen or heard from again. Then 8yrs later, as the fog returns so does Jack. When one college student comes home late one night, he can't remember where he was and wonders if HE is the killer? Only the cargo in the trunk of his car can answer that question.

Doveed's version of this horror tale of murder and mayhem was very entertaining, creepy, and true to the original tale told by Stephen King. I did feel that I would've liked to have seen more since it is extremely short, however, Doveed's version gets right to the point and is effective. It is well done and very eerie.

Here is my Exclusive Interview with Doveed Linder.

Anthony Northrup: Out of all the Stephen King short stories, what attracted you most to this one?

Doveed Linder: *Strawberry Spring* was actually the first movie I ever made. I shot it on 8mm film in 1995. It was a project for film class. I re-made it in 2001, because at that point I had access to better equipment, I had matured as a filmmaker, and I wanted to see what I could do with it. I was (and am) attracted to this story because a lot happens in a short period of time. It's almost like a novella that only lasts ten pages. This story reads like a movie. When I read it, I can see the scenes in my mind. With the fog that is described in the Stephen King story, I saw an atmosphere that I wanted to create. Basically, *Strawberry Spring* is a very visual and thought-provoking story, which is why I think it makes for good cinema.

AN: What changes did you make to make this your own as opposed to King's original text?

DL: The biggest change I made is that I told the story in present tense, opposed to telling a story that happened several years before. I chose to do it this way, for starters, because I wanted to avoid making a "period piece". If I talked about events that had already happened, I would have to make sure all of the cars, clothes, etc. were accurate for the early 90's, or even accurate for the 1960's, which is when King's story is set. I also think there's a certain tension that exists when you're telling a story in present tense than telling a story that already happened. Because of the choice I made, there is a scene in the movie between the Narrator and his father that wasn't in King's story. In the movie, the dialogue between the Narrator and his father leads to the Narrator thinking that something unnerving might be in his trunk. In King's story, the Narrator is reading a newspaper article (with his wife in the next room) when he has the same thought. The father/son scene gave me a chance to make it a little more visual, but the idea is pretty much the same.

AN: So many Stephen King fans want adaptations to be as close to the book as possible, how do you handle the pressure to keep the fans happy?

DL: As a filmmaker and as a fan of Stephen King's work, I want the same thing as the audience. So, I made the movie with the intentions of satisfying that personal need, just as I wanted the viewers to be satisfied. When making an adaptation, I think it's more important to capture the feeling of the story, more than it is to follow every plot point that exists in the original written material. There could be certain events in a Stephen King story that work very well, but if you try to craft them into the movie, it just doesn't fit. So what it comes down to, in my opinion, is that if you have a story that makes you think, you want the movie to make you think as well. If you have a story that's creepy, you want the movie to be creepy, too. It's about the emotion you generate, not necessarily the specific plot points.

AN: What was your main goal you wanted to achieve about this film?

DL: When I first started making this movie, I had just finished production of a feature film and I was anxious to get back on the set and make something else. I was doing it for the love of the craft and no other reason. But after a while, I developed a vision for a Stephen King anthology. I wanted to make a feature film consisting of five of his short stories. The name of the movie was to be *The Reaper's Image,* which is a short story from King's *Skeleton Crew.* The mirror from "The Reaper's Image" was to be something of a bridge from story to story. I wanted for "Strawberry Spring" to be an example of what I was capable of in hopes of getting the rights to make *The Reaper's Image. I* went so far as to write the entire screenplay for the proposed movie which I sent it to King, along with a VHS of *Strawberry Spring.* After a year of trying to get a response, King's assistant eventually told me that he had denied my request. A couple of years ago, ironically, I read that a filmmaker was in the early stages of developing an anthology based on King's work entitled *The Reaper's Image*. I'm sure it's pure coincidence, but I was shocked to read that. As a fan, I'm really looking forward to seeing it!

AN: Where were the school scenes filmed and were there any difficulties filming on location such as that?

DL: We shot on the Washington University campus in St. Louis, MO. I called the main office and was referred to a woman who is in charge of making decisions regarding projects like mine. She was absolutely spectacular. She did everything she could to make the experience as smooth as possible and she even let us wave the location fee!

AN: Was there any particular reasons for the film to be just little over 6 minutes and were there any scenes you would've liked to completed that didn't make it in?

DL: I did not make the movie with a running time in mind. It just happened to be six minutes. I shot everything I set out to shoot. If there was a scene that didn't make it in, it was because I felt that was the best decision. If I made the movie again today, I would probably do a few things differently. One thing I would do is make it gorier! At the time I made it, I wanted to keep it light and whimsical. But the subject matter is so brutal and I think I should have gone for the jugular just a little bit more.

AN: What is your greatest moment so far with the success of *Strawberry Spring*?

DL: *Strawberry Spring* was accepted into the Cinematographers Showcase, which led to a screening at the Cannes Film Festival. That was a great time and I felt a tremendous sense of pride. While at Cannes, I was passing around trailers of a feature film that I had just made. A sales agent picked it up and they went on to sell the film to Lionsgate. So, the showcasing of *Strawberry* Spring proved to be beneficial in a number of ways.

AN: What Stephen King story would you like to adapt on a large scale?

DL: If I was given the opportunity to adapt King's work on a larger scale, I would love to make an anthology consisting of about four of his stories. I love anthologies like *Creepshow, Cat's Eye, The Twilight Zone, Sin City*, etc. I think a line-up of four short stories by Stephen King could be a tremendous thing. One of the stories I would like to include, believe it or not, would be *Children of the Corn*. As a movie, that's a story that I believe should be told in 25-30 minutes. In my opinion, it just doesn't work as a feature. When you try to develop it into a 90-minute piece, it takes away from the mystery of King's story. At this point, however, I'm not so sure it would work as a short segment, because of the fact that it has been made into a feature so many times. It's a very well known story and it may have run its course. *One For the Road* and *Mrs. Todd's Shortcut* would make for good short segments as well.

AN: Lastly, What's next for Doveed Linder?

DL: I am currently in production on my second feature film, which is an anthology called "The Box". It's four stories surrounding a mysterious box, which is the link from story to story. It's of the sci-fi genre, similar to *The Twilight Zone*. When I'm finished with that movie, I want to go on to the next feature right away. I wanted to explore different subject matter and different formats, not just anthologies of the strange and bizarre. I have a script ready to go for a crime drama, but who knows? I'm just looking forward to staying busy as a filmmaker and doing what I love to do.

I want to thank Doveed for his time to do this interview and giving me this opportunity. I wish him well in his future projects. Copyright 2014.

The Boogeyman

Jeff Schiro
June 18, 2014

OUR NEXT DOLLAR BABY comes from the very FIRST Dollar Baby filmmaker ever! Although it's been debatable who was first, Frank Darabont or Jeff Schiro, it appears Jeff was the very first and I am honored to present to you our interview and my review of the very first Dollar Baby, *The Boogeyman*.

Our feature director is originally from Bangor, Maine (home of Stephen King himself and most of his stories take place there as well). Jeff studied at NYU and graduated in 1982. He has directed many short films, television films, and documentaries. He has worked on such films such as, *Secret Worlds, Manhunters, True Tales of the Texas Rangers, The Deadliest Warrior*, and of course, the very first Dollar Baby; *The Boogeyman*. He is a writer, director, and currently works as the Senior Editorial at MorningStar Entertainment.

Here is my review of… *The Boogeyman*.

The short story of *The Boogeyman*, was first published in March of 1973 in *Cavalier* magazine and in 1978 published in Stephen King's collection of short stories book, *Night Shift*. The story is about a husband and father of three, Lester Billings (played by Michael Read), who comes home only to find his 4yr. daughter dead in the bathtub. Later, his 5yr. son dies in bed. The police and coroner call them both "crib death" and contusion on their head. The police

The Boogeyman by Jeff Schiro

can't get any information from the wife and Lester can barely speak, let alone make any sense to them. Once Lester gets to the psychiatrist office, he opens up more and tries to explain to the doctor that it wasn't him or anyone else, but it was…THE BOOGEYMAN! As Lester goes over and over of the events that took place in his home and the death of his children, the question begins to rise: Is Lester the murderer of his children or is it indeed the Boogeyman himself? Or is it something… else?

I was beyond thrilled that I had the honor of seeing the very first Dollar Baby film, *The Boogeyman*. It is certainly dated, first released in 1982, it had a very low budget/grindhouse type look to it that made the film feel more eerie. The way the lead actor went from father, husband, paranoid, and possible murderer was quite interesting. And of course, that questionable ending stays in your mind even after the credits roll. I enjoyed watching this film, but it is dated quite a lot and that brings the quality down just a little. However, it is well told and a very good adaptation of King's tale.

Credits:
Filmed on 16mm
Budget: $20,000
28 min. running time
Released 1982

Here is my Exclusive Interview with Dollar Baby filmmaker, Jeff Schiro.

Anthony Northrup: Out of all the Stephen King short stories, what attracted you most to this one?

Jeff Schiro: Ultimately there were probably 3 things that attracted me to *The Boogeyman*. The first was the surprise ending. Growing up I was always a big fan of *The Twilight Zone*, because you knew each show would end with a twist. Second, I was always a big fan of psychological horror and this seemed to fit into that category. And third, I can remember being a child and thinking that "something" might be in my closet!

AN: What changes did you make to make this your own as opposed to King's original text?

JS: Well, for one the short story never leaves the psychiatrist's office, while the film does. The story works brilliantly within the confines of the office, but cinematically it would have probably been a bit boring to keep it there. So, I brought in a couple other characters and added some scenes that I thought would be visually and dramatically interesting.

AN: So many Stephen King fans want adaptations to be as close to the book as possible, how do you handle the pressure to keep the fans happy?

JS: This is the only King story I have done, but I can understand that point of view. Stephen King is a very visual storyteller. So, when his films are adapted, people tend to want that same feeling as reading the book. On the other hand, the written word and pictures on a screen are two very different mediums, and sometimes you just have to take liberties to make things work.

AN: What was your main goal you wanted to achieve about this film?

JS: Making a film is always a personal journey. When I started *The Boogeyman*, I think what I really wanted to achieve was to make a watchable film! It was about bringing a creative vision to life.

AN: Where were the house scenes filmed at and were there any difficulties filming on location such as that?

JS: I made the film while I was a college student in NYC. The house, which was in Brooklyn, belonged to the family of a classmate. They weren't originally so keen on having me film there, but as it turned out, my cinematographer was renting one of the rooms for the semester, so he pulled a few strings.

AN: There is a debate of just what was the first Dollar Baby film ever: *The Boogeyman* or Frank Darabont's *The Woman in the Room*, Can you shine some light on that debate and clarify which is truly the first one?

JS: I suspect both films were being made at nearly the same time. I finished *The Boogeyman* in 1982, while *The Woman in the Room* was completed in 1983.

AN: This film has a very "grindhouse" early 80's horror look to it which I loved, do you prefer "old school" horror to today's "paranormal" and "reboots" of this generation's horror films?

JS: I think either "schools of horror" can work equally well. *The Boogeyman* has that gritty look, partially due to the fact that it was shot on 16mm. The truth is, these days you can shoot something and make it look like just about anything. But, as always, a film is only as good as its story.

AN: There have been many Dollar Baby versions of *The Boogeyman*, do you feel the father was just really imaging all of it or did he really do it?

JS: That's almost a trick question! And it will always be up for interpretation. But, if I had to choose one… I don't think the father was imagining.

AN: You are one of the "godfather" filmmakers of Dollar Babies, tell us what those early years were like for a filmmaker and do the new Dollar Baby filmmakers have more advantage now?

JS: The original deal I had with Stephen King asked for $1 and a Betamax copy of the film. (Just to show you how long ago it was!) For years I thought I had a special deal because I grew up in Maine. It wasn't until much later that I found out there were loads of dollar-deals! As for making the film, it was a challenging proposition since I was a student and was on a limited budget. It was shot on 16mm film, and edited on what was known as a flatbed. It ultimately took two years to complete. If I made the film today, I suspect the shooting days would have been the same, but the time and money spent on post production would have been cut by 2/3rds. For today filmmakers, I believe technology has made the process much more efficient and allowed for smaller budgets. You can shoot a film on a DSLR and edit a film on your desktop. Of course, making a good film is still as hard as ever.

AN: What is your greatest moment so far with the success of *The Boogeyman*?

JS: I think the greatest moment was probably actually finishing it! That said, one highlight was when Stephen King showed up to a screening I had in Maine. Also, that he liked the film enough to allow it a commercial release. And recently I had someone track me down who told me that when he was a kid, he practically wore out the VHS tape he had of *The Boogeyman*.

AN: What Stephen King story would you like to adapt on a large scale?

JS: Well, I always thought *The Running Man* could use a remake.

AN: Lastly, What's next for Jeff Schiro?

JS: I'm a working editor in Los Angeles, so I'm generally surprised at what comes my way!

I want to Thank Jeff for his time and patience and giving me the opportunity to do this interview and wish him nothing but success in the future.

All That You Love Will Be Carried Away

James Renner
February 1, 2014

OUR NEXT DOLLAR BABY comes from the Buckeye State of Ohio.

The film is called, *All That You Love Will be Carried Away*, directed by James Renner.

James Renner was born on March 30, 1978 in Diamond, Ohio. Attending Southeast High School and after graduation he attended Kent State University. He is a former writer of Cleveland Scene magazine and editor of The Independent. He was also a founding member of Last Call Cleveland and in December 2004 was named one of Cleveland's Top 30 Most Interesting People. In the 2004's, *All That You Love Will Be Carried Away* was named an Official Selection at the 2005 Montreal World Film Fest. In October of 2006, Gray & Co. published his book, Amy: My Search, a 2-year investigation about the abduction of 10-year old Amy Mihaljenic in 1989. In July of 2009, James did an online documentary called, *Catching Salinger*, a story about the reclusive author, J.D. Salinger and some behind the scenes look at his famous book, *Catcher in the Rye*.

Renner's first book was, *The Man from Primrose Lane*. In January 2011, he announced plans on a project about the disappearance of Maura Murray, a nursing student of Massachusetts Amherst, who went missing after only one car accident in New Hampshire. Currently, James Renner is an American investigative reporter, film producer and director, and teaches at the University of Akron as an English Instructor.

Here is my review of *All That You Love Will Be Carried Away*.

All That You Love Will Be Carried Away by James Renner

All That You Love Will Be Carried Away was first published in *New Yorker* magazine on January 29, 2001. That next year in 2002, it was published in Stephen King's collection of short stories, *Everything's Eventual.* The story is less horror and more about… human living. It is about Alfie Zimmer (played by Joe Bob Briggs), a traveling salesman who goes from one part of the country to the other selling all sorts of things his whole life. At this point in his life, he is selling gourmet frozen foods across the midwest. Even tho he has a home, a wife, a daughter, a dog, and a job: Zimmer had been doing the same routine of traveling, selling, going from one hotel to the next, seeing the traffic go by on American's highways and byways day in and day out of his sad, yet routine of a lifestyle.

Somewhere in Nebraska, Zimmer pulls in a hotel knowing that he has had enough. He can't do this same routine again so he decides to take the gun in his traveling bag and kill himself. As Zimmer put's it: "he couldn't go on living the way he had been living." While Zimmer was on his travels, he kept a notebook full of… graffiti. Graffiti he saw on bathroom stalls or walls in dirty truck stops, maybe on candy machines, or even road signs as he passed them by on the Interstate. He chose this as a hobby to log these colorful notes and phrases in a notebook he kept near him. The hobby grew and was fascinated by them. Phrases like, "Save Russian Jews, collect valuable prizes". After a while, they became his companion, his "voices of the walls, his friends that spoke to him". As he sits on the hotel room bed, he knows that a shot in the mouth with his gun would be living proof that there was something wrong with him as the cops discovered his body. He didn't want to be remembered as that. So, he tries to figure out what to do? He wants to write a book about the graffiti he has seen and explain to people what they might mean and about his travels. As he puts it: "telling would hurt". So, Zimmer goes outside and sees a farmhouse across the way. He decides that if the light in the house comes on by the time he counts down to 60, he will write the book, if it doesn't he will go back into the hotel room and end his sad, yet bland life as a traveling salesman.

I have seen a good handful of these Dollar Baby films and I must say, I think this is one of the best ones yet in the sense that it's not "horror", but real. I, for one, have been in sales for a long time and I can tell you Renner nailed it when it comes to the details of being a salesman. He also nailed the details of the film. The way he films and describes the hotel rooms, the highways, the bathroom, everything is spot on. Joe Bob Briggs did a very good performance as Zimmer.

He portrayed him the way a salesman talks and sometimes acts, perfectly. I was quite surprised to see Joe Bob in a Dollar Baby film, but glad because he really did a great job. For Stephen King fans, I can tell you there are "nods" to King that only a true fan will notice such as, the number "19" and "Gilead" on the road sign among others.

The graffiti phrase: "Save Russian Jews, collect valuable prizes" is also found in King's book, *IT*. I found the film very realistic and could relate in ways. Renner really made you want to feel for this character and more importantly hope that light came on at the end before he got to 60, but we will never know and sometimes that's the best ending of all. I was very impressed with this Dollar Baby and hope you will too at a film fest near you.

ALL THAT YOU LOVE WILL BE CARRIED AWAY
Zimmer: Joe Bob Briggs
Directed by: James Renner
First released: September 24, 2004

Here is my Exclusive Interview with filmmaker, James Renner.

Anthony Northrup: Out of all the Stephen King short stories, what attracted you most to this one?

James Renner: This is one of those rare Stephen King stories that does not include the paranormal. It's a very human story, like the *Shawshank Redemption*. I liked the exploration of the character of Alfie Zimmer. Also, it was a cheap story to film.

AN: What changes did you make to make this your own as opposed to King's original text?

JR: It's pretty close to the story, down to the vague ending. We tried to stay as true to the source material as possible.

AN: So many Stephen King fans want adaptations to be as close to the book as possible, how do you handle the pressure to keep the fans happy?

JR: I threw in a bunch of easter eggs for avid King fans. The number 19 comes up a lot. And there is a Castle Rock road sign which my father had a lot of fun making.

AN: What was your main goal you wanted to achieve about this film?

JR: Honestly, I wanted to gain experience working with professional actors. And to learn more about directing.

AN: You were able to get Joe Bob Briggs to star in this film, How did this come about?

JR: It took me a long time to figure out who to cast in the lead role. I got to talking with my old man about old monster movies and that led to a discussion about Joe Bob, who used to host monster movies on cable. He seemed perfect for the part. I reached out to him through his official website and he was excited to be a part of it. He is terrified of planes, though, so we had to bring him out on a train.

AN: I was quite impressed by the details in this film, tell us about the research process that you had to do for the film?

JR: Just a lot of pre production. Storyboards to get a sense of camera placement. I spent a lot of time figuring out how we could get everything we needed shot without having to move the camera more than three times in a scene.

AN: What is your greatest moment so far with the success of *All Things You Love Will Be Carried Away*?

JR: The short film premiered at the 2005 Montreal World Film Festival. It was amazing to go there and to walk around and see all these people in love with different films and to be a part of that.

AN: What Stephen King story would you like to adapt on a large scale?

JR: I have a soft spot in my heart for *Lisey's Story.*

AN: Lastly, What's next for James Renner?

JR: My second novel, *The Great Forgetting,* is scheduled to come out in 2015. I'm also working on a nonfiction book about the strange disappearance of UMass student, Maura Murray.

I want to say Thank You to James Renner for taking the time out of his busy schedule for doing this interview and giving me the opportunity to watch and review his very entertaining film. I wish James the best of luck in his future projects.

Everything's Eventual

J.P. Scott
May 16, 2014

EACH AND EVERY DOLLAR BABY FILM has its own unique past. There is something special about each one. In the case of *Everything's Eventual* by J.P. Scott, his Dollar Baby adaptation is the very first full-length Dollar Baby film ever made. When Stephen King received a copy of the film back in 2009, he was so impressed with the film he Ok'd the right to have the film have a theater release. Quite impressive and history making for J.P. Scott in the Dollar Baby program. Let's get to know a little more about J.P. Scott and his Stephen King Dollar Baby adaptation of Everything's *Eventual*.

J.P. Scott was born October 28th, 1985. He was born and grew up in Phoenix, Arizona. His backyard was the biggest backyard one could ever have: a golf course. At the age of 12 years old, he began his love for film and filmmaking. His father helped by taking J.P. to big blockbuster films like *Butch Cassidy and the Sundance Kid, Jaws,* and *Good, the Bad, and the Ugly* just to name a few. He attended Arcadia High school and graduated in 2004. He later continued his education at the Arizona State University and graduated in 2009. There were no film classes at that university at the time, so J.P. had to study the craft elsewhere. J.P. has worked with the Boy Scouts of America and teaches film at the University of Missouri. With a few short films on his credits, he is best known for the feature-length Dollar Baby film, *Everything's Eventual*. J.P. currently lives with his family in Arizona.

Here is my review of J.P. Scott's Stephen King Dollar Baby adaptation of *Everything's Eventual*.

Everything's Eventual by J.P. Scott

The Stephen King novella, *Everything's Eventual* first appeared in the October/November 1997 issue of *The Magazine of Fantasy and Science Fiction*. It later was published in his short story collection, *Everything's Eventual* in 2002.

The story is about Richard "Dinky" Earnshaw, a 19 year old who tries to live a normal teenagers life. However, "Dinky" has a special gift, he can manipulate people with special drawings that only he can understand. When a certain "group" hears of his talents, he is hired by Mr. Sharpton to use his "gift" to dispose of certain people… permanently. In return, Dinky gets everything he could ever want: home, car, CD's, movies, food, anything all for free! When Dinky looks into the background of some of those he is "disposing of", he realizes he was lied to and turns the tables on Mr. Sharpton before leaving the new life he was given. Fans of this story know that this story isn't the last time they'll see the character, Dinky. Dinky Earnshaw returns in Stephen King's *The Dark Tower* series.

I have seen different versions of this adaptation and I must say, I can clearly see why Stephen King OK'd the release of this Dollar Baby film for movie theaters when it first was released. It is filmed very professionally, the actors are top drawer, very intense and suspenseful. It also has the best opening animated credits of any Dollar Baby I've ever seen. J.P. Scott truly captures King's story beautifully and intensely.

Here is my exclusive interview with Dollar Baby filmmaker, J.P. Scott.

Anthony Northrup: Tell us what it was like growing up in Phoenix, Arizona?

J.P. Scott: I had a great childhood in Phoenix. I was lucky enough to grow up in a house on a golf course so I essentially had the biggest backyard any kid could have. I have memories of epic games of hide and seek, catching my first whopper of a fish in the nearby pond, and walking to the pool every day of summer.

From an early age I had a great love for movies. I vividly remember watching Sergio Leone's "spaghetti westerns" with my dad. I would wear a western style holder he had and put a bit of SlimJim in my mouth pretending it was a cigar. I remember seeing *Jurassic Park* for the first time when I was 8 years old and nearly bolting from my seat when the T-Rex made its first, booming appearance. I then saw the movie another 10+ times in the theater, I loved it so much.

When I was in 4th or 5th grade I started seriously using the family camcorder to create films of my own. Usually, these were for class book projects where submitting a video instead of a paper report was accepted. My first video projects were adaptations of Michael Crichton stories like *Andromeda Strain* and *Sphere*. I then adapted *Saving Private Ryan* and *The Trench* by the time I was in 8th grade.

We moved around that same time and I started creating little stories and films of my own just blocks away from where the legendary Stephen Spielberg made his first films as a kid. I went on to Arcadia High School, again, following in Mr. Spielberg's footsteps. There I learned how to edit on a computer for the first time and this accelerated my filmmaking significantly. Whenever there was an opportunity to do a video for an assignment, there was no question.

AN: When did you first discover the works of Stephen King? Your first King book and film?

J.P.: My first Stephen King book was *The Dark Tower: The Gunslinger.* My much older brother-in-law is a huge Stephen King fan and he suggested I give that a try. I have always been a pretty voracious reader. *The Dark Tower* series would go on to have a significant impact on me. I read the series from age 14 years old to about 20 years old, ingesting many, many other King titles along the way. Looking at my collection, I am especially likened to audio books as they let me do housework or drive while enjoying a story. I have read at least 38 novels and short collections by King.

As far as films go, I would say that I had seen and loved many Stephen King adaptations before even knowing they were adaptations of his. *Misery, Stand By Me, The Green Mile, The Shawshank Redemption* were all significant in my cinematic psyche all before I even knew who Stephen King was.

AN: You attended Arizona State University and later took film classes. What do you feel you took away from that education that has helped you the most in your career?

J.P.: I was a bit of a lost sole in college as far as a major was concerned. I nearly majored in history when they announced that a film degree would be offered at Arizona State University. I was in my 3rd year at the time and immediately detoured my education and energy towards getting accepted into the school and majoring in film and media production.

One of the best parts about being a 3rd year student was that I had completed all my required and elective courses completed so 100% of my class load for the remainder of my scholastic career was focused on doing what I loved. I'm sure my professors would agree that I was one of the most determined students they ever had. I dare say I even had some talent as well. Though, I always felt that there were many other students that easily outshined me. My best skills were organizing complex projects, technical prowess in cameras systems and editing, and persistence. That last one was what really gave me my edge. I was something of an unstoppable force when I started a project.

To graduate and earn your degree, students had to create a short capstone film project. These were usually films of 10-20 minutes. So, naturally, I ultimately decided to direct and produce a full-length feature film. A project that would certainly use all of what I learned in my time studying film. I had the support of every one of my professors though several were concerned about me taking on a seemingly impossible project.

My first film production class taught me how to organize a film. I have kept all of my film binders ever since that class. My internship in the school's equipment cage gave me access to great gear and additional time to learn the tools. My directing classes taught me how to focus more on the creative vision rather than the technical, something I have always struggled with. Most importantly, all of my classes allowed me to make mistakes and learn. I was allowed to try new things and find what worked and what was a disaster. In life, as well as film, making mistakes is how you learn and film school allowed me the opportunity to make a ton of critical mistakes with the support of my teachers and fellow students. This taught me so much and, in the end, geared me up for the monumental task of my final year in film school.

AN: Let's talk about your Stephen King Dollar Baby film, *Everything's Eventual*. How did you first discover the Dollar Baby program?

J.P.: I was preparing for a summer internship at 20th Century Fox in Los Angeles. I would be shadowing the director of the hit show, *Prison Break* during its 4th season. I had the Turner Classic Movie channel on the TV in the background as I packed my suitcases for the 6 weeks I would be gone. Frank Darabont's masterpiece, *The Shawshank Redemption* was playing. From time to time, text boxes would appear giving some fun facts about the making of the film. One of these boxes, which I only caught for a moment, described how Stephen King gives adaptation permissions to students for a dollar. The text disappeared from the screen before I could read everything and I jumped onto the computer and started googling things like, "Stephen King, short story adaptations, students, one dollar." I inevitably discovered the Dollar Baby program and just like when I instantly decided to major in film, I knew I was making a Dollar Baby.

Knowing I would have a decent drive to California as well as a significant commute every day to and from the studio, so I grabbed a bunch of King short story collections on audio. I planned on listening to as many as I could to find the best one. And that's what I did.

AN: Out of all the Stephen King short stories, what attracted you most to this one?

J.P.: I started with the collection of shorts called *Everything's Eventual*. And, though I got through dozens of shorts over the next 6 weeks, I ultimately loved the first short story I read about a young man who possessed the power to kill with a letter filled with mysterious symbols.

I really identified with Dinky's character, a loner/loser, who finally finds some validation and self worth albeit through ultimately nefarious and tragic means. I also couldn't help but be a bit entranced by the connection to *The Dark Tower* series as Dinky makes an important appearance in that terrific epic.

AN: What changes did you make to make this your own as opposed to King's original text?

J.P.: I knew I couldn't, or shouldn't, write the script adaptation myself. I went online to various filmmaking forums to find a writer. Enter Chad Callaghan, a great person, huge King fan, and a most excellent and dedicated writer. We spent many nights on marathon calls talking through the details of the plot and characters. Ultimately, Chad delivered a fantastic first draft. The problem was, it came in at 40+ pages. At that point, I was still trying to make a short film, around 20-30 minutes. Script pages typically translate to a minute of screen time per script page. Chad's script would run much longer than that. Not only that, but many of the great moments were gutted from the draft of the script.

After some long discussion and heart to hearts we came to a three-pronged fork in the path. Either we find a new short story, further gut the existing script to get to the needed length, or go full tilt and commit to a feature length film to tell the entire story of Dinky Earnshaw. My aforementioned determination and persistence kicked in. We were making a feature and there was never any doubt that it would happen from that point on.

We, of course, made several changes to the script that deviated from the original material. The largest was the expansion of Dinky's friend, Pug. Pug was a minimal character in the written story but a very significant part of the film. This character, and his role in the plot, drives Dinky's personal journey to the climax of the film. We also significantly increased the severity of the character, Skipper, an early and short lived (literally) antagonist in the short story. We made him much more aggressive and dangerous in the film though his end was the same.

Apart from that, as well as some easter eggs here and there, we remained pretty faithful to the original short.

AN: So many Stephen King fans want adaptations to be as close to the book as possible, how do you handle the pressure to keep the fans happy?

J.P.: I did not intentionally make this film for fans of King's work. I made the film that I wanted to see and included what Chad and I felt were the core parts to the story. Since we were both big King fans, that meant much of the script closely followed the short story for the most part. Certainly in essence.

I was a young adult learning how to direct and produce a feature for the first time. There were so many considerations on just the logistics of the production that I really followed my own compass when it came to the creative. This didn't really leave much room for what others would think. That's not to say that I intentionally shunned their thoughts of fans, I felt that myself and Chad the writer were fans enough to make sure we were proud of the final product.

AN: What was your main goal you wanted to achieve about this film?

J.P.: I wanted to direct my first feature film. I wanted to direct the first feature length Dollar Baby, which to my knowledge, *Everything's Eventual* is. I didn't want to wait for one to land in my lap so I decided to make one happen myself. I loved the challenge and I felt the story deserved a feature length telling. My ultimate goal was to impress Stephen King, which (*spoiler) I did. I also wanted to prove to myself that I could do it. A necessary step in the journey of becoming a filmmaker.

AN: Where was the movie filmed specifically and were there any obstacles to overcome while filming there?

J.P.: We shot a feature length film in 13 days and had 16 locations. The entire film was shot in Arizona and included factories, private jet hangars, resort pools, bars, motels, libraries, and more.

Remember when I said I got to make a lot of mistakes in film school before making this feature film? Well, trust me, there was still plenty more to be made. One saying in independent filmmaking is to avoid shooting in many locations, casting children, and working with animals. We had a short production schedule, multiple locations, kids, animals, and a small budget to boot. Coupled with the fact that I had never done this before, we were in for a very interesting project.

But, and I can't say this enough, I had an amazing crew who were as resilient as they were patient. They were professional and so flexible working with me, a first time feature director and producer. They are what made this film possible and through our collective will, we managed to pull off the production. What's more we did it without any major issues which was damn near a miracle.

That is not to say there weren't any hurdles. Every production of any scale has issues. The wartime adage of "no plan survives contact with the enemy" is also true in filmmaking. You spend months and months planning out as many details and contingencies as possible but when the first day of production comes, planning is done and you have to ride the wave to the end, wherever it takes you. The key is to be flexible.

Dinky spends a lot of his time at his house in our story and so the first three days of filming were dedicated to these scenes. The 4th day was one of our wow locations, a private jet hanger and jet interior. But, on day two or early on day three of shooting, I learned that the owners of the jet and hanger were pulling out of the deal and we were losing the location. All the keys, department heads, and myself brainstormed solutions. Ultimately, the art director, Jim Aiken, came up with a contact he had at Dillon Precision, the guys who make the gatling gun among other things for the military. They also had a private hanger and small jet.

So, at lunch on day three, about 24 hours before we would be shooting the now homeless jet and hanger scenes, I ran over to Dillon's offices and toured their hanger. They were incredibly understanding and willing to help. The next day the entire cast and crew were shooting the scenes as scripted without any changes. It is a great example of how flexible and helpful my crew was who were real professionals and problem solvers dedicated to making the best film possible.

Another funnier example, though Cavin (Pug) might disagree, was the bar scene where Dinky gets in an argument with Pug and hits him. We rehearsed the punch many times and it was our first shot of the day, as it was the most technical. And as the camera rolled on the first take and Michael (Dinky) punched Cavin right in the face for real. It was an accident, of course, and Cavin wasn't seriously hurt. But now we had a quickly swelling actor on our hands. We quickly got a lot of ice (at least we were at a bar so there was plenty in quick supply) and we did all that we could to minimize the swelling. If you look closely, you can see in other shots how Cavin's face has swollen a bit but it is hard to catch. We continued on with the rest of the day's shooting schedule and we ended up using the "hit" take in the final film.

Overall, the biggest hurdle was time. We didn't have much of it to shoot this feature length Dollar Baby. Usually, feature films shoot a few pages of script a day, sometimes just one or two. We had to shoot about 5 pages per day to keep up. There were a lot of shots on my shot list that had to be dropped due to time. Greg Pilon, another titan of this project who can't be thanked enough, was the Director of Photography and this was his first feature film as well. Together we made the most of everyday and selected the shots needed to make the film work. I think any filmmaker, even those who have months to shoot a film, would always want more time. This project was no exception but we still managed to create something really special in just 13 days.

So often hurdles are the focus of the behind the scenes of making a movie. I would also like to call some of the notable wins, lucky takes, and "happy accidents" that made this production special. The shot where the letter is dropped from 3 stories up over Dinky and it lands in his lap. That was done practically, no CGI. And, it was the first take! We must have dropped 10+ more letters to see if we could do it again. Not even close. We had it in the can on the first one. The airport scene in the final shots of the film could not have turned out much better. It was also our cheapest location, if you can believe it. The local airport only asked that we pay the onsite security guard with hourly wage. We were there for 5 hours and the location cost us about $100 bucks! Talk about production value. And all the extras in those scenes were volunteers organized by Patrice Farner at MovieWork Now Casting. I also remember how I failed to get a permit to shoot at my university where we shot some critical exteriors and the library scenes. I had permission to shoot in the library but not for the exteriors around campus. It was too late to try to figure it out so I decided to just show up with all of our cast, crew, and equipment and roll with it. I would ask for forgiveness instead of permission. We showed up, about 30-40 of us with our 3 ton grip truck and gear. I remember setting up for the first exteriors and campus police coming over. And I was worried. Turns out, we looked so legit with all of the crew, equipment, and lights that the campus police didn't even question our validity to shoot there. They just assumed that we looked so professional that we must have permission. They just wanted to get a glimpse of a Hollywood production. I think that our f-ing amazing Unit Production Manager, Margaret Schrader, asked them to help with crowd control to keep the university students from getting too close. Amazing.

AN: How long was the film shoot and process from start to finish?

J.P.: I started the project in August of 2008, immediately after returning to AZ from my director's internship on *Prison Break*. My first step was to find a writer, the aforementioned Chad Callahagn, and that happened very early on. We drafted the script by early October. I also started working to plan the project. I looked for a company to partner with that could help organize this project. Enter Greg Pilon of Assembly Foundry, he took on the incredible task of shooting, editing, and compositing this entire film. It would not exist without Greg.

From there we soon found Margaret Schrader, our Unit Production Manager, who would help immensely with finding crew and being an absolute rock during production. Robert Gutherie was critical in the organization of the schedule and production as a whole. Jim Aiken, was an incredible art director. Dinky's office was a custom built set and you would never know it! Mirko von Berner did an amazing job designing all of the cool symbols that Dinky uses. Richard Anderson, John Mahoney, Skip Beck, Nathan Thompson, Josh Gill, Jennie Gryder, Liana Hubbard, Stephen Harrison, Siddhartha Barnhoorn and so many more all made this film possible with their skill and dedication. I would ask that anyone who can see the film to just look at the credits and watch them through. Hundreds of names appear and all of them helped make this project a reality. I owe them all a great debt and thank them all for what they did to make this project a reality. I also owe a great deal of thanks to those who financially contributed to the making of the film. Shoestring as we were, the film could not have happened without their contributions. Most importantly, I need to thank my wife, Anissa, who was an anchor throughout this project and my entire life. Her support and belief in me means more than I can say. At the time of this writing, we have been married for 11 years and together for 18, we are high school sweethearts. Throughout that time her support in my dreams, goals, and endeavors has never waivered. Anissa, I love you and thank you for all that you are, all that you've done, and so much more.

We were in pre-production for about 4 months and started shooting on Monday, February 16th, 2009. We wrapped about 2 weeks later and post production began. Greg and his team worked incredibly hard over the next 7 months to complete the film. Editing, color grading, compositing all the VFX computer screens into the film, were all done by Greg. It was a herculean task that Greg took on with grace and perseverance. I'd also like to shout out Stephen Harrison of The Audio Suite who created the sound mix as well as Siddhartha Barnhoorn and my brother John Scott who created the amazing score for the film.

In the end, the final film was mailed to Stephen King on October 23rd, 2009. We held a private cast and crew, friends and family screening of the film on November 11th. In all, it took about 15 months to produce this feature length Dollar Baby.

AN: I noticed a few "nods" to other King stories in this film such as. *Men in Yellow Coats* and a few others. Was this part of the tie-in to *The Dark Tower* books?

J.P.: I guess when I said earlier, that I didn't give any thought to pleasing the fans of King was not entirely accurate. We did add in some *Dark Tower* universe references. The eye of the crimson king and a flashy classic car driven by low men. These elements were not in the original short but with Dinky's tie in to the *Dark Tower* series, we thought it would make sense to work that in a little bit.

AN: The opening animated credits were absolutely amazing. Share with us who did those and how you came up with that opening?

J.P.: Thank you. But, really, the thanks needs to go to Jennie Gryder who animated it. I created and storyboarded the title sequence but Jennie brought it to life! She worked on the title sequence for weeks and weeks. It is a highlight of the film and something that many people note upon watching the film. I would also recommend a repeat watch after you complete the film as more will come to light with a second viewing of the title sequence.

AN: What other tie-ins to *The Dark Tower* are in your film?

J.P.: The only other tie would be the character Ted Brautigan who is the "friend" who drops the letter to Dinky and makes an appearance in the final scene of the film. Ted is a significant character in *The Dark Tower* series who makes his appearance alongside Dinky in the books.

AN: What is your greatest success moment so far with the success of *Everything's Eventual*?

J.P.: It would definitely have to be the response from Stephen King after he saw the film. He was "very impressed" and surprised as he wasn't expecting it to be as good based on most of the Dollar Babies that he sees. So much so that he decided to allow me to try to sell the film as a commercial project! I was elated by this and was able to share it with the cast and crew at the private screening just 2 days later. That was an awesome moment for the film.

Ultimately, an agreement was reached and signed. In order to sell the film we would need to secure a wide theatrical release as well as some cash upfront and a percentage of sales for King. I won't go into specifics but it was going to be a daunting task to reach the terms of the deal. I will say that Stephen King likely had little to no idea of the details of the deal. That is the job of his entertainment lawyer, Jay, and talent agent, Rand. They are the folks I interacted with on this agreement.

In hindsight, I should have tried to negotiate. But I was a naive kid of a filmmaker that was so excited to even have this chance to sell the film that I accepted what they presented without question. Having said that, Rand and Jay are very good at their jobs and knew they held all the cards. Rand was even nice enough to help get my film out there and sent it to several film studios for consideration. He did not have to do that to help my chances but he did and I appreciated it very much!

In the end we did receive an offer, which was beyond belief. It was to release the film in 300 theaters across the US with some cash upfront. However, it was not enough to meet the agreement and so the offer was declined. That would be the closest the film would ever get to being commercially released. This is very common in the film industry. Hundreds of feature films are made every year and so many never see the light of day. I was still proud of everyone who worked on this film and I was proud of the finished product. Even having the chance to be sold commercially was an accomplishment that I am grateful for.

AN: What Stephen King story would you like to direct on a much larger scale?

J.P.: Honestly, I would love to remake *Everything's Eventual* with an expanded story to include Dinky's escape and eventual recapture which bleeds in *The Dark Tower* series. I think it could make a fantastic sci-fi thriller. I envision the bulk of the film I made would be condensed into the first act of the film. Then Dinky's escape, evasion, and ultimate capture would be the core and climax of the film.

AN: Where can fans see this film? Will it play any film fests across the country?

J.P.: The film won the best sci-fi feature at the 2010 International Horror and Sci-Fi Film Festival. It was also accepted at Shriekfest, Spooky Movie Film Festival, Cinefamily's Annual Horror Film Festival, and others. *Everything's Eventual* also still screens from time to time at Dollar Baby festivals which I hope continue for a long time.

AN: Lastly, What is next for J.P. Scott?

J.P.: It has been more than 10 years since the film was made. It was ultimately responsible for getting me out to California to try to be a filmmaker. It got me my second feature director job, a small horror/thriller film that I would not have gotten had I not made *Everything's Eventual*. The film also helped me spark friendships with many film industry professionals who were willing to watch a young filmmaker's work and offer their encouragement, advice, and friendship.

I still love filmmaking and developed a number of scripts and projects in my time in California beyond my 2 feature films. Though none have sold, you never know what could happen. After years of trying, I decided to transition into marketing and now and the Director of Multimedia at a marketing agency. I still get to create everyday and tell stories which, naturally, appeals to my nature. I feel in my heart that I will return to filmmaking some day. I continue to write and stay in contact with my friends in the industry. So, who knows what will happen in the future. But, looking to the past, I am so thankful for the opportunities I have been allowed and the chances I was able to take. This film, a feature length movie, was a stone few filmmakers get to step to. And being able to say that I directed two full length movies is a point of pride and gratitude.

We look forward to J.P.'s return to filmmaking and thank him for taking the time to speak with us today.

Night Surf by Tony Pomfret

Night Surf

Tony Pomfret
January 16, 2015

THE DOLLAR BABY PROGRAM has covered a lot of King's stories and this time we have what I call a "Side-quel" story, *Night Surf*. The story isn't a "prequel" or a "sequel", but takes place roughly the same time period as Kings Mega-Epic Masterpiece, *The Stand*.

The director of *Night Surf*, Tony Pomfret, born March 1, 1973 from the UK. Tony attended the University of Westminster and graduated in 2001. He spent his childhood educating himself on classic horror films and tried to get around the Video Nasty Act of 1984 with the intention to write, direct, and have a glittering career in the film industry. Tony is currently teaching film studies to 16-18 year olds and pushing them into the film industry to help with the next generation of filmmakers. He believes when you're not filming, teach the art of film to those just starting out.

The short story Tony's film is based comes from the Stephen King short story book collection, *Night Surf*. It was originally published in 1969 in Urbis magazine and later in the short story collection in 1978. The story takes place during the same time as King's over-sized book, *The Stand*. This post-apocalyptic story is about a killer virus known as A6 or "Captain Trips", which wipes out a very large amount of the world's population. A small group of survivors camp out on the beach thinking they are safe and exempt from the virus. As time moves on and very little survivors are left in the world, the group captures one. They think if they sacrifice him they will not be cursed with this virus. However, some in their group survived an earlier strain of the virus known as A2. By surviving this they feel they'll not die from A6 which is much stronger. When one of the survivors begins to show symptoms of the A6 or "Captain Trips", they realize it's just a matter of time before their time is up as well.

Tony did a very fine job adapting this short story of *Night Surf*. He captures the atmosphere and fear of the story nicely. The actors did fine performances and the film leaves you guessing and wanting a little more.

Here is my Exclusive interview with Dollar Baby filmmaker, Tony Pomfret.

Anthony Northrup: Out of all the Stephen King short stories, what attracted you most to this one?

Tony Pomfret: I have always been taken with *Night Surf* more than any of Mr. King's other shorts. I read it some time after reading The Stand and was taken by the fact that the universe was expanded. It reinforced, for me, the horrific concept that Captain Trips had conquered the world. There were other stories involving people that had no idea of Randall Flagg or Mother Abigail. People that were trying to live a life in a horrible new world. Remembering my childhood and that of my friends, seeing kids where I lived with nothing to do despite entertainment being at their fingertips, and I didn't live in an impoverished area by any means; kids just hanging around bus stops and street corners, chatting, drinking booze that they'd managed to get, occasionally getting out of control because they felt there was nothing else to do and situations presented themselves. I realized that if the apocalypse came, it wouldn't be *Mad Max* or *Dawn of the Dead*. It would be *Night Surf*. After six months of being a teen and able to take anything you wanted and just hang out, you would be bored. This catastrophic event and this desolate landscape would be bone-crushingly dull very quickly. I liked that idea and hadn't seen or read anything that had communicated that to me to that degree. Not a bang, but a whimper. A slow drawn out exhale.

AN: What changes did you make to make this your own as opposed to King's original text?

TP: The major change, and one that I had always intended was to set the story in England in order to reinforce the idea of a pandemic, of a dead world rather than a dead United States. I also decided to change the timeline so we get everything happening in one night. I did this because if I followed the story slavishly and kept with characters talking about something they did the night before I felt I would have to resort to flashback and narration and that the hindsight would distance the viewer too much from the horror of the situation. However, I loved the writing in that Alvin's death, by being depicted as recollection made the characters experience of the world the most important aspect of the tale rather than Alvin's murder and I made sure and the digging of the grave and lighting of the bonfire meant that the horrific event was present but did not overshadow the film.

Other changes tended to be due to budgetary considerations or expedience, although the producer and I were always very careful to make sure that they fit with our original interpretation rather than to cope with a best-case scenario. I had originally envisaged the characters to be much younger, early to mid-teens, because I saw parallels to The Lord of the Flies and, in the beginning, I thought the terrible event with Alvin happened so quickly, it made more sense to me if they were more obviously younger, as children, without the mediating influence of an adult, can find a simple situation spiraling out of control very quickly. When developing the script I realized that young adults, with no responsibilities, and the presence of Needles in place of that adult mediator, someone I saw as de facto leader simply because of his strong personality and who is angry at his imminent death and taking revenge on the virus the only way he can; I realized that these characters would devolve into a more childlike perspective and quickly succumb to the mob mentality.

AN: So many Stephen King fans want adaptations to be as close to the book as possible, how do you handle the pressure to keep the fans happy?

TP: To be honest, and I know this sounds like a hoary cliché, the producer and I had spent so long wanting to get this made (more of that later) that we were happy that we made the film that we wanted to see. We took for granted that nobody might see this and so determined to develop something personal to us, although staying true to what I saw as the spirit of the story. To this day, if the film never gets seen by anyone other than friends and family, I will be happy and proud.

AN: What was your main goal you wanted to achieve about this film?

TP: When we first thought of this (in 2001!!) upon leaving university the main goal was to use it as a tool towards getting a foothold in the industry, however as time moved on, as I've mentioned above, we started to regret not being able to make the film and the goal at that point became one just having the opportunity to make what we thought was a very good adaptation and to be able to say to each other: "look at this: we made this."

AN: Where was the movie film specifically and were there any obstacles to overcome filming by the ocean?

TP: It was shot in Druridge Bay, Northumberland. It is a beautifully desolate and unspoiled seven-mile stretch of beach in the north east of England. It is owned and protected by the National Trust as an area of natural beauty and, we felt, leant itself perfectly to the emotional core of the film. The morning's reveal of the wide, cold, and barren expanse at the end of the film was designed to impact the viewer given the more claustrophobic nature of the scenes of the night before. We decided to shoot the entire film there to take the cast and crew out of the confines of London and the comfort of what easily could have been a studio shoot to help bring everyone together and allow the young actors more of a personal experience of the loneliness that was at the heart of the film.

We all slept in four caravans at a local family holiday resort and so would get odd looks from holidaymakers going to the bar for the evening while we packed the kit and drove off to the beach and they got up in the morning to see us return, tired, unpack the kit and sleep for the rest of the day ready for the next evening. Of course, filming miles from anywhere on a cold shore-line from 10pm to 6am, when the incoming tide chased us up the beach, for five nights straight could have gone horribly wrong, and we were at our budget's limit so if it didn't work the film was lost to us. We were getting reports of extreme weather warnings every night (we had just come out of a heat wave the week before) so we were filming on the understanding that a massive thunderstorm could wreck everything we had worked so hard to accomplish but the cast and crew were remarkable and gelled incredibly well. We had a campfire built every night on the sand around which everyone would congregate and eat chili that had been made and brought to us so despite the stress that we all should have been under it felt like a camping break. By the way, the thunderstorms did finally arrive – on the very last shot, a pick up that as it turns out we didn't need anyway.

AN: How long was the film shoot and the process from start to finish?

TP: The shoot was five nights, over the Easter holidays in 2013, but the entire process started in 2001. My producer, David Ridley and I had just graduated from university and found out about the Dollar Babies. I had already written the script, just as an exercise in screenwriting with no intention of doing anything with it but when the opportunity came up he suggested we put it forward and see if we could do anything with it. We sent it off but it was rejected because it had been "optioned for a movie, which will be a pilot for a series" (I have the letter framed on my wall) and so we shelved the idea. We found we kept talking about it whenever we would meet up, and kept regretting that we couldn't do it because we liked the idea so much. Cut to 2012 and David finds out that we could have another chance and would I want to do it? I quickly pulled the script backup and had another look at it and sent it off. This time we were given the go ahead and got the rights late 2013 for a calendar year for that amazing one dollar. We knew we wanted to shoot over Easter so spent the months before that making contacts, managed to secure the location and get a great deal on a Red Epic (we were all very excited about that one), developing the script and then had three months after the shoot to edit, grade and finish.

AN: What is your greatest moment so far with the success of *Night Surf*?

TP: As you can imagine, finally getting it finished and taking delivery of DVDs and BluRays. If it plays anywhere, all well and good, but what makes me most happy is that I can look at my shelf and see it sitting there, and that hopefully, somewhere, Mr. King can look at a shelf and see it sitting there as well.

AN: What Stephen King story would you like to adapt on a large scale?

TP: My preferred period is his early work and they've already been nabbed, but I do really like *The Long Walk* and have thought long about that one. Thinking about it, I would love to have a go at back-to-back adaptations of *Desperation* and *The Regulators* with the same cast.

AN: Would you say this is a "sequel" to *The Stand* or a "side-quel" (takes place same time as *The Stand* just a different location)?

TP: Side-quel. As I said earlier, I definitely feel it takes place in the expanded universe of *The Stand*.

AN: How much of *The Stand* did you want to put into your story?

TP: I didn't feel it necessary to push *The Stand* too much into it. Mr. King doesn't do it in the original short story beyond the nomenclature of the virus so I opted for the same approach. I did take the original on-screen title, delineating the virus, it's mortality rate and familiar names it is known from from *The Stand*, but didn't add anything beyond that. If someone was enough of a Stephen King fan to see the film, I figured they would know enough about his work to make the connection. People that have seen it that don't know *The Stand* have all understood the film so it seems to stand well enough alone to make sense.

AN: Where/when can fans see this film? Will it be playing in any film fests in the USA?

TP: It has submitted it to various festivals in the UK and around the world but are still waiting to hear back from many of them. We will certainly let you know when we hear more about it showing in your neck of the woods.

AN: Without giving too much away, explain that ending a little bit if you can?

TP: Not sure I can… Let me explain but you can edit so as to not give too much away: I have said about the impact of the sudden bright open space after the claustrophobic night before, when shooting I likened it to God's flashlight after the event. I wanted to have everyone separated given what we have learned. Each of the characters react in their own way: Needles is cut off physically and emotionally from the others throughout the film and, given his condition, takes Alvin's place in the car; Kelly stands at the shore, wide-eyed and horrified at what she has taken part in; Corey is oblivious and doesn't care, sleeping peacefully, as does Susie, they are, after all, the emotional children of this dysfunctional family; and Bernie, finally understanding his fate and knowing that he must soon step up as leader, tries to make some form of meaningful connection, an anguished hand-clench with Susie communicates his emotion while making her think he is saying what she wants to hear, because to not tell her what she wants to hear, knowing what is to come, would just be too cruel. Whether that is all communicated successfully is for you to decide – that's what I told the actors, anyway.

AN: Lastly, What's next for Tony Pomfret?

TP: Teaching, paying the rent, putting food on the table. I have other finished short film scripts that I would like to film but right now, I am still content that I have finally been able to complete this. That helps when you have to spend the time saving up for the next one!

I want to thank Tony for taking the time out of his busy schedule to speak with us today and wish him success in all his future projects.

Rest Stop

Patrick Abernethy
December 12, 2015

MY NEXT DOLLAR BABY INTERVIEW comes from a young filmmaker from Charlotte, North Carolina and his adaptation, *Rest Stop*. Here is my exclusive interview with director Patrick Abernethy and my review of his Stephen King adaptation of *Rest Stop*.

Patrick was born March 4, 1983 and from the southern city of Charlotte, North Carolina. He attended Central Cabarrus High School, later attending Appalachian State University where he studied Computer Information Systems. It wasn't long before Patrick's love for films would lead him to be a part of the Stephen King Universe by making a Dollar Baby of his own and his vision of King's short story, *Rest Stop*.

Stephen King's short story, *Rest Stop* was first published in the December 2003 edition of *Esquire* magazine. It was later added to King's short story collection book, *Just After Sunset*. The story won the National Magazine Award of Fiction in 2004. REST STOP is a story about a writer, John Dykstra (his pen name is Rick Hardin) (played by Jonathan Foust) who has a bit too much to drink after leaving a special writer's group. Feeling intoxicated, James decides to pull into a Rest Stop. While he is there, he overhears a domestic abuse argument between Lee (played by Nick Alexander) and Ellen (played by Bella Bellitto). James must decide if he should put a stop to the violent boyfriend or is it James' other side that comes out to stop him?

Writer Michael Welsh first requested permission from King's office to get the Green Light to adapt to *Rest Stop*. After lining it up, he asked Patrick if he would like to direct it. Working together on the script, both Patrick and Michael pulled off the King adaptation nicely. I felt the film was very well done, creepy, fine performances all around, and quite enjoyable.

Rest Stop by Patrick Abernethy

Here is my Exclusive Interview with Dollar Baby director, Patrick Abernethy.

Anthony Northrup: Out of all the Stephen King short stories, what attracted you most to this one?

Patrick Abernethy: *Rest Stop* was a story that could be produced fairly inexpensively and had a compelling premise that was easy to expand on. We wanted something we could make our own to an extent, and it was the right choice for that.

AN: What changes did you make to make this your own as opposed to King's original text?

PA: We tried to stay pretty true to the story. We dropped some aspects of the story to make the movie flow better, and added some. The meat of the story is the same, though.

AN: So many Stephen King fans want adaptations to be as close to the book as possible, how do you handle the pressure to keep the fans happy?

PS: In the end, we're fans making a movie. We really just tried to make an adaptation we would enjoy, and we hope other fans will agree.

AN: What was your main goal you wanted to achieve about this film?

PA: We wanted to tell a great story in a different way. We wanted to keep the experience of reading Rest Stop the same and just apply it to a different medium.

AN: Where was the movie filmed specifically and were there any obstacles to overcome while filming there?

PA: The film was shot primarily in the Charlotte, NC area. The only obstacles came from using a rest area that was still open to the public, so we had to work around people coming in and out. The North Carolina Department of Transportation really helped us out. The rest of our locations were all available thanks to friends and family, so it was no problem at all.

The story is actually set in Florida, but we made the choice early on not to worry about that. The story holds up, no matter where it's set.

AN: How long was the film shoot and the process from start to finish?

PA: From planning to a final cut, the film took almost two years to finish. The shoot itself took us 4 days, and then one day of pick-up shots. We had a small window where everyone was available, so we crammed it into those 4 days. We were working around school, jobs, and other things that made it take longer than we hoped. We had a great cast and crew, and its really thanks to the team effort that the movie came together like it did.

AN: What is your greatest moment so far with the success of *Rest Stop*?

PA: Just being a part of the Dollar Baby family is wonderful. There are so many talented people working on these films, and we're glad to add our film into the mix. We are looking forward to having Stephen King view our movie as well, even if we don't get any feedback from him on it, it's an honor either way.

AN: What Stephen King story would you like to adapt on a large scale?

PA: I have always wanted to adapt a new version of *The Girl who Loved Tom Gordon*. I love that story so much, and I think it deserves a killer film. I'm also a fan of the Bachman Books, so any of those would be a blast.

AN: Where/When can fans see this film? Will it be playing many film fests across the USA?

PA: We are currently submitting Rest Stop to festivals, so hopefully it'll be all over the place before long. We're already accepted to a Dollar Baby Festival in the Netherlands, so we're super excited about that.

AN: Tell us about your lead actor, Jonathan Foust. Was he your first choice when casting and what did he have that the other actors who auditions didn't have to win the role?

PA: We actually developed the story with Jonathan in mind. He is a great actor and a great friend of ours, so it was a no brainer. He had an amazing ability to play both the light and dark sides of Dykstra/Hardin, and he pulled it off beautifully.

AN: Lastly, What is next for Patrick Abernethy?

PA: I'm currently in pre-production on an original short film that a friend of mine had the concept for. We're currently finishing up the script for that, and hope to shoot it some time next year.

I want to thank Patrick for his time and patience and wish him much success in his career.

The Man Who Loved Flowers

Drew Newman
January 25, 2015

DREW NEWMAN WAS BORN March 17, 1976, in St. Louis, MO. He was a typical child of the 80's, enjoying the films and music of the era he was growing up in. He also enjoyed going to summer camp, where he first discovered the world of Stephen King. One particular summer, while at camp, a friend let Drew borrow one of his Bachman books, (of course we know Bachman better as Stephen King's alter ego), and Drew was hooked! Who would've thought years later that Drew would be part of the Stephen King universe, through the Dollar Baby Program.

Drew attended college in New York, at the University of Syracuse, majoring in film, with his minor in drama. He also spent 5 years in Los Angeles CA, working on films, and eventually moved back to the midwest. It was however, while in college, Drew had an assignment to make a short film, one that had to have a twist that would make it uniquely his own. Drew says "the story always appealed to me for a short film, and I considered doing an adaption my Sophomore year. Glad I waited". Drew instead, worked at various places, including Gateway Media, and the St. Louis Holocaust Museum and Learning Center.

He finally made his Stephen King Dollar Baby film, *The Man Who Loved Flowers*, in 1996.

Drew is close friends with Dollar Baby filmmaker, Doveed Linder (*Strawberry Spring*). Drew also enjoys life with his wife Margo, and his family, but his love for film continues, and he is proud that he was able to contribute to the Dollar Baby film program.

Here is my review of Drew Newman's *The Man Who Loved Flowers*.

The Stephen King short story, *The Man Who Loved Flowers*, was first published in August 1977, in Gallery magazine, and then in 1978, published in King's collection of stories in his book, *Night shift*. *The Man Who Loved Flowers* is about a man who walks the city streets without a care in the world, stopping by a vendor to buy flowers for his true love Norma.

However, every woman he tries to give the flowers, tells him they are not Norma, that he is mistaken. It turns out his beloved Norma had passed away many years earlier. In a state of sadness, he becomes crazed with the notion that he must continue to buy flowers to give to Norma.

This short story has been adapted several times by Dollar Baby directors. Each filmmaker brings his own unique vision to the final product, however in Drew's case it is quite a different vision. Filmed in what is termed "grindhouse" fashion, with the lead character dancing, singing, not a care in the world, easing down the city streets, to the tune of Van Morrison's, "Brown Eyed Girl", is where this quirky story begins. Along the way he encounters several situations, which of course leads to his buying flowers, for Norma. This film is witty, funny, and full of satire. As I say, Drew makes a cameo as the flower vendor. It's clear to see that all who participated in this short film had a wonderful time doing so.

Out of the many adaptations I've seen, I found this one to be the most funny, and unique in its ability to convey that of a horrific act, as humorous. Drew Newman adapted this short story to film in 1996, with a budget of only $2,000. However, it took Drew 14 years to get the rights to the film. It was then released in April of 2011, and played at film festivals. It was filmed on location, entirely in Syracuse, New York.

Here is my Exclusive Interview with filmmaker, Drew Newman.

Anthony Northrup: As a child, what was it that captured your attention as far as films were concerned? Secondly, when did you first begin reading Stephen King?

Drew Newman: My dad took me to see my first movie when I was around five years old. It was a re-release of *Star Wars*. Soon after, my mom took me to *Raiders of the Lost Ark*. Not a bad start, eh? I've been hooked on movies ever since. Also my introduction to Stephen King came several years later at summer camp, when my bunkmate lent me his copy of *The Bachman Books*. I borrowed it because I wanted to read *The Running Man*, but he insisted I start with *Rage*. If you were lucky enough to read it before King took it off the shelves, you know that was good advice. Almost 30 years later, and I've read just about everything he's written.

AN: You majored in film and drama at University, did you ever want to act full time, or did you feel more comfortable behind the camera?

DN: While I do enjoy acting, it's not something I want to do full time. Cameos are fun, though.

AN: Tell us how you met filmmaker, Doveed Linder (director of the Stephen King Dollar Baby *Strawberry Spring*)?

The Man Who Loved Flowers by Drew Newman

DN- We've known each other since we were kids, and went to junior high, and high school together. I think we first met playing soccer in a youth league. It was a total coincidence that we both did adaptations of, *The Man Who Loved Flowers*.

AN: Can you tell us where you were, and your reaction when you first heard back from Stephen King, giving you the "OK" to film, *The Man Who Loves Flowers*'?

DN: My experience was a little different from most of the Dollar Baby Filmmakers. I shot *The Man Who Loved Flowers*, back in 1996, while in film school at Syracuse University. My professor said I didn't need to get the rights since the project was a requirement for my degree. I actually found out about the Dollar Baby concept after the film was completed, but I figured it was too late at that point. It wasn't until about five years ago, when Bernd Lautenschlager contacted me, and suggested I make it official.

AN: What was the budget of the film, and how did that affect the running time of the film?

DN: The budget was around $2000, and had no impact on the running time. I think 5-10 minutes is the ideal running time for a short.

AN: What was the audition process like, and what did lead actor, Seamus Mulholland bring to your attention that won him the lead role?

DN: This was the second of three films Seamus and I collaborated on. I hand-picked him for the role because I knew it was something he could do. There aren't many actors who can exhibit that kind of range and willingness to go over the top, not to mention sing! He won a regional Emmy for the performance.

AN: Why did you choose Van Morrison's song, 'Brown Eyed Girl', and was there any other song you thought of going with?

DN: It just sort of occurred to me. The whole idea of making it a musical and using that particular song. I had the, *Born on the Fourth of July* soundtrack in my car and listened to it quite a bit, so I'm sure that had something to do with it.

AN: What was it about Los Angeles that turned you off, and took you back to New York?

DN: Well, it was St. Louis I moved back to, although I would pick New York over LA in a heartbeat. It's all about the people. Of course I'm generalizing, but New Yorker's tend to be more real, while Angelenos are fake. I'd rather get shot in the face than stabbed in the back. Don't get me wrong, LA has a lot of great qualities. I still have good friends there. St. Louis is home. Always has been, always will be.

AN: Out of all the Stephen King short stories, what attracted you most to this one?

DN: I think it's perfectly suited for a short film, that's probably why there have been so many adaptations. One of my professors, Thomas Friedmann, compared the structure of the story to telling a joke. King put a lot of thought and detail into the set up and delivered a pitch perfect punchline.

AN: What changes did you make, to make this your own, as opposed to King's original text?

DN: Well, obviously turning the story into a musical was a big change. I also rewrote the dialogue between the Leisure Suit Man and the Flower Vendor, because I wanted it to match the overall wackiness of the singing and dancing.

AN: So many Stephen King fans want adaptations to be as close to the book as possible, how do you handle the pressure to keep the fans happy?

AN: Ultimately, you have to believe in your vision. I think Stanley Kubrick's, *The Shining,* is one of the all-time great horror films, but also a terrible adaptation of King's novel. There's room for both. Perhaps some King fans will take issue with turning *The Man Who Loved Flowers* ,into a musical. If I can get them to laugh in spite of their misgivings, though, then I'll consider it a success.

AN: What was the main goal you wanted to achieve about this film?

DN -To create something entertaining. (And to get a good grade.)

AN: Where was the movie filmed specifically, and were there any obstacles to overcome while filming there?

DN: Downtown Syracuse, New York. Weather was the biggest obstacle. Syracuse gets a lot of snow, so we had to wrap shooting while it was still nice out. That basically gave us the month of October. We only had to cancel one day of shooting due to rain, and the temperature dropped a bit when we went back for reshoots, but other than that the weather was perfect.

AN: How long was the filming process from start to finish?

DN: One semester, or about four months. Pre-production in September, production in October, and post-production in November and December.

AN: What is your greatest moment so far with the success of *The Man Who Loved Flowers*?

DN: Participating in my first Dollar Baby Festival back in 2011 in LA. It's the only festival I've been fortunate enough to attend. I enjoyed meeting the other Dollar Baby filmmakers, and being on the Q&A panel was a trip.

So, there you have it, another great adaptation of a Stephen King short story, to a short film through the Dollar Baby Film project. I am always amazed to see these fine films, and never grow tired of them, no matter how many times some of them are done. There is always a new way of looking at them through the vision of each director. I have certainly enjoyed this adaptation of *The Man Who Loved Flowers*, by director Drew Newman, and can honestly say I will never be able to listen to the song 'Brown Eyed Girl', by Van Morrison, again, without envisioning this film.

I want thank Drew Newman for taking the time out of his busy schedule to speak with us today and wish him much success in his career.

The Man Who Loved Flowers

Justin Zimmerman
March 22, 2015

THE DOLLAR BABY PROGRAM has covered a lot of King's stories and this time we have a young filmmaker from Oregon, Justin Zimmerman, who has adapted the Stephen King short story, *The Man Who Loved Flowers* from the King collection, *Night Shift*.

Justin Zimmerman was born August 16, 1977 and is originally from Greenwich, Connecticut. He went to college at Ohio State University majoring in English and Film and later got his Master's degree in Film from Ohio University. He has always enjoyed film specifically and storytelling as well. His first film in 2001 was *Meeting Again* followed by 2002's *One of Five* (a story about mental & physical handicaps and the families who have to deal with it). Justin has led a very impressive life in high education including receiving two grants from the Ohio Art Council. He has studied various parts of film including screenwriting, directing, lighting, editing just to name a few. His next film, *The Calling* about the continuing rivalry between Yale vs Harvard, won Justin two Telly Awards. He has a long list of short films and documentary credits to his name as well as many awards including Best Non-Fiction Short, Silver Award for Cinematography, SXSW, Sundance, Portland International, Ohio International, Seattle Lesbian/Gay Film Fest, and Long Beach Film Fest just to name a few. Not only is Justin a very talented director, producer, writer, screenwriter, editor, teacher, and other titles, but he also writes comic books. His graphic novels include titles such as, *The Killing Jar*, *Other Worlds*, and *Safe*. Justin's latest film is a short story adaptation of Stephen King's *The Man Who Loved Flowers* part of the Stephen

King Dollar Baby Film Program. When I asked Justin how he got into the Dollar Baby Film Program, here is what he had to say, 'I've been to Acadia National Park in Maine almost every year of my life. I grew up with Stephen King's works. I helped a college peer gain the short rights to a King story around 2000. I also adapted a Stephen King short into an official and commercial feature length script circa 2005 or so. So I was familiar with King's office. When my team and I decided we wanted to adapt the short story, it was a quick process, and we got right to work. We put our hearts and souls into the project.'

Justin has a promising future in the film industry, a talent to keep a lookout for, indeed.

And now, here is my review of Justin Zimmerman's adaptation of *The Who Loved Flowers*.

The Man Who Loved Flowers was written by Stephen King and originally first published in Gallery magazine in 1977. It was later added to the short story collection book, *Night Shift* in 1978. The story is about a young man walking down the street, various daily routines of people around doing their jobs or business just like any other day. A radio can be heard in one of the stores with breaking news of a dead woman's body being found. The young man stops in a flower shop to buy some flowers for that special someone in his life. He clearly looks completely in love based on his facial expression. When he later sees a woman in an alley, he thinks she is her beloved "Norma" and tries to hand her flowers. However, she is not Norma and what comes next can only be told in typical Stephen King fashion. Justin's version of this story was spot-on. He kept his vision close to the original story and added his own personal flare to the mix. With impressive camera angles, cinematography, and locations that fit perfectly, Justin's version of '*Flowers*' is entertaining and leaves you hanging for more… until the credits. Creepy images and questions are answered during the closing credits and I found this revealing surprise nicely done compared to revealing them during the film itself. Very unique in his storytelling. I found this to be one the more entertaining and well-done Dollar Baby films I've seen so far. I recommend Justin Zimmerman's *The Man Who Loved Flowers*.

The Who Man Who Loved Flowers can be seen at film fests and you can go to Bricker-Down Productions webpage for more details.

Here is my Exclusive Interview with Dollar Baby filmmaker, Justin Zimmerman.

The Man Who Loved Flowers by Justin Zimmerman

Anthony Northrup: Out of all the Stephen King short stories, what attracted you most to this one?

JZ: *The Man Who Loved Flowers* is a perfect short story. But I also felt that it could be adapted in a cinematic way, something that is decidedly NOT true for a number of written works, King's or otherwise. *TMWLF* also reminds me of another favorite short story of mine, *The Daemon Lover* by Shirley Jackson.

AN: What changes did you make to make this your own as opposed to King's original text?

JZ: I was very faithful to the source material, but did deviate in some respects, though always in the spirit of the original. The crew and I tried to create a timeless, beautiful world of nostalgia through cinematography, production design and costumes. It's a small town Americana rather than a specific large city Americana. The central dialogue scene is abbreviated. The foreshadowing radio's been cut. The dead girls are not revealed during the attack. They are placed throughout the credits. And last but not least, key lines at the end are delivered by the Flower-Vendor and his wife, rather than a new couple. Again, it's up to the audience— and King—to decide if I did or adapt the source right. But I'm happy to say early reactions have been great. I felt I could truly bring it to life on screen.

AN: So many Stephen King fans want adaptations to be as close to the book as possible, how do you handle the pressure to keep the fans happy?

JZ: In general—and I've been making films and comics for well over a decade—I try and put ego aside and objectively try and make the best possible project I can. And work isn't made in a vacuum. I had an incredible team with me every step of the way. The only pressure I feel is to lead a team to do our very best. And we poured our hearts and souls into *TMWLF*, absolutely.

AN: What was your main goal you wanted to achieve about this film?

JZ: While I've directed many award-winning films, they've all been documentaries. I've written, produced and edited narratives, sure…but I'd never directed a narrative film. Until *TMWLF*! So my goal was to take one of my favorite short stories from one of my favorite writers and write and direct a great adaptation.

AN: Where was the movie filmed specifically and were there any obstacles to overcome while filming there?

JZ: We shot on location in Estacada, Oregon. We shut down their main street for multiple days and we battled a sudden rainstorm on an incredibly important day of shooting. But the crew and cast prevailed and you'd never know every second on set wasn't gorgeous. It was a challenging but amazing experience.

AN: How long was the film shoot and the process from start to finish?

JZ: We worked for almost 6 months pre producing the film. The shoot was 5 days, and we spent over 3 months editing, working on visual effects, sound design, score, mixing and color-correction. You can see all kinds of process photos at our Facebook page here:https://www.facebook.com/TMWLFlowers.

AN: What is your greatest moment so far with the success of *The Man Who Loved Flowers*?

JZ: The film literally wrapped last week, and it's already being accepted into film festivals and getting nice reviews. This pleases me to no end.

AN: What Stephen King story would you like to adapt on a large scale?

JZ: I would LOVE to adapt *The Regulators*. Man is that one right up my alley. In every way, shape and form. Second choice? *The Long Walk*, but I think Darabont's got dibs on that one. Third choice? *Cell*, but I hear that's already happening. So…*The Regulators*!

AN: Where/When can fans see this film? Will it be playing many film fests across the USA?

JZ: TMWLF will be entered into fests across the US, and I'm hoping the awesome network of Stephen King film festivals will reach out so that I can get as many eyes on the project as possible. I'm proud of the film, and I'm proud of everyone who helped make it happen. It's easy to get in touch with me through my website here: http://brickerdown.com

AN: You also do comic books, tell us how you got into that and where can comic book fans buy yours?

JZ: I've been writing comics for years, and have several self-contained series featuring some INCREDIBLE artists. Interested? There's a store tab on my website, but physical books can be snagged through Etsy: https://

www.etsy.com/shop/BrickerDown and ComiXology has digital copies of my work: https://www.comixology.com/Justin-Zimmerman/comics-creator/7845

AN: What makes your comic so unique? Have you been a fan of comics all your life?

JZ: I love storytelling, and I love comics. Fans of King's work might really dig *The Killing Jar*. Or *Safe*. Or hell, *Other Worlds*. If you're a King fan, you're my kind of reader.

AN: What made you want to get into films?

JZ: Why do I love film? Good question. Shaping reality, I suppose. Documentary or narrative, you're crafting a world for someone. An experience. What's cooler than that?

AN: Lastly, What's next for Justin Zimmerman?

JZ: I didn't plan this, but I have three films coming out in 2015. *TMWLF* is first. A 30-minute documentary I've been working on for over a decade with a survivor of a Colorado school shooting—*Sara's Columbine*—comes out in a couple months. And last but not least my first feature-length film—a LA rescue doc I've been working on for almost 3 years called SMART—wraps in June. Then I'll be taking a nap and hopefully supporting these projects in a lot of fests.

I want to sincerely Thank Justin for taking time out from his busy schedule to talk with us about *The Man Who Loved Flowers* and his future projects. Look for his film and other "Dollar Baby" films at festivals near you.

Suffer the Little Children

Corey Norman
April 17, 2015

STEPHEN KING HAS WRITTEN many tales about children. He has had them with special powers, looking for a dead body, defeating their ultimate nightmare in the form of a clown, and some tales of kids being abused, bullied, or in some sort of danger. However, one of his most disturbing children's tales is, *Suffer The Little Children* and filmmaker, Corey Norman brought that story to the screen with his adaption of King's terrifying tale.

Corey Norman was born March 19, 1981 and grew up in the same state as Stephen King: Maine. He attended Windham High school and graduated in 1999. He continued his education attending many colleges such as, Southern Maine Community College in 2001, University of Southern Maine in 2006, and Lesley University graduating in 2011 in Cambridge, Mass.

His studies included such subjects as, English Literature, Creative Writing, Education with a focus on Curriculum Instruction. He turned from education to filmmaking with his Stephen King Dollar Baby adaptation, *Suffer The Little Children*. Currently, Corey is a full-time professor at the Southern Maine Community College. When he is not teaching, he is playing in his band, Unscarred. Corey is happily married to his wife, Haley and they live in Portland, Maine.

Here is my review of Corey Norman's Dollar Baby film, *Suffer The Little Children*.

Suffer the Little Children was first published in the February 1972 issue of Cavalier magazine. In 1993, it was published in the Stephen King

Suffer The Little Children by Corey Norman

short story collection, *Nightmares & Dreamscapes*. The story is about a school teacher, Miss Emily Sidley, who teaches first grade. One day, one of her students stares at her, torments her, and tells her that he is not who she thinks he is. Each day over and over he torments her and simply stares. He tells her that he and all the students are really doppelgangers and that the real children in the class are gone. After a leave of absence, Emily returns to the school with a gun and plans on shooting all of the children. Later, as she is in a mental institution, Emily fines her own solution to her on-going nightmare.

Without question, *Suffer the Little Children* is one of the very top most disturbing stories he has ever written! He has put children in some of the scariest and worst scenarios ever written, but in this story, having children being shot was very hard to read. It was even harder to watch, as Corey Norman did a very good job with this adaptation. He built up the suspense, transferred the horror from the page to the screen nicely, and certainly made it uncomfortable for the viewer to watch that horrifying scene of the shootings. This was a very well done film even with a disturbing subject matter.

And now, here is my exclusive interview with Dollar Baby filmmaker, Corey Norman...

Anthony Northrup: Tell us what it was like growing up in Maine?

Corey Norman: Growing up in Maine was a unique experience, though it was not nearly as creepy as Mr. King would have you believe. Even our biggest cities have a small-town feel, and the sense of community is inspiring. I love the woods, and spent a lot of time there, but felt enjoyment rather than fear. The biggest thing about growing up in Maine was that we were always in Stephen King's shadow. Whether we were going to the grocery store that was featured in *The Mist*, fishing at Runaround Pond in Durham from *The Dead Zone* or driving past The Shiloh Temple that would inspire the Marsten House, where we're living in the world that inspired Stephen King.

AN: When did you first discover the works of Stephen King? What was your first Stephen King book and film?

CN: My father was a huge horror fan. He also lacked a lot of the discretion that parents today have. That being said, I saw my first Stephen King film, *Cujo*, with him before I was five. We were at the Bridgton (Chester's Mills) Drive-in. I was supposed to be asleep when I popped up from the back seat in tears... not because *Cujo* was killing people, but because I didn't want them to hurt the dog! My lifelong addiction with King began in that moment. I'd go on to begin reading King in High School. By the point, I had worked my way through his film library and I wanted more. I was given *Night Shift* as a gift, and I devoured it.

AN: You wear many hats: director, producer, professor, editor, outdoorsman, and musician. Which of these is the most challenging?

CN: I think the most difficult hat to wear, and one I only wear out of necessity, is that of the producer. As an independent filmmaker, in most cases, you don't have the luxury of a real budget, so you have to get really creative as you line up the resources needed to make these films. I find this very stressful, but without it, I wouldn't be able to do what I truly love; directing.

AN: You play bass in the band, The Unscarred. How long have you been in the band and what type of music is it? Do you tour? And who are your musical influences?

CN: I've been playing bass with my band The Unscarred since the early 2000's. When we started out, we were signed to an independent record labeled and toured heavily up and down the east coast. After several years of this extensive touring, we went on a 15 year hiatus. Three years ago, we decided to give it another go, and have been playing together again ever since. Our sound is very metal, and blends influences like 36 Crazyfists, Killswitch Engage, Sevendust and Life of Agony. You can check out our newest album, Prelude, on Spotify, Apple Music and GooglePlay.

AN: When did you first hear about the Stephen King Dollar Baby program?

CN: I first found out about the Dollar Babies program from my director of photography Ben Heald. While shooting my first feature film *The Hanover House*, he told me he had attempted to adapt *Gray Matter*, but was never able to raise the funds he needed to do it justice. Several years later, he and I would finally get the opportunity to do a Dollar Baby film with *Suffer the Little Children*.

AN: Out of all the Stephen King short stories, what attracted you to this one?

CN: I had never read *Nightmares & Dreamscapes* before doing my research on the Dollar Babies. When trying to select which story we wanted to adapt, I simply began reading every available story, one by one. Then I got to *Suffer the Little Children*. As I reached the final paragraph, I found that my jaw was literally hanging wide open. It was such a shocking ending, and controversial topic, that I had to do it!

AN: What changes did you make to make this your own as opposed to King's original text?

CN: We tried to stay as faithful as possible, but there was one big change we had to make, and that revolves around the locations or the climax. These days, most schools no longer have a mimeograph room, so we had to adapt. We asked ourselves, where could we shoot a bunch of children one by one, and not cause alarm. Our first solution was to introduce enough noise to cover the sound of the gunshots. We used the sound of the school band for this. We then needed a location for the murders. When a building, like the library in the school we chose, is under renovation, it provides an out of the way location that people would avoid. We felt that these two elements working in tandem would be a realistic replacement for the mimeograph room.

AN: So many Stephen King fans want adaptations to be as close to the book as possible, how do you handle the pressure to keep the fans happy?

CN: I am one of these fans. So, when we set out to make our short, we wanted to stay as faithful as possible. Most of our dialog comes directly from the text, and we tried to include as many small details as possible, right down to what Ms. Sidley was eating for dinner. The only time we deviated was in regards to the mimeograph room that is no longer present in schools. We also hid some small King inspired Easter eggs throughout the film specifically for the fans. The "baseball boys" team name is the St. Bernards as a nod to *Cujo*, Ms. Crossen is drinking from a mug that says "Got Coffey" as a nod to The Green Mile, and there's a quote from 11/22/63 on the principal's wall that says, "When all else fails, give up and go to the library."

AN: What was your main goal you wanted to achieve with this film?

CN: To be honest, I just wanted to make a Stephen King film. Since I was a little kid, it's always been my dream, and I finally got the opportunity through the Dollar Babies program to make it a reality. Everything past that was just icing on the cake.

AN: Where was the movie filmed specifically and were there any obstacles to overcome while filming there?

CN: After being hung up on by over 14 superintendents, we finally found support for our film at Sanford High School. They welcomed us with open arms, not only at the school, but in the whole town. Local businesses donated food for the cast and crew, and so many of the child extras were from the town itself. Because of this, it was only right that we brought the film back to Sanford for the Maine premiere during the Sanford International Film Festival. Apart from filming in Sanford, our other filming locations were on the Southern Maine Community College campus. The Juniper Hills observation room with the double side mirror was in our early childhood education department, and Ms. Sidley's hospital room was a vacant dorm room.

AN: How long was the shoot and the process from start to finish?

CN: We spent 6 weeks in pre production leading up to our 4 day shoot. We premiered the film less than two months later at the HorrorHound Film Festival in Cincinnati, OH.

AN: In the film industry, they always say it is hard to work with animals and kids. Was it challenging working with such a young cast?

CN: This is one of those statements that I always hear, but totally disagree with. We tend to work a lot with child actors in our films, and I find it to be unbelievably enjoyable. The children bring such an imagination to the set, and generally have so much fun with everything they do. They make it fun for me.

We had just over 20 kids in the classroom scenes, and even after close to ten hours in their seats, they were still more focused and well behaved than many adult actors I've worked with.

AN: What is your greatest moment so far with the success of *Suffer The Little Children*?

CN: There have been so many great moments that I can't limit it to just one. First, it was such a pleasure to work with Anne Bobby (*Nightbreed, Born on the Fourth of July*) again. She brings so much thought to her character portrayals and she's so easy to collaborate with. I couldn't have done this film without her. During our funding campaign, we received some very unexpected support from writers Chris Claremont (Uncanny

X-Men) and Neil Gaiman (Sandman, American Gods). Both took to their social media channels to help promote the film. My inner fanboy was over the moon. The biggest moment came during our premiere at the HorrorHound Film Festival where a room of 250 rowdy horror fans sat silently as Ms. Sidley euthanized her students one by one. The room erupted with applause at its conclusion. As we were leaving the room, Robert Kurtzman (Gerald's Game, Army of Darkness, The Devil's Rejects), whom my wife was nominated alongside for Best Special Effects, stopped to congratulate us on the film. It was so surreal to be supported by these people we had admired since childhood.

AN: What Stephen King story would you like to adapt on a much larger scale?

CN: From King's short stories, I've always wanted to adapt Nona. I really love the sense of impending dread in that one. I'd love to do this with a legitimate budget so we could bring all those rats to the screen. I'd also love to do a remake of *Christine*. That's my all time favorite King book, and while I can appreciate the John Carpenter version, I'd love to have the chance to both modernize the film, while making it more closely aligned with the book. Mr. King, if you're reading this, I'll donate my services to direct anything you write.

AN: Where can fans see the film? Will it play at any film fests?

CN: Unfortunately, our one year license for screening the film has come to an end. During that time, we screened the film at 16 festivals, received 20 nominations and won 9 awards. We currently have no screenings planned, but if someone would like to program us, and if Mr. King would be willing to issue an extension, then we would gladly screen it.

AN: Lastly, What is next for Corey Norman?

CN: By day, I'll continue to teach in the Communications and New Media department at Southern Maine Community College. But by night, I'll be returning to the horror world. I've recently signed on to direct a New Year's Eve slasher film called *Time's Up* starring Damian

I want to thank Corey for taking the time to speak with us today and wish him great success in the future.

Everything's Eventual

Maxwell Heesch
May 18, 2015

FROM THE NORTHERN PLAINS to L.A., filmmaker stardom can come from anywhere. Such is the case of my next Dollar Baby interview. This time it is with filmmaker, Maxwell Heesch.

Maxwell Heesch grew up in the upper plains of Sioux Falls, South Dakota. He studied Film at the Minnesota State University of Moorhead class of 2010. Once he moved to Los Angeles, Maxwell worked as Production Assistant and Post Production on films such as, *The Terror, Pure Genius, Rise,* and *Olive Forever* just to name a few. He turned his filmmaking talents to the Stephen King universe when he decided to make a film adaptation of the Stephen King *Everything's Eventual*. He currently is Post Production Coordinator at Tacoma FD and lives in Los Angeles, California.

Here is my review of Maxwell Heesch's Stephen King adaptation of *Everything's Eventual*.

The story of *Everything's Eventual*, first appeared in the October/November 1997 issue of *The Magazine of Fantasy and Science Fiction* magazine. In

Everything's Eventual by Maxwell Heesch

2002, it was published in the book *Everything's Eventual*. The story is about Dinky, a 19yr old teenager who has an amazing life. He has his house, car, and everything you could ever imagine paid for by a secret source. He even gets an allowance and even music CD's before they are even released. In exchange for all of this, he is told to kill specific people via emails by unique and strange designs that only Dinky can do. He doesn't know what they mean, it is just a "gift" he has. When he is recruited by a stranger, Mr. Sharpton, to assassinate specific people, Dinky realizes after doing research, he is killing people he shouldn't be killing. And Mr. Sharpton might not be who Dinky thinks he is.

This tale is connected to the epic Stephen King *The Dark Tower* series. Without spoilers, *Everything's Eventual* isn't the last time we "may or may not" see Dinky. Maxwell Heesch's adaptation was done very well. It had an intriguing and suspenseful feel about it that keeps the eeriness of King's original text.

Here is my exclusive interview with Dollar Baby filmmaker, Maxwell Heesch.

Anthony Northrup : Share what it was like growing up in Sioux Falls, South Dakota?

Maxwell Heesch: Well, coming from the Midwest certainly is an isolated experience, but thankfully Sioux Falls is a "big city" in comparison to the rest of it. If I didn't have a movie theatre readily available, I would have gone nuts.

AN: When did you first discover the works of Stephen King? What was your first Stephen King book and film?

MH: Pretty sure my first exposure to King was through the TV version of *The Stand* in middle school, which was proper spooky enough to me to pursue the book version right after. From there I found *The Dark Tower* series and that sucked up most of my reading time through high school.

AN: You studied film at the Minnesota State University of Moorhead. What key lessons and advice helped you there once you started making short films?

MH -"Film what you know" was a popular maxim, but so was "film what you have", which was incredibly helpful when writing for a realistic production. Making short films in the Midwest is also the best, because you don't have the entitled LA-types who are more than willing to let you film anywhere, no permit necessary.

AN: You later on moved out to Los Angeles and worked on films such as, *The Terror, Pure Genius, Rise*, and *Olive Forever*. What are these films about and did you have a favorite in particular you enjoyed working on the most?

MH -As far as my time in LA in concerned, I've had my share of experiences as a Production Assistant behind the camera, most good, some bad (cough*The Terror*cough). So far my time in Post Production as a Coordinator has been great, especially when I get to run around a movie studio lot.

AN: When and How did you first hear about the Stephen King Dollar Baby program?

MH: I think I learned of the program after reading more about Frank Darabont after digging his work on *The Mist* (and everything before). He did *The Woman in the Room*, and I just started thinking about the possibilities of what stories I could adapt.

AN: Let's talk about your Dollar Baby film, *Everything's Eventual*. Out of all the Stephen King short stories, what attracted you most to this one?

MH: Since getting heavy into King's works, *The Dark Tower* has always held my imagination more than any of his other works, so I wanted to have a connection to Mid-World for sure. *Everything's Eventual* fits that criteria to a tee. Plus Dinky Earnshaw is just a fun character.

AN: What changes did you make to make this your own as opposed to King's original text?

MH: I originally wrote an entire feature for EE, but (1) that would be incredibly difficult to pull off for no money, and (2) J.P. Scott was already in the process of that very feat. So with that I went the opposite direction and put the whole thing in Dinky's head and made it a little weird.

AN: So many Stephen King fans want adaptations to be as close to the book as possible, how do you handle the pressure to keep the fans happy?

MH: To be honest, I never even considered what fans would like, as the nature of the Dollar Babies means few will see it away. I just made what I wanted to see and went from there.

AN: What was your main goal you wanted to achieve about this film?

MH: I wanted to make a Dollar Baby unlike any of the others, both visually and narratively, and I think I succeeded.

AN: Where was the movie filmed specifically and were there any obstacles to overcome while filming there?

MH -We filmed the whole thing in a warehouse in West Fargo over 3 days in August 2010, so the heat was intense. We also had to empty out the warehouse and paint the entire thing.

AN: How long was the film shoot and the process from start to finish?

MH: It was a 3 day shoot, but the post took the better part of six months, as I had to do it while I was moving to Los Angeles, which was a bit taxing.

AN: Tell us about the casting process and what your two main lead actors brought to the table that won them the role?

MH: I had my actors in place while I was writing. Billy Schnase was a friend through the MSUM theatre department who was up to the task and Bill Dablow was a friend from my senior thesis project. Both brought great energy. Billy was a fantastic smartass and Bill was made to menace.

AN: This story has many ties to *The Dark Tower* series. Are you a fan of the series and if so, what do you like the most about King's epic story?

MH: Huge fan of the series (maybe not the 2017 movie so much). I love how, whether in subtle or obvious ways, all of King's work is connected to the series.

AN: What is your greatest moment so far with the success of *Everything's Eventual*?

MH: Knowing that a copy of the short is sitting on Stephen King's shelf is a pretty high honor in my book.

AN: What Stephen King story would you like to adapt on a much larger scale?

MH: Going back to *The Dark Tower,* I would love to do *The Wolves of Calla*. A full on King western would be the best.

AN: Where can fans see this film? Will it play at any film fests?

MH: I'd love to be able to show it in more festivals, but it's been a bit since I've submitted it. Until, it hides on Vimeo.

AN: Lastly, What is next for Maxwell Heesch?

MH: I'm currently rocking the world of TV Post Production in Los Angeles while I attempt a living in screenwriting.

I want to thank Maxwell Heesch for taking the time to talk with us today and wish him great success in the future.

Maxwell Edison

Warren Ray
September 21, 2015

THE DOLLAR BABY PROGRAM has covered a lot of King's stories and this time we have a young filmmaker from Louisville, Kentucky, Warren Ray, who has adapted the Stephen King short story, *Maxwell Edison* aka *The Man Who Loved Flowers* from the King collection, *Night Shift*.

Warren Ray was born on September 17, 1965, in Corydon, Indiana. He attended Corydon Central High School, later attending the Louisville Technical Institute (Robotics Engineering). Warren has worked at Ghost Age Films, LLC, and through the entertainment industry as editor, actor, and director among other titles. Warren has worked on films such as, *100 Proof* (1997), *Super Rocket* (2009), *Nothing in the Flowers* (2011), and *Maxwell Edison* aka *The Man Who Loved Flowers* (2012 and Dollar Baby based on Stephen King's short story from the book, *Night Shift*. Warren has had a career in country music as well. Back in the early 1990's, he was a singer-songwriter in the alt-country/punk scene. It was never trendy and no one ever danced to my music. The line race scene was very square compared to the CBGB atmosphere of the clubs I was playing; only dancing was mosh or pogo. The line dance crowd would never step foot in the punk clubs I played in. Not his or his type of music at all. Warren was in the Indy Alternative /Punk music scene never Country mainstream . It was called country punk then / alt country nowadays. Country music became a "trendy" style of music and was the "it" thing to listen to and go to country bars line dancing. His music was right at the highlight of that craze. Even though he had great success with it, he returned to his love of film and acting soon thereafter. It was then he would be part of Stephen

Maxwell Edison by Warren Ray

King history by being part of the Dollar Baby film program and with his adaptation of *The Man Who Loved Flowers* but changing the name for his own reasons to, *Maxwell Edison*. Warren recently participated along with 19 other filmmakers in the new book about the Dollar Baby film program called, Dollar Baby: The Story of the Stephen King Dollar Baby Filmmakers by Shawn S. Lealos. Warren was kind enough to take some time out of his busy schedule to let me interview him and his part in Dollar Baby history and his own career.

Here is my review of *Maxwell Edison* aka *The Man Who Loved Flowers*.

This story based on Stephen King's short story is from the book, *Night Shift*. It is about a man who walks the streets on a sunny day and buys flowers for the one he truly loves. However, every woman he comes across isn't her and it's not the flowers he delivers but a silver hammer and brutally kills each one he encounters. I have seen other versions of this film, but this one was quite enjoyable! Warren stars in the film playing the young lover and makes the performance creepy and believable. The soundtrack is from the 60's/70's influenced and had a very "Quentin Tarantino" feel to it. I found it well directed, stylishly filmed, and the only complaint is that it was too short! *Haha! I would have loved to watch a full-length film version of this, that is how entertaining it was. Warren has talent and an eye for style while trying to entertain. I was quite impressed with this version of King's story.

Here is my Exclusive Interview with Dollar Baby filmmaker, Warren Ray.

Anthony Northrup: Out of all the Stephen King short stories, what attracted you most to this one?

Warren Ray: It was short, with not a lot of dialogue. When I read it ,right away it reminded me of the Beatles song *Maxwell Silver Hammer*. So it sparked some ideas.

AN: What changes did you make to make this your own as opposed to King's original text?

WR: Well I added names to the characters. Taken from the Beatles tune, *Maxwell Edison,* Joan, and pc31. Mr. King's original character was a nameless everyday average Joe. But I melded the stories together.

AN: So many Stephen King fans want adaptations to be as close to the book as possible, how do you handle the pressure to keep the fans happy?

WR: I don't worry about the fans. You can never make everyone happy. I'm a fan of Mr. King myself, so all I need to do is please myself and get to a point where I feel like I'm doing him justice. Only the most hard core King fans will ever see this film because of the contractual restrictions anyway. I just need to feel like I'm doing right by Mr. King.

AN: What was your main goal you wanted to achieve about this film?

WR: To have an official Stephen King project on my film reel and of course impress my friends and chicks.

AN: Where was the movie filmed specifically and were there any obstacles to overcome while filming there?

WR: We shot in Louisville Ky. Under a skyway on the edge of town, Downtown during rush hour, and in the Highlands area of town it's a hip spot with lots of cool shops and restaurants. It was all done commando style on the fly hand held. We rarely used a tripod. Only obstacles were folks shouting congratulations. People assumed I was getting Married and that we were doing a wedding pictures shoot because David Brewer, my camera man, was using a Canon DSLR to shoot video with and it just looks like a still camera he was holding. Haha.

AN: How long was the film shoot and the process from start to finish?

WR: Well it took over a year to pull it all together. My first camera man had to leave because of family stuff. I had to recast a few roles because of typical BS. I had a friend come down with cancer who has since passed away (punk rock icon from the band the end tables) Chili Regot was going to be the bag lady in the film and we held off on production for a while in hopes he would be well enough to participate. It didn't happen so I just left that part out. My friend Theo was also going to portray the smoking pregnant women on the street. But sadly she got sick and also passed away unexpectedly , so it was a bumpy road with lots of snags along the way. But all in all it took 3 days to shoot another 3 or so days to edit once it was shot. I was also dressed up in a suit and carrying a flower box, so I can see how it looked that way to people. haha.

AN: What is your greatest moment so far with the success of *Maxwell Edison*?

WR: I was stoked when it played a DB festival at the red square in Russia. It's played like 8 or 9 countries now but I guess the greatest moment was having Shawn S. Lealos book about the dollar baby program come out with a 15 page interview of me about music in film. Frank Durobont was interviewed as well so that's pretty good company. Feels like validation I suppose.

AN: What Stephen King story would you like to adapt on a larger scale?

WR: *Cycle of the Werewolf.* I thought Silver Bullet kinda sucked compared to the book the adaptation was stupid with the changes it made to the story and it's original structure. The whole calendar idea as story chapters was brilliant and you didn't know who did it till the end. The film gave it up way too early on. And the film didn't do the calendar chapters if I recall.

AN: Where and When can fans see this film? Will it be playing many film fests across the country?

WR: I believe it's playing the Dollar Baby festival at Crypticon in MN this October 23-25th 2015.

AN: Growing up in the mid-western state of Indiana, what was life like for you there and how early in life did you discover the love of filmmaking?

WR: It was boring as you may expect, I was into Syfy and practical effects as a young kid. *The Planet of the Apes* franchise was big when I was a kid, pre-*Star Wars.* As well as the Universal Monster movies. My father was a successful theater director and set designer. So I was around all the behind-the-scenes aspects of show business, sets, costumes, practical effects, lighting, sight lines, and acting. I was a professional child actor in 1977 doing summer stock theater in front of audiences that were over a thousand strong on a nightly basis. I recall reading *Starlog* magazine and the like backstage while around to go on stage. I did my first film ever on a super 8 film with little *Star Trek* models hanging from thread in front of a painted starfield on black poster board in the dressing room of Stephen Foster Story with another child actor. While the adults were all on stage, we were shooting Syfy movies. I was 10yrs of so but always loved movies and wanted to make them ever since I can remember.

AN: What was your first Stephen King book and Why did you choose this particular short story?

WR: There was a copy of *Carrie* around the house when I was a kid as well as *The Shining.* But "my first" King book was *Cycle of the Werewolf.* I was working as a carney one summer in my early 20's. I picked it up while in a drug store in Damone, Iowa. I recall setting in the back of reefer truck and reading it in one setting, the art was so cool and even though I was on an adventure in the heartland of America, I still needed some kind of an escape from the shit service job and constant smell of onions on your body and in all your worldly property. *Cycle of the Werewolf* did that. It was like a Rockwell painting or a werewolf coming to Mayberry! It really spoke to me. That's why I was so disappointed when the film adaptation was so different then the vision. The book provided me.

AN: You studied at the Louisville Technical Institute in Robotic Engineering, how did you go from that profession to writing/acting/directing?

WR: Well, I went to Louisville Tech to study Robotics because I really wanted to learn about hydraulics and pneumatics because I wanted to get into practical effects building for film but I found that the school was really intended to create maintenance workers for assembly line robots, so after the first year of robotics theory and geometry I dropped out. I wanted to create and that was the wrong school for that. It was really a grad school but the only place to study robotics without going to a full blown University. I was already into doing film effects and theater acting before I studied robotics. It was really a "trade" school.

AN: What do you find more challenging: directing, writing, or acting and which do you prefer more of?

WR: Writing is the toughest for me. I have dyslexia so I can come up with ideas all day long, but having to write it down is the problem for me. I prefer to act for directors I trust because I'm a bit of a control freak, so if I can just worry about my role in the film it's a real cakewalk compared to all the worries of the director. I use flashcards to separate ideas and scenes or storyboarding before I ever get a script together. So folks have to trust my vision there isn't always a complete "script' so to speak. It's all in my head for the most part and always subject to change depending on location, mood, and random events. Worries of the director.

AN: The film, 100 Proof, was your first film in 1997. Tell us about that first film experience?

WR: It was interesting. I drove to Lexington to meet the director. I was trying to get some music I had done in the film score (I was a singer, songwriter, recording artist for the 90's, part of the alternative country movement. Well, an actor they hired wasn't working out, the unit production manager knew me and told the director, 'Warren used to be an actor, when he was a kid". So, one thing led to another, next thing I know, I'm getting paid to be Tommy the Liquor Store Guy. Cool thing is that Jim Varney was in that film and I had the opportunity to hang out with him for a bit. Super nice fellow. He had a beagle dog back home in Tennessee that he missed and w as showing off a photo of his beloved pet. Then when the camera rolled he played the nastiest mutha f**ker you'd ever want to meet. He was trying to make a departure from his typecast cast as Jed Clampett and 'Ernest' does whatever films. He was playing a real bad person in this psychological thriller. It was one of the last live action films he did before he passed, he did the Slinky dogs voice for the Toy Story film. I was on set for 2 or 3 days. It was shot on film. I did not see the final product for well over a year or so. It took so very much longer to see a done film project back then before the advent of HD video. They edited with a razor blade and tape back then, what a headache.

AN: I personally found your version of *The Man Who Loves Flowers* (aka *Maxwell Edison*) to be very "1960's/1970's" influenced and a sort of… Tarantino feel to it. Was this something you envisioned the story to be when you read it or a style of filmmaking you prefer?

WR: Well, l grew up in the 60s/70s so all my influence was tv and movies of my youth. I love Tarantino. He is in my Top list of fave directors. He is older than me but as a child actor I was hanging out with college age theater kids, so I was exposed to adult themes and dialogue earlier than most kids were. I think at first I wanted to do a Hitchcock style black and white. To keep it simple. But I think I saw that *The Man Who Loved Flowers* had been done before more than once so I decided that shooting the text verbatim would be boring and probably had already been done. So I decided for a more mod kitch feel with a bit of a Steve McQueen homage built in.

AN: Lastly, What's next for Warren Ray?

WR: I play an Apollo Era astronaut in the film "Orbs, They are among us" by jkfilms that movie has distribution and should be out on digital and DVD this winter. A sequel is planned to shoot next year called "Orbs Apollo 21 " in Which I will star and we find out what happened to the 2nd lieutenant from the first film. After his encounter with the Orbs.

I want to take this opportunity to Thank Warren Ray for his time and patience out of his busy schedule to do this interview.

I Know What You Need

Shawn S. Lealos
October 11, 2015

JUST ABOUT EVERYONE in the world knows who Stephen King is. He is well-known around the world for scaring us with his books, movies, and television series. He is one of the biggest authors of our generation and with over 60 novels, over 50 films, and many well deserved awards under his belt – King has earned his spot in writing history.

However, back in 1976, King had the idea to have film students adapt his short stories into short films. These films were called, "Dollar Babies" because it cost the filmmaker $1.00 to be paid to King himself. The program still goes on to this day almost 40 years later and over 80 films have been made which have played around the world at film fests everywhere. These are very rare gems indeed for any Stephen King fans to witness and they can be at film fests near you. Just check the Dollar Baby webpage for details. With all those films, talent, and knowledge someone had to capture it all and share with the world all that information so they too can learn about the Dollar Babies especially if you're a Stephen King fan. Author Shawn S. Lealos did just that very thing.

Shawn's new book, captures the amazing talent known as Dollar Babies by interviewing 19 of them for his book. Inside we hear from the biggest and the best, how they brought their visions to the screen, and the struggles along the way. This book is packed with tons of information about the Dollar Baby film program, the history, details on films that were adapted, and the future of the Dollar Babies themselves. As one of the biggest Stephen King fans around, I have witnessed some of these films at films fest and I found it very interesting getting the backstories of them by reading this book. Some fans won't have that great opportunity to see these films and this book captures everything you need to know next to seeing the film itself.

I Know What You Need by Shawn S. Lealos

I found this book very entertaining, educational, funny at times, and a true gem to have in my personal Stephen King collection of books and collectibles. If you would like to learn more about the Dollar Babies and these films as well as support an Independent author, then I recommend picking up *Dollar Baby: The Story of the Stephen King Dollar Baby Filmmakers* at Amazon and remember to leave your thoughts on the book there as well to show your support.

One of the joys of being a writer and supporting Independent talent is the amazing discoveries you make along the way. It doesn't matter if it's an Artist painting, a new young face on the music scene performing at a club, a short film being played at a film fest, or in this case, an author releasing their new self-published book. As a full supporter of Indie's, I get a lot of joy spreading the word when I, myself, discover these types of talents. Case in point, author Shawn S. Lealos new book: *Dollar Baby: The Story of the Stephen King Dollar Baby Filmmakers.*

Shawn S. Lealos was born August 11, 1970 in Yukon, Oklahoma. He attended Yukon High School and then Oklahoma City Community College. He graduated from the Gaylord School of Journalism at the University of Oklahoma studying professional writing. He has been a journalist for over 20 years and film critic before making his own films. Shawn is the Creator/Owner/Writer at Renegade Cinema and Producer/Director at Starving Dogs Productions. He made his Dollar Baby in 2005 called, *I Know What You Need*. Followed by 2006's Les Chansons and 2008's *The Final Detail*. Shawn has hosted Dollar Baby film fests in Texas and Washington. Shawn is currently married to Johanna and lives in Norman, Oklahoma.

Here is my review of *I Know What You Need*.

I Know What You Need was first published in *Cosmopolitan* magazine in the September 1976 issue. It was later published in the Stephen King short story collection, *Night Shift* in 1978. The story is about a young college student, Elizabeth Rogan, who has a fellow student, Ed Hamner, Jr. in love with her. Well, more like obsession, really. How obsessed? Well, he uses black magic to kill off her boyfriend and manipulate her emotions so that she will fall for him instead.

Shawn's adaptation of this tale was done very well. The cast were all top drawer. And I found the film very entertaining and interesting. Shawn did a wonderful job bringing this King nightmare to life.

Here is my exclusive interview with author Shawn S. Lealos.

Anthony Northrup: You grew up in the middle of America in Yukon, Oklahoma. Tell us about those years growing up, did you always want to be a writer at such a young age or was film making your first love.

Shawn S. Lealos: My first love was always writing. When I was a kid, I was a huge comic book kid. This was back in the late 70s and early 80s, so Marvel was where it was at for me and I read everything. I hit the comic store the day they came out and grabbed every issue that came out every week. I always wanted to write comic books. Then, when I went away to college the first time, I stopped reading comics, but about the same time, I started reading Stephen King. That would have been 1989. By this time, I was starting to party with new friends and there were a lot of haunted places out in the country. I ended up writing short stories about the places and we would pass the stories out to newbies before heading out to the haunted places, and they usually worked perfectly to scare people. I turned in one of those stories to my English Comp class and that is when my professor asked why I was a business major when I was talented at writing. On her advice, I went to the University of Oklahoma and majored in professional writing. It wasn't until my capstone class as a senior in college that I discovered my love for screenwriting, and then filmmaking after that.

AN: You swept the Columbia University Gold Circle Awards by winning 1st, 2nd, and 3rd Place for Sports Journalism. Tell us what the article was specifically about and how did it feel being a three-time winner in one shot?

SL: I did sweep those awards one year, and it was for three different articles, one for each place. I was pretty successful at those collegiate awards for my sports writing. In 1998, I took third place for a story about the Oklahoma-Texas rivalry, in 1999, I took first place for an article titled "Living the Dream," and in 2001, I swept the category of Sports Reporting with three articles ("Sweet Victory," "Road to Independence," and "Superior Leadership.)" Basically, when I started writing for student publication, I was writing for the Yearbook and student paper. When I broke a story about a former player (Brian Bosworth) starting a new charity organization, the paper wanted to give the story to someone else, but the Yearbook told me to run with it. I got an interview with The Boz, wrote the story for the Yearbook and then asked the paper how their story was coming. They said they were having trouble getting in touch with Bosworth and I told them I already interviewed him. I ended up writing the story for them as well and it was the cover story of the game day newspaper. I also sold a story about it to a national sports magazine at the time. That earned me an Honorable Mention at the actual Oklahoma Society of Professional Journalists awards, which is still my most proud moment since I was competing with actual professional journalists, while I was still a student.

AN: You hosted two Dollar Baby film fests: Comicpalooza in Houston Texas and Galacticon in Seattle Washington. How did that come about and what do you like most about Horror/Syfy/Comic Book conventions like that?

SL: I was covering Comicpalooza in Houston as a journalist for a couple of years and one year reached out to the guy who created and ran the convention. He seemed interested and we set up the festival for the next year's convention. I reached out to Dollar Baby filmmakers and everyone seemed interested. We ended up having three days of screenings, stretching back to the first known Dollar Baby (*The Boogeyman* by Jeff Schiro) to brand new ones like *In the Deathroom* by Damon Vinyard. It was exciting. That same year, *Battlestar Galactica* had their convention in conjunction with Comicpalooza and I met the guy who helped run that and he called me about a year later and asked if I wanted to bring the Dollar Babies to Galacticon in Seattle this year. I agreed and we set that up.

As for conventions, I love to attend them and really enjoyed working as a journalist at them. Interviewing people like Tony Todd (*Candyman*) and Michael Biehn (*Terminator*) was just a real treat. Also, meeting lesser known people like Terrance Zdunich (*Repo: The Genetic Opera*) made it all worthwhile. However, working the convention as an invitee is a lot of hard work and manning a table is very long hours and often discouraging. Overall, I love the atmosphere of the conventions, especially as a journalist and fan.

AN: When was your first introduction to Stephen King? Which book of his has made an impact on you the most?

SL: I never watched movies growing up because my religious upbringing didn't allow me to go to movies. When I left home for college the first time, I started going to movies all the time. I really don't remember if I saw a Stephen King movie before I read a book, but if I did it was probably *Misery*. But, what I do remember clearly was reading my first Stephen King book – *The Stand*. It was the long unabridged version and I loved it. Absolutely loved it. I joined the Stephen King book of the month club after that and read the books as I received them (instead of in order) and couldn't get enough. But, *The Stand* is still my favorite story by King.

AN: Before we get into the Dollar Baby Q/A, tell us a little bit about your other two films you've done: *The Final Detail* and Les Chansons? Was one more difficult to film than the other? Were these shown at film fest, if so where?

When I discovered my love of screenwriting, I decided to stick around OU after I graduated and started taking film studies classes, which was basically a film history and writing course. I took a couple of screenwriting classes, one in the journalism college and one in the film college, and thought about making a movie. I learned about the Dollar Babies and wanted to make one of those, but at that time, you had to send in a request via mail and wait (unlike now with the Internet application). While waiting, I teamed up with my friend Rob McIlrath, and we made our first film *Three Piece Combo*. That was for a class that I was taking that Gray Frederickson (the producer of *The Godfather*) taught. He let us either take a final exam or make a short film for our final grade. I chose to make the film and it was a dumb comedy about a drunk redneck who kept interrupting the shoot of a melodramatic film. It got laughs from the audience when it screened and I made an "A" on the project. We next decided to shoot a short film based on my short story "The Devil's Playground," which was both one of the stories I wrote about the haunted places back in Yukon as well as the story that impressed my college English teacher years before. We were shooting that when the contracts from Stephen King arrived and we dropped everything and started *I Know What You Need*. As for *Les Chansons*, that was at a period of time where I was wanting to really establish our production company and I asked our contributors to submit some ideas. That was one submitted by a girl named Anne Haider. I adapted her idea into a screenplay and let her direct the entire film. I then made a decision as a producer to have it all in black and white and then hired someone to score the film. *The Final Detail* was the next one that I wrote and directed myself, a drama about a man contemplating suicide who sets out to see his friends one last time. It was influenced highly by the French film by Louis Malle called *The Fire Within*.

I never submitted either film for festivals, although I did hold private screenings. Those three non-Dollar Baby films were not really hard to make because I had some great people working with me. However, there was a zombie movie called WWZJD that was extremely hard and is still not finished because of the mistakes made while shooting it. There was also a movie I tried to shoot twice called *This is Hell* that was not completed either time because I was not happy with different aspects of the films. I am my own worst critic.

AN: You picked the Stephen King short story, *I Know What You Need* as your Dollar Baby. Out of all the Stephen King short stories, what attracted you most to this one?

SL: I was working as a sports reporter for OU and I was taking the screenwriting class where I wanted to test my adapting skills on the writing of the King Dollar Baby. I had no idea what I wanted to shoot, so before I set out for a road trip to Kansas City for the Big 12 football championship game, I bought *Night Shift* on audio and listened to it on the way to and from the football game. I had three main criteria for what I chose. First, it had to be a story with locations that I could use Norman, Oklahoma for. Second, it had to have limited casting roles to make it easier to manage. Third, it couldn't have special effects that I knew I was unprepared to make and couldn't afford to pay for. There were two finalists: *Last Rung on the Ladder* and *I Know What You Need*. *Last Rung* is still my all-time favorite King short story, and I did not trust myself to do it with the talent and respect it deserved, as my first ever short film project (which at the time, it would have been). That left *I Know What You Need*, which had three characters (Ed, Elizabeth, and Alice), limited locations (mainly at the university and living accommodations), and had no special effects. My decision was completely based on financial decisions.

AN: What changes did you make to make this your own as opposed to King's original text?

SL: Well, the biggest thing about Stephen King's writing is that most of the stories are internalized thinking – you are inside the head of the protagonist. You can't show that on the movie screen. With *I Know What You Need*, the biggest problem was that this was a story about Elizabeth telling the story of talking to Ed, talking to Alice, talking to Ed, talking to Alice, confronting Ed, the end. That is boring to watch in a movie, although fascinating to read. So, I knew I had to make some decisions. First, I added a new character of a detective. In the story, Alice hires a detective to search into Ed's past and tells Elizabeth. Instead of telling, I showed Alice and the detective and then showed the detective investigating the case. That also allowed me to show Ed at his most evil when he gained some revenge against the detective for interfering. Next, I added a nightmare scene for Elizabeth that was just added to give some horror elements to the story.

AN: So many Stephen King fans want adaptations to be as close to the book as possible, how do you handle the pressure to keep the fans happy?

SL: It's just about telling the story that Stephen King wanted to tell, but doing it in a way that works on screen. I can't make changes to the characters that go against what King created. I could add the character of the detective because King mentioned in the story that there was a detective. I can have Ed use his powers to kill the detective because King showed in the story that Ed had used his powers to kill in the past (and present) of the story. I can add the nightmare scene where Elizabeth is scared of her boyfriend Tony because King shows in the story that she has relationship issues. As long as the additions to make the movie more entertaining line up with the story, I don't think fans have a problem with them.

AN: What was your main goal you wanted to achieve about this film?

SL: My thought was all about my future in the entertainment industry. When someone makes a short film, that film may never get seen anywhere. When I made *The Final Detail,* I figured that I might get it into a festival or two, but that is it. No one would see it. However, by making a Dollar Baby film, I have something that has Stephen King's name attached to it. It has been shown in the Netherlands, Argentina, King's home town of Bangor, Maine, Houston, Los Angeles, Seattle ... I have allowed this film to be screened in more places than any of my other shorts have been screened together. Much like other Dollar Baby filmmakers, using the King movie is a way to get your name out there. I never took the step to go to Hollywood like others, but this movie helped me release my book and now I have gone full circle and am starting my writing career up again after years of filmmaking (although I am not finished with filmmaking yet).

AN: Where was the movie filmed specifically and were there any obstacles to overcome while filming there?

SL: The best thing about shooting a film in Norman, Oklahoma is that people there are more than willing to help. I was able to shoot the nightmare scene in a park by campus and when the police showed up, I just said I was a student making a student film and they left me alone. I shot at a couple of restaurants, at a recreation park, at a theater, at the university, and more, and no one wanted money for it. Oklahoma doesn't require permits to shoot on public property or in private places where we have permission. My actors all worked for free because this was a Stephen King project. My DP Boots Kennedy worked for free, and was awesome. I had a great guy named Tony Moyer who did all the paperwork so I could focus on shooting the film. There was an obstacle originally. We tried to shoot it back in 2001 and things just went wrong. The lead actress was not right for the role and things just stalled out. When we started the second time, we recast everyone except for Kevin Real, who played Edward in both versions, and it went off almost without a hitch. There was some controversy on set a couple of times with one cast member, and that causes one scene in the movie to still remain disappointing for me, but overall it went off well.

AN: How long was the film shoot and the process from start to finish?

SL: We got the contracts back in 2000 or 2001, and tried to shoot it then. We started up again a couple of years later and finished it. The release date listed on IMDb is 2005, but it was finished a couple of years before that. That puts it at three years from contract to final edit and then a short wait until the first screenings. The film was actually 40 minutes when we finished it, but after a rough test screening, I cut it down to 30 minutes. I still think it is too long. If I was to remake the short, it wouldn't be longer than 15 minutes.

AN: What is your greatest moment so far with the success of *I Know What You Need*?

SL: At first, the biggest moment was having the film show in different countries. However, I think the biggest moment for me was being able to use the film to meet all the other Dollar Baby filmmakers and write my book. These days, I am almost more excited to talk up the films of Rodney Altman, Juan Reinoso, Warren Ray, Jay Holben, and James Cox, than to talk up my own film. I love my film, and it is my baby, but so much time has now passed, that I see it as a nice part of my past as the main key to opening up things in my future.

AN: What Stephen King story would you like to adapt on a large scale?

SL: That is a tough one. Most of the filmmakers I talked to mentioned *The Long Walk,* but I don't think I would enjoy that. I loved *The Stand,* but that is way too big of a project for my taste. Same thing with *The Dark Tower.* I really don't think I would want to remake something that was already made, so really that just leaves some of his short stories and newer stuff. I really enjoyed *Revival* and think that could be a nice, down and dirty, horror movie. *Doctor Sleep* was great as well and it would be fun to shoot the sequel to *The Shining.* I also liked *Throttle,* the novella that King wrote with Joe Hill, and that might be fun to shoot as a stretched out feature length film in the vein of *Duel.*

AN: Where and When can fans see this film? Will it be playing many film fests across the USA?

SL: At the moment, there is nothing scheduled for *I Know What You Need*. I am currently considering another Dollar Baby festival in Midland, Texas, but I don't plan to show my film due to time constraints.

AN: Let's talk about your book, DOLLAR BABY: The Story of the Stephen King Dollar Baby Filmmakers. Basically, how did it all begin? What inspired you to write about Dollar Baby films something very few people know about with the exception of King's fans?

SL: I was trying to figure out what to do with my career in entertainment, as the filmmaking itself was becoming expensive and time consuming. I knew that I could not afford to make a feature length film and making short films was fun but seemed to be just running in place. I was bartending at a casino in Oklahoma and I always used the time bartending to come up with ideas (most of my short films were developed through the time either bartending or driving, I just seem to think better when doing something monotonous). That is where I thought of the idea of writing about the Dollar Baby filmmakers. My thought was two-fold. First, it is something few people know anything about, and even a lot of King's fans don't know about it. I thought it would be something interesting that no one had ever written about at length before. Second, the stories of the filmmakers are so interesting, especially seeing the success so many of them have enjoyed. These are inspirational stories about people who chased their dreams and, in many cases, succeeded, all thanks to Stephen King. It is stories that I assumed people would want to read about.

AN: You have 19 Dollar Babies who helped you with this book by interviewing them and talking about their films. How did you narrow it down to just 19 and was it hard to choose who would be in or not?

SL: When I first started wanting to write the book, it was about 2008. I sent out feelers to the Dollar Baby filmmakers that I had contacted before (Jay Holben, James Cole) and then Bernd Lautenlager sent out emails to everyone he knew and I got a limited number of responses. I sent out questionnaires to the filmmakers and got almost nothing back. A couple of years later, I had quit bartending and was working as a writer fulltime and decided I would try it again. I sent out feelers to everyone who responded last time and Bernd sent out emails again. This time, I got a ton of responses. Since the question lists went so poorly last time, this time I decided to make it more personal. I wanted to interview the people personally, so I set up times to call everyone and all the interviews in the book were done over the phone. This allowed one Stephen King Dollar Baby filmmaker to talk one-on-one with another Dollar Baby filmmaker, and I think that allowed me to get a lot more personal information and real talk than I would have with someone just writing out precise answers to questions. I wanted to talk to everyone, so the responses from outside of America were sadly passed on, including some great filmmakers like Elo Quiroga, who made the animated *Home Delivery* thanks to the help of Peter Jackson's animation studio. That is the one story I regret not including in the book. There were also a couple that were left out due to not being able to get in touch with them in time for the book, like Billy Hanson (*Survivor Type*). I also wanted to see the films before interviewing the filmmakers, and sadly Mr. King's attorneys contacted me when one of the filmmakers queried told them I was asking and put a stop on that, saying that asking to see the films was in violation of our contracts. Luckily, film festivals allowed me to see every film for every filmmaker I interviewed before speaking to them. If I couldn't see the film, I didn't interview the filmmaker.

AN: I read the book and very much enjoyed it. I found it very informative. Out of all those interviewed, what tidbits of information did you learn that surprised you the most? Something you didn't know about Stephen King or the Dollar Babies themselves?

SL: I enjoyed talking to some of the filmmakers who actually met Stephen King. Robert Cochrane had two Stephen King films on his resume, and I had no idea that "Roland Meets Brown" (based on a scene from *The Gunslinger*) was for a contest. He met King thanks to that contest and actually got a chance to contact and possibly work with Frank Darabont, although that ended up falling apart in the end. I also loved how King helped Jeff Schiro get a job making a music video for The Ramones because he loved the adaptation of *The Boogeyman* so much. King is really a generous man, and it is great to hear these stories.

AN: Tell us the process of the book, how long from start to finish did it take? Was this self-publishing or through a publishing house? And is there a chance of a Volume 2?

SL: Once I started the book the second time, it took a few months to do all the telephone interviews, each one between 30 and 90 minutes in length. After that, it took a long time to transcribe the audio. Then, life kept getting in the way because when you write for a living, it is hard to work on something that is for future earnings because the bills to pay are due now. By the time, I got around to reading the transcribed interviews, I realized that letting the Dollar Baby filmmakers tell their stories through the interviews was better than me re-telling them. That made the actual completion of the book quicker. It then took over a month to copy edit the entire book and get it ready for fresh eyes to copy edit it. Overall, it took 6 years from conception to completion, and two years from interviews to publication. After that, I decided to forego the publishing houses. I was told that I could get a nice advance for the book but then selling it was in the hands of those who I signed with and they would control the book completely. By self-publishing the book, I control all rights, including the pricing of the book. I also hold the right to do anything I want with it, and I liked that control. It makes it a lot harder to promote it and get the word out, but I expected that. As for a second volume, that all depends on how well this first volume sells. At the moment, there has not been enough interest in it to put in the time for a second book, but I have some marketing plans over the next three months and depending on how that goes, we will see.

AN: You have many titles: Journalist, Producer, Director, and now Author. Which of these do you find more challenging and which do you want to focus more on?

SL: I would say that producer/director is the most challenging. As a producer, it is all about planning a project, hiring the people needed, finding the money needed or figuring out how to do it without the money, and then making sure the project is completed. When it comes to filmmaking, a film is created three times – on paper as a screenplay, on video as a film, and on the computer in the editing stage. I love all three of those areas, which is why I prefer to shoot films that I write and then I want to edit them myself (which is incredibly fun). Those are all hard jobs, but very satisfying (and sometimes frustrating) to do. As for the future, I am going to be working more as an author. Filmmaking is fun and I don't ever want to stop that, but that is a group effort and there comes a time where it gets harder and harder to get everyone together to make a movie – especially with no financing. Writing a book is normally just me and my computer. The Dollar Baby book required a lot of interviews and transcribing and took a few years to finish. I am starting work next month on my first actual fiction novel that will be self-published. Now that I have learned the process of self-publishing thanks to Dollar Deal, I have a business plan in place for this start to my fiction writing career.

AN: Tell us a little about Johanna, your wife, how much of a supporter has she been throughout your career?

SL: She has been a huge supporter. We met a few years after I got the original Stephen King contracts, but when it came time to make it the second time around, we were together and she was a great help through that. She has also been very supportive of all my filmmaking endeavors as well as my goal of being a full-time writer. I try to pay it back by making sure to help out around the house while writing since she is working full time to provide a steady paycheck and insurance while I try to make my career in writing a reality. I make good money freelancing, so I am pulling my weight, but she is 100 percent behind me trying to get my career as an author going now that my filmmaking dreams have stalled out a bit.

AN: You ask this throughout your book so now it's your turn, If I may: What advice would you give to filmmakers and writers just starting out?

SL: Be ready for a lot of work. Making a movie is not easy and it requires not only a lot of work from you, but also a lot of trust in the people you surround yourself with. Find collaborators that share your vision of what it means to make a movie. Once you have that team together, everything else is easier. Don't go into a project thinking that you can do anything in the world, because you have to work within your means. Anyone who starts a project thinking the sky's the limit will often quit when they realize they can't move forward anymore. Next, know how to work with people. I had two problem children on my films *I Know What You Need* and WZZJD. One was a case of immaturity and the other a case of arrogance, and both people thought they were bigger than the project. Learn how to deal with these people to get the project done properly while not alienating them and putting yourself in a hole. Finally, don't quit, don't take no for an answer, and finish the damn movie.

AN: Lastly, What's next for Shawn S. Lealos?

SL: I am ready a lot right now in preparation for my journey back into fiction novel writing. That is actually what I was studying in college before I stepped into a filmmaking career. It has been 15 years since I sat down to write a fiction novel, so I am getting ready to start that up again in

October. After that, I am just going to concentrate on fiction writing for a while (mystery/thriller novels). I had an idea for another non-fiction book based on comic book movies, but after the slow sales for Dollar Deal, I am going to move in a different direction for now. I will return to the non-fiction book, but that will have to wait for now. I also have plans to attend some more conventions with the Dollar Deal book in 2016, so keep an eye open for that.

I want to thank Shawn for taking the time to speak with us today and also Thank him for contributing copies of his book as contest prizes for the 2nd Annual Stephen King Dollar Baby Film Fest at Crypticon Horror Con MN on October 23rd-25th, 2015. I wish Shawn great success in his future projects

Love Never Dies by Peter Szabo

Love Never Dies

Peter Szabo
December 13, 2015

PETER SZABO IS ORIGINALLY FROM Toronto, Ontario, Canada. Attending St. Martin Secondary School, later studying English Literature at the University of Toronto. After receiving his B.A., Peter appeared as an extra in TV and films. In 2006, he wrote, produced, and directed his first short film *A Day in the Life of a Psychopath*. Also in 2006, he produced the documentary *Change Now for the Future: Perspective from Guelphs Street Youth, Numb,* a music video, and feature film *Dead Genesis* for Foreign and USA distribution.

In 2008, he produced and directed his second short film *Moma & Theo*, 2010's *Too Low,* and 2012's *Love Never Dies*. Peter has many other credits to his name as well as other educational experience. Peter is the owner/Producer of Possibility Films and currently living in Ontario with wife, Irene.

Here is my review of *Love Never Dies*.

Stephen King's short story *Nona* was first published in 1978 as part of an anthology called, *Shadows*. It was later published in 1985 in King's short story collection *Skeleton Crew*. Even though Peter changed the title to *Love Never Dies*, the story is the same: a story about a college dropout drifter, Steve (played by Reese Eveneshen) making his way through Maine to Castle Rock.

A beautiful young woman called, Nona (played by Erin Stuart) mysteriously appears and leads Steve through a night of madness and murder! However, not everyone is who they appear to be and not everyone is so innocent. Repeating the line: "Do you love?", Nona is a force to be reckoned with.

Although the title has been changed and the ending is slightly different from King's original text, Peter Szabo has brought, in my opinion, one of the very best Dollar Baby adaptations ever to the screen! The film was top notch! The actors were perfectly cast, especially Erin Stuart as 'Nona'. She reminded me of a female version of Stephen King's Needful Things character, Leland Gaunt. The film was scary, thrilling, and kept my interest to the very end. *Love Never Dies* was made on a $10,000 budget and under 35 minutes, but you wouldn't have known any better because it had the look and feel of a full-length film. Peter has the eye for storytelling without losing King's flare to scare.

I very much enjoyed this film and even though all of the Dollar Baby filmmakers are all very talented and bring their own style and vision to King's works, this film is one of my Top Favorite Dollar Baby Adaptations I've ever seen. It was a hit this year at the 2nd Annual Stephen King Dollar Baby Film fest at the Crypticon Horror Convention in Bloomington Minnesota this October as well

Here is my Exclusive Interview with filmmaker Peter Szabo.

Anthony Northrup: Out of all the Stephen King short stories, what attracted you most to this one?

Peter Szabo: *Nona* was not my first choice to adapt. My first choice, *Mrs. Todd's Shortcut,* was not available on the Dollar Baby list. So I read most of the stories that were on the list and *Nona* really resonated with me. What appealed to me was that the story focused on the inner psychology of the protagonist rather than on some horrifying or supernatural gimmick. To be clear, I have loved Stephen King's writing for years, but there was a difference between reading a story for entertainment and integrating a story into my own creative process. In *Nona,* I was fascinated by the protagonist's obsession with this strange woman he meets one night and about how she can inspire or bewitch him into committing violent acts in a twisted form of chivalry. I liked the psychological obsession of the main character, and his susceptibility to suggestions from Nona. I easily imagined a suspense thriller movie and thought the story had a lot of interesting visual scenes.

AN: What changes did you make to make this your own as opposed to King's original text?

PS: The biggest change was to remove many of the bizarre supernatural elements, and in particular, the giant rat imagery. It's difficult to make supernatural creatures look realistic on film. Plus I knew it would simplify the filming and post-production process without special effects or CGI creatures. For me, it grounded the film in a more human story, too. I also eliminated the killing of the utility workers. I decided that viewers would see enough killing in the film to get the point that the main character had gone too far down a dark path to return. Oh, and I changed the title! I wasn't sure if movie watchers would know what genre of film I had made with the title NONA. It could be the name of a drama or a comedy about a grandmother (Nona is a common European name for grandmothers), and clearly my film was something quite different.

AN: So many Stephen King fans want adaptations to be as close to the book as possible, how do you handle the pressure to keep the fans happy?

PS: I have to admit that I didn't think about the fans when I first chose to make a Dollar Baby. I was more interested in filming a Stephen King story as a personal, artistic challenge. Adapting someone else's writing is tricky because I think you should only do it if you can take the story into your mind and heart, and make it your own. But I did feel that I had to keep the integrity of the story by maintaining the original story arc and the main character's journey. I'm grateful to Mr. King for providing the inciting story ideas and inspiration to develop and express my own art. Hopefully, something in the film resonates with fans in such a way that compliments King's ideas and leaves my expression as a variation on recognizable ideas.

AN: What was your main goal you wanted to achieve about this film?

PS: My main goal was to have the experience of filming a longer film as a stepping stone to filming a feature length movie. I have made short films with a few characters and scenes, but I wanted to take on something complex with multiple locations and a range of characters/actors. A secondary goal was to make a film based on a story that was not written by me. Rather than hunting around for a script that I could like, I thought I'd go straight to the source of some of the best storytelling in the world.

AN: Where was the movie filmed specifically and were there any obstacles to overcome while filming there?

PS: The movie was filmed in and around Guelph, Ontario, Canada, a small university town about 60 miles east of Toronto. The biggest obstacles were related to weather. Nighttime exterior temperatures were unseasonably cold. We had to bring a sleeping bag on set to keep the lead actress warm between takes. We also had to reschedule shooting on scene twice because it snowed in the middle of the production schedule and we had to wait for the snow to melt to maintain continuity. We also had a minor injury on set. During a night shoot, the fog-machine effects technician jumped into a ditch to avoid being seen while filming; he twisted his knee and tore his ACL. An on-set nurse examined the injury and declared it wasn't too serious. A P.A. drove the technician home and shooting resumed.

AN: How long was the film shoot and the process from start to finish?

PS: We shot on weekends in March and April of 2011. Editing and post-production lasted from April 2011 to October 2012.

AN: What is your greatest moment so far with the success of Love Never Dies?

PS: Screening the film in Toronto at the Blood In The Snow Canadian Horror Film Festival was a rush. Many of the cast and crew were there to share in the glory. The theatre was full with horror fans, other regional filmmakers, and *Fangoria* magazine writers. The film looked great on the big screen and I was relieved and proud to see that fans and critics liked the film a lot.

AN: What Stephen King story would you like to adapt on a large scale?

PS: I would love to make a feature length version of *Mrs. Todd's Shortcut*. Or maybe a trilogy of King short films that would include *Love Never Dies* (NONA), plus film adaptations of *Willa* and *Mrs. Todd's Shortcut*. I imagine the same actress playing all three female characters, as if the characters are all different manifestations of the one being.

AN: Where and When can fans see this film? Will it be playing many film fests across the USA?

PS: It's played at the BLOOD IN THE SNOW Canadian Film Festival in Toronto and the Macabre Faire Film Festival in Pennsylvania a couple of years ago, but there are no more scheduled film fest screenings, so this could be the last one!

AN: Your lead actor, Reese Eveneshen, is also very involved in the film with other responsibilities such as Producer, Editor, F/X Make-up; tell us how he got involved with the film?

PS: Reese and I have been helping each other with each other's movies for a few years now. We take turns directing while the other does whatever they can to help complete the project. We held casting sessions for the lead role in *Love Never Dies,* but I wasn't sold on the actors who auditioned. When I cast Erin Stuart as Nona/Betsy, Reese, who happens to be Erin's boyfriend, offered to play the lead role to have both lead roles conveniently accessible to the locations. When I saw his audition, I was sold that he could channel the perfect transition from weak and fragile to strong and deadly.

AN: Is it safe to say the female character in the film, *Nona* is almost a "spawn" of Stephen King's *Needful Things* character, Gaunt?

PS: I'll be honest…I haven't read *Needful Things* so Nona isn't a conscious spawn of Gaunt. Stephen King writes books faster than I can read them, and I haven't caught up to *Needful Things*, yet.

AN: Lastly, What is next for Peter Szabo?

PS: I directed a short film last spring and am just finishing the post-production sound mix and colour grading. It's called LIGHT AND SILENCE, and it's about a young woman who discusses her murder with God while watching the killing on a movie theater screen. And I'm producing a feature length science-fiction/action movie called DEFECTIVE, written and directed by my filmmaking colleague, Reese Eveneshen. We plan to start shooting over this winter and have it ready for festivals and sales agents by Fall 2016.

I want to thank Peter for his time and patience and wish him much success in his future projects

One For the Road

Jacob Sanders
May 7, 2016

THE STEPHEN KING DOLLAR BABY PROGRAM has been going strong for over 30 years and doesn't seem to be slowing down. More and more up-and-coming filmmakers are rushing to adapt one of Stephen King's short stories and be part of King history. The latest filmmaker to be part of the Dollar Baby family is Jacob Sanders. Jacob chose one of Stephen King's very early short stories in his career, *One For The Road*.

Jacob Sanders was born in Manitowoc, WI, son to Paul and Edie . Jacob came from an entertainment background for his parents were in that field. His father, Paul, a professor of music education and Edie an educator, actor, and theatrical director. Jacob moved to Newark, Ohio and graduated from Newark High School. He continued his education at Ohio State University graduating in 2011 with a Bachelors in Film Studies. Jacob is a screenwriter as well as director and is continuing his filmmaking career to date.

Here is my review of Jacob Sander's *One For The Road*.

Stephen King's short story, *One For The Road,* was originally published in the March/April of *Maine* Magazine in 1977. In 1978's short story collection, *Night Shift.* The story is a "sequel" to the Stephen King classic novel, *Salem's Lot.* On a cold , blizzard night, a young husband enters a small bar in a town not too far from Jerusalem's Lot where the events of Salem's Lot took place a few years earlier. The man is frozen to the bone, tired, and half dead from the cold winter storm outside. He tells the old men in the bar his car broke down and he must get back to his wife and child he left there. The old men fear the worst as they remember the events and horrors that took place in Salem's Lot before. They fear

One For the Road by Jacob Sanders

and have heard rumors that vampires still lurk in the area and something might have happened to his family. They head out to the abandoned car and what awaits them is a horror beyond this world!

I found this Dollar Baby adaptation very entertaining. I enjoyed seeing a "sequel" to one of King's stories and it was done right. Jacob captured the feel and vision of King's story, but putting his own spin on the tale. The winter outdoor scenes were very eerie and creepy, keeping the suspense building for the viewer. The cast all did a fine performance and well done. Very few King adaptations stick to the original story, but there are some that are adapted very well and Jacob's *One For The Road* is one of those.

And now, here is my exclusive interview with filmmaker, Jacob Sanders.

Anthony Northrup: Your parents both were employed in the education field and musical/acting background. Did this influence you and help prepare you for your film?

Jacob Sanders: My mother has acted in plays my entire life. As a child I have countless memories of cast parties and going to see her in plays. Directing films requires a certain degree of knowledge in several disciplines. You have to appreciate films, music, acting, writing, etc. Without the upbringing I was given I would have never thought to be a director, it would have never occurred to me. My father is a very humble man. He is talented and knowledgeable but he always lived a rather simple life, more simple than he could have, and I admire him for it. Filmmaking is a hectic and chaotic world with lots of emotions and egos. Standing on firm foundation is essential to success, I saw that in my father.

AN: What was your major in college and what made you decide to get into film?

JS: When I first went to college my declared major was Philosophy. Over time I realized I often enjoyed the Philosophical implications of novels, films, and art in general. During my senior year of high school I read Brave New World and decided I would set out to adapt it to a screenplay. I sat down and adapted the novel word for word, which of course is not how you adapt a novel. The end product was useless but the process began the demystification of screenwriting and that was valuable. At some point in college I took a Beginning Screenwriting class. I wrote a script that was very well received and that changed my direction.

AN: Just how cold was it while filming the night scenes in the snow?

JS: I still have the call sheets. The coldest reported temperature was 0 degrees Fahrenheit. An interesting story, after the first night of shooting the snow that had been trampled on was no longer good for use in our shots. At one point during the second night of shooting it snowed so much in about six hours that you couldn't see any of the tracks we made. It was almost like we had never been there at all, it was remarkable.

AN: Out of all the Stephen King short stories, what attracted you most to this story?

JS: There were three main reasons I was attracted to this story. First, it's an early Stephen King story. There aren't many stories left from that early in his career which are available to adapt as Dollar Babies. The second, it's a straightforward horror story. As King's career has progressed his work, including his short stories, have become more "literary" and less genre specific. Thirdly, and this isn't something to gloat about, it was difficult to shoot. I suspected that few filmmakers had attempted to preserve the snow storm element of the original story. In true over-ambition I decided to tackle an incredibly challenging short story to adapt. My thought was if I'm going to do it, I should do it all the way.

AN: What changes did you make to make this your own as opposed to King's original text?

JS: The first major difference is that the film is set in the present day. I liked this idea because it meant that Booth and Tookey had a more intimate attachment to *Salem's Lot* because they grew older with the legends. I included an AMC Eagle which is an interesting vehicle and very fun to drive in the snow. I am part of a weird community of people who collect AMC cars. It's my own personal touch. The music in the short, *Ghosts I – IV* by Nine Inch Nails, was influential throughout the production. I originally conceived of much of the short while listening to different tracks. I also wrote the script to the music, envisioning scenes with the music in my ears.

AN: So many Stephen King fans want adaptations to be as close to the book as possible, how do you handle the pressure to keep the fans happy?

JS: Ultimately it's impossible to preserve the essence of the story in an adapted film. One person may envision a character in one way and another may not. In the end the filmmaker will always lose. That being said there are great adaptations of many stories, but what generally sets them apart is that they're great films not necessarily faithful reproductions. Sometimes, rarely, those goals align and everyone is happy. Take for example Stanley Kubrick's *The Shining*, a movie Stephen King has made very clear he strongly dislikes. Of course, Kubrick is a master filmmaker. There are few filmmakers who have produced so many significant films. I personally love Kubrick's *The Shining*. That being said Kubrick was an asshole to King while making the film. He called King up in the middle of the night to ask him his thoughts on God and then publicly claimed that the novel was not literature. There is no substitute for having a strong personal vision, beyond that only time will tell whether the adaptation succeeded.

AN: What was your main goal you wanted to achieve about this film?

JS: My main goal was simply to make the short film. It was about seeing something through to completion. When I thought about making the film I thought in terms of my intentions and saw it as something to check off my list. Something I didn't anticipate was how much the finished short film would affect me. I feel much more emotionally involved with this short now that it's finished than I ever did while making it. I'm immensely proud of it.

AN: Where was the movie filmed specifically and were there any obstacles to overcome while filming there?

JS: There were three locations in the short. I hired a special duty officer to close a no outlet road so I could load the Eagle on a car trailer. I used a special suction cup rig to attach the camera to the outside of the car and then we pulled it up and down the road until I got my shots. The second location was the Red Brick Tavern in London Ohio. It sits on the old National Road and was visited by six presidents. I chose it because it had two working chimneys in the bar area, something surprisingly hard to find. The outside sequences were shot at the Dawes Arboretum in Newark Ohio. Aside from hiring a special duty officer for the car sequence, I rented fans and bought six hundred pounds of potato flakes to create some of the snow seen in camera. Working in the cold with a cold cast and crew is stressful. People think it'll be fine until they get out there.

AN: How long was the film shoot and the process from start to finish?

JS: I decided I was going to do this nearly two and a half years ago. Production really started January of 2015. We had five days of principal photography. Some of the footage used as the beginning of the film was stock footage graciously donated by Doug Jenson. After those five days of production it took me about six months to get the cut I wanted and then it was on to ADR and then color correction.

AN: What is your greatest moment so far with the success of *One For The Road*?

JS: Honestly, doing this interview and the general response of the short since it's been completed. It never really occurred to me that people would want to watch it or care about watching it. We live in a time when most people go to YouTube for their short video satisfaction. It almost feels like short films are completely irrelevant. I'm excited to see it go to festivals and what happens next.

AN: What Stephen King story would you like to adapt on a larger scale?

JS: I'd love to adapt *Salem's Lot* as a feature film. However, the idea of telling a new story based on the events of the novel *Salem's Lot* would also be interesting too. I think an adaptation of *Doctor Sleep* would be super cool.

AN: Where and When can fans see this film? Will it be playing any film fests soon?

JS: I've submitted it to some festivals and plan to submit to more. Eventually I'll release it online or something if permitted. My Facebook page for *One for the Road* is the place to get all the info on festivals and general updates.

AN: Lastly, What is next for Jacob Sanders?

JS: My next production is original and is a more personal story. It's a satire of Community Theater in a style reminiscent of Robert Altman. The script is finished. That project is a little far out, but I should get started on it soon.

I want to thank Jacob for his time and patience and wish him much success in his future films and look forward to seeing what he does next from this very talented filmmaker .

The Road Virus Heads North

Dave Brock
July 24, 2016

IT'S TIME ONCE AGAIN to take a walk into the world of Stephen King.

This time, I bring you a filmmaker from West Virginia, by the name of Dave Brock, and his adaptation of King's *The Road Virus Heads North*.

Dave Brock was born in Logan County, West Virginia on August 3rd, 1974. He attended Logan County High School and graduated in 1992. From there, he moved on to attend the West Virginia State University, where he majored in Communications, and graduated in 1998 with a Bachelor's in Science Communications.

Dave took a couple of years off, and once again continued his education at Ohio University. He graduated there in 2004, with a Masters of Fine Arts in Film Production, and Screenwriting.

Dave currently teaches at the West Virginia State University, and lives in Mount Gay, West Virginia.

And now, here is my review of Dave's adaptation of…*The Road Virus Heads North*.

Stephen King's short story, *The Road Virus Heads North*, was first published in 1999 in 999 Anthology. In 2002, it was published in King's short story collection: *Everything's Eventual*.

King himself has said he is a personal fan of "moving pictures" type stories (like in the TV series *Night Gallery* which starred Roddy McDowell). He has also said that the story was inspired by a painting in his house that only HE loved, everyone else in the family hated it.

This Dollar Baby film adaptation was directed by Dave Brock, and the screenplay by his sister, Rebecca Brock, and filmed on location, near

The Road Virus Heads North by Dave Brock

to where they lived in West Virginia, on a $10,000 film budget. Dave used locals, and some of the local businesses to cut costs. It was released on May 10, 2004.

The film later would be nominated for the Student Academy Award, by the Academy of Motion Pictures Arts and Sciences, in 2005. It would go on to play with other Dollar Baby, and other short films across the country at film festivals.

Here is my review of The Road Virus Heads North.

The story of *The Road Virus Heads North*, begins with a retired writer, Richard Linnell, who purchases a very creepy painting at an estate sale, he then suffers from nightmares as he continues his road trip from Boston to Derry, Maine.

As his journey continues, the painting itself changes along the way, with graphic and disturbing images. Several people die along the way, for the painting is cursed and has its own violent, scary backstory. Once Richard arrives at his destination, clues have been revealed, and the final outcome is not always a pretty one.

Dave Brock brings his story to life with his own take on this eerie tale that leaves you scared, and keeps you guessing all the way to the very end. Well acted, disturbing images, and a respect to King's original text, Dave brings new life to the tale.

I enjoyed this adaptation, and can see Dave Brock is not only a fine director, but a true visionary, and I look forward to his next Stephen King adaptation: *Woman In The Room* coming soon!

Here is my Exclusive Interview with filmmaker, Dave Brock

Anthony Northrup: What inspired you to major in film production and screenwriting?

Dave Brock: Oh, that's been a lifelong dream, to either make movies or be involved with the production of movies in some capacity. I'm from Southern West Virginia, so back in the late 80s/early 90s there weren't a lot of outlets for anyone who had the itch to make movies. Equipment was cost-prohibitive and it certainly wasn't as available (or portable, or budget-friendly) as it is now. My brother Matt, my sister Becky, and myself would instead write and produce plays throughout high school and my early college years, and I think that was probably one of the best ways to learn how to work with actors, since performance can make or break any film. It was also a good primer in learning how to maintain a composition for two hours; I always pretended as if I was composing a two-hour long master shot whenever I directed plays. Anyway, once I got into college, I transferred to West Virginia State University, which was the only university in the state at the time that offered any sort of courses in filmmaking. From there I went on to the School of Film at Ohio University in Athens, OH, and it was there that I really became interested in screenwriting; it was during my training there that my eyes were really opened, and I discovered that there was a lot more to film than cinematography and directing. Once I started tinkering around with narrative structure, a whole slew of filmmaking possibilities opened up.

AN: How did you get the nickname "B-Rock"?

DB: You know, that was given to me by some friends of mine in film school. It just sort of stuck. I consider it a gift by my peers, so I wear it like a badge of honor.

AN: On the film's credits, Rebecca and Matt Brock were listed. How are they related to you, and how did they first get involved in the film?

DB: Becky is my older sister, and Matt is my twin brother. I can't think of a time when I didn't work with them in some capacity in whatever film project I happened to be doing. I've written a lot of stuff with Becky (who is an exceptionally talented writer; I'm not just saying that because we're related), and I cast Matt in pretty much everything I do. He's my good luck charm. I know some filmmakers like to cast themselves in their own films, but I could never do that. I'm too camera shy. Matt is my cameo-by-proxy. He's also the monster in the Road Virus paintings, one of which I have hanging in my apartment. I gave another one as a gift to my mom.

AN: How many paintings were used for the film and who painted them?

DB: There were a total of seven paintings used in the film, and there were two that were made but we didn't use because we felt like it would have been too much. We also had two stunt paintings that were destroyed by either water or fire. They were actually photographs that were blown up and digitally altered by a talented artist by the name of Ocean Eiler, and my insanely brilliant production designer Krista Thomas applied a sort of lacquer to the finished "paintings" to give them texture and then mounted them onto canvas before framing. We shot the images in the middle of a large field, and Ocean added in the rest of the scenery for each painting digitally.

AN: What did you think of the 2006 version on the *Nightmares & Dreamscapes* TV series?

DB: I loved the cast, but my biggest gripe was how they handled the paintings. One of the creepiest parts of the original story to me was that Richard Kinnell never actually saw the paintings change; rather, they changed in some form while he wasn't looking. That kind of leads the reader to believe (for a while, at least) that maybe the whole thing is in his head. That was really important to me while we were shooting, that we never see the paintings change. The audience sees the change when Richard does. Also, the Road Virus needed sharper teeth. That was the thing that drew Richard in at the yard sale: the TEETH. The ending was also a little bizarre, but the ending to the original short story was also bizarre; I had trouble adapting that myself when I was doing my own version.

AN: Out of all the Stephen King short stories, what attracted you most to this story?

DB: The idea of paintings or photographs that change, that's always been something that's traditionally given me the heebie-jeebies. My sister Becky is actually responsible for the whole thing: she called me back in 1999 and told me about this creepy story that Stephen King wrote for an anthology called "999" (before it was published in *Everything's Eventual*) that dealt with a n evil painting that changed. She sent me a copy and I read it at, like, 3 in the morning and was completely creeped out by it. I knew I had to do a film version of it.

AN: What changes did you make to make this your own as opposed to King's original text?

DB: I'm not the type of filmmaker who feels the need to put his "stamp" or "mark" or "signature" or whatever you want to call it onto a film. At the end of the day, the film isn't about me; rather, it's for the audience to hopefully enjoy. That was one of the larger concerns I had when I sat down to try to adapt it: will the fans like it? Stephen King has a loyal fan base for a reason, and it's because of the way he tells a story. I felt that it was my responsibility to try and be as faithful to the source material as possible, because I thought it was terrifying enough as it was without me putting a flourish or whatever on it. So aside from some necessary alterations (the indoor estate sale as opposed to an outdoor yard sale, for example, because we shot in December), I tried to stick as close to the original story as possible. I added the nightmare sequence at the end as a way of introducing Bobby Hastings into the fold and visually establishing the mess he made of things when he dabbled with things he shouldn't have dabbled with, and the ending, well…I just had to end it. I think the story ended with Richard naked right out of the shower, which I understand that it makes the character seem more vulnerable toward the end, but I thought it would have been too gratuitous to film that as it was originally written. Since the ending of the story was a little open-ended, I decided to leave the ending to the film a little open-ended. Originally, we were going to end the film with an estate sale at Richard's house, and a little girl comes across an odd painting of a muscle car with Richard's head as a hood ornament (I actually have that painting, by the way), but we never shot it because it just seemed too much.

AN: So many Stephen King fans want adaptations to be as close to the book as possible, how do you handle the pressure to keep the fans happy?

DB: Well, I think it helps that I'm a HUGE fan of Stephen King myself, so I have my own barometer of what I think makes a good Stephen King adaptation good and what makes one…not so good. I put a lot of pressure on myself to try and deliver something as close to the source material that I can, so if I can somewhat satisfy my own needs as a lifelong fan, then hopefully others might enjoy the work as well. I always love to hear what other fans think of the work as well, and I consider every comment that's made, good or bad.

AN: What was your main goal you wanted to achieve about this film?

DB: I wanted to go for the creep out, first and foremost. If it's something that gets under your skin after you finish watching it, then I've done my job! I think there's a larger message about dealing with the inevitability of death, but I didn't want to get too heavy-handed with that. I've had people take away different things from the movie after they screened it, which I think is great. Audiences should draw their own conclusions about the meaning of any given work. I feel like talking too much about the reasoning behind the making of something takes away from it somewhat.

AN: Where was the movie filmed specifically and were there any obstacles to overcome while filming there?

DB: We shot the entire film in Athens, OH, which is just a filmmaker's dream, really. The locations are so diverse that you could substitute Ohio (and West Virginia, for that matter) for any other location in the country. We shot the nightmare sequence in the basement of an abandoned lunatic asylum, believe it or not, so that was fun. We left the insane scribblings of Bobby Hastings on the wall where we filmed with the hope that a tour group would walk through later and think an actual patient had written those things. Other locations included a local park (the lake shots), a rest stop, a university-owned alumni center that was based in an old, historic house (the estate sale), and for Richard's home we rented an empty house that was on the market for a few days. Interesting thing about that location is that we had to cheat and shoot all of the coverage for the living room scenes across two rooms to get the onscreen layout that we wanted, and that was again due in no small part to the brilliance of Krista Thomas (the production designer) and some tricky editing. Since wanted actors who were either SAG or SAG-eligible, we entered into a low-budget film agreement with SAG in order to make it legal all-around. The downside to doing that was we then had to adhere to SAG union rules in order to have professional actors for no pay. That meant we had to strictly adhere to an 8-hour shoot day,, meals had to be called within a certain time period after shooting started each day, actors had to be signed in and out etc. It was an extraordinary amount of paperwork that my wonderful producer Vicente Cinque handled every day without complaint. The paperwork had to be filed by a certain deadline, and if we violated any of these rules, then the salaries of the actors we used would have been due and payable, along with penalties. It was a little stressful, but we were super organized and got it done. The biggest obstacle we had to overcome was having to reschedule and redesign the entire shoot because we had managed to cast a very well-known horror personality: who shall remain nameless because my ears feel like they'll burst into flames every time I hear his name: for the part of Richard, and he had committed; we had the financing set and his deal was in place and everything was ready to go, and then he simply decides to not return our phone calls after he explicitly agreed to do it. We tried to get in touch with him up until a week before we were scheduled to begin shooting, but we heard nothing. This was in summer of 2003, so luckily I had an AMAZING crew and an awesome cast that we had coming in from New York City who took everything in stride and agreed to shoot in the winter instead. That meant Krista had to redesign EVERYTHING from scratch, which meant several more months for her in Athens instead of back at her home in New York. Meanwhile, the big shot horror guy who screwed us was off on another project, but in retrospect he did us a huge favor because I can't imagine anyone else in the role of Richard other than the one that we cast, the wonderful Denny Dalen, who taught acting for years at Ohio University. It really was a blessing in disguise.

AN: How long was the film shoot and the process from start to finish?

DB: The film was shot over seven consecutive days in December 2003; I remember the last day of filming vividly because that was the same day that Saddam Hussein was captured. Not counting the false start and redesign thanks to Big Shot Horror Guy, we spent about two months in pre-production and I edited the film over a period of four months during my last quarter of graduate studies. So all in all, maybe about six months, not counting the year it took to contact Stephen King for the Dollar Baby rights. Another Dollar Baby filmmaker by the name of Justin Zimmerman really helped me out with that one; we were both at the Ohio University School of Film at the same time, and he was pretty active with the project during its early stages. We originally planned to shoot in Maine and even went up and scouted in Bar Harbor and the town where *Storm of the Century* was shot. Justin went on to do his own Dollar Baby adaptation of *The Man Who Loved Flowers*, which I hear is really good.

AN: What is your greatest memory so far with the success of *The Road Virus Heads North*?

DB: You know, I think it has to be the day that I found out that it was nominated for a Student Academy Award, and it was exciting because I couldn't wait to share the nomination with everyone who had worked so hard on the film. I'm really proud of the film, but I'm more proud of the incredible effort that everyone put into it. Also getting to screen it alongside the premiere of a Tobe Hooper film at the 2005 New York City Horror Film Festival was pretty great, too!

AN: What Stephen King story would you like to adapt on a larger scale?

DB: Well, I would say *The Long Walk* but I think George Romero has the rights locked up on that one. I've had Dollar Baby rights to *The Library Policeman* for a while now (I requested it right after I finished Road Virus), which I'm dying to do, but I'm having trouble adapting the story. That would be the one I'd love to do, and I think it'll happen at some point. It's looking like *Nona* will be next; after we wrapped, *The Woman In The Room* a few weeks ago, I had students in my Stephen King class do presentations on other potential Dollar Babies, and *Nona* was selected by popular vote (*I Am The Doorway* and *Rest Stop* were the other contenders).

AN: Where and When can fans see this film at film fests?

DB: I'd like to get '*Road Virus*' back out there, though I seem to keep missing deadlines for some of the Dollar Baby fests. I have a terrible memory. With any luck, *The Woman In The Room*, will be finished in October, and I hope to hit the festival circuit shortly after.

AN: Lastly, What is next for Dave Brock?

DB: *Nona,* then a feature project that I'm currently writing, and hope will come together over the next few months (also based on a well-known horror story), then, the Adaptation Gods willing, *The Library Policeman.* If I could make Stephen King movies for the rest of my life, then I would die a very happy man!

I would like to thank Dave for taking the time for this interview and wish him much success in his future projects.

Rainy Season

Vanessa Ionta Wright
April 28, 2017

STEPHEN KING, KNOWN AROUND THE WORLD for over 40 years, as one of the "greatest writers of our time", has brought us some of the most frightening, intriguing, and mind bending stories. Also, over 60 of these stories have been adapted for the big screen, as well as television. It is with great pleasure, I bring you yet another… Dollar Baby… film review and interview, this time with a female director. I understand there aren't that many female Dollar Baby directors, and this in fact, is my second interview with yet another talented lady behind the camera, and her extraordinary vision of the story she chose.

Vanessa Ionta Wright, is one of the most energetic, enthusiastic, and talented directors I've had the recent pleasure to speak with. Her love for all things Stephen King, her knowledge of horror films, her excitement of filmmaking, all prove to make Vanessa the real deal! Vanessa has brought the Stephen King short story… "Rainy Season"… from the written page, to life on film. However, before I give you my review, let's learn a little a bit about Vanessa!

Vanessa Ionta Wright was born June 10, 1976, and grew up in Dayton, Ohio. She went through grammar school, eventually graduating from Stebbins High School in 1994. She continued her studies at the University of Ohio, graduating in 1998, with a degree in video production and film. After enjoying a bit of travel, Vanessa married, and now shares a happy life with husband, John Wright, since October 29, 2005, and their family.

She is the founder, and festival director of… Women in Horror Film Fest… and the owner of… Above The Line Artistry, LLC. Her film, *I Baked Him a Cake*, got Vanessa's feet wet, so to speak, as a director, but it was in 2016,she decided to join the Stephen King Dollar Baby program, and

Rainy Season by Vanessa Ionta Wright

bring the short story, RAINY SEASON, to the big screen. When I asked how she originally became interested in film, more specifically directing, she says, "how I got into film?" I always wrote and directed, I just didn't know that's what I was doing. I was always writing scripts, performing skits and plays for class, and family gatherings. When I was in high school, I would always ask the teacher if I could make a movie instead of creating dioramas, or making speeches. I wrote my first feature screenplay in college, it was wonderfully terrible! Outside of student projects in college, RAINY SEASON, was my directorial debut." And what a debut it is, but how good is it? Well, here is my review of… *Rainy Season*!

RAINY SEASON: 2017

There are so many wonderful, entertaining, and frightening Stephen King short stories. Stories such as, *The Mist, The Body, The Library Policeman, The Monkey, Survivor Type,* and *The Shawshank Redemption,* just to name a few. Personally, I feel *Rainy Season* is one of the top scary short stories King has ever written. When I heard I was getting the opportunity to see the adaptation of it, my expectations were very high , and I was NOT disappointed!

Rainy Season was originally published in *Midnight Graffiti* magazine, in the 1989 Spring issue. It was later published in the Stephen King short story collection, *Nightmares & Dreamscapes* in 1993.

The story is about a young couple who rent a vacant home in Maine, during the beginning of the summer season. Every 7 years, on June 17, a sacrifice must be made, so the locals can be spared to live yet another 7 years in peace. The couple were warned, they had their chances to leave, but they didn't listen. What comes later that night on the 17th, is horror of the most unspeakable kind, a storm, not of rain, but FROGS!

Like I said, my expectations of this short story being adapted to film were very high, and as I said, Vanessa's vision certainly did not disappoint! The lead actors did fine performances, the locations made you feel like you were really there in Maine during the balmy summer season, and this was one of the closest adaptations to a King story I've ever seen!

So, what makes Vanessa's direction different from the rest? Well, remember the classic horror film, *Jaws*? You didn't actually see the shark for quite some time, in fact not until later in the film, right? However, the anticipation of what was to come was actually intensified by the music, sound effects, suspense, and most importantly, your… imagination. That's exactly what Vanessa did, she built up the fright and horror of this story by using what I will call, "old school horror storytelling", and I loved it! You don't exactly SEE the frogs, but you hear them, giving you that creep factor of almost being able to feel them. This in itself, is worse than actually seeing them! In many cases, the anticipation of what comes next, is actually much more magnified and intense by leaving it to the imagination. Vanessa knew that, and this is why *Rainy Season* is what I consider to be one of the top best Dollar Baby films I've ever seen, and perhaps, one of the best film adaptations of any of his work!

It is based on a short story, yes, but it is not hyped up with what I call, fillers, meaning constant additions to the story to lengthen it. Rather, the story is in its most pure form, and it is executed perfectly. Short and sweet, no compromising the original story!

Here is my Exclusive Interview with *Rainy Season* director, Vanessa Ionta Wright.

Anthony Northrup: Out of all the Stephen King short stories, what attracted you most to this one?

Vanessa Ionta Wright: I actually did not know about the Dollar Baby program until someone on Facebook mentioned it and I thought "WHAT?... King will let you adapt a story for $1? No way!" I headed over to StephenKing.com, and checked out the list of available stories. Some of the stories I was very familiar with, and had actually seen that there were many adaptations of certain stories.

It was important to me to pick a somewhat less familiar story, and one that hadn't been adapted many times. I saw that Rainy Season had been adapted by Nick Wauters, in 2002, and it seemed he had taken a much more tongue and cheek approach, paying homage to the creature features of early horror. I knew I would have a very different film, and comparisons would more than likely not be made. When I picked up my copy of *Nightmares & Dreamscapes,* I was instantly hooked on this story. It reminded me of Shirley Jackson's *The Lottery,* which is one of my favorite short stories of all time. When I saw that King referenced that story in Rainy Season, I knew immediately that I had to adapt this one.

AN: Two songs by Ross Childress were used in the film. How did Ross get involved, and what was special about those two songs particularly that made you decide to use them in the film?

VW: First of all, I gotta say, Ross is an absolutely amazing musician, and I still can't believe he wrote 2 original songs, and did the entire score for us! Ok, here's how it went down. Bryan Dickerson (who played 'Man in Store'), was a huge supporter of our film from the very beginning. I finally meet Bryan face to face, and he says to me "Do you know Ross Childress?", and I'm like "The guitarist from Collective Soul?, yeah, I've heard of him".

Bryan proceeds to tell me that Ross is a huge fan of Stephen King, and heard about our little film, and wanted to write an original song for us. Enter the long, stunned pause by me. I reply with a resounding "YES PLEASE!" Working with Ross was amazing, he made it so easy. I explained that I wanted this big opening with amazing aerials and without being overly specific with titles, I wanted the audience to feel transported to around 1976. He and I had discussed some music, and he completely understood where my head was musically, and he delivered that amazing opening song. We were still in need of a composer and a song for the closing credits.

I wanted to license "I can see clearly now", by Johnny Nash, but the process was arduous and too expensive for our tiny budget. I went to Ross for musical guidance, and he said in the simplest terms "I'll write another song for you, and I would like to do your score too". Who says no to that? Not me. It was such an honor to work with him. We actually collaborated on my other short film 'I Baked Him a Cake'. He's a brilliant musician, I can't say it enough.

AN: Your two lead actors, Brian Ashton Smith, and Anne Marie Kennedy, were quite impressive. Tell us about their auditions, what did they bring to the table that won them their roles?

VW: Grant McGowen actually did the first round of casting and sent me the audition videos. I was immediately drawn to Brian. He has a great charisma, and I knew he would breathe the extraordinary life into this character. We were still in need of "Elise", so I did an open casting call online and set up callbacks. Brian was kind enough to join us so I could get him to read with the potential actresses and gauge their chemistry.

Anne Marie Kennedy actually auditioned earlier in the day, before Brian arrived, and I was very impressed by her performance. We were limited on time and I really wanted to see her read with Brian, but felt at the time it just wasn't going to happen. She left and we continued with our auditions. We saw Brian read with a few different actresses and something was missing. I kept thinking about Anne-Marie, so I called her, and luckily she wasn't too far away. I asked her to come back and read with Brian, and I watched them together and knew we had found what we had been looking for. Their chemistry was perfect. We had given them a pretty dark backstory to work with which gave us some beautiful tension on screen. So proud of these two, they really made my job easy!

AN: In *Rainy Season*, you went "old school" horror by letting the audience depend on suspense, sound, and imagination. Why did you go that route instead of "in your face" horror like today's films?

VW: I don't find "in your face" horror scary. I can appreciate a good gore fest, but I didn't want to cheat the audience out of the beautiful subtext of this story that I think would have been lost if we focused on the blood and guts. This could have very well been a very gory film, but that wasn't what this story is about. At least, it is not how I interpreted or envisioned this story for the screen. I grew up on Alfred Hitchcock and Rod Serling. Suspense has always been the key to building fear. I think that is the reason so much of King's work is so terrifying. He has such a gift for building suspense and allowing your imagination to take over. Hitchcock said it best, "There is no terror in the bang, only in the anticipation of it."

This is exactly how I approached *Rainy Season*. Sound was crucial in this film, and I wanted to play with the senses and create a very visceral experience for viewers. The way we approach the climax of the film is all sound, so it's completely dependent on the viewer's imagination as to how scary it really is. You don't see this a lot in horror because so much is given visually. I wanted to see if we could scare and disturb with just sound. I wanted the audience to be afraid of what wasn't being seen.

This is why we took the focus off of the toads, and never even mention them by name. We wanted the audience to imagine the monster and build it up. This makes for a different viewing experience for everyone, which is an amazing thing to create as a filmmaker.

AN: What did you use for the sound effects for the thunder and the various frogs?

VW: This question actually needs to go to our phenomenal Sound Designer, Dave Wilson at Crawford Media. What talent! I handed over the film and explained the plan. When I wrote the script, I knew that sound was going to play a crucial role. This film was not going to work without amazing sound design and music. Dave has an extensive library of sound, and he created a brilliant soundscape for us. He also created the entire audio of the film in 5.1 surround sound, so it should be explosive and terrifying in theaters that are set up for this.

AN: The actors you used for supporting roles were quite impressive, what former acting experiences did they have, and did you use any locals as extras?

VW: Both Jan Nelson and Kermit Rolison, had quite a bit of film/television/theater experience. Jan brought a beautiful darkness to the role. In King's story, there was something playful between Henry and Laura. I wanted to keep the story dark, so I reworked the tone of the scene at the mercantile. We even wrote out the dog, but mostly for safety reasons. It was one of the hottest days in middle Georgia, and I just couldn't, in good conscience, have an animal in that heat. The funny thing about Kermit, is that he was not originally cast as Henry. Alpha Trivette was set to play the role, but at the last minute was requested by Tyler Perry to join him in LA. How are you going to turn down Tyler Perry? We were a day away from shooting the mercantile scene, and I was in a mini panic. My awesome, problem solving producer Stephanie Wyatt, was like "it's fine. I know a few actors. I got this" She pulled up an actor's reel on my laptop about 30 minutes before our call that evening. I was like "who is this guy! He's great! Is he available?" Her reply... "His name is Kermit Rol... " STOP. "His name is Kermit? We are making a film about a man eating toads, and our "town local" is named Kermit?" I found the entire moment serendipitous.

As far as the extras, our jump roping girls, and the man in store? Short answer, yes, they are all local to the Atlanta area. We had gotten a little creative with raising money for the film and hosted a red carpet silent auction last June. All in, our budget came to $18k, and we had raised around $7700 on Indiegogo, and needed quite a bit more to pull this off. Many of the local businesses in Senoia, GA donated items to our auction, and then I had the bright idea to auction off a role in the film. I had no idea people would be in a bidding war over this. Bryan Dickerson won the role, however I was so impressed with the tenacity of 10 year old Lillian Gray. I had an idea of adding something original to the mercantile scene, and what's creepier than children chanting obscure schoolyard rhymes?

I felt like a pair of children would work better, and my daughter Emma had begged to be in the film, nepotism as its finest. I actually really love the addition of the children, adding a whole additional layer of strangeness to the town.

AN: I noticed there were a few "nods" to Stephen King throughout the film, was this done on purpose?

VW: Absolutely! This was done for the die hard King fans, and the off chance that King himself would actually see the film (fingers crossed). Our license plates on the picture cars, the names in the guestbook, the make of the couple's car, even composition of some of the shots. All of these playful winks to the Master of Horror! I personally love little details in film, and as a viewer, I am always looking for them. These details usually go unnoticed by most, but I appreciate them and I know others do too.

The Missouri plate on the Buick reads SK1-237, a little nod to Stephen King, and the room number from Kubrick's version of the Shining. The Maine plate on Laura's truck reads 217-019, a nod to the recurring number throughout *The Dark Tower* series, and the room number from *The Shining* novel. The Buick was a happy accident, we were looking for period cars and we lucked out with the Buick, and it seemed so fitting since King had written an entire novel around a Buick. Majority of the guest book was filled with the cast and crew, but we tossed in 2 names that King fans would recognize. R. Flagg and B.E. Smith, one referencing the infamous villain that pops up in several of King's novels, and the other referencing the man who literally, almost took King's life.

AN: In one scene, your lead actor is typing, as he plays a writer in the film, did you have him watch other Stephen King films for inspiration, such as "Jack Torrance", in *The Shining*?

VW: It is widely known that King is not a fan of Kubrick's version of *The Shining*, however, there were some amazing shots in that film. My favorites being the opening with the VW Beetle winding through the mountains, and the shot of Jack typing in the lobby of the hotel. I used those two scenes as inspiration for the corresponding scenes in *Rainy Season*.

Tom Black did a wonderful job capturing the aerial footage from the beginning of the film, giving us that isolation we were going for. The lonely Buick on these isolated roads stretching into the "cursed" town of Willow. I did reference the scene where "Jack Torrance" is typing in the lobby of the Overlook and spoke with Brian about that scene. We set up this great scene between "John" typing and "Elise" relaxing in the bath. I think the silence and space between the characters created some great tension, and a disconnect in their relationship. I love how this scene opens on Brian Ashton Smith. There is something quite off-putting when a shot is straight on and perfectly symmetrical, it creates a wonderful uneasiness. Our DP, Mark Simon, crafted it perfectly. These are easily my two favorite scenes in *Rainy Season*.

AN: What did you use as the "frog goo"?

VW: I don't want to give away any SFX secrets, and I actually don't know what all went into the "goo" recipe, but I know the main ingredient was lube. Our SFX makeup artist, Nadine Al-Remaizan had some great, budget friendly ways to create what we needed. I can only imagine her going from store to store buying up all the lube. I wonder if Costco or Sam's carries it in bulk?

AN: There was a quote in the film from the Bible, Psalms 106:38, why did you pick that particular quote?

VW: To me, when there are stories of sacrifice, it always feels biblical. Even though the original story by King makes no literal reference to anything biblical, I still had a sense that there was some underlying, old-testament stuff happening here. I mean, we already had the frogs which according to the bible was the second plague. Psalms 106:38 had a very literal mention of sacrifice, which is what *Rainy Season* is about.

This small town is plagued with terror every seven years, and a sacrifice must be made in order for the town and its inhabitants to prosper. I think this particular bit of scripture fits quite nicely with the story.

AN: The ending of the film sort of leaves the story open, would you do a sequel if you could?

VW: Absolutely. Actually, I would maybe want to do a prequel and see how we got here. There are so many directions this story could take, expansion would be a lot of fun.

AN: What changes did you make to this story to make it your own as opposed to King's original text?

VW: I had never adapted anything before and I wasn't sure what the rules were. King's work is tough to tackle as so much of it is internalization. How do you show this? I started my first draft with a very true to the original story, scene by scene, line for line adaptation. Then I started to wonder about John and Elise and their relationship. Maybe it wasn't perfect. Maybe there was a reason they needed to get away, other than time for John to write his novel. Maybe they needed to rebuild something that had broken. There were so many places that I wanted to explore with them to create this beautiful tension. I thought it made it more desperate, there was so much more to lose. I kept it vague, as I thought it made it more interesting and more relatable for the audience to try and decipher what might be going on between them. By pulling the focus off of the town and the toads, it created a sadness.

In the 20 minutes of this film, we feel for the Grahams, and it makes the climax of the film that much more impactful. I tried to rely on visuals and subtext, and remove any dialogue that I felt wasn't absolutely necessary. I wanted the theme of the story to remain intact, of course. I am a huge fan of Stephen King, and I wanted a film that fans would enjoy.

I darkened the tone up a bit from the original text. I found the original story to have a lighter side to it, which creates a nice balance, but for the film I wanted it dark, I wanted the seriousness of the situation to come through. King describes these toads with such colorful visuals, but I still wasn't sure how we would ever create these monsters and live up to how they were imagined. So that is where I left them, in the viewer's imagination.

AN: So many Stephen King fans want adaptations to be as close to the original story as possible, how do you handle the pressure to keep them happy?

VW: I think as long as you stay true to the tone and the meat of a story, you'll keep them happy. I also wanted a film that Stephen King himself would enjoy. We had tremendous talent behind this film, from the actors to the crew, to the post production team. I knew we would have a beautiful film, the pressure was to make a film that was unmistakably King. Some things were changed due to logistics and budget. If there was a way to get information across visually, I did it, so we dropped quite a bit of dialogue from the original. Honestly though, I tried not to think about making King fans happy, because you really can't please everyone. We took some big risks in our adaptation and I think there are fans that are going to really love it, and there will be some who will hate it, and there will be fans in between.

I wanted a film that everyone involved in making it would be proud of. This film was my directorial debut, so the pressure was really to make a great film, and prove I had the directing chops necessary to pull this off.

AN: What was the main goal you wanted to achieve with this film?

VW: The main goal was to create quality film that entertains. I was not willing to cut corners, and we didn't have to. The level of experience amongst the cast/crew was astounding. I wanted high production value and we got it. I wanted a film that looked big budget, but would cost very little. Look what we can do for $18k, imagine what we can do with a million!

I also really enjoy the challenges that come along with independent film production. I think it makes you appreciate everything just a little bit more, and I think ultimately, it makes you a better filmmaker and storyteller. At the end of the day, I wanted a film that showcased everyone's talent and would lead to more opportunities doing what we love most.

AN: Where, and when was the movie filmed specifically, and were there any obstacles to overcome while filming there?

VW: The film was shot in Senoia and Haralson, GA in August of 2016. We must have scouted a few dozen homes searching for the perfect "Hempstead House". We knew we probably wouldn't find everything in one location. The perfect basement might not be attached to the perfect living space, and the perfect exterior might not have the right interiors. I had heard from someone on Facebook that the film Lawless (2012 starring Tom Hardy & Shia LaBeouf), was shot in Senoia, and they had built a location for the film that was still there and vacant. This location was exactly what we were looking for, and to top it off, it was surrounded by an abundance of lily pads covering a majority of the water. The amount of frogs and toads at this place was unbelievable, I thought we might have been punk'd! There is no way this place could exist and be available to us! Our art department did a wonderful job creating the sets. They turned the location from a depression-era saloon, into a quiet cabin in Maine. The biggest obstacles to shooting there… snakes, and no running water or electricity. We were able to rent a generator and a portable bathroom, which covered 2 of our issues. The snakes… well no one got bit! Our mercantile location was actually a working store in Haralson, and was open for business during the shoot. I think the biggest obstacle during the mercantile shoot was the heat. That was by far the hottest day, and keeping everyone cool and hydrated was our priority.

I think the biggest challenge for the entire shoot was… time. We had two day shoots, and two night shoots, and we did our best to keep to a 12 hour day. This was an ultra low budget non-union shoot, but we did our best to keep it running professionally, and as close to union guidelines as possible.

AN: How long was the film shoot and the process from start to finish?

VW: I think the previous question was meandering into this one. So, we had originally scheduled a five day shoot, but I kept reworking scenes based on possible weather, location constraints, etc. Once I finally locked the shooting script and reworked the shot list we realized we would be able to do this in four days if we stayed on schedule. Our AD had his work cut out, but he kept that crazy train on schedule. This turned out to be the best thing that could have happened, because cutting a day of shooting saved some money that we were then able to put into post production.

So, start to finish… I acquired the rights to the story in July of 2015, launched crowdfunding in February of 2016, shot the film August 11, 12, 13 & 15, 2016, began post production in December 2016, and had the final film in my hands March 10, 2017. With that timeline, this should have been a feature! There were so many moving parts, it was like being the ringmaster for a six ring circus. Ross Childress was writing and composing music, while our sound designer was building a terrifying atmosphere of sound, all while our visual FX artist was creating the "rain". It came together beautifully.

AN: What is your greatest moment so far with the success of *Rainy Season*?

VW: Each moment seems to get better than the last, so I think the greatest moment is still ahead. It was so great to be able to showcase the film for the community that supported us. We wanted to share the screen with other indie filmmakers, and just have a fun night, so we launched the… Rainy Season Short Film Independent Showcase… and invited filmmakers to screen with us. I think the greatest moment so far, actually, was seeing the finished film. To see the evolution of the entire project from original published story, to adapted screenplay, to film. It was great to see it come to life.

AN: Which Stephen King story would you like to adapt on a large scale?

VW: So much of his work has been adapted for the screen, maybe more than any other modern author that I'm aware of. There is still so much I haven't read! And every time I finish a book, or a collection of tales I think, 'This should be a movie', then BAM, it's already in development. I really enjoyed *Doctor Sleep* and thought it would make a great film, and I do think it is already in development. If not… I'm available to help!

AN: Where can fans see this film? Will it be playing at film fests across the country?

VW: As you know, Dollar Babies cannot be distributed or screened publicly outside of a festival, however, I am entering the film in festivals around the world, and will keep the website (www.rainyseasonmovie.com), and social media pages updated on where and when it screens.

AN: You said once, quote: "I love scary movies and scary stuff, and I love scaring people, but I don't like to be scared… " What scares you? What is your favorite horror film, also, what is your favorite Stephen King book, and why?

VW: You are right, I did say that. I do love the thrill of watching a film and having the hair on the back of my neck stand up. I also really love exploring all those dark places in my imagination, and creating frightening stories. But I'll be honest, I startle very easily, and I will not investigate strange noises, and I am terrified of haunted houses. Not real ones, I'll take a paranormal experience any day, but those novelty attractions that pop up during Halloween. I am terrified! I despise being chased, or surprised with chainsaws, or other power tools. I guess that leads into the next question of what scares me. At the core, I think losing control scares me. I'm not in control in those places, and I think that scares the hell out of me. I don't know where the monsters are hiding, or when they're gonna pop out. Just talking about it has me jumpy. I hope no one is creeping up behind me!

Favorite scary film… are you kidding me? So many choices. Favorite slasher? Favorite psychological thriller? Favorite supernatural? This one is hard. I love so many for so many different reasons. I really love the original *Halloween* (1978), *A Nightmare on Elm Street* (1984), *Poltergeist* (1982), *The Exorcist* (1973)… I feel like I am giving you such a clichè list of films, but they really are great. I LOVE the original *Twilight Zone* episodes, and I really love the films of Alfred Hitchcock. A more modern film that I really enjoy is *The Strangers* (2008). Maybe it would be easier for me to send you a Billboard Top 100 style list! Favorite Stephen King Book?… another tough one, but I think I have to go with, *IT*. That book really resonated with me, and scared the shit out of me! Maybe because I was younger when I read it. Creating an entity that is everything you ever were afraid of! Brilliant! I'm actually very excited about the new film, and to see what they have done with the story.

AN: Lastly, What is next for Vanessa Ionta Wright?

VW: I want to enjoy the success of *Rainy Season,* and see how it does in festivals. I was able to direct another short last summer called *I Baked Him a Cake,* which was written by Samantha Kolesnik (Executive Producer of *Rainy Season*), and that will be making the festival rounds as well. The next big thing is the film festival that Samantha and I co-founded called, The Women in Horror Film Festival. We are so excited about this fest, and so proud of the growth so far. Sam and I also want to make more films together. She has written a really fun gothic horror that she has offered to me to direct, and hopefully we can bring Mark Simon back on board to DP. It's a magical team when we all work together! One thing that would be amazing, that I would love to happen next… I would love a phone call from Stephen King, saying he saw Rainy Season, and that he loved what we did. Then I would love for that call to end with him saying "we should work together." In all seriousness, I want to continue writing and directing. Small scale, large scale, I want to make films. If you were looking for a literal answer to the question of what is next for me… lunch, a sandwich to be more specific. I love sandwiches! There you have it, the director's perspective!

I want to thank Vanessa for this opportunity, and with the "fan girl excitement", she has for horror and filmmaking, I have no doubt she will have great things to come in the near future. Look for *Rainy Season* at a film fest near you!

I Am the Doorway

Joe Kowalski
August 16, 2017

THERE ARE PLENTY OF STEPHEN KING adaptations, however, the very talented Dollar Babies that adapt King's short stories are some of the very best, which leads me to my latest Dollar Baby interview. This time it's from a young director in the Great Lakes region of Ohio, who has had a love for films and filmmaking since he was a young child.

Filmmaker Joe Kowalski, has brought his vision of Stephen King's short story, *I Am The Doorway* to the screen, and here is my review of the film, and exclusive interview, but first, let's find out just who Joe Kowalski is.

Joe Kowalski was born on March 19, 1995, and lived in Oberlin, Ohio, and lived in the big city of Cleveland as well. He attended St. Paul High School in Norwalk, Ohio, and graduated in 2013. After graduating, Joe attended Lorain County Community, and later graduated from Cleveland State University. Joe majored in Film Digital Media, and graduated in May 2017.

As a child, Joe played around with video cameras and watched endless DVD's, particularly the "special features" sections so he could learn more about films. He enjoyed Pixar films, and still does.

Joe heard about the Stephen King Dollar Baby program from his former girlfriend. She helped him write the initial story treatment. According to Joe, she is a HUGE Stephen King fan, and suggested he give it a try, and adapt his own vision of King's works, so that being said, Joe chose *I Am The Doorway*, one of King's few Sci-fi stories.

Joe wears many hats, he is a director, actor, editor, and occasional Youtuber.

Along with his Stephen King adaptation, he has also worked on stop motion, CGI, and four other short films: 2014's *One Day: A Musical*, 2015's *Billie Bob Joe*, 2016's *Prism*, and 2016's *I Am The Doorway*.

I Am the Doorway by Joe Kowalski

Here is my review of Joe Kowalski's, Stephen King's... *I Am The Doorway*.

Stephen King's short story, *I Am The Doorway*, was first published in 1971's March issue of *Cavalier* magazine. It was later published in King's short story collection, *Night Shift*.

The story is about a disabled astronaut who is exposed to a toxic chemical during their mission to Venus. The lead character has his hand bandaged, it itches him something terrible, and suddenly eyeballs appear on his body as "doorways".

It's an alien life form who wants to take over by annihilating all mankind!

Joe's vision of this story is simple, but eerie. The music throughout the film plays a key role. The actors did a fine job capturing the story line and bringing it to life.

Toward the end of the film, the F/X are very *Twilight Zone ish*, which I personally enjoyed and found to be very clever. I felt it leaves the audience with an open ending, however I feel most viewers are looking for a more conventional and definitive ending. I still found the adaptation very entertaining, and done on the budget that was allowed, it was amazing to say the least.

Here is my Exclusive Interview with Joe Kowalski.

Anthony Northrup: When did your love for films and filmmaking first begin?

Joe Kowalski: It really began when I first picked up the family video camera as a youngster. Ever since then I was writing scripts, filming videos with my siblings as actors, and creating my own stop-motions.

AN: You told me the "special features" section of a DVD is what attracted you also to filmmaking. When did you first discover that this was of interest to you, and are there any special features that stand out in your mind as your favorite, or helped you?

JK: It was really the special feature on the *Monsters, Inc.* disc. That was the first DVD my family bought, and it blew my mind. Pixar was incredibly thorough on their DVD releases to show how they went through every single step of their process, and in a very fun way at that.

AN: Growing up watching a lot of films, who were your inspirations?

JK: I was really inspired by a lot of influences many other people are inspired by... Spielberg, and Citizen Kane and all that... but I particularly like the work of Charlie Kaufman. I enjoy movies that are high-concept but still accessible. I also love really clever family affairs, like the work that Jim Henson did, and Pixar and Disney continue to do.

AN: How did you first hear about the Stephen King Dollar Baby program?

JK: I had heard about it years ago, but had long forgot about it. It was only when my ex–a huge Stephen King fan–brought it up to me when we were still dating, that I considered doing something with it. She's credited as a co-director because she was so influential in the early stages of it.

AN: I understand you are quite the fan of Pixar, and have worked with CGI and computer animated shorts. Do you enjoy, or find it more challenging working on those type films, rather than live-action films?

JK: All of my animation expertise has been quite rudimentary. Although I fiddled with CGI, I much prefer live-action for my workflow. It's much more efficient on a low-budget.

AN: Out of all the Stephen King short stories, what attracted you most to this one?

JK: Out of all the Dollar Babies, it seemed the easiest to turn into a no-budget affair when a few changes were applied to it! I also thought it was quite a fun little read.

AN: What changes did you make to adapt this as your own, as opposed to King's original text?

JK: The biggest change was when we added a framing story with two characters discussing the original story, in order to give an excuse to show only the scenes we could afford to shoot from King's text. The framing story adds a nice parallel to the events of the original story as well.

AN: So many Stephen King fans want adaptations to be as close to the book as possible. How do you handle the pressure to keep the fans happy?

JK: I believe that an adaptation has to work within what's best for its medium, and that doesn't always mean following the original story note-for-note. *The Wizard of Oz* could only be a great movie because it adapted the story in a way that worked best for the film, as opposed to what works for a novel. The same goes for any adaptation. It's more important to capture the feel of the original work, than it is to capture every detail.

AN: What was the main goal you wanted to achieve with film?

JK: It was a fun side project that we could show alongside the much bigger film I was working on at the time, called *Prism*. My main goal was to stop worrying about the big film and give my brain something else to chew on temporarily!

AN: Where was the movie filmed specifically, and were there any obstacles to overcome while filming there?

JK: It was filmed throughout the Cleveland, Ohio area. The biggest obstacle was that we filmed the outdoor scenes on a frigid day in October. To make matters worse, we filmed by Lake Erie, which made the sound unusable. We had to redub all of those scenes in post.

AN: How long was the film shoot and the process from start to finish, and was the budget really only $250?

JK: It really was! The entire film was shot in a weekend, although the full film took several months through its complete conception. Like I said, it was something of a no-budget way of relieving my mind a bit, and giving us something to show alongside our other film.

AN: What is your greatest moment so far with the success of *I Am The Doorway?*

JK: Well getting this interview is definitely a high point! Also showing it to an audience was a great deal of fun.

AN: Which Stephen King story would you like to adapt on a larger scale?

JK: I think *The Stand* would be an interesting challenge.

AN: Where can fans see the film? Will it be playing at film fests?

JK: We're trying to get it in some, so stay tuned!

AN: There have been other Dollar Baby versions of this story. What do you feel makes yours separate from the rest?

JK: I like that we weren't afraid to tinker with the story a bit. Most of the adaptations I've seen of the story stick pretty closely to the original, but it was fun (and daunting), to play around with what Mr. King did first.

Well there you have it, another great short story by author Stephen King adapted to film. It always amazes me to see these films from each of these great directors for the Dollar Baby Films. This time Joe Kowalski showed us his vision from behind the camera. Thanks Joe!! It was a pleasure to view your film, and to do this review and interview with you and wish you great success.

The Doctor's Case by James Douglas

The Doctor's Case

James Douglas
August 20, 2018

IN THE LATE 1970S when author Stephen King created his Dollar Baby program, it allowed for three things: helped independent filmmakers bring their love and vision of Stephen King short stories to life, gave opportunity to amazing filmmakers from around the world to showcase their work, and gave viewers a chance to see some of their favorite Stephen King short stories on the big screen (if they were lucky enough to make it to an independent film fest).

I have had the honor of seeing many of these adaptations of King's work brought to film , as well as the privilege of reviewing, and interviewing many of these fine directors. This brings me to my latest Dollar Baby review from a Canadian filmmaker, who has brought us a short film based upon a Stephen King short story surrounding the legendary Sherlock Holmes. This story is, *The Doctor's Case* directed by James Douglas.

The Doctor's Case was first published in 1987 in the Centennial Collection of *The New Adventures of Sherlock Holmes*. It was later reprinted in the Stephen King short story collection, *Nightmares & Dreamscapes*, in 1993. The story is narrated by an aged Dr. Watson, who tells the tale of the murder of Lord Hull, which brings the famous Sherlock Holmes out of retirement to solve what just might be his last case.

It's Inspector Lestrade, who calls on the famous duo to solve this murder of a wealthy, not well liked man, who has a family that is out for one thing: his money! However, how can there be a murder when it seems impossible for anyone to have gotten in or out of the scene of the crime? Only from the mind of Stephen King, and through the vision of James Douglas, can we obtain the answer, and what an answer it is!

I have seen many Stephen King Dollar Baby films, and without question, this is one of my top favorites! It's very impressive for James Douglas's first film as a Dollar Baby independent director. The locations and sets are amazing, the musical score lends an eerie quality, and the casting is great! James not only features new upcoming actors, but also has the support of two veteran actors, who have both been in prior King films, Denise Crosby of *Pet Sematary,* and William B. Davis, who was in *The Dead Zone,* and the 1990 version of *IT,* but is most noted for his long standing role as the "Smoking Man", on televisions *The X Files.*

The Doctor's Case is the only Stephen King short story about the famous Sherlock Holmes, and the film will appeal to both King and Holmes fans alike. James did do something with this Dollar Baby which I've never seen before in the short films category , he added a scene after the credits! I loved that extra touch! I can honestly say that I hope all of you who have the opportunity to attend the next, "It's a Dollar Baby Independent Film Festival", will look to see if this fine film is among those presented, as you will thoroughly enjoy it.

Without further ado, here is my exclusive interview with this down to earth filmmaker, who is now a part of the Stephen King universe with his adaptation of, *The Doctor's Case.*

James Douglas was born in Oshawa, Ontario Canada, and currently resides in Barkerville, British Columbia. He's also spent time in the United States, studying acting in New York City. He studied Theatre History at the University of Victoria, as well as English Literature. When James switched from acting to screenwriting, his love for film and Stephen King collided, and in 2017 he brought Stephen King's short story *The Doctor's Case* to life.

When he isn't filming, he's busy writing, working as a manager for the Visitor Experience and Public Relations, in Barkerville Historic Town & Park. However, with the support from his wife, Danette Bee, and his own passion, James is becoming an unstoppable talent.

And now, here is my exclusive interview with Dollar Baby filmmaker, James Douglas.

Anthony Northrup: You are originally from British Columbia, Canada, what was it like growing up there, and at what age did you first become a Stephen King fan? What was the first King book you read?

James Douglas: Growing up in BC was magical, really. I was born in Oshawa, Ontario but moved across the country to the Okanagan Valley with my mom at a young age, so I definitely consider myself to be from British Columbia (and I couldn't be happier about that). Living in Vernon, BC for the bulk of my early years meant equal parts outdoor recreation, indoor pursuits like music and theatre, and a healthy dose of striving to leave what I considered to be small town drudgery, for the bright lights of a big city somewhere. It's funny, because when I go back to Vernon as an adult, I am reminded of what a progressive, exciting, and growing city it really is. Back then it seemed terribly small and boring. Now I very happily live in a secluded mountain town of 250 people. Go figure.

As for my Stephen King fandom: it began in earnest for me in the eighth grade. I had seen The Shining when I was ten or eleven years old (some friends and I stayed up late one night at a sleepover to watch it on TV), and I remember it scaring the hell out of me, but I hadn't' read any of King's writing until I was thirteen. I can very clearly recall the circumstances, too.

In grade eight I was forced to take an Industrial Arts course because at the time they frowned upon boys taking Home Economics (which, to be honest, would have been much more useful to a latch-key kid like me). One of the four units of the course was on electricity, and I just couldn't get into it. As a result, I never had my homework finished in time for class, as was required. Our teacher had a strict no homework policy: if you showed up to class and the work wasn't done, you sat out in the hall for the remainder of the hour. I sat in the hall a lot, so a good friend of mine lent me a copy of Stephen King's *IT* to help pass the time. I had hardly even seen a novel that big before, let alone read one that size, but I had nothing better to do. The second I started reading *IT* I knew I was in for the long haul. Three times a week during that class I sat in the hall devouring that book, and it fueled my subsequent passion for both Stephen King and literature in general. I wound up with an English Lit degree many years later, and I attribute that to my early exposure to reading (thanks, Mom and Dad), and specifically to those freshman afternoons reading *IT* in the hallway of the high school IA building.

AN: I learned in my research that you were an actor before you became a director. Why did you switch gears, and which position do you find more challenging?

JD: I was (and am, in some respects), a working actor for a number of years. I have always been interested in directing, however, right from my earliest days of fantasizing about what it would be like to make movies out of my favorite comic books and novels, to the mini-plays I would produce and direct in elementary school, to Fringe Theatre Festival projects later in life, and so on. I have spent time writing, producing, and directing stage shows since then, and have written a bit, and produced a bit more for documentary films and narrative shorts. Feature film directing was a secret burning desire of mine, but it took a very long time for the right project to come along that would shake the fear out of me once and for all, and demand that I make the movie I wanted to make, with the folks I wanted to make it with, right here and right now; a project that would not take no for an answer. That project was *The Doctor's Case*.

AN: You moved to New York for a while, was that while you were learning your craft as an actor?

JD: For the most part, yes: I started my career as a professional stage actor after leaving Vernon in the early-1990s. I took a year of English transfer courses at the local community college, but when it came time to go to university I decided theatre was my calling. I had spent a lot of time in community and high school musicals up until that point: performing, directing, building sets, what have you: and like so many star-struck kids before me, I wanted to see if I could make it to Broadway! So I took two years of theatre at the University of Victoria on Vancouver Island before transferring to the American Academy of Dramatic Arts in New York. It was a life-changing experience.

I learned a tremendous amount about the craft of acting in NYC, and even more about myself as a person. One of the most important things I learned there (although it took a few years to really take hold), was that I honestly didn't want to be an actor in the traditional sense. The bright lights of the big city I had dreamt about for so long didn't enthrall me as much as I thought they would, and the day to day grind of what it takes to be a consistently working actor in places like New York or Los Angeles woke me up to the realities of that lifestyle. I really love performing, but it is not the only thing I love to do, and I started to feel that in order to make any kind of sustainable career for myself as a jobbing actor, I would have to devote everything I had to the pursuit of that one thing. That realization kind of turned me off of the whole thing, to be perfectly frank.

Don't get me wrong, I have the utmost respect for those friends and colleagues of mine who devote their lives to the craft, and as a director, I am particularly happy they choose to do so because it means I get to know and work with some of the best in the business, but I have always had difficulty sticking to one thing and one thing only. I need to do lots of different things to keep myself occupied.

After a year in New York I eventually made my way back to BC to complete an English Literature degree before accidentally falling in love with a little town in the central interior of British Columbia, called Wells. Wells is a crazy mixture of gold miners, forestry workers, artists, musicians, actors and writers nestled in the foothills of the Cariboo Mountains, with a history of mid-20th century hard rock gold mining that followed hard on the heels of a 19th-century placer gold rush centered around nearby Barkerville, BC. Barkerville is now a fully restored living history museum (the largest in Western North America, in fact), that employs professional actor-historians to deliver a variety of immersive and interactive educational programs in period costume throughout the original wooden town site, which consists of 140 restored buildings.

In the summer of 1998 I came up to Barkerville and Wells for what I assumed would be a unique but temporary summer acting gig. Twenty years later I am still here, although I have traded seasonal work as an historical interpreter for a full-time gig as the Director of Public Programming and Global Media Development. My wife, Danette (who I met at Barkerville, all those years ago), helps to produce and deliver award-winning educational programs here with me, and our twin daughters have just finished grade three at the Wells-Barkerville Elementary School (which boasts a total of 20 children, kindergarten to grade seven). From Wells I have managed to talk my way into some of the most amazing professional experiences of my life, including an internship at the National Theatre of the Czech Republic in Prague, with renowned avant-garde theatre director Charles Marowitz, and some short film projects, and a broadcast documentary that ultimately laid the groundwork for *The Doctor's Case*. It's an incredible situation to be in, and I feel very blessed to have found myself here.

AN: Out of all the Stephen King short stories, what attracted you most to this one? How did you first get involved with the Dollar Baby program?

JD: I remember listening to the three-part audiobook of *Nightmares & Dreamscapes* when it first came out in 2009, and was instantly flooded with memories of reading the collection back in 1991 during a transition year between high school and university. Back then I had two major literary loves: Stephen King and Sherlock Holmes. Imagine how excited I was to learn that King had written a Holmes story, in the style of Conan Doyle! The audiobook brought all that back to me, years later, with the added bonus of listening to Tim Curry, Pennywise himself! I read both *The Doctor's Case* and *Crouch End* (my second favorite story in *Nightmares & Dreamscapes*). It also happened to be right at the time I was returning to Wells to work for Barkerville full-time, with six-month old twins in tow, and looking for something creative to do in my (very limited) spare time.

As I walked around Barkerville that summer I began imagining what it would be like to turn *The Doctor's Case* into a film, using the variety of Victorian interiors at my disposal in this restored 19th-century gold rush town I had returned to after a couple of years away. At the time it was merely a creative exercise: after all, I did not have the authors permission to attempt an adaptation, and even if I did I could only shoot the interiors of any resulting project at Barkerville, since the exterior locations in a wooden mining town nestled in a mountainous valley covered by distinctly Canadian trees would hardly convince the viewer that he, she or they were in London, England (where the entirety of Kings story takes place). I still toyed with the idea though. Good ideas rarely stay quiet. But over the next few years it was relegated to a what if that I would dust off over a few beers with friends from time to time.

Then, in April of 2016, I happened to run into an old friend in Vancouver and, requisite beers consumed, started yacking about my unrequited desire to adapt *The Doctor's Case* into a short film, and explained (as I usually did), how it would always be an unfulfilled dream because of the reasons outlined above. At which point she (the old friend) said: Have you ever heard of a Dollar Baby?

I had not. Which now seems utterly strange to me. How on Earth did I not know about a program King has administered since 1977 that granted limited rights to emerging filmmakers who want to adapt his unlicensed short stories? I still have no idea how that one slipped by me, but it did. Until April 2016. By May I was hanging out with Michael Coleman at Northern FanCon (an entertainment expo produced by my friend and colleague Norm Coyne in Prince George, BC), and casually mentioned the Dollar Baby idea to him. I wanted to know if he would consider playing Watson if we were successful in a hypothetical bid. He was enthusiastic about the idea so I promptly did nothing about it for nearly six months.

The following November I was shooting some promotional video in Barkerville with one of our immensely talented historical interpreters, JP Winslow. As I was transferring the captured video to my office computer, I started to think I had found a very interesting choice for Sherlock Holmes. One we'd definitely never seen before, but one that would work in a shared Stephen King/Sherlock Holmes universe, based (if nothing else), on the combination of JP's inherent skills as an actor, and his own passionate interest in the history and writings of Arthur Conan Doyle. I asked JP the next day if he'd consider it. He called me crazy but still said yes. That afternoon I applied for the Dollar Baby program, and prepared to wait the suggested 4 to 8 weeks for a response. Which instead came three days later, contract attached. The game was afoot!

AN: What changes did you make, if any, to make this your own as opposed to King's original text?

JD: There are two obvious deviations we made from King's original story. The first and I imagine most noticeable is the framing device we created as a means of telling the story within the story of *The Doctor's Case*. In Stephen King's short, the tale of Lord Hull's murder and its subsequent investigation by Holmes and Watson is written like the majority Conan Doyle's Holmes stories were, in the first person narrative by Doctor Watson some time after the events he's describing have occurred. In this case, Watson tells the reader he's nearing his 90's and figures now is an appropriate time to record the one and only mystery he can recall solving before his slightly fabulous friend, Mr. Sherlock Holmes. The story then jumps directly to the meat of the matter. I knew I wanted to keep the older Watson's voice throughout the film, both as an instrument of exposition and as a means of preserving as much of Mr. King's actual writing as possible. I also knew I wanted something a little more dramatic than having the older Watson sitting at a desk with pen in hand, literally writing the story as we went along. So I thought it would be best to have him talking with someone. The Captain Norton character evolved out of that idea, and I had a lot of fun creating a backstory for her once I knew Denise Crosby was on board.

The second change we made also includes a female character not in the original story, sort of. Fans who are familiar with King's version of *The Doctor's Case* will remember that Lord Albert Hull, diabolical Englishman and well-deserving murder victim, has three sons: William, Jory, and Stephen. I knew I wanted there to be a stronger female presence in our film than there is in the story (where there are only two women, Lady Rebecca Hull and Mrs. Hudson, neither of whom say much), and found it surprisingly satisfying to change the youngest child, Stephen, into a daughter and still have the plot make sense from a historical perspective. In doing so, I also selfishly guaranteed that I would be able to invite my cousin, Joanna Douglas, to play this new Hull daughter, which was important to me because she is a successful Canadian actress in her own right (with a principal role on a popular TV show called Being Erica, as well as a supporting role in another Stephen King project: Hulu's 11/22/63). I hadn't seen Joanna since she was three months old, so I was particularly thrilled when she agreed to be in the movie. Since Stephen King had probably named the Stephen Hull character after himself, I decided to call our female version Tabitha Hull, after Stephen's wife and fellow novelist, Tabitha King.

AN: *The Doctor's Case* has a very impressive cast which includes actress Denise Crosby (*Pet Sematary*), and William B. Davis ('The Smoking Man' in *The X Files*). How did these actors first get involved with a Dollar Baby film, and what did they bring to the table that impressed you enough to cast them?

JD: Denise Crosby was the key. She agreed to participate (I think), as a personal favor to me, which is amazing. I had met her back in 2013 when we held a mini-fan expo at Barkerville called, Lost in Time. Denise and I kind of hit it off then, and stayed in touch a bit via email. When I found out we got the Dollar Baby license I immediately asked Denise if she'd consider playing a role in the film (her pedigree being what it is, coupled with the fact that she is an extremely pleasant person to be around). It took a flight down to LA to work out the details, but she said yes without even seeing a script (which was great because I didn't have one written at the time).

As I mentioned before, I knew I wanted a couple of female characters beyond Lady Hull and Mrs. Hudson, and the idea of an older Doctor Watson talking with someone rather than sitting down and writing the story was already forming, so I was presented with the extraordinary opportunity of developing the Captain Norton character with Denise in mind (not something I was expecting to do on my first kick at the can).

A family friend works at William Davis's agency in Vancouver, so once I had Denise confirmed I immediately sought Mr. Davis out, as I knew we needed someone of Denise's caliber to play against her in the

1940 framing scenes I had written (with input from Andrew Hamilton, our Lord Hull, who acted as creative consultant on the film). I am also a huge fan of *The X-Files*, so I had to take the shot. Thankfully, Mr. Davis said yes almost right away, and was very generous with his time and expertise on set.

It was literally a dream come true. When I was a teenager, *Star Trek: The Next Generation* and *The X-Files* were my two favorite TV shows, *Pet Sematary* was one of my favorite movies, and Stephen King and Sherlock Holmes books filled my shelves. Suddenly, here they all were colliding together right in front of me!

Michael Coleman (ABCs *Once Upon A Time*), was an old friend from my days as a working actor in Vancouver, Joanna Douglas (*Being Erica, 11/22/63*), is my cousin, and Erin Fitzgerald (*Monster High, Ever After High, Ask the Storybots*), is a dear friend from my days at the University of Victoria. The rest of the cast was made up of people I have known over the course of my careers in theatre and historical interpretation, and all of them said yes to the project without the slightest hesitation. I didn't have to hold a single audition for any of the roles in *The Doctor's Case*. I simply asked my friends and colleagues to participate, and am incredibly thankful they all said yes (including my wife, the incomparable Danette Boucher, who plays Mrs. Hudson in the film).

I have to admit that I was excited by our cast for another, totally geeky reason (one that I'm sure fellow King fans will appreciate). We had a remarkable number of veterans of other Stephen King adaptations on our set. Denise Crosby played Rachel Creed in *Pet Sematary*, William B. Davis was in David Cronenberg's *The Dead Zone,* and the 1990 television miniseries Stephen King's *IT*, we had another *IT* alumnus in the first cut of the film, Gaelan Bleasdale (now a Canadian hip hop artist called Evil Ebenezer, Gaelan played one of the Bowers gang as a kid; sadly, his short scene in *The Doctor's Case* was ultimately cut), and my cousin Joanna played Doris Dunning in *11/22/63*. Not bad for a Dollar Baby.

AN: So many Stephen King fans want adaptations to be as close to the book or story as possible. How do you handle the pressure to keep the fans happy?

JD: To be honest, I didn't feel a lot of pressure to keep those Stephen King fans happy because I am one of those Stephen King fans! Seriously. I wanted this to work as a film as much as any fan would, and I was determined to keep as much of King's writing in the script as possible. I mean his actual writing. Not just the plot and characters and themes, but whole passages of text. I think some adaptations of King's work struggle to connect with audiences because they ignore the very thing (intentionally or otherwise) that makes a Stephen King story transcend its genre: his choice of words. King's plotting is masterful, to be sure. His characters are more sharply drawn than most. But the glue that holds everything together, the thing that makes you want to keep turning the page no matter how late into the night you've been reading: is his narrative voice. Without that authentic voice to guide an audience through the turbulence of his imagination, it becomes easier to focus on the surface aspects of a Stephen King story: to trade important thematic details for jump scares, for example, or cut too quickly from one scene to another without allowing concepts to fully develop.

Preserving that voice can be very difficult when transitioning from page to screen, however. Movies are not books. It's normally better to show than to tell on film. It is unrealistic to think that the majority of filmmakers will have a chance to work with a story that requires near-perfect transcription of not only dialogue but entire descriptive passages to ensure the whole thing makes sense, and to ensure the Stephen King-ness of a story set in another author's world is upheld.

Fortunately, *The Doctor's Case* is exactly that kind of story. It's very nature allows for a massive amount of tell on screen. It's a Sherlock Holmes story. It's meant to be wordy. Our collective fantasy version of the Victorian era in England and abroad, thanks in large part to Hollywood versions of Charles Dickens and Arthur Conan Doyle we've all grown up with, involves a lot of standing around and talking. Therefore, it doesn't seem out of place to have these characters do precisely that.

As Sherlock points out, Inspector Lestrade relays a remarkably large body of information in a remarkably short period of time while standing in 221b Baker Street, and not only does it play as natural to have him do so in a 19th-century setting, it is absolutely vital to the presentation of the murder mystery plot that he does. I wouldn't necessarily approach every King story that way, but for my first adaptation I was buoyed by the fact that my inner fan was going to be very pleased with our choice to be slavishly faithful to the original text of The Doctor's *Case*.

To be honest, I feel more pressure to appease the Sherlock Holmes fans out there. By necessity we've taken slightly non-canonical approaches to a couple of the finer details of our shared King-Conan Doyle universe. While I firmly believe these choices are justified given a) our budget, and b) the fact that this is our version of King's version of Conan Doyle's character (at least, that's what I keep telling myself), but I'm always a little nervous about how Sherlockians will react to certain choices.

Those folks can be ruthless (just kidding).

All joking aside, I do feel a responsibility to our audience: many of whom will be lovers of Stephen King, Sherlock Holmes, and/or movies in general: and while I suppose I can't expect everyone to agree with every choice we've made, I believe there is enough in *The Doctor's Case* to surprise and delight casual observers and diehard fans alike.

AN: There were a lot of things I was impressed with in your film: the music and the sets, both were amazing. Tell us about both of them.

JD: Serendipity has been our friend and mantra throughout all of our work on *The Doctor's Case*. So many of the incredible opportunities we've been able to take advantage of have literally walked into the room at exactly the right time, as if to keep daring us to dream bigger and work harder. The music and the locations both started as one thing, then quickly became something much bigger than we would have dared dream of at the very beginning of this process.

As soon as we realized *The Doctor's Case* was a go, my producing partner Norm Coyne and I started talking with a musician friend of ours, Jeremy Breaks, about helping with the score. Norm and Jeremy have been tight for years, and when not touring as lead guitar for the Dallas Smith Band, Jeremy (or Jer, as we call him), has recently started writing music for short film and video projects. As we were sifting through Jeremys schedule and trying to decide whether he would tackle the entire score for *The Doctor's Case* himself or bring in some collaborators, I happened to be presenting a reading of Charles Dickens' *A Christmas Carol* during Baskervilles Old Fashioned Victorian Christmas event. After the reading, a couple who had originally been sitting at the back of the auditorium but who had slid further and further toward the front seats as the reading progressed, came up to me afterwards to introduce themselves and let me know how much they had enjoyed the presentation. Ken Marshall and his partner, Maria Lui. They told me their names and my jaw nearly hit the floor.

It just so happens that, as a teenager, I went through a short but glorious industrial music phase while trying and failing to break into the local skateboarding scene. I listened to a lot of hard-core music back in the day, and for a couple of years my absolute favorite was the music of a pioneer industrial band called Skinny Puppy: and Skinny Puppy's music was produced by a guy named Ken Hiwatt Marshall. This guy. Standing in front of me. A guy with a platinum record hanging on his studio wall (thanks to a collaboration with Linkin Park), was standing there telling me how much he'd enjoyed my show. I couldn't believe it.

Before we said goodbye, I found myself telling Ken and Maria that there was another project I was working on that I would love a chance to tell them about sometime. They told me to tell them about it right then and there. So I told them about *The Doctor's Case* and what we wanted to do with it. They said they wanted to help with the music. Right then and there.

From that point forth our trio of composers, Ken, Maria, and Jer, worked in tandem on the soundtrack, with Jer writing guitar and banjo riffs, while Ken experimented with a room-sized analogue synthesizer he had access to in LA in between tour dates with his new industrial band, Black Line (who in turn opened for Depeche Mode all across Europe last summer), and Maria began scoring our overture. To top it off, the three were completely open to incorporating the melody of a song my aunt had written for me back when I was a baby, which became the tune Sherlock Holmes plays on his violin at the very end of the film. Another dream had, serendipitously, come true.

It was kind of like that with our locations, too. Or, at least, the National Historic Site equivalent of meeting the producer of one of your favourite bands and having him volunteer to supervise your music team. A couple of weeks before I met Ken and Maria in Barkerville, I was in Jasper, Alberta at an annual tourism industry conference. While there, I ran into an old friend from Victoria, Kate Humble. Like me, Kate had transitioned from a traditional theatre career into a career in historical interpretation, and at that time was the visitor services coordinator at Craigdarroch Castle National Historic Site, a spectacular Victorian mansion and former home to the wealthy industrialist Dunsmuir family, designed and built in the 1880s to resemble a four-story Scottish castle.

As I mentioned earlier, my original idea was to shoot the interiors of our film in Barkerville, and find some other places to film the exteriors. If we were able to use Craigdarroch Castle as Hull House (I found myself saying out loud to Kate), then we'd be able to shoot interiors and exteriors in the same place. To my utter astonishment, she said she would talk with her team about it. Now, I wasn't ever expecting to film *The Doctor's Case* at a place like Craigdarroch. Major studio movies like

Little Women shoot there, and their location day rate is (deservedly) very high. We would never be able to afford it, even if they did say yes. And yes, they did say yes. They even did one better. As long as we promised to shoot between 5:30 pm and 2:30 a.m. each day (which we regularly pushed to 5:30 am and the good folks at Craigdarroch were kind or crazy enough to allow it), then our location fee would be drastically reduced, in light of our meagre budget, and their desire to showcase the castle in our film.

Once we knew we were bound for Victoria to shoot at the castle, it seemed only logical we should try to shoot as much of the rest of the film there as we could. Another colleague from BC's heritage tourism industry is Jan Ross, who operates Emily Carr House National Historic Site, the birthplace of renowned Canadian painter and writer, Emily Carr. Jan was extremely helpful, and let us use the dining room of Emily Carr House as our Baker Street apartment, as well as an impressive set of interior stairs that allowed us to create the illusion that the apartment was on the second floor of a building, which Holmes and Watson's residence famously is, but Emily Carr Houses dining room is not. We then managed to get a permit from the city of Victoria to shoot the exterior of Baker Street in Bastion Square, which is full of 19th-century stone buildings.

We saved one interior scene to film in Barkerville, which we did several weeks after the Victoria shoot. It's a flashback scene depicting the birth of Jory Hull, Lord Albert Hull's middle child. For that we used an authentic 1860's country doctor's office in Barkerville, which also happens to be a National Historic Site of Canada. So, in the end, we were able to showcase three separate National Historic Sites in British Columbia in one 65-minute Stephen King film. Sites that are all spectacular places to visit, by the way (shameless tourism plug).

AN: What was the main goal you wanted to achieve with this film?

JD: My main goal was to finally make the film I had been dreaming about making, and make it with a group of people I was thrilled to team up with every day. Of course I want people to like it, heck, I just want people to be able to see it, but honestly the fact that I was simply able to make this movie to the best of my ability, at this particular time with these exceptional people means my real goal has already been met. Having Stephen King watch it and (hopefully), like it is an associated goal, and I'm working on that, but even if that never happens I must say I have been completely satisfied by this experience so far.

AN: Where was the movie filmed specifically, and were there any obstacles to overcome while filming on location?

JD: Specifically, the movie was filmed on location at Craigdarroch Castle, Emily Carr House, Heritage Acres and Bastion Square in Victoria, British Columbia, and at Barkerville Historic Town & Park in Barkerville, BC. There were many obstacles to overcome in all of our locations. As I mentioned before, we were shooting at Craigdarroch Castle all night long. This meant shooting our Baker Street scenes at Emily Carr House and Bastion Square, as well as the interior carriage scenes at Heritage Acres, during the day: then shooting the Hull House scenes at Craigdarroch at night. We had a very small crew, so this meant everyone was pulling double and triple shifts, fueled by great catering (thanks to Sara Mushansky), lots and lots of coffee, and sheer force of will. It was a challenging shoot for that reason alone. Throw in the fact that the majority of the interior Hull House scenes we filmed at night took place during the day, and suddenly we have serious lighting challenges to deal with.

We were also shooting in Victoria in April, which meant expensive accommodations for our cast and crew, and no rain. You'd think no rain would be a good thing, but in our case it was a real challenge. Anyone who has read Stephen King's *The Doctor's Case* will tell you that rain is practically its own character in the story. So much depends on, or is affected by, the rain. And in Victoria in April there is no rain, only bright, beautiful sunshine, and acres of spring flowers (another shameless tourism plug). We wound up having to be very creative with how we invented rain for our version of *The Doctor's Case,* and although it was both a practical and digital challenge to do so on a micro budget, we managed to pull it off.

When we got to Barkerville in June things ran pretty smoothly. Although we were only there for a day shooting one short scene there was still the challenge of filming the one flashback in the movie that takes place significantly prior to most of the main action. This meant we had to de-age Lord Hull a bit, and find another actor to play a younger version of Lady Hull. Serendipity was our friend once again, however, and while we were preparing to shoot I ran into a young woman I knew who was traveling to Wells to visit family, would be here when we needed her, had some acting experience, and looked remarkably like a younger version of Michelle Leiffertz, our Lady Hull (and production designer, by the way). We needed to use an actor other than Michelle not because we didn't want to keep her for the scene, but because by June of 2017 she'd returned to Italy, where she'd been travelling with her family on a year abroad adventure when I hauled her back to Canada for two weeks to design and act in *The Doctor's Case*. We also didn't have a real baby to use as the newborn Jory Hull. We had to be creative there, too, and rely on some dramatic conventions that fit the purposefully theatrical nature of the majority of our Hull family flashbacks.

AN: How long was the film shoot and the process from start to finish?

JD: We shot for twelve days (and looooong nights) in Victoria, and one day in Barkerville for a total of thirteen production days. We then spent nearly seven months in post-production. We managed to get it all finished within the year allotted by the Dollar Baby contract, however, and that was a pretty astonishing feat in retrospect.

AN: You did something in this Dollar Baby I have never seen before: you added a scene after the credits. Was this on purpose as a teaser for a possible sequel, or just a treat for King fans once the credits were over?

JD: I put in the post-credit scene for a couple of reasons. The first reason was I wanted to give some resolution to the Captain Norton/Older Watson story we'd invented for our framing device, without having it interfere with the main plot of the film. It does tease a possible sequel, or provide the jumping off from a pilot episode of some sort to the remainder of a hypothetical series, but that was more for fun than out of any expectation of actually being able to continue the story (as much as I would love to). It also seemed to fit with the 1940's setting of the Norton/Watson scenes, and harken back to a time for moviegoers when cliffhanger endings were a regular part of the serialized short films that would often play before feature presentations at movie theatres a generation or more ago; the same kind of movie theatres a young Stevie King might have found himself frequenting back in Maine in the 1950's. So, yes: a treat for the fans, and for one fan in particular.

AN: What is the greatest moment so far with the success of *The Doctor's Case*?

JD: There are too many to count. I think, to be totally honest, it was the day I placed a Blu-ray disc containing the final version of *The Doctor's Case* in the mail, addressed to Stephen King. I have no idea if he's watched it yet (I suspect he hasn't had the chance), but that accomplishment alone actually finishing the film and sending it to Stephen King was worth all of the work and stress and education and raw determination that had gone into making *The Doctor's Case*. If I had to choose one moment, that might just be it. But there really have been so many.

AN: Which Stephen King story would you like to adapt on a much larger scale?

JD: There are so many of those, too! I would probably be happy for the rest of my life making nothing but Stephen King movies. Really, I would. If I had to pick just one, though, and the budget was sufficient to do it properly, then I would have to say my dream project would be an adaptation of King's 1987 novel, *The Eyes of the Dragon*.

AN: As a Stephen King fan, what are your thoughts on the film adaptations that are coming out recently, and his new novels compared to his older works?

JD: I love it all. I really do. Some of the new adaptations have been great (the new *IT*, *11/22/63*, and *1922* come to mind), some have been so-so (*Gerald's Game*), and some have missed the mark completely (I still haven't been able to get past the first act of *The Dark Tower*, I am ashamed to admit; but I will keep trying). Regardless, I still love them all. It's the same with his newer novels and stories. I am still having a blast reading them. I think *Dr. Sleep* and *The Outsider* contain some of his finest work. And when it comes right down to it, they are Stephen King. Bad Stephen King is better than no Stephen King, and except for a few of the films there really isn't that much bad Stephen King. Even *The Tommyknockers* is better than most of the genre novels I was reading at the time of its release, and King barely remembers writing that one!

AN: Where can fans see your film, and will it also be playing at film fests around the world?

JD: Anyone who wants to see the film can come to Barkerville and I will personally show it for free. I'm actually allowed to do that, so start making your vacation plans, everybody (final shameless tourism plug)! As for other opportunities: according to our Dollar Baby contract with King, we cannot distribute the film commercially, so the only place other than Barkerville it can be seen is at established film festivals and under certain not-for-profit conditions. We've applied for more than 30 international festivals over the past six months, and have been fortunate enough to be officially selected by a number of them already. We're still waiting to hear back from more than a dozen that take place this fall, but so far we've screened at the Julien Dubuque International Film Festival (our world premiere), the Adrian International Film Festival, Cinema CNC Festival, Cariboo Chilcotin Film Festival, Mid-Tennessee Film Festival (where we won awards for Best Feature and Best Actor), Comicpalooza Film Festival (where we won for Best Cinematography, Best Costumes, and Best Actress), the Penti-con Festival, and the New Hope Film Festival (where we won for Best Period Film). Next week we head to the Kew Gardens Festival of Cinema (and are nominated for Best Cinematography and Best Editing there), and the week after that we're at three more: the Regina International Film Festival, WorldCon 76 Film Festival, and the Diamond in the Rough Film Festival.

AN: What is the best advice you can give to future filmmakers and those who wish to make a Dollar Baby film someday?

JD: Don't panic. Learn from everyone. Don't be afraid to admit when you don't know something, and don't feel ashamed to ask advice from someone who does. If you're offered a chance to work on a Dollar Baby film and you love Stephen King, do it.

AN: Lastly, What is next for James Douglas?

JD: Over and above my day job at Barkerville and ensuring I spend quality time with my wife and kids, there are a few projects on the horizon. Andrew Hamilton (Lord Albert Hull), Stu Cawood (William Hull). and I am writing a vampire western we hope to shoot in Barkerville this winter. I am also directing a short film written and starring JP Winslow (Sherlock Holmes) in September, and I am currently writing historical scripts for a television documentary that my co-director on *The Doctor's Case*, Len Pearl, is producing and directing for broadcast in 2019. Other than that, I could use a little more sleep!

I'd like to thank James Douglas for his wonderful film, and his great enthusiasm with this interview. I truly cannot remember when I have interviewed someone with such passion for his craft. This truly made this exciting for me as well. I hope all of you will enjoy this article, and remember, if you get the opportunity to find an Independent Film Festival near you, look to see if *The Doctor's Case*, a film directed by James Douglas, is among the agenda.

Dedication by Selina Sondermann

Dedication

Selina Sonderman
May 5, 2019

It's amazing that the Stephen King Dollar Baby program has been around for over 40 years! This program has helped so many up-and-coming filmmakers, not to just take their vision of a Stephen King story and put it on the big screen, but it has also opened many doors for them to bigger projects within the film industry.

I have enjoyed the Dollar Baby program for many years now, taking on new interviews, and Dollar Baby reviews with joy and excitement. Meeting these independent filmmakers is truly an inspiration. My latest Dollar Baby interview comes all the way from Germany! Not only is this a young woman who has passion and a love for film, but has something to say, and she does it through her work. Selina Sondermann is an amazing filmmaker, and a joy to talk to. However, before we get to the interview, let's find out just a little bit about this new generation filmmaker.

Selina Sondermann was born in Austria, and has a very impressive upper educational background. She attended Europagymnasium in 2011, in Linz Austria, Linz International School in 2011, JKU Linz, from 2011-2012, studying sociology, Kingston University, class of 2015, studying filmmaking in Kingston, New York University in July 2015: August 2015, studying screenwriting and creative writing in New York City, NY, and Metfilm School Berlin, studying directing, class of 2018.

After working at various jobs, some at film companies, Selina got behind the camera in 2015 with her first film, *Aurheopophilie,* followed by her films, *Ginger* (2016), *Three-Wheel Stroller* (2018), and the Stephen King adapted short story, *Dedication.* Selina has a strong love for film, and her talents clearly show in her work. Here is my review of her adaptation from book to the Stephen King Dollar Baby short film, *Dedication.*

Dedication first appeared in the June 1988 anthology, Dark Visions. It was reprinted in Stephen King's collection of short stories, *Nightmares & Dreamscapes*. This story is about a Black woman who has left a very violent and senseless relationship, who goes to work at an exclusive hotel as a maid. There's a repeat guest, an alcoholic, but talented writer stays to do his writing. The maid finds him annoying and disgusting, yet a slow amicable relationship begins.

However, the maid has her own agenda, a child. After the previous failed relationship, she decides to go to someone who might be of help. A black magic spell is cast, and she can now fulfill her ultimate desire. She chooses the writer as the father , but the circumstances surrounding the situation, well let's just say, are highly unusual.

Considered the most grotesquely shocking of all of Stephen King's works, this film tells this story in an enjoyable and touching way. The story is filmed and set in Berlin, instead of the original setting of New York, and a few small changes were made, but that's good because Selina's vision of *Dedication* is well told, and is visually stunning in regards to its location.

The camera angles, and lighting lend to the quality of this film. The actors did a fine job of depicting the characters, and I found this to be one of my favorite Dollar Baby films so far, as it is very close to seeing a big budget film, however financed by means of a more conservative independent budget.

I believe Selina has a very bright future in filmmaking, and this film proves her talents are outstanding.

Here is my Exclusive Interview with director Selina Sondermann.

Anthony Northrup: I want to start off by saying, thank you Selina, for joining us today. Tell us what it was like growing up in Germany, and when did you first discover the writings of Stephen King?

Selina Sondermann: Thank you for having me!
I am a Berliner-by-choice, but was actually born and raised in Austria. Despite how often I complain about the country, I realize how privileged I am, having grown up in a place where things like public health care, and access to education are a given. A place where I can hop onto a train and have breakfast, lunch and dinner, in three different countries if I feel like it. A place where people don't get stoned to death for loving who they love. Even the fact that I can criticize Austria's government without fear of punishment, is proof of the freedom I enjoy in Europe.

I first discovered Stephen King when I was about 12 years old. In a discussion about the uncanniness of clowns, a school friend mentioned a film about a clown, who eats children. Hence in the summer break that followed, I spent my vacation reading my first King novel. I have quite vivid memories of reading *It* by the pool and having goosebumps despite the warm weather.

AN: You have attended many universities around the world (Austria, Germany, the United Kingdom, and New York in America). Which did you enjoy the most, and which one helped you more prepare for the world of filmmaking?

SS: All of these experiences contributed to who I've become as a person and a filmmaker.

My summer term at NYU's Tisch School of the Arts was without a doubt the most invaluable lesson I had in terms of my writing practice. It was more like a bootcamp, not quite comparable to the degree courses I completed in London and Berlin, but over the short amount of time I learned so much. It's obvious why NYU is regarded as one of the best film schools.

AN: What was the first Stephen King movie you saw, and what is it about King's stories that draws you in?

SS: I think the first movie was *It* (1990) as well, I don't precisely remember whether I saw it before or after I read the novel. The first one that really stuck with me emotionally was *Dolores Claiborne* however. What caught me back then, and what still draws me in are the characters first and foremost. Stephen King has the ability of creating fictional people that are just as real as the people we see on the streets every day, if not more so. In a few entertaining scenarios, when we aren't looking, he shares with us their hopes, their dreams, their shortcomings. He makes us care, which is why we fear for the characters, when he puts them in harm's way.

AN: Before we get started about your Stephen King Dollar Baby film, *Dedication*, let's talk a little about some of your earlier films: *Ginger, Three Wheel Stroller,* and *Anthropophilie*. Share with us a little bit about what they are about, and which one you enjoyed most working on?

SS: *Anthropophilie* and *Ginger* were both made within the same year so they're quite similar in terms of approach: one is about consensual cannibalism, the other about the women targeted by the serial killer known as Jack the Ripper. Both sound like classic horror films at first, but in truth, are dramas that deal with people's personal struggles and desires.

Three-Wheel-Stroller is a story about a threesome that results in a pregnancy.

Asking me to choose between my films is a bit like asking a parent which of their offspring they prefer, but *Anthropophilie* is the one closest to my heart. If there is only one story I can ever tell, this is it. I am currently writing the feature length script for it.

AN: How did you first learn about the Stephen King Dollar Baby program? What attracted you to the story, *Dedication*?

SS: I first heard about the Dollar Baby program just when I was finishing *Ginger*, which was my BA graduation film. If I'd found out about it any earlier, I probably would have wanted to participate back then. *Ginger* wouldn't exist, and neither would *Dedication*. At the time I didn't have the confidence or experience to fully grasp what it means to adapt somebody else's source material: let alone Stephen King's! I remember seriously looking into the program in early 2016. Frankly, what stood out to me about *Dedication* at the time was that it was the only story that hadn't been adapted.

(Tyna Ezenma was the first to turn it into a film in 2017, according to my research.)

Upon reading the story I realized why. Originally published in 1988, it really didn't age well. The characterization of Martha, a black maid, is problematic and also the story didn't make sense to me. In the following two years I spent a lot of thought on it and came to the conclusion that this was actually an opportunity. Instead of dismissing *Dedication* as one of Stephen King's few slip-ups, I thought maybe I could revamp the story.

AN: What changes did you make to your version of the story as opposed to King's original text?

SS: Warning: From here on out, there will be spoilers!

What irked me in the original story was that Martha was so passive. She was basically just a bowling pin, waiting to be hit by verbally abusive guests staying at the hotel she worked at (metaphorically), or by her husband (literally). In no way do I mean to make light of domestic violence, but we need to stop portraying women as helpless victims everything just happens *to*.

Martha ends up at a witches' house and is forced (!) into a magic ritual to change the paternity of her unborn child, because that way her son will not end up "no good" like his biological father, but a famous writer like his "natural father": one of those abuse guests who is a particularly despicable human being!

Even if we suspend disbelief that oral intake of sperm can have an impact on a pregnancy, this is simply not how genetics work. I will not bore you with the details, but I believe in magical realism, so the changes I made were that I gave Martha a voice of her own. My Martha is so dedicated to her child she makes an active choice to seek out Mama Delorme's help, even of the supernatural kind. I also changed the circumstances that made the in-utero father transformation necessary to the child's well being and not a naive luxury.

AN: *Dedication* is considered the "grossest and most disturbing" of all of Stephen King's works. Did it make you nervous to tackle such a grotesque story?

SS: I am not scared of the grotesque, but I was nervous about not being able to redeem the story.

What makes the short story gross isn't the semen or the consumption thereof. That can be quite a beautiful and romantic element as *Call Me By Your Name* shows. What is "gross" about *Dedication* is that Peter Jeffries is such a vile person, that the whole ordeal is degrading. It's one of the most humiliating things Stephen King has ever written, but I think he wasn't aware of how hurtful the implications of this scene were to women of color.

So while Peter Gottfried is still an entitled straight white man, he is not the misanthrope of King's story. This way I could rationalize Martha choosing him as the "sperm donor": his regular emission on the sheets makes him a convenient means to an end for her.

AN: So many Stephen King fans want adaptations to be as close to the book as possible. How do you handle the pressure to keep the fans happy?

SS: It was a cause for concern, because it is very easy to see it that way. Before I studied film, I often criticized literary adaptations for straying too much. But one has to understand that these are two different art forms. To adapt is to translate from one media into another.

As is the case with languages, often you will not find an exact equivalent for some of the words. There is no English term for "Weltschmerz", for instance. You can dissect the word's origin and find a literal translation for the parts it is made up of, but will it have the same impact? You can try to find a phrase that embodies a similar sentiment or attempt to describe this one specific word with an abundance of other words. There are different ways to approach an adaptation.

But to simply copy/paste the words from the book into a script format and expect it to work the same way, is unrealistic.

That aside, yes, I was particularly liberal in my adaptation of *Dedication,* but what would be the point of making a film where my input wasn't relevant?

AN: What was the main goal you wanted to achieve with this film?

SS: My goal was to make a film about women helping each other. I wanted my film to reflect the beauty of a multicultural environment and how rewarding it is to make a choice for oneself, to embrace change. I wanted to tell a story about a woman who prevails over the demons of her past.

AN: Where was the movie filmed and was there any challenges to overcome while filming there?

SS: The movie was filmed on location in Berlin. The challenge was that there just aren't enough hours in the day when you're trying to make a film, but that is the case wherever you shoot.

AN: Was the hotel management and staff excited when you chose their hotel to film in? Did you use any of the staff as extras?

SS: We shot in two different hotels: the canteen was actually not in the same place as the rooms and hallway. We were very lucky that we got permission to film in both of these wonderful establishments. Because our budget didn't allow us to rent out the entire dining facility, we agreed with management that the F&B staff could continue their work in the kitchen. Our sound guy wasn't happy but yes, we got some free extras out of it.

AN: How long was the shoot and process of the film from start to finish?

SS: The filming period itself was just under a week. Pre-production started in early 2018, and post-production took us half a year.

AN: What is your greatest moment so far with the success of *Dedication*?

SS: Being asked to speak about the film :)

AN: Which Stephen King story would you like to adapt on a larger scale?

SS: Rose Madder. It's a story that doesn't answer all of the questions it raises, which is why it intrigues me. There are quite a few similarities to *Dedication* as well.

AN: You are actually the third female Dollar Baby director I have interviewed. Tell us your thoughts on the rise of women filmmakers, and their position in film in the future? Do you find it challenging for women being in the film industry?

SS: Three out of thirty-three? That's actually a larger number than I thought. Still, 9%, when we make up 50% of the population?

Obviously, I cannot speak for all women, but I have had some experiences that I doubt men setting out to become filmmakers face. Women are actively discouraged from being assertive, so often we have to work harder to be respected in a position of authority. Yet I believe we are on a good path. It is so important to have storytellers from different backgrounds. Women, people of color, LGBTQIA… Representation matters. The best way to ensure that our stories are being told in a truthful matter is to give us a seat at the table.

AN: You have many titles: director, producer, writer. Which of these do you find more challenging?

SS: Every position brings a specific set of challenges. I never particularly wanted to produce, but it is just something that comes naturally to me. I'm good at organizing, over-thinking, coming up with all the things that could possibly go wrong and then finding solutions for it. But it also takes up a lot of energy.

When it comes to directing, I find it challenging if I haven't written the script myself, and when it comes to writing, I find it challenging to start.

AN: You have a cameo in *Dedication,* who did you play?

SS: Yes, indeed. I was one of the maids Martha sees in the canteen on her first day at the hotel.

AN: Now our final question: Where can fans see your film? Will it be playing at film fests around the world?

SS: That is the plan. We submitted to festivals and are waiting to hear back.

There you have it, another wrap on yet another great Dollar Baby film adaptation. I'd like to thank Selina for taking the time out of her busy schedule to do this interview, and wish her the very best. Keep an eye out at your local film fests for this very well executed and entertaining film, *Dedication*. If YOU are interested in making a "Dollar Baby Film", go to the Stephen King Dollar Baby webpage, or on Facebook.

Beachworld by Jackie Perez

Beachworld

Jackie Perez
July 25, 2019

ONE OF THE JOYS of doing film reviews, especially Stephen King Dollar Baby films, is the excitement these filmmakers have. Jackie Perez is no exception. She is full of energy and excitement, not only for filmmaking, but for the horror genre as well. This includes the love for the master storyteller himself, Stephen King.

Jackie Perez was born in San Antonio, Texas but claims Los Angeles, California as home, as it's the longest place she's lived. Jackie moved many times as a child, as she is what they call a military brat, and also as an adult, while she too, was in the Navy.

Jackie has always loved film, especially horror, and movies were her escape. She started writing and making narrative shorts in college, as she was inspired by the film Hostel, during a Q&A session with Eli Roth. It was in high school though, in Jacksonville, Florida, that she began playing around with a camera, documenting events with friends, soon becoming hooked on filmmaking!

Jackie finished her undergraduate studies at MIT, for environmental engineering, then spent 5 years as a nuclear engineering Naval Officer. While working in Hollywood, she completed her MFA in Television and Screening, at Stephens College.

Now that *Beachworld* is through post, Jackie is finishing up rewrites on a few feature scripts that she's been working on, and has been commissioned to write a biography on Sally Ride, who NASA recognizes as the first American Woman in space. Wow, congratulations are in order, and this will be published in 2021.

Here is my review of Jackie Perez's, Stephen King's Dollar Baby film, *Beachworld*.

There are actually a few versions of the Dollar Baby film, *Beachworld*. I have personally seen only one other version, and that was animated, by Dollar Baby filmmaker, Maria Ivanova, so this was the first time seeing a live-action version of this story.

Beachworld is a short science fiction story by Stephen King, which was first published in *Weird Tales,* in 1984, and later featured in King's *Skeleton Crew.* This story takes place in the future, when a spacecraft crashes on a remote and unheard of planet, which is a sandy desert. When one of the three crewmen dies, the other two sit and stare at the isolated planet, endlessly watching the dunes.

While in this trance-like state, one of them becomes distracted, and decides to head back to the ship to escape the monotony. Eventually another ship lands, the Tarrives, hoping to rescue the stranded survivors from this desolate wasteland. One of the two stranded crewmen doesn't believe the ship and crew are real, and doesn't want to leave, caught in the planet's strange spell.

Jackie takes this short story to high levels with her professional filmmaking talents, amazing vision, and beautiful locations. With a talented cast, an intriguing story, I found Jackie's version entertaining and nicely done, with minimum expense.

I had the pleasure of speaking with Jackie about her life and career, and here is my exclusive interview.

Anthony Northrup: You traveled quite a bit as part of a military family. How and when did your love for film first begin? Also, what is it about the horror genre that attracts you so?

Jackie Perez: My love for horror began in the womb! My mom read *IT, Christine,* and *The Stand* when she was pregnant with me, so I think I started to love it via osmosis. I read voraciously, and film was another way to escape reality. My parents let me watch whatever I wanted, except *Beavis and Butthead,* so I have home videos of me watching stuff like *Hellraiser,* and *Rocky Horror Picture Show* when I was like 5 years old. I've always loved the adrenaline rush of being scared. I'm a very analytical, non-emotional person, so I love horror, it invokes such an emotional response in me that I don't normally have in everyday life.

AN: What were some of your favorite books and films that inspired you growing up?

JP: I loved Upton Sinclair's *The Jungle,* and *Ender's Game* by Orson Scott Card. I've revisited each several times throughout my life. I guess you can say I'm drawn to hopeless situations and very dark endings. Filmwise, I am a sucker for 1980s horror-comedies. *Dead Alive,* and *Terrorvision* were staples. Still are!

AN: Going from environmental engineering, and nuclear engineering ,to filmmaker, is a really big change of career. What happened to make such a drastic change, and would you ever leave filmmaking to go back to the engineering field again?

JP: After watching Chernobyl, there were a few moments where I missed that world, and missed being an expert in that world. I went to Hollywood because I love film, and love horror. Now I'm becoming an expert in my craft, and what I love about writing is that I get to learn new things every day, including diving into science and engineering for research. I've learned a ton about the early days of computing, for a new screenplay I'm working on about Grace Hopper, and I'm learning about a whole new world for my biography on Sally Ride. Between Hollywood, the Navy, and MIT, it's kind of crazy how many people I already know who are astronauts, or work in the space industry, and now I get to pull all those strings together and create something that will hopefully get young people excited about STEM. So I still feel very involved in a way.

AN: What type of short films did you make while attending college?

JP: No budget ones! I'd grab a camera, grab my engineering classmates, and we'd spend a few hours shooting. No lights, no sound gear... we just made use of what we had around us for production design. I don't think I even bought them pizza or anything, and honestly, I don't think I even knew what production design was. The third short I made, I did buy pizza, because I had actors I found through Craigslist. I was totally winging it.

AN: You said you were inspired by horror director Eli Roth to pursue filmmaking, where was that Q/A at specifically? Was it a convention, or a special event at your college? Did you get to meet with him?

JP: It was a Q&A he did in Boston for Hostel. His dad was there. Eli's from Boston. I was already a big fan of Cabin Fever from watching it in high school, and even though I was studying my butt off at MIT, I still went to a ton of horror films and midnight premiers. I remember going to see SAW at an advance screening, and then dragging all my friends to see it on opening weekend. I even got a cool Jigsaw stuffed doll. Back to your question... no, I didn't get to meet him, but not for lack of trying. I wanted to do an interview for our school newspaper, and he was doing a breakfast interview with different colleges. I told the paper my plan ahead of time and that I was going to submit as a guest post, and they called and told them I didn't work for the paper and to not allow me to attend. So instead of getting an awesome interview with Eli Roth (which I secured), they got nothing. All thanks to some clueless editor who knew nothing about film, on a power trip. Lesson learned: better to ask for forgiveness than for permission.

AN: When did you first discover Stephen King, and what are some of your favorite books and films by him?

JP: My first foray into a Stephen King book was *Desperation*, in 5th grade. My absolutely favorite book of his is, *The Girl Who Loved Tom Gordon*, and I think *Misery* is the best adaptation for the screen of his work.

AN: You live in Bahrain in the Persian Gulf. It must be very hard to get Stephen King books or latest news, correct? How did you first hear about the Stephen King, Dollar Baby program?

JP: Not at all! It just takes a bit longer. There's a few bookstores, and luckily the library I live near has a whole shelf full of Stephen King books. Those coupled with my personal collection... I'm set! I still follow all the trades every day to stay up on entertainment news. Most movies come out the same release date, and some I have to wait a bit. I had to wait two weeks for Midsommar, and I was so sad to be out of the loop on all the online discussions! I moved to Bahrain (where the US has a Navy base), a few weeks after we wrapped production, and I'll be back in the States permanently in early 2021. I first heard about the Dollar Baby program at a friend's barbeque in LA, by a guy who had optioned *Strawberry Spring*. He never ended up getting into production with that one.

AN: Out of all the Stephen King short stories, what attracted you most to *Beachworld*?

JP: Three things: no children, no snowy setting, and the location! We lived a manageable drive to the largest dunes in California. That and the limited character count sealed the deal. I picked something that I enjoyed reading, but was also a practical decision about budget. It was also a plus that Beachworld doesn't have a ton of adaptations. I think we are one of four that I know of.

AN: What changes did you make in order to adapt this film as your own, as opposed to King's original text?

JP: The original story had all male characters, and I wanted to update that. When I started thinking of a woman at the center of the story, that snowballed into other ideas. I started out with a very straightforward adaptation of the original story, but again, the limited budget forced us to make some creative changes, and each draft I had to chip away at things. There's no wrecked spaceship that slowly fills with sand. I loved that aspect of the story, but the numbers just didn't work for us to build something like that. But it ended up working great because we gotta make the most of our amazing dunes setting ,and set everything outside. Also we adjusted the ending. I will say… Frank Darabont's *The Mist* was a big inspiration. You'll have to watch to see.

AN: So many Stephen King fans want adaptations to be as close to the book as possible, how do you handle the pressure to keep the fans happy?

JP: I just have to make something I love. Filmmaking is too hard to try and please others. There's always going to be people who don't like your content. But you have to be comfortable enough with yourself and your work to tune them out and just keep making what you want to see.

AN: What was the main goal you wanted to achieve with this film?

JP: My main goal was to push myself. To make something bigger and more challenging than I've ever made, and I got through it! I learned a lot along the way, and now feel ready to make a feature. In a perfect world, this calling card will help me get representation.

AN: Where was the movie filmed specifically, and were there any obstacles to overcome while filming there?

JP: We filmed one day in the Glamis Sand Dunes, near Imperial County, CA which was a huge logistics undertaking. We had to caravan down there and do two overnight trips. But the biggest obstacle was the unpredictable environment. We're dealing with wind, sand, heat, and an $80K camera. We couldn't have picked a better day to shoot. The day before was way too windy for droning, and the day after the temperature shot up more than 10 degrees. And although the dunes are a destination spot for dune buggies, we chose a spot and a day where there were barely any tracks. That was the biggest concern, so we tried to do our best with planning around weekends and spring breaks, but it was still a total crapshoot and we somehow got it right.

AN: How long was the film shoot, and the process from start to finish?

JP: We had 2.5 of actual shooting for 12 pages of script. 1 on the dunes and 1.5 on the green screen, and one build day in our LA studio. I had renewed the option a few times because things kept popping up. A new full time job, I got married, honeymoon, holidays. My producer and I had been planning for a while, but then it was time to move, and it was now or never. The specifics came together extremely fast at the end. I know now how to plan things different for next time.

AN: What is the greatest moment so far with the success of *Beachworld*?

JP: Honestly I'm just so glad it's DONE, and I'm happy with it, and the cast and crew are happy with it. Everything else is icing on the cake.

AN: Sadly, there was tragedy with the loss of one of the actresses from the film, can you share with us your thoughts about that?

JP: It was a shock to receive the news. Lyn Ross, who played Captain Reyna, was such an incredible talent and a joy to direct. She had to run to a table read right after wrapping the day we shot, and still let us cover her with blood. She was incredibly gracious. Her passing was unexpected, and an incredible loss to the world. I'm very sad that she never got to see the film. She is amazing in it. It was a very sharp reminder how fleeting life is, and puts everything in perspective of what to truly value. It makes me value this experience even more because her legacy is a part of it.

AN: What Stephen King story would you like to adapt on a larger scale, and why?

JP: *The Girl Who Loved Tom Gordon*! It's the story of a young girl who survives a week lost in the woods. It's a beating the odds story, and one that explores the idea of self-worth. When you are all alone and in the shittiest situation, there's no one who can save you but yourself. It has a lot of the same themes of isolation as Beachworld.

AN: Where and when can fans see this film? Will it be playing at film fests around the world?

JP: We have a few festivals lined up so far: Dragon Con in Atlanta, Adirondack Film Festival in Glens Falls NY in October, a Dollar Baby Film

Fest in Rijen, Netherlands. We are still waiting to hear about many more! Our website www.beachworldfilm.com and FB page www.facebook.com/beachworldfilm will stay updated with all the screening dates. We can't wait to get this out into the world for fans to see.

AN: Lastly, what's next for Jackie Perez?

JP: As for me, I'm focusing on completing some new scripts and coming up with an idea for a feature film to shoot in Bahrain. I'm looking forward to a visit back to the US for some *Beachworld* screenings!

Thank you, Jackie, for a wonderful interview, and for taking the time out of your schedule to speak with me. I know my readers will really enjoy getting to know a little more about you and your work.

A Very Tight Place

Stephen Tramontana
August 2, 2019

STEPHEN KING HAS SCARED US countless times over 40 years, and has done so every way imaginable. However, there are two short stories in particular that are not only frightening, but considered gross. One of those is the short story *A Very Tight Place*. This story is about a man trapped in a porta potty. Director Stephen Tramontana took this story, and has now brought it to the big screen, and I must say his adaptation is great!

Stephen Tramontana was born in Durango, Colorado on February 9, 1980. After completing his elementary and high school years, he went on to study at the College of Santa Fe. He later settled in New York, working at NBC before moving on to Los Angeles, California. In 2005, he joined FWE Entertainment, where he coordinated post-production at the Syfy Channel. In 2009, he was recognized for his film *Exit Strategy*, and in 2011 he wrote the film *Welshgate*, a final in the Austin Film Fest. By 2014, Stephen co-wrote, and directed the horror/comedy, *Killer Pinata*. He then turned his talents to the comic book world with his first comic, *Anya*. In 2017, his film *Norman* was a quarterfinal Bluecat Screenwriters Competition contender. He continued his comic book work with *GR-8* in 2018. However, with all of these credits to his name, it seems befitting that just this year, 2019, Stephen Tramontana would step into the Stephen King universe, directing the Dollar Baby short film *A Very Tight Place*. At present he is living in Chicago, Illinois with his wife, and their dog Tom Hanks (yes, Tom Hanks).

Here is my review of one of the more grotesque Dollar Baby films to date: *A Very Tight Place*.

A Very Tight Place by Stephen Tramontana

Stephen King has run the gamut of every scenario possible with his stories, and with characters ranging from vampires, werewolves, killer clowns, cars, dogs, cats, and monsters from other worlds, and nearly everything else we can think of. However, Stephen King has at times had a very twisted imagination, or so it seems. The short story *A Very Tight Place* was first published in the May 2008 issue of McSweeney's, and later appeared in King's 2008 collection of stories entitled, *Just After Sunset*.

This story is about Curtis, a middle-aged man who is lured to a construction site by his very unfriendly neighbor. The two have had numerous confrontations with one another regarding legal disputes over property rights, and the death of Curtis's dog, whom he blames his neighbor for. Once Curtis is at the site, he is then forced into a porta potty, locked in, and is left to his demise, along with the most disgusting and foul odors one can imagine, not to mention other creepy encounters. Poor Curtis, I wonder how all this will turn out for him?

This Dollar Baby was disgustingly entertaining, and well done. With an interesting soundtrack, enjoyable performances, especially the two main actors, a bit of quirky humor, and actually seeing the amazing, but difficult way of filming in a porta potty, I think Stephen Tramontana hits the mark with this adaptation. This is a Dollar Baby film you won't want to miss. I do however, recommend viewing it… after lunch!

I had the privilege of doing this interview with director Stephen Tramontana, and I hope you will enjoy it as much as I did.

Anthony Northrup: Growing up in the small town of Durango Colorado, your love for film began at a very young age. Tell us about some of the things you filmed with your friends, and what were some of your inspirations back then?

Stephen Tramontana: They were all horror-related, haha. I think we were probably 9 or 10 when my buddy and I picked up that camcorder, but I remember one of the earliest shorts we made was called, *The Sterling Massacre* , and we played both the victims and the masked killers, and just kind of switched out who was killing, and who was getting covered in ketchup. My earliest inspiration was definitely Wes Craven. I just fell in love with the creativity of *A Nightmare on Elm Street,* and Freddy-mania in general, which led me to go down the franchise rabbit hole of *Halloween, Friday the 13th,* etc. I was a huge B-movie fan, even at that age. The Charles Band Full Moon films became kind of a guiding light for me, this idea that you could churn out low budget horror films, but they were really cool. I would read about them in *Fangoria* and immediately bike down to the video store to try and find them. Non-Full Moon things like *Ticks, Dolly Dearest, Return of the Living Dead III,* etc.

AN: You worked in television, and making films for the Syfy Channel. What is more challenging: television or feature films, and why?

ST: I would call it a draw, they both have unique challenges. I was in post production on the Syfy films and the budgets were decent, but we still had the classic issues of "fix it in post": which, as we know, is the worst idea, haha. So we would inherit all the issues stemming from pre-production and production, and that just made our job 10 times harder, because we still had our regular post work, which was also time consuming. I remember we were filming Stan Lee's Lightspeed, and that production was in Utah, the first movie we tried shooting in the States and not Romania. We're shooting on film, and the first footage comes back to LA with no sound. I call the Unit Production Manager, ask where the sound is, turns out the recording equipment malfunctioned, so they decided to shoot the entire day without sound, and it's ALL dialogue scenes, haha. So we had to edit dialogue scenes without sound, then bring the actors back to re-record everything from that day. It was that kind of thing all the time.

AN: You wrote a comic book in 2018, GR-8, share with us some of your thoughts about the late Stan Lee, and how your love of comics came about?

ST: It's tough to say something that hasn't been said already about Stan "The Man" Lee. I'm just very thankful that destiny kind of put him at Marvel during its worst period and, much like his creations, he rose to the challenge and built something amazing. I discovered Marvel comics when I was 10, and I had probably read them for about a year or two before realizing who Stan Lee was, which is a testament to him. I mean, don't we all want our creations to outlive us? Funny story about Stan Lee, I actually got to work with him a bit on Lightspeed. That was his story, 100%. The villain was originally supposed to turn into this man/snake creature, similar to Serpentor in GI Joe, and we didn't have the budget: it was a good budget: it just couldn't afford that particular effect. So our office is trying to figure out how to deliver this news to Stan Lee, and I'm the only one in the room that is a comic book nerd. So I raise my hand and explain that we need to couch it as an evolution of character. Happens all the time in comics, Beast evolves into a furry blue creature, Brainiac goes from alien to robot, etc. So I go with Jeff, our producer, to visit Stan and I'm explaining this to him, and that we can have the villain become the full man-snake in the sequel. Stan gets it and loves the idea, and I'm like, I learned it from you, man! That was a really cool moment. But I've always loved comics. I have a ton of them, I pay artists for independent commissions, and one day I'll probably transition from making films to just making comics. It's something that's been in my DNA since birth, I was the kid running around with a bath towel on my back pretending to be Superman or Batman. Superheroes are a unique American creation, representing the best of our ideals and intentions. Obviously, there are flaws, but I think they are one of our finest creations.

AN: In 2019, you made the Stephen King Dollar Baby short film, *A Very Tight Place*. When and how did you first learn about the Dollar Baby program?

ST: In film school. At least when I was in film school, the infamous Frank Darabont Dollar Baby was talked about. We were about five years away from YouTube, so there was no real way to see it, but the story was out there. If you wanted to option a Stephen King short story, you could.

AN: Out of all the Stephen King short stories, what attracted you the most to this one?

ST: I remember, even on first read, thinking it was tailor-made for a short film. I don't think it could be sustained as a feature, but I always felt that if I were brought in on some anthology show like *The Twilight Zone*, and they asked me to pitch an episode, this is one that I would make the case for. It has humor, it has tension, it's gross, and everyone likes a good revenge story. I was just kind of surprised it never happened. So I just decided to do it myself.

AN: What did you change to make this your own version of King's story?

ST: So the biggest change is that I switched out Tim Grunwald for Ginny Grunwald. Ginny is not really a character in the short story, there's a passing mention of her as kind of this younger trophy wife with plastic surgery who leaves him, so I had to create Ginny and apply what I could of Tim to her, while still making her her own character. Part of this motivation was that I feel general audiences aren't that familiar with this story, so this may be the first time they're seeing this. If you have these two guys who hate each other, and one calls the other up and says "meet me in this random place", you know it's a trap. You would never go. Whereas, by having Ginny, at least it keeps the mystery of the story a little longer. Also, I think she's a much more nuanced antagonist than Tim. I want to make it clear that I'm NOT suggesting I'm a better writer than Stephen King, haha, I'm just saying that, from a film story perspective, a grieving widow is a little more sympathetic. So that was the big change. The second change was the ending, which was more of a tiny adjustment. In King's original text, it's kind of just a vague threat and Curtis leaves. My feeling was, in a revenge story, someone has to get theirs, frontier justice must be dealt. It brings the story full circle, we start on Curtis reading Tim's obituary, and end with him watching Ginny die. Death of a Grunwald surrounds him.

AN: At what age, and how did you first discover Stephen King (his books, films)? What is your favorite of both of these?

ST: Very early. I remember my mom reading *IT* to me as a bedtime story around the age of 7 or so (and yes, she skipped over the sewage gang bang). I remember bringing Bachman books with me to second grade. In the 80s, every elementary school was filled with kids secretly reading their parent's King novels, haha. In terms of favorite stories, I love *Pet Sematary, Cujo, Firestarter, Blaze,* and *Needful Things*. In terms of films, I love *Christine, Misery,* the 1989 *Pet Sematary,* and *Cujo*.

AN: So many fans want adaptations to be as close to the book as possible, how do you handle the pressure to keep the fans happy?

ST: I think you have to look at what appealed to you about the story, and hope that appealed to other people, too. I've adapted Shirley Jackson as a screenwriter, and now King, and in both cases you look for the waypoints, the things that fans will be looking for, and then what you can do with the material outside those waypoints for clarity or timing. Besides the character swap, I tried to keep as close to the material as possible within the time constraints of a short film. I would say the dialogue is 80% King's. I know King's dialogue grates on some people, but I like it, and I really like something pulpy like this. But I figured as long as we kept the classic elements like Betsy, why they were fighting, his escape, etc, we were in good shape.

AN: What was the main goal you wanted to achieve with this film?

ST: I wanted to make the movie that had been in my head for 10 years, and I feel we did that.

AN: Where was the film made specifically, and were there any obstacles you had to overcome while filming there?

ST: We had a REALLY difficult time finding a Durkin Village location. We probably talked to 8 or 10 different construction sites around Chicago and Indiana and no one wanted to give us permission to film. Which I understand, it's a construction site, but we've made a couple of films at this point, we know what we're doing, and we have production insurance, haha. So it was really frustrating and kind of scary, because we had about three weeks left before we had to shoot the Durkin stuff and had no location, which meant my prep time was winding down. Finally, we were able to get permission from the city of Chicago to film at Lathrop, which is the oldest housing project in Chicago. As luck would have it, they were rebuilding it, so it was abandoned when we were filming, which helped with both the production design and just not have a bunch of people around while we were trying to film. Some Lathrop residents even came in and helped out, so it was a fun day. It was hot, it was like 80-something degrees, haha, but we got through it. The other issue was filming in the porta potty itself. We bought ours fresh from the manufacturer, and trying to tear it apart to get film and lighting equipment in there was a real challenge. It's all rivets and the plastic is harder than you realize. Trying to get just one piece of it off was insane. There were days where I was just staring at this thing, going what was I thinking? Why did I want to do this? I'm an idiot.

AN: How long was the film shoot, and the process from start to finish?

ST: All in, we shot for 6 days, from October to December. The last day was all of Danny's stuff inside the porta potty, which was interesting. His exterior stuff in Durkin, we filmed that in October in the heat, and here we were, you know, two months later shooting the interiors in 40 degree weather. When he's upright, we were actually outside, so before each take, Danny had to hold ice in his mouth so we wouldn't see his breath. In terms of the overall process, about two years. We originally optioned the material when we were making *Eyelash,* because I thought we would wrap *Eyelash,* then immediately move to prepping *Tight Place.* But *Eyelash* had a much longer post than I anticipated, so that pushed this one and I actually had to go back to King's office and request an extension. We showed them *Eyelash,* and I think that gave them the confidence that we knew what we were doing. Our post was January through April, we literally locked print about two weeks before our debut in the Windy City Horrorama, haha. So, 0 to 60. Always 0 to 60.

AN: Tell us a little bit about the auditions, and what specifically did your lead actors bring to the table that won them the role?

ST: So we didn't really have to audition for this one, which was nice. We knew from the get go that Joette was going to be Ginny. We've worked with Joette on multiple projects, starting with *Killer Piñata,* and we've used her in every movie since. She's just such a joy to work with, such a calming presence on set, and the other actors just adore her. Generally, when I'm prepping a movie, I'm thinking, what do we have for Joette? I just knew, having worked with her, she could deliver on this, and she does, some of her line reads are my favorite. "Tim turned to me and said, there is justice in this world", is probably my favorite line delivery in the whole thing, I just love how she relishes that line. In terms of the lead, I pretty much knew that I wanted Danny. Danny came really close to playing the jerk boyfriend in Eyelash, and when we didn't use him for that, I kept him in mind for other things. We auditioned a couple of other actors, just in case Danny wasn't available, but it turned out he was! Danny surprised me. First, in real life, he's the nicest guy in the world. But he kind of developed what he called Donald Trump Jr. for Curtis, and once he explained that to me, I was fully onboard. For Vinton, I had known Joe DeBartolo for a while. I actually met him at a screening for Killer Piñata, he was in the movie before ours and I definitely wanted to work with him, so this was a nice way to do that. For Tim Grunwald (aka TMF), that was really tough. We just couldn't find anyone we liked, and I was starting to think we wouldn't. Then Joette says to us, I just worked with this guy who played my husband and he was great. Then she shows us some of the set dressing photos they took together for the other film, and it was perfect. So that's how we got Ron Beecher to join us. He came in close to the end of production, so it was a real save. I've never had that happen before. We're usually full cast before we start production.

AN: What is your greatest moment so far with the success of *A Very Tight Place*?

ST: I'm not sure that we've seen it yet, we're just getting started. But I will say, so far, so good. We've had some good reviews and write ups, and we were just invited to take part in a screening series at the George Eastman Museum, which is a real thrill for me. I'm just looking forward to continuing to get this in front of people, I'm very happy with how it turned out.

AN: *A Very Tight Place* is considered one of the top two gross Stephen King stories he's ever written. What did you use for the "human waste" in the porta potty scenes? How difficult was it to film in (dare I say it), a tight place? Haha.

ST: The human waste was created by our great effects person and production designer, Catherine Woods. She had worked with Joette before, and Joette referred her to us, and I think Catherine did a great job. She made some plastic fake poops for the logs, so to speak, and the rest was this mix that had a potting soil base. Catherine was very considerate about Danny, and using things that wouldn't irritate his skin, as she knew he would be in there for a while. As a last step, we would add bits of toilet paper, random paper, and blue gel for that blue sanitizer that you always see in those bowls. In terms of shooting, once we were in the porta, VERY difficult ha, for the reasons I previously stated.

AN: What Stephen King story would you like to adapt on a larger scale?

ST: It would either be *Blaze* as a feature, or *Hearts in Atlantis* as a feature or limited series. If it was a feature, then I would adapt the actual story *Hearts in Atlantis*, about the college kids and Vietnam. I think that has a lot of potential to be a *Stand by Me*, coming of age story. If it were a limited series, then I think you could adapt each section as its own episode. But those are the two I would be most interested in.

AN: Where can fans see the film? Will it be in any film fests this year?

ST: So we're still sorting the fests. They'll be able to see it in Rochester in October, and our fans in the Netherlands can see it in September there. We'll hopefully announce more dates soon!

AN: You have a pet with a very unusual name. Can you tell our readers his name and why? (haha)

ST: Haha, I think you mean my dog, Tom Hanks. We call him Hanks. My wife and I both love Tom Hanks, because we're human beings that exist in this time and space.

AN: Lastly, What is next for Stephen Tramontana?

ST: For next projects, we're just finishing our last day on our new short as I write this. It's called *Grief Counseling,* and it's probably the grimmest thing Angry Mule has ever produced, so we'll be lightening it up going forward. We have a couple of cool web series ideas that we're starting to firm up, and I'm definitely ready to make another feature, so I'm just getting my head around that to hopefully film next year!

That sounds great Stephen, a lot of work ahead for you. I want to thank you for taking the time out of your busy schedule to do this interview with me. I enjoyed it immensely, and I know my readers will as well. I look forward to all of your future projects, and wish you all the best.

Here There Be Tygers

Bryan Higby
September 1, 2019

STEPHEN KING HAS WRITTEN many stories about kids dealing with bullies in school. Classic novels such as *Carrie, IT,* as well as short stories, such as, *The Body* (*Stand By Me*), *Cain Rose Up, Sometimes They Come Back*. These stories show us the ugly side of growing up, and the fear of being bullied. King wrote one particular short story, *Here There Be Tygers*, that's also a story about bullying, with an unusual bizarre twist.

To the best of my knowledge, there are two *Here There Be Tygers* Dollar Baby films, and this is Bryan Higby's take on this quirky little short story. I had the pleasure of interviewing Bryan as well, and discussing his vision of Stephen King's tale, but before we get to the interview, let's get to know Bryan a little bit.

Bryan Higby was born May 17, 1974 in Lowville, New York. He studied at the Lowville Academy Central School, and continued his studies at the State University of New York, at Potsdam, where he graduated with the class of 2000. He has a Liberal Arts degree from Jefferson Community College, and a Bachelor's degree in theater arts from Suny Potsdam, in Potsdam, New York.

Bryan was also the co-creator/co-owner of the off Broadway Black Box Bunbury Theater Company, in Jamestown, New York, from 2001-2006. Bryan has directed several plays, including a theater version of Stephen King's *Misery*. Along with plays, Bryan has produced two short films: *Speaking But Not Actually,* and *Billy Gone Home*. After moving in 2009, he co-produced/directed three more short films: *Buffalo Style, Morgue Pi*, and *How I Learned To Stop Worrying And Kill My Mom*. He's also an acclaimed author of 35 novels and counting. Bryan currently lives in East Greenbush, New York, with his wife Amy, and their family.

Here There Be Tygers by Bryan Higby

Here is my review of Bryan Higby's adaptation of the Stephen King short story, *Here There Be Tygers*.

This is one of the very first short stories Stephen King had ever written in his career. He wrote it while in high school, and was first published in 1968, in Urbis magazine. It was later republished in King's short story collection *Skeleton Crew*, in 1985. Considered one of the very shortest King stories he has ever written, it tells the tale of a little boy in elementary school, Charles (Charlie), who urgently needs to use the bathroom. His teacher, Miss Bird, is extremely mean and cruel, and belittles Charles about having to go. Eventually she gives in.

Upon entering the bathroom, he hears strange noises coming from one of the stalls. Finally, after working up enough courage, he ventures in and takes a look. To his utter surprise, there's a tiger in one of the bathroom stalls. When one of the classroom bullies comes to check on Charlie, he too hears strange noises. The boy ventures toward the stall as Charlie waits to see what happens next. Sounds of terror and horror can be heard coming from the stall. Hmmm, Charlie feels a bit vindicated. This story is considered one of King's most twisted tales.

In Bryan Higby's version of this Dollar Baby, he changed the genders of some of the characters, but the story remains intact. His unique usage of sound and music lend to the imagination of the viewer as to what is happening in the bathroom stall. This definitely makes it creepy. With a talented young cast, and true to King's original text, Bryan Higby's vision of *Here There Be Tygers,* was definitely a Dollar Baby film that was well-done and enjoyable.

Here is my exclusive interview with Dollar Baby director, Bryan Higby.

Anthony Northrup: What was it like growing up in the historic state of New York, and when did you first discover the works of Stephen King?

Bryan Higby: Northern NY was great. I spent my childhood fishing and camping, and watching movies at the Town Hall theater, which is an old 1920's movie house. My parents also took us to the drive in theaters all the time. My parents got me into movies from an early age. They actually owned their own video store, Cutting Edge Video, from the early 1990's until the place burned down in 2007. I knew Stephen King through the films based on his works; *Carrie, Salem's Lot, Christine, The Dead Zone, Silver Bullet* (one of my mom's favorites). I started reading King when I was 16. I bought a paperback edition of the unabridged version of *The Stand* in 1989, and never looked back. My parents actually bought me a subscription to the Stephen King library for about a year, and I got several hardcovers through that.

AN: You've worked a lot in theater and plays. Is it more of a challenge than working with film, and if so how so?

BH: Theater was my back up plan, LOL! I wanted to be a writer and filmmaker, but didn't have a film reel for NYU, and couldn't afford it anyway. My cousin and writing partner Ricky Snyder, was planning to go to Suny Potsdam for theater, so I figured why not. I acquired a bachelor's degree in theater. Theater has its own challenge in that you receive immediate feedback from your audience. There are also lots of block restrictions with theater that you don't have with filmmaking. I've always heard the saying that: Television is a producer's medium, theater is an actor's medium, and filmmaking is a director's medium. What they don't tell you, in all three you need a writer to start the engines of creativity. That's me!

AN: You directed the Stephen King novel *Misery*, as a play. Share with us your memories of that project?

BH: Misery on stage was fantastic. The play was a very loyal adaptation of the novel, going as far as severing Paul Sheldon's foot. We actually did that on stage, but came up with a way to stage it so that the cutting of the foot was between flashing of lightning. We also had a great artist Greg Peterson, who is known for his Lucille Ball murals, create an entirely realistic axe head made of foam rubber attached to a real wooden axe handle. The actress I cast as Annie Wilkes, was not an actress at all. Funny story. I was working at a donut shop in Jamestown NY where we had our black box theater, The Bunbury Theater company. One day while working, this big farm girl came into the store and I immediately thought—Holy Cow I'm seeing Annie Wilkes. She was big, creepy, and loved *Misery* the novel and the film. I offered her the role right there in line at the donut shop. She was thrilled, and she killed it. Our theater was in the industrial basement of an old folks home, and we built a huge rotating stage. This allowed us to build the entire interior of Annie Wilke's home, and then stage hands pulled out long steel bars that were slid into the stage, and rotated the stage on cue. It was amazing. I think I might still have video of that production. I'll send you some stills. We received rave reviews in the local paper, and as far off as Buffalo.

AN: When did you begin your career in writing? Was it before, or during the time you worked in theater?

BH: I wrote my first novel when I was 17. This would have been about a year after reading King's novels *The Stand, The Gunslinger, Drawing of the Three,* and *Needful Things.* I knew this was what I wanted to do. So I took about a year and wrote a Horror/Fantasy novel titled *The Lighthouse.* It was written out in longhand in like five notes books. I still have them in a lockbox at home. My second book was written in 1996. I was maybe 22. This story was titled, The Diary of a Logos, and was inspired by Franz Kafka and William Burroughs. That novel was the first one I ever published in 2005 with a small press in Maryland. The sequel, *A Logos At Large,* was published in 2006. Neither were commercial successes. Also from the early 1990's until the late 1990's, I wrote, and shot several no-budget short movies on analogue, and digital video. That was a huge learning experience. I don't consider my writing career starting until 2013, when I met bestselling author Joe Konrath, of the Jack Daniels thriller series fame. By then I'd written maybe six traditional genre novels. Joe was the writer who inspired me to self-publish. I was like, are you serious that's for losers. LOL! What I didn't realize was that through self-publishing, there were no gatekeepers, no one to say no. I could write what I wanted, how I wanted, and then have the books professionally copyedited, and I could then publish as many as I'd like. It's proven good. It's also given me motivation to keep writing. In the last 6 years I've written 29 novels in the Horror/Fantasy/Thriller genres. I love every day I can write.

AN: Who are some of your writing and filmmaking inspirations?

BH: Stephen King, Jack Kerouac, William Burroughs, Joe R. Lansdale, Bentley Little, Franz Kafka, just to name a few writers who inspire me. David Lynch, Stanley Kubrick, The Coen Brothers, Frank Capra, Billy Wilder, John Carpenter, George Romero, George Lucas, just to name a few filmmakers that inspire me.

AN: How, and when did you first learn about the Stephen King Dollar Baby program?

BH: I'd heard a story that Stephen King sometimes offered students, or independent filmmakers, the permission to do film versions of his short stories, at least 20 years ago. I didn't think about it again until one day I looked at my life and said, 'well you've written 35 novels, produced nearly 100 podcast episodes, directed theater, and film productions. You oughta have a higher profile than what you have now.' Then I asked myself, 'who could help? Which authors could help?' So I emailed writers I liked. F. Paul Wilson, Joe R. Lansdale, William Hjortsberg, Barry Gifford, Joe Konrath, Hugh Howey, and Blake Crouch. Some of these writers have become friends, but none of them have the pull that Stephen King has. So I visited King's website and looked at the millions of posts and despaired. Finally I noticed a section titled – Self Promotion, and thought that sounded kind of sleazy, but there were only 500 entries, so what the heck. I did a post, all in caps – DROWNING WRITER LOOKING FOR A LIFE JACKET!!! In this post I said I had three Horror EC Comic style novels, Pizza Man, Taco Bandits, and Chuck A Chik , that I think Mr. King would get a blast out of. Could I send them for the heck of it? Later that day the domain master contacted me and said if I was serious, she'd send me King's Bangor office address. That was Marsha DeFilippo, King's personal assistant since the late 1980's. I sent my three novels, and Marsha assured me they were in Steve's office, with no guarantee when he'd read them. Speed ahead a few months later. I read about some students in England who just got permission to do *Stationary Bike*. I emailed Marsha asking if I could do, *Here There Be Tygers*? She said go to the site, fill out the form, and we'll see. I did. Not long after, Margaret Morehouse, King's secretary sent me the contract. I signed it, and sent it back, and received a confirmation on November 2nd, 2018.

AN: Out of all the Stephen King short stories, what attracted you most to the story, *Here There Be Tygers*?

BH: *Here There Be Tygers,* just rang with truth for me. I read it as a small child who was bullied, and finally fate steps in and the bullies get theirs. It was simple and direct. I never looked deeper. It wasn't until after we shot our version that I read all this stuff about how Charlie was nuts and all this. So my version is very pure. I used actors who were Charlie's age, and did not over dramatize the subject matter. Filmmakers for some reason think they need to change King's source material and I'm always saying – WHY?! Stephen King is the most bankable writer to date. Don't change a thing. Especially when your story is only two and a half pages long. LOL!

AN: What changes did you make that made it your own, as opposed to King's original text?

BH: The only changes I made were in the sexes of the characters. Charlie became a girl, and her bully became Jenny Griffen, not Kenny. I also changed Miss Byrd to Mr. Byrd. These changes were all made for practical reasons. I decided to do the film because of my daughter Harper, who played the lead, my niece Sophia, who played the bully, and my long time collaborator, and actor friend, David Wilder.

AN: What was the main goal you wanted to achieve with this film?

BH: My main goal for this film was to tell King's personal story about bullies as purely as I could, as well as have a heck of a lot of fun doing it. There was also the alternative motivation, and that was to play in King's sandbox, and help promote my own work to King fans, because I know they'd love my stuff.

AN: Where was the movie filmed specifically, and were there any obstacles to overcome while filming there?

BH: We shot the film at Hudson Community College in Troy NY. We cast the film using Drama Kids International. The casting process was quick and easy. Securing the location presented a problem at first because the original elementary refused to allow us to film there. Debbie Gardner, at Hudson Valley Community College was a God send. My major problem, I was the only crew. My wife, and actor friend David Wilder helped set the location, but I did all the technical work, which turned out to be a problem because the original audio recording did not come through. I had to go back to HVCC and record all the foley sounds myself. I also had to record the actors voices again, and loop it into the film, which is why the audio sounds kind of funky. The cast was outstanding. Everyone did such a stellar job.

AN: How long was the film shoot and process from start to finish?

BH: The screenplay took maybe 2 hours to write. We're talking about 2 and a half pages short. I arranged a shoot at Hudson Valley Community College, in Troy NY, on March 26th. We shot one Saturday for about 4 hours. I did have to go back a couple of weeks later to record more audio.

AN: Share with us some of the challenges and behind-the-scenes funny moments working with kids?

BH: Well all the kids were great, but there were a couple who really played it. The boy at the very end, who looks from Charlie to Jenny's empty chair said to me, 'Maybe I should look at the missing students chair.' I said great, let's do it. We also had the cast decide that they wanted to do some crazy stuff while Mr. Byrd was out of the classroom. So we did a couple of takes of complete improvement, which didn't make it into the film, lol!

AN: Explain to us some of the challenges of creating the tiger for the film?

BH: The tiger was tough. Initially I thought that there was no way we could show any of the tigers. Just kind of hint at it. Actually at that point I started thinking maybe we should do more of an existential version, where everything is a projection from this crazy kids perspective. Then I thought no, that changes my initial love for the story. Then I played with the idea of using prop tiger parts. Like show a paw here, or a tail there, and include the sound effects. Then I said screw it, let's see if we can get a real tiger, and cut that in. We did.

AN: What is your greatest moment so far with the success of *Here There Be Tygers*?

BH: Well, *Here There Be Tygers,* hasn't had it's official debut yet, but we do have a Stephen King Dollar Baby Film Festival scheduled, at the historic Town Hall Theater, in Lowville NY on October 19th, at 10:00. We will also be playing 8 other dollar baby films there. Also Hudson Valley Community College booked me for a speaking engagement on November 22nd, at 7:00 PM, where *Here There Be Tygers*, will show along with three other Dollar Baby films. The most surprising thing was Jared Case, the curator for the George Eastman Museum in Rochester, contacted me. He said that he wanted to do a Stephen King film retrospective in October, and got some of my contacts for the other dollar babies. My version of *Here There Be Tygers* , will be archived in the Kodak film archives forever. That's pretty cool. Also we might have a special guest for our October 19th festival in Lowville, fingers crossed.

AN: Lastly, what is next for Bryan Higby?

BH: I have two new novels that I'm working on now. One is a horror novel: *The CarLowDen Chronicles*. The second novel is a literary novel that I'm very proud of titled, *Old Men*. It's a novel about faith and magical realism. I'd like to play more in Mr. King's sandbox, and would love to meet the guy just for a chat. You can also listen to a 90 minute podcast between David Wilder, who played Mr. Byrd in our film, and myself at the podcast link below. Also you can find out more about me, and work here:

https://www.amazon.com/Bryan-Higby/e/B00CWEFNVS
http://thelatlateshow.com

Thank you Bryan for taking the time to do this interview. Again to those of you reading, I hope you've enjoyed this article about Bryan Higby, and found his work as interesting as I did.

To see this fine short film adaptation of Bryan Higby's, *Here There Be Tygers,* look for a Dollar Baby film fest near you.

Here There Be Tygers by Jennifer Trudrung

Here There Be Tygers

Jennifer Trudrung
September 24, 2019

The Stephen King short story *Here There Be Tygers,* as far as I know, has only been adapted twice in the Stephen King Dollar Baby Program. It's been a privilege watching the adaptation of this story to a short film, directed by Jennifer Trudrung. However, through my interview with Jennifer, I've found she's no stranger to film and television. Her resume is quite impressive. In fact, one show she's had the pleasure of working on is one of my personal favorites, *The Walking Dead*. But before we get to the many endeavors Jennifer has taken on, let's get to know a little bit more about my latest Dollar Baby filmmaker, Jennifer Trudrung.

Jennifer Trudrung grew up in Pensacola, Florida. She attended Florida State University, where she earned her Masters Degree in English. From there she worked for the National Park Service before becoming active in the entertainment industry. She's also a parent, and at one point decided to stay at home to enjoy raising her little one.

It didn't take long though, before Jennifer became interested in acting. She began attending acting classes, found an agent, and went on auditions. Those classes and auditions paid off, and she began working in independent commercials. This soon led to becoming an extra in several television programs, such as *The Vampire Diaries, Homeland, Banshee,* just to name a few. However, she was extremely excited to land a recurring part as an extra in one of the biggest series on television, *The Walking Dead*. Jennifer also appeared in feature films such as, *The Hunger Games*, and the sequels as well.

Soon Jennifer's acting coach encouraged her to move away from being an extra, feeling it was time for her to do what might be best, writing and directing. It was at this time Jennifer began her career writing short films. As of this interview, she has made 10 short films.

Through connections in the Independent film industry, Jennifer heard from another Independent short film director, Vanessa Ionta Wright , who had directed her own Stephen King Dollar Baby film (*The Rainy Season*). Vanessa also shared with Jennifer that she headed her own festival, "Women In Horror Film Fest", and Jennifer contributed her short film, *Unbearing* to the lineup.

From that moment forward Jennifer knew, writing/producing/acting/directing was definitely for her, and has made quite the career for herself. She has also been a devout Stephen King fan all her life, and part of that fandom came true when she made the Stephen King Dollar Baby film, *Here There Be Tygers*.

Here is my review of Jennifer Trudrung's short film… *Here There Be Tygers*.

Here There Be Tygers is a very short story written by King while he was in high school. It was first published in 1968, in Urbis magazine, and later republished in his short stories collection *Skeleton Crew*, in 1985. The story is about a little boy in elementary school who really has to go to the bathroom. Having a very strict and cruel teacher, the little boy barely makes it to the bathroom. Once there, he is soon checked on by one of the bullies from the class, as well as the teacher, who are both greeted by a huge tiger! Is the tiger real, or just imagination? With a typical Stephen King twist, this is yet another tale of revenge against bullies who prey on the innocent.

In Jennifer Trudrung's version of this tale, the genders of the lead character Charlie, and the teacher, Mr. Bird, were both changed to female characters. Jennifer herself plays the very strict Ms. Bird, and does a fine job. Scary in fact. The film had a decent budget, thus lending to a movie theater feel and quality. With exception of the teacher, the rest of the cast are children, including Charlie, and they are very professional.

I enjoyed the special effects twist of the tiger itself, and the ending had its own unique and very eerie twist as well. This is one of the Dollar Babies that is sure to please and entertain those who love to leave a bit to the imagination.

I hope you will enjoy getting to know Dollar Baby filmmaker: Jennifer Trudrung, a bit better through my exclusive interview.

Anthony Northrup: While growing up in Florida, tell us what it was like, and when did you first discover Stephen King?

Jennifer Trudrung: Growing up in Florida as a child was amazing. My Dad would take me fishing all the time. We would go pompano and mullet fishing, and we would also gig (a type of spearfishing) flounders. The beach and coast were pretty magical, but as a teenager I pulled away from enjoying living so close, as I felt the pressure of having to look a certain way in a bathing suit on the beach. Middle school was really hard for me, and that was when I really got lost in reading, especially reading horror books. The first book by Stephen King that I read was *Night Shift*. The story *The Boogeyman* absolutely terrified me! I believe the first Stephen King movie I saw was *The Shining*.

AN: Tell us what it was like doing behind-the-scenes, and extra work on the *Hunger Games* films, *Homeland*, *Vampire Diaries,* and especially *The Walking Dead*? As I am a major fellow *Walking Dead* fan, what are your thoughts on the show currently, and do you have a favorite character?

JT: Doing background work on *The Hunger Games* movies was really cool, as I loved the books, and it was amazing to see the world from the books come to life. I was lucky as in each movie I worked on, I got selected to be in smaller scenes, and therefore got to see a more intimate look of how the actors and production worked. In the first movie, I was picked for a featured role (it didn't make the final film), but it was super cool as Jennifer Lawrence's hair and makeup people created my look. Also, *Homeland* was super fun, as I was in the scene from the first season, where Brody was going to detonate a bomb in the VP's bunker. Damien Lewis was brilliant to watch. He's a phenomenal actor. *The Vampire Diaries* was by far my favorite though, as I had a speaking role, got my own trailer, and worked one on one with Ian Somerhalder, and several other amazing actors, including Evan Gamble. They blew me away. Now for *The Walking Dead*. I LOVED working as a zombie, but it was a very long drive for me to get there, and very long days on set, so I kind of burned out after working on the show after three seasons. I did get killed by Rick twice, and I was also featured in that infamous dumpster scene with Glenn. That was my favorite day on set. I have to admit, I stopped watching the show after season 7. It kind of lost me. My favorite character is Daryl. The makeup and wardrobe people on *The Walking Dead*, were by far, my favorite part of being on the show though. The level of talent there is mind-blowing.

AN: Out of all the Stephen King short stories, what attracted you most about this one?

JT: When I looked at the stories that were available for Dollar Baby films, I was torn between *Lucky Quarter* and *Here There Be Tygers*. I knew I wanted to act in the film, so I was trying to choose one that had a role I would be interested in playing. *Here There Be Tygers*, won out because I liked the challenge of the tiger in the story, and because Ms. Bird is such a fun role to play.

AN: What changes did you make to this film to make it your own, as opposed to Stephen King's original text?

JT: Once I got over my fear to change anything that Stephen King wrote, I knew I wanted to do a gender swap for the lead role of Charlie. My daughter is also an actor, and I feel that there are a lot of shows and movies that feature middle school aged boys, and they have maybe one of two token girls, so I wanted to change that. I also wanted to show a young girl claiming her power, which is what I think is the core of the story. Charlie fights back to cruelty and suppression, and the idea of how a woman is supposed to be by the more conservative aspect of our society.

AN: So many King fans want adaptations to be as close to the original as possible. How do you handle the pressure to keep the fans happy?

JT: I honestly wanted to make this a film that Stephen King would watch and get a kick out of. I think he would like the gender swap and some of the political jabs that I incorporated. I love Stephen King, and I love how outspoken he is, and what an advocate he is for gender equality, among so many other things. I think I also kept the story line close enough that his fans will like it also. I hope so!

AN: What was it like working with an all children cast, and directing your daughter as she played the lead character, Charlie?

JT: Working with kids made me very nervous at first. The two leads, my daughter Penny, and Selah were complete pros though, and I wasn't worried about them. When I say I was nervous, it was more about keeping the featured background kids happy and engaged, as most of them didn't have any acting experience. This was the first time on a set for many of them. But they were all exceptional and engaged. I was so impressed! Penny and I quite honestly had a lot of fun playing such mortal enemies. Having such a close bond made it such a safe environment for us. Also

Penny and Selah are close friends, so there was laughter after every take. It was really a fun set.

AN: What was the main goal you wanted to achieve with this film?

JT: My main goal was to impress Stephen King, and to create a film that I could be proud of. I had the best team ever to work with, and we are all Stephen King fans. I think it's a love piece, and thank you to him.

AN: Where was the movie filmed specifically, and were there any obstacles you had overcome?

JT: We filmed at my daughter's school, and it was actually really awesome to film there, as the setting was perfect, and we had the complete trust of the school administration, as they knew me and my family. Shane Meador, our Production Designer, was able to walk into the school and pick out the best rooms and settings, and we painted a wall in the bathroom. His eye and expertise made the location and setting every better.

AN: How long did it take to make the film from start to finish?

JT: We filmed *Here There Be Tygers* in two days. They were long days, and we had to be very aware of working with kids and making sure of their hours. But we did it! Also Polly Schattel did an amazing job editing the film. She took her time with it, and I was able to assist her and learn from her as she edited. I'm so grateful to her for being such a gifted director and editor, and for bringing this film to life.

AN: What is your greatest moment so far with the success of *Here There Be Tygers*?

JT: My greatest moment is that every time I watch the film I'm proud of it. I love the way it looks, sounds, all of it. I'm actually sending the disc to Stephen King this week, and I'm just really proud of my whole team.

AN: What Stephen King story would you like to adapt on a larger scale?

JT: I would love, actually love to create a feature length version of *Here There Be Tygers*. It would be a challenge, but now that I know the characters I would love to create their backstories, and what led up to that moment in the bathroom.

AN: You have many titles: director, producer, screenwriter, actor, mother. Which of these is the hardest and most challenging?

JT: I have to say acting is the hardest for me. Every time I get an audition I get so excited. It's like playing a game at an arcade. You see this amazing prize and you are completely invested. You play your absolutely hardest and wait to see what happens. Then nothing. In acting, you rarely get that ultimate prize. You have to learn to stop asking why, and just keep plugging ahead, and keep playing.

AN: Where can fans see this film, and will it be playing at any film fests across the country? Lastly, sum up your experience making *Here There Be Tygers,* and what is next for Jennifer Trudrung?

JT: We are awaiting our premiere status. I have to admit I was pretty selective about our film festival submissions for this year, so I'm honestly not sure where it is going to premiere. It has been sent to numerous film festivals, and I'm hopeful it will have many showings all around the world over the next two years. We should know pretty soon about it's first screening, and I will keep screenings updated on our, *Here There Be Tygers,* a short film Facebook page. What is next for me? I'm going to hopefully be going to a bunch of film festivals over the next year! Also, I'm currently revising a feature length horror screenplay that will hopefully be going into production this Fall. I plan to really focus on writing feature length screenplays. Right now I have so many ideas in my head. Wish me luck!

We most certainly do wish you luck Jennifer! I want to thank Jennifer for taking time out of her busy schedule to do this interview, and I look forward to her many projects in the future.

You can find out where *Here There Be Tygers* will be playing at a film fest near you on its Facebook page, and follow Jennifer there as well for information on any of her upcoming projects.

Cain Rose Up

A.J. Gribble
October 14, 2019

I'VE INTERVIEWED MANY Stephen King Dollar Baby filmmakers, but to my knowledge this is the youngest. A.J. Gribble was only 17 years old when he made his film adaptation of this short story, written by author Stephen King. But before we get to the interview, let's learn a little more about A.J. Gribble.

A.J. Gribble was born August 13th, 2001. He grew up in Wilkes Barre, Pennsylvania, where he went to grade school, before attending James M. Coughlin High School. He later studied at the Wilkes Barre Area Career and Technical Center. During his college years, he was a rock n roll/Heavy Metal music DJ, at Deep Cuts Radio on 88.5 FM WRKC, at King's College. From 2016 through May 2019, he worked at Sheil's Supermarket. A.J. studied writing, directing, and editing, and eventually graduated from Wilkes Barre Area Career and Technical Center, specializing in Audio Visual Communications. A.J. currently lives in Saint Augustine, Florida, where he continues to pursue his film career.

However, A.J. began making short films at the young age of 13. Before he made his first Dollar Baby debut, he made several short films, which included, *Torment Of The Mind*, and was also co-director, and writer of, *My Frightful Night*. He already had a passion for making films, and he first heard of the Stephen King Dollar Baby program, in an article entitled: "50 Things You Didn't Know About Stephen King". A.J. knew right then and there, he wanted to adapt one of Stephen King's stories for the big screen.

Here is my Stephen King Dollar Baby film review of A.J. 's adaptation of, *Cain Rose Up.*

Cain Rose Up is one of Stephen King's earlier short stories. He wrote it in 1968, and it was first published in the Spring 1968 issue of Urbis magazine, and later republished in King's short story collection, *Skeleton Crew*, in 1985. This story is somewhat dark, and the subject matter is disturbing . The story centers on a young college student, Curt Garrish, who goes on a shooting spree to kill as many as he can at the campus. A.J. Gribble takes care to tackle this very serious subject matter with caution, yet still maintains the integrity of Stephen King's work. The gender change from a male lead, to that of a female, is one A.J. feels makes for a more interesting version of the story. The film was made well, but does leave the viewer unsettled in some respects.

With today's headlines full of tragic, real life circumstances of shootings at schools, malls, and concerts, this is once again another example of Stephen King's fictional work, imitating life, through storytelling.

I hope you will enjoy my exclusive interview with this young up and coming director, A.J. Gribble.

Anthony Northrup: What was it like growing up in Pennsylvania, and now living in Florida, and when did you first discover Stephen King? (book and movie).

A.J. Gribble: Growing up in PA is something I'm going to miss. Just turning 18 years old, and moving down to Florida is a huge change. But, it is so exciting! I grew up in Wilkes-Barre/Scranton… yes like in, The Office. It's nothing like the show, it's more run down than anything. I was lucky to move when I did, but it'll always be home to me. I first discovered King as a kid, thanks to my sister. She has every single one of his books, and she was always reading them. I always knew the name as a kid, but never really knew anything else about it. It wasn't until I was older, when she showed me Kubrick's *The Shining*, that I was blown away by it!

AN: Tell us about your experience working as a college radio DJ, and when you first start making short films?

A.J. G: It's funny you mention being a "college" radio DJ, because I was in high school when I started! I was the host of a rock/metal show every Tuesday, from 4-6pm, and it recently ended when I moved, but it was so much fun! I always took it seriously, and I had fun with it. I ran it for 2 years, and I was able to play whatever I wanted, I just had to keep it clean. That was the only rule. I am so grateful for having that opportunity at a

Cain Rose Up by A.J. Gribble

young age because I met a really great friend, and also the composer of *Cain Rose Up*. OneManStanding, or Brian Kutzor. I first started making short films when I was 13, by using my iPod camera. My brother and I would just make so many videos. Some good, and bad, but it was the start of something great!

AN: What are your short films *Torment of the Mind* and *My Frightful Night* about? Were they played at film fests, or was this just while you were at college?

A.J. G: *Torment of the Mind,* is about a student who falls asleep in detention, wakes up, and starts to face the darkness in his mind, but will he ever actually wake up? *My Frightful Night* is about a teen who must relive the same day over and over again, after being killed in nightmares, by a deranged masked killer. Yes, both were played at festivals, and won a few awards, and both were made when my friends and I were in our A/V class in high school. Our team was named "The Cinema Boyz". We have so many other films that we have done that we are all proud of, the latest one *The Hunted,* is our most successful.

AN: Out of all the Stephen King short stories, what attracted you to this one?

A.J. G: What attracted me to *Cain Rose Up,* was the story, and how relevant it really is. Especially when I first purchased the rights in February 2018, that's when every week there was a new school shooting. So I felt that to make this, even though it was incredibly risky, was the right choice, and right story to use.

AN: What changes did you make as opposed to its original text?

A.J. G: The biggest change that I have made was to change the gender of the main character, Kate. In the original, the character is Curt Garrish, a boy who goes on a shooting rampage. I felt that to change the gender of the main character was a must, because in the news you never see a girl shooter, always a guy. So, I wanted to see what would make a girl want to do it? What goes on inside their heads? Little changes were just taking out some characters, putting different ones in, changing some dialogue, and adding a few more scenes to make it longer.

AN: So many Stephen King fans want adaptations to be as close to the book as possible. How do you handle the pressure to keep the fans happy?

A.J. G: I really don't haha! As a fan myself, I always want adaptations to be close to the original material. As a filmmaker, it's hard to keep things close ,because sometimes things just don't work on the screen as they do in a book. Some things are just not able to be filmed, so I try to keep the best of both, keep the main story and details from the material, and also add some original things to make it my own.

AN: What was the main goal you wanted to achieve with this film?

A.J. G: What I wanted to achieve from this film, was for people to be more aware of what's going on in other people's lives. I also wanted people to enjoy the film.

AN: Where was the movie filmed specifically, and were there any obstacles to overcome while filming there?

A.J. G: It was mainly filmed at King's College in Wilkes-Barre, PA. No there weren't any obstacles, just little hiccups. The college gave us permission to film, and everything went great, but it was campus security that gave us a little trouble in the beginning. They stopped us a few times, but that was mainly it, filming went pretty smoothly.

AN: How long was the filming process from start to finish?

A.J. G: Bought the rights in February 2018, writing took a few months, after, filming started in May/June. Editing took a few months, then music took until January/February, which is when it premiered.

AN: With the headlines today full of deadly shootings, and innocent people dying (like the recent shootings in Texas and Ohio), was it difficult to choose this story of King's, since it involves a college student who goes on a deadly shooting spree? Was there tension on-set because of this, or did you handle this project with special care?

A.J. G: Not really, it wasn't difficult choosing it. The main reason I chose it was to bring awareness to it (mass shootings). The tension was a little high on set, but everyone was respectful of it, and treated it with care.

AN: What's the greatest achievement so far with the success of *Cain Rose Up*?

A.J. G: Some people might say "awards, festivals, nominations, wins", as the greatest achievements for their film. I might say that also. But honestly, the greatest achievement so far has been the friends and the relationships the cast and I have made. They are the best friends, and most hard working people I've ever met, and I'm so thankful that I got to make this with them.

AN: Which story of Stephen King's would you like to adapt on a larger scale?

A.J. G: Ah… now that's a tough one. If I ever got the chance, I would make a proper adaptation of *The Dark Tower* series. It totally deserves to be done right.

AN: You began making short films at the age of 13, and you made your first Stephen King Dollar Baby film at 17. You are the youngest Dollar Baby filmmaker I have interviewed, and know of. Do you feel age does, or doesn't matter when it comes to creating films, and getting your vision out there for others to enjoy?

A.J. G: Not at all! If you have stories to tell and want to make films, then go for it! No matter how old you are.

AN: Where can fans see your film, and will it be playing at any film fests in the near future?

A.J. G: Well, I'm sure people know that you can't release the film publicly online, but if anyone wants to view it, contact me for private viewings. In the near future, it could be! It's still in the festival circuit, so it could be at a few more in the future.

AN: Lastly, what's next for A.J. Gribble?

A.J. G: I am currently editing a new film that I have directed, so be on the lookout for that. A I'm also writing a feature length film, and hoping production can begin within the next few months, or early 2020!

Well, we are certainly looking forward to that, and any other future projects A.J. has in store for us. I want to thank A.J. Gribble, for taking the time from his busy schedule to talk with us today, and it has been so refreshing to interview such a young, and ambitious filmmaker, with such passion and excitement for the art. We certainly wish him the best of luck.

Popsy

Jon Mann
October 19, 2019

STEPHEN KING DOLLAR BABY filmmakers have covered a very wide range of King's short stories, but this short story, *Popsy*, is technically a semi-sequel to another Stephen King story, *The Night Flyer*. When I found out the two stories were connected, I couldn't wait to see this adaptation of the story to film.

Here is my review of Jon Mann's short film ... *Popsy*.

The short story *Popsy*, was first published in Stephen King's short story collection, *Nightmares & Dreamscapes,* in 1993. It's a story about a man named Sheridan, who is a compulsive gambler, who finds himself in deep debt to a man known only as Mr. Wizard. Mr. Wizard threatens Sheridan with serious bodily harm if he doesn't pay up, and has a way of paying off his debt is through child trafficking, sending the children on a boat to another country. Sheridan doesn't want to know anymore than he has to, only wants his debt paid off, so he complies with Mr. Wizard's sick request. When Sheridan kidnaps a child from the local mall, he grabs the wrong child, meaning he has met his match, and then some. This story by King is scary, creepy, and entertaining , a good read, especially around Halloween time.

Jon Mann's vision of this tale is spot on! He grabs his viewers, and draws them in with this disturbing scenario of stalking and kidnapping. He brings the characters to life with a cast that completely embodies those in the story. As the terror escalates we want more. All this eventually leads to death, but whose death?

Jon did a wonderful job with this adaptation of one of the more disturbing subjects that King has broached. This film, as I say, draws the viewer in, and you can't help but wonder what comes next.

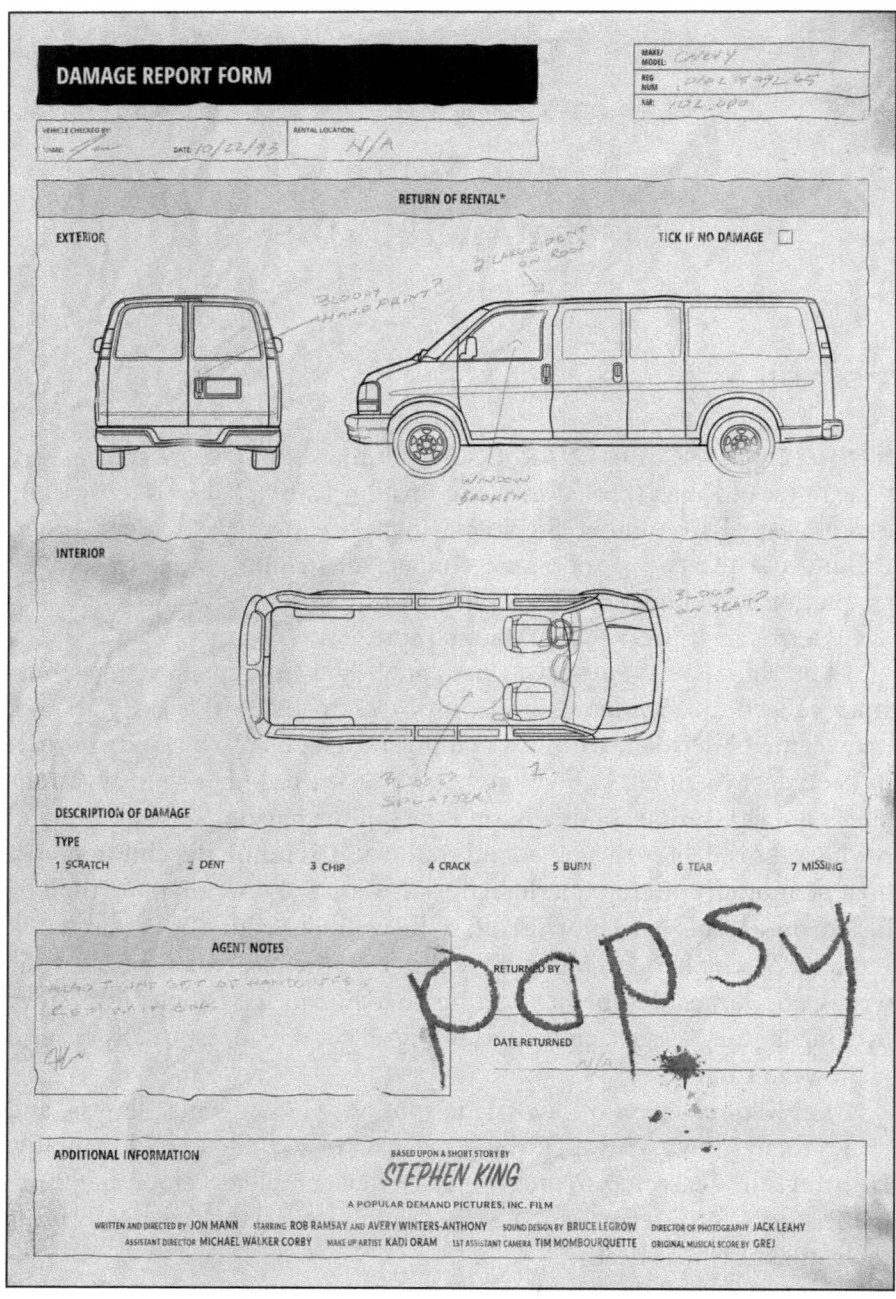

Popsy by Jon Mann

Let's get to know a little bit about Jon now.

Jon Mann was born on October 31st, 1989.. Halloween, and was born in Fredericton, New Brunswick, Canada. After grade school, he attended Leo Hayes High School, in Fredericton, and graduated in 2007. Jon continued his higher education at Acadia University, majoring in Political Science. He graduated in 2011. Jon also attended the New York Film Academy, majoring in screenwriting, in 2013.

In 2017, Jon, and production partner, Rob Ramsay won at the 2018, National Screen Institute's Totally Television program for their project, Wolfville, optioned by Take the Shot Productions. Jon's film Cahoots, won Best Film at the Canadian International Comedy Film fest, in 2019. His 2019 film, *Missy*, was purchased by the Canadian Broadcast Company for distribution, and premiered nationally.

At one time, Jon was also the Communications Correspondent at Acadia's Men's Hockey. He also founded Popular Demand Pictures. Currently Jon lives in Halifax, Nova Scotia, and his Dollar Baby film *Popsy*, is being presented at the Silver Lake Film Fest in Fredericton, New Brunswick.

I hope you will enjoy my exclusive interview with Stephen King Dollar Baby filmmaker, Jon Mann!

Anthony Northrup: You were born in, and grew up in the province of New Brunswick, Canada. Share with us some of your early memories of living there, and you first discovered Stephen King's books. Which is your favorite King book/film?

Jon Mann: One of my earliest memories of growing up in Fredericton was my mom taking me to see *Jurassic Park i*n theaters. That was the summer of '93, which would put me at three-and-a-half. Going to the rink for hockey, and the soccer field in the summer also comes to mind. I'm still best friends with the guys and girls I grew up playing sports with. When I was about 10 years old, my family moved from one side of town to the other, and I didn't really have many friends right away, so I was reading a lot. I read *IT*, and *The Shining* in middle school, and had seen Kubrick's *The Shining*, even before that. Reading *IT*, reminded me of my friends, on our bikes getting into lame trouble. It completely changed what I thought it meant to be a kid. I hate to say it, but I think *The Shining* is still my favorite adaptation. It feels almost sacrilegious to say so. *Stand By Me*, is a very close second. Mr. King is so good at writing about the idiocy and confusion of boyhood, and young manhood. I think he got me at the right time (laughs).

AN: What made you decide to change from a political science major, to screenwriting, eventually leading you to filmmaking?

JM: Honestly, more than anything I was sort of told to. I'm an English drop out. I did a year-and-a-half with English as my major. I was writing creatively in high school, and as a hobby through my undergrad, and I thought it would be a lot more creative writing, which is my own fault. I got a really bad mark on what I thought was an awesome essay, on Frankenstein, then had a really embarrassing moment in front of my class talking about, The Road, then wrote a terrible essay on Eleanor Rigby. Those were all within 2 weeks of each other. That's really when I knew it wasn't for me. I tried to argue my voice too much, without knowing what I was trying to say. I took a really great class from a professor I really admire: The Politics of Water. The department was much more keen on argumentative essays, so it was a pretty natural fit. By fourth year, I was starting to read more and more about film, and film theory, and I was starting to get bored with school. I was a terrible student. I wrote a short story called Ethan, about a young boy in the hospital whose roommate ends up trying to ruin his life. I had such a passion for film, but never thought it would ever be a career choice. I always had a fire in me about movies, but I don't think I really recognized it until the last year of my undergrad. I was fortunate to get into a great film school, and all of a sudden, I was an A+ student.

AN: Your short films, *Cahoots* and *Missy*, have won some awards, share with us what they are about, and how that led you to the Stephen King Dollar Baby program?

JM: Yeah! Cahoots is a comedy, about a guy who reaches out to two old acquaintances to tell them about his new job. They're happy for him, because he's had a bit of a rough stretch, but their patience runs thin with him when he tells them his new gig is doing social media for Isis.

It's a ridiculous concept, so I wrote it trying to make it as heartfelt as possible. It's a weird look at contemporary friendship, and what it means to take care of yourself in 2019. It won Best Film at the Canadian International Comedy Film Festival, and I'm incredibly proud of it. I love that movie. *Missy*, was recently purchased by the Canadian Broadcast Company (CBC), for distribution, and is available on their streaming service, CBC Gem. It's about a man living in the woods who finds a mannequin, and how his life starts to unravel after finding it. It's a bit of a psychological drama. Rob Ramsay is the star of both films, and absolutely crushes it! Rob is such a talent, and some of the scenes between him and the mannequin are unbelievable from an acting perspective. Rob has a great part in *It: Chapter 2,* actually. Both films gave Rob and I a lot of validation as to what types of stories we are trying to tell, and I know they went a long way to being accepted into the Dollar Baby Program.

AN- Out of all the Stephen King short stories, what attracted you most to this one?

JM: The ending! I think it's the quintessential King story. It's like being led down a hallway, and each passing door has something creepier and creepier behind it. Then all of a sudden, the real monster has been crawling on the ceiling behind you the whole time.

AN: What changes did you make to *Popsy*, in order to make this your own, as opposed to King's original text?

JM: Not too much. A big part of the short story is that Sheridan is motivated by a mob boss to pay off some gambling debts. I didn't find it necessary to establish why he was trying to find a kid to kidnap. I think the not-knowing is pretty creepy, too. I wanted to keep the world small, and really just focus on the kidnapping itself. I felt that revealing too much of Sheridan's motivation would become distracting in an 11-minute short. I had to make some dialogue changes, because obviously in film, you do not have the luxury of knowing a character's every single thought, the way you do in a novel or short story.

AN: So many Stephen King fans want adaptations to be as close to the book as possible, how do you handle the pressure to keep the fans happy?

JM: I think with the success of *It: Chapter One* (2017), and *It: Chapter 2* (2019), we are seeing that it's not completely necessary to stay absolutely true to intellectual property. Hell, look at *The Shining*. Some things work in a novel, but would never work on screen. I think Muschietti did an incredible job with It. At the end of the day, I wanted to make a movie that I would want to see, using a story I admire, from my favorite author. Of course I want everyone to like *Popsy*, and as a Stephen King fan myself, the pressure I listen to is mostly between my own ears to begin with. I think the fans will be happy, and true fans will pick up on a lot of easter eggs in the film. I don't think anyone will be disappointed. Pressure is an interesting thing, especially in art. All you can do is bring your eye and your taste to a project, and hope that people will get behind it. So far, I have been fortunate that people have enjoyed what I have to offer!

AN: What was the main goal you wanted to achieve with this film?

JM: It's probably cheesy, but I really wanted to do the story justice. This is such an incredible program, and I owe so much to Mr. King in my development as a story-teller, and story-digester. The least I could do, is not screw up one of his best short stories (laughs).

AN: Where was the movie filmed specifically, and were there any obstacles to overcome while filming?

JM: We started filming on a Friday night, and we had a mall lined up who backed out on Tuesday afternoon. We had everything signed, and then they read the script. Go figure. Other than that, things were great!

AN: How long was the film shoot, and the process from start to finish?

JM: The filming process itself took about 3.5 days. Fredericton was really accommodating, and the business community there was very welcoming to us. New Brunswick has a great film community, and even though I have been living in Nova Scotia for a few years, I find comfort knowing that New Brunswick will always support my projects.

AN: What is the greatest moment you've had so far with the success of *Popsy*?

JM: Some of the reviews that have come in for the film have made me really proud of what we were able to accomplish. We screened at the FIN: Atlantic International Film Festival in September, and to be there with so many other great films was really special. A lot of the crew, family, and friends were able to attend as well, and that is what is most important to me.

AN: What Stephen King story would you like to adapt on a much larger scale?

JM: Well, it was *The Girl Who Loved Tom Gordon*. I think that would be an interesting challenge. *A Good Marriage,* was another story I would have loved to have a stab at. As far as those that have yet to be done, I'd love a chance with *Fair Extension*. It's another stereotypically King story, in all of the best ways. It reminds me of Hemingway's short stories. *The Night Flier,* too, of course. That story has 'feature' written all over it.

AN: Where, and when can Stephen King fans see this film? Will it be playing at any film fests across the globe?

JM: We have some screenings approaching that haven't been announced publicly yet, but I can't wait for people to find out. I wish I could say more!

AN: Lastly, What is next for Jon Mann?

JM: I'm currently writing a feature film based on a folktale from New Brunswick, about a woman who meets the devil. I'm always writing with my production partner Rob Ramsay, and we are getting together to write our next project in November. I have another short written that I am trying to find a producer for, so if anyone out there is looking for a script, let me know (laughs).

Well, there you are. I have no doubt this talented filmmaker will find plenty of producers to do his future projects. Thank you Jon, for taking the time to do this interview for us all.

If you can't see this new release at a film fest near you, then by all means, read this Stephen King tale *Popsy*, in *Nightmares & Dreamscapes*, and find out the basis of what motivated Jon to choose this particular short story.

Uncle Otto's Truck by Dan Sellers

Uncle Otto's Truck

Dan Sellers
November 3, 2019

STEPHEN KING IS NO STRANGER to "haunted" vehicles. With stories such as, *Mile 81*, *Trucks* (aka *Maximum Overdrive*), *From A Buick 8*, and the queen of "haunted" vehicles: *Christine!* But there was a short story first published in Yankee magazine in 1983 and later published in Stephen King's short story collection, *Skeleton Crew* in 1985. A talented filmmaker, Dan Sellers, has brought this short story to life.

Dan Sellers is originally from Wadesboro, North Carolina. He attended University of Charlotte, Class of 2007, and also attended University of Greensboro Class of 2009. Dan also attended the Chicago School of Professional Psychology for graduate school. Dan created his production company, Wreak Havoc Productions about 6 years ago. He released his first film in 2014, *Hank vs. The Undead*, a zombie horror/comedy feature film. Dan also produced the documentary, *Samie The Comic Book Man* and the documentary short, *Trouble Will Cause*. He also produced *Midnight Shift* and *Countdown To Midnight*. Havoc Productions also publishes podcasts and hosts an annual international film festival. Dan currently lives in Greensboro, North Carolina with his family and has plenty of film and writing projects he is currently working on.

Here is my review of Dan Sellers adaptation of Stephen King's short story, *Uncle Otto's Truck*!

Uncle Otto's Truck is a short story written by Stephen King that first appeared in Yankee magazine in 1983 and later appeared in King's short story collection, *Skeleton Crew* in 1985. The story is about an abandoned truck owned by Otto Schenck and George McCutcheon, Castle Rock businessmen in the post-depression era. After Otto purposely crushes

George beneath his truck, the murderer becomes obsessed with the truck. Otto insists that the truck is not only moving on its own, but plans to kill him. He becomes a recluse, living in a house he built across from the truck itself, and generally begins to lose his sanity. In Dan's version, the niece tells the story and makes a horrifying discovery at the uncle's house.

I really enjoyed Dan's adaptation of Stephen King's *Uncle Otto's Truck*. It was creepy, interesting, scary, and intriguing. It was filmed beautifully throughout Virginia and North Carolina. and Dan knows how to tell a tale and keep you interested. This is a great story by Stephen King but one of the better Dollar Baby adaptations.

Uncle Otto's Truck has been adapted by artist Glenn Chadbourne for *The Secretary of Dreams,* a collection of comics based on King's short fiction by Cemetery Dance in December 2006.

Here is my exclusive interview with Stephen King Dollar Baby, Dan Sellers!

Anthony Northrup: What was it like growing up in North Carolina? Were you always a horror fan? And what was your first Stephen King book and film?

Dan Sellers: North Carolina is a fairly segmented place: geographically you've got very distinct types of places from the Atlantic ocean to the Appalachian mountains, and very rural landscapes and big cities in between. But there's also a darker side to North Carolina that I've always been intrigued with: it's steeped in folklore and ghost tales, which was the inspiration of a podcast I produce called "Carolina Haints." I've always been a horror fan, ever since I was a small child. I was allowed to watch all kinds of horror films and things that I probably shouldn't have been exposed to, but was, and I've always gravitated toward dark and macabre things. The first Stephen King book I read was *Different Seasons* at the age of 13. At a young age I fell in love with *The Shawshank Redemption* and naturally sought out the source material. Which leads to reading other works of horror.

AN: What made you decide to go from Psychology to filmmaking? Share with us how your production company, Wreak Havoc Productions got started?

DS: I'll answer both of these questions with this response. I've always been a film fanatic and even at a young age was fascinated by movies and filmmakers and the process of filmmaking. As a teenager, I even tried to make a horror film but that fell through, as so many projects do, unfortunately. However, as an adult, the idea of making a film just kept gnawing and pulling at me until I couldn't ignore the urge. These days, the tools to make a film are very accessible to most people: with the technology being available, I really ran out of excuses to not follow that dream. In 2013, I set out to make my first film, a zombie-comedy horror film, which eventually became *Hank vs. The Undead* (2014) and it was essentially just an exercise in filmmaking. I just wanted the experience of making a film, and to learn just by the process of doing. And I absolutely learned a lot! I'll never discourage anyone from attending film school or seeking some formal way of studying film, but for me, it took making a decision to make a film and to go through the steps of getting it done, to really learn. So, what started out as just a self-indulgent exercise has become a strong passion.

AN: You said you attempted a Stephen King Dollar Baby film, *Beachworld* before you made *Uncle Otto's Truck*, but it fell through. What did you do differently to get *Uncle Otto's Truck* made this time?

DS: I was briefly involved in an adaptation of *Beachworld* as a producer. I was not involved in the day to day decision making and work on that film, which had not even gotten into production, besides some 2nd unit footage. The biggest thing I did differently with Uncle Otto was that I not only was the producer, but served as the Writer and Director as well.

AN: Out of all of the Stephen King short stories, what attracted you most to this story?

DS: I've always found myself attracted to stories of obsession. Vertigo is one of my all-time favorite films. Something just struck a chord with me about Uncle Otto that I couldn't ignore. There's also a playfulness to it that resonated with me as well. As I read the story, I couldn't stop envisioning how I would make the film and I too became obsessed with getting the rights. I also loved the idea of telling a story that takes place in Castle Rock and being able to have fun in that little world that King created was just too much of a grand opportunity to pass up.

AN: What changes did you make to make this your own as opposed to King's original text?

DS: There were quite a few things here and there that were modified or condensed from King's story into my script. The most notable is the decision to change the narrator from Otto's nephew to his niece. I thought that this was something that could easily be done without changing anything at the heart of the story. It just seemed to work better for the film too to have that male/female dynamic between the two main characters. Besides that, I think our film is a fairly close adaptation to King's text.

AN: So many Stephen King fans want adaptations to be as close to the book as possible. How do you handle the pressure to keep those fans happy?

DS: I don't worry at all about Stephen King fans. Primarily when I'm making a film, I'm concerned about pleasing myself as an audience member. I try to make films that I would like to see. My films are not for everyone, and Uncle Otto is no exception: it's certainly based closely on King's short story, but it's through my filter and is my point of view. Not all King fans will likely love it and I'm Ok with that. The right people will enjoy it. Secondly, I was more concerned about making a film that Stephen King himself would enjoy and recognize as being a faithful or at least serviceable adaptation. I figured if I could make myself happy and then Mr. King, then his fanbase would follow along.

AN: What was your main goal you wanted to achieve about this film?

DS: My main goal was to simply make an enjoyable and entertaining film. Plain and simple. I knew we had great source material to use and I didn't want to mess things up by half-assing it. I probably worked harder on it than anything else I've ever made and have pushed people harder and asked for them to deliver more than I've typically done. It was important to me to get the film right. That was really the main goal: just to do it well.

AN: Where was the movie filmed specifically and were there any obstacles you had to overcome while filming there?

DS: Principal photography took place in Patrick County, Virginia which is a very rural, mountain location. It was a beautiful place, but there was no running electricity, water or cell service. So that presented a ton of logistical issues that my producers and I had to work on tackling every day. It felt like camping a lot of the time but my cast and crew worked very hard during the shoot and we all made the best of it. The rest of the film was shot between a handful of locations in North Carolina including Mount Airy, Danbury, Madison and Greensboro.

AN: How long was the film shoot and process from start to finish?

DS: From the point of signing the contract with Mr. King to the premiere, it was right at a year. Pre-production by far was the longest stretch of this film. Finding the right shooting locations, casting, and finding the truck were all major hurdles. We also had a pretty significant crowdsourcing fundraiser that took several months to implement. But we reached our goal and raised $3000 to make the film. The main production was done over the course of four days while other scenes were shot over the course of several weeks. Once production was finished, I worked on the film in post-production for about six weeks. Between editing the film myself, recording ADR, working with a composer, etc. there was a tremendous amount of work being done in a short amount of time.

AN: What is your greatest moment so far with the success of *Uncle Otto's Truck*?

DS: That's hard to say because this has been such a great experience that it's hard to choose a greatest moment. However, I'd have to say that there was a lot of relief in seeing a special effects apparatus operate as planned. We had spent a considerable amount of our budget on essentially one special effect shot and a lot was riding on it. Our amazing special effects supervisor, Matt Patterson created a mechanism that worked beautifully in the film. It was amazing to be on set and shooting this effect in person. Matt was so relieved once it was finished. I think the combination of seeing it work in person and seeing it work in-camera was a great feeling of success.

AN: What Stephen King story would you like to adapt on a larger scale?

DS: I honestly don't have a good answer to this question. I have not thought about personally making another Stephen King adaptation until just now. However I was thinking the other day that I wish some talented filmmaker would remake *The Dead Zone* and do a really great job with it. I feel that we're at an interesting time politically to see how that might play with a wide audience. Cronenberg's 1983 adaptation is a particularly well-made film and one of my favorite King films, so whoever lands that task has their work cut out for them.

AN: Where did you get the actual truck used in the film and what happened to it when the film was finished?

DS: The truck's name is Festus and it's a local truck from the area in which we filmed the movie in Patrick County, Virginia. Festus's owner was a very kind gentleman who assisted in a major way throughout filming. Festus was a running automobile which we were delighted to use. Initially we thought we would have to find a real derelict truck and have it towed to the set. But we got extraordinarily lucky to find Festus. I don't know that luck had so much to do with it as the incredible producing skills of my producing partner, Sammie Cassell. He was the mastermind behind finding the truck and getting as much out of it as we did.

AN: Stephen King has had many films and television shows from his books adapted in North Carolina, such as, *Firestarter, Silver Bullet, Maximum Overdrive, Under the Dome,* and many others. What is it about North Carolina that brings filmmakers to your state to make their projects?

DS: That's hard to say: at one point, NC was known as one of the biggest filmmaking states in the country. Due to some really bad political decisions to cut tax incentives in NC, most productions have moved to Georgia. My hometown was used to film Spielberg's The *Color Purple* and the horror classic, *Evil Dead 2*. So it's always been part of North Carolina lore for me. Having Screen Gem Studios in Wilmington helPS: they're currently filming *Halloween Kills* and soon, *Halloween Ends* there right now.

AN: Where can viewers see the film? Will it be playing at a film fests and if so, Where?

And Lastly, What is next for Dan Sellers?

DS: We plan to submit *Uncle Otto's Truck* to as many film festivals as we can afford. So far we're 3 for 3 and I definitely hope to keep that streak up as long as I can. Audiences in North and South Carolina will be able to see it this month and next at the Horror Movie Freaks Film Festival, the Stranger Days Independent Film Festival and at AtomaCon Short Film Festival. We also plan to host a few free screenings around North Carolina over the next few months.

I'm currently in talks to direct a short horror film here in NC. Besides that, I plan to spend the majority of the next year doing some writing. I've got a few feature length screenplays that I need to get on paper. There are also two books I'm working on that are both connected to ongoing projects of mine. I'm also very involved in the day to day running of my company, Wreak Havoc Productions. We're readying a new film for its upcoming release, entitled *Sea Salt Wind,* and we have ongoing shows called the Wreak Havoc Production Film Buffs Podcast and The Carolina Haints Podcast, both of which I host and produce. There's also the annual

Wreak Havoc Horror Film Festival, which is an international showcase of independent shorts and feature films in the genre. All of these projects are certainly enough to keep me busy over the coming year.

I want to thank Dan Sellers for taking the time to speak with us today and wish him great success in his future projects.

All That You Love Will Be Carried Away by Hendrik Harms

All That You Love Will Be Carried Away

Hendrik Harms
February 15, 2020

ONE OF THE MOST ENJOYABLE parts of doing Stephen King Dollar Baby interviews and film reviews is meeting talented filmmakers, not only from the United States, but from all over the world! My latest Dollar Baby interview is with a talented director from the UK, Hendrik Harms.

Hendrik Harms studied at Keele University and graduated in 2o11. With various jobs and experience under his belt, Hendrik eventually started his own production company 'Harms Way Studios' in 2018, in Worcester, Worcestershire. He is a writer, producer, director, and he is now a part of the Stephen King Universe with his Stephen King Dollar Baby film, All That You Love Will be Carried Away.

Here is my review of *All That You Live Will Be Carried Away.*

All That You Love Will Be Carried Away was first published in the January 29th, 2001 issue of the *New Yorker* Magazine. In 2002, it was published in the short story collection, *Everything's Eventual*. The story is about a traveling frozen foods salesman. While staying at a hotel, the salesman is debating with himself whether or not to take his own life.

During the course of his travels he keeps a journal filled with different sayings and graffiti he has seen in bathrooms. He feels these sayings have meaning, and speak to him in a way no one else can. As he waits outside the hotel, he lets fate decide if he should kill himself, or not.

Hendrik Harms version of this Dollar Baby has an amazing cast of actors that prove their talents are above and beyond. The film has a different take on the Stephen King short story, however, it keeps you intrigued, entertained, and amazed all at once. I enjoyed this version of Stephen King's short story, and it showcases Hendrik's amazing talent and vision, which definitely does King's story justice.

Here is my exclusive interview with Dollar Baby director, Hendrik Harms.

Anthony Northrup: What was it like growing up in Worcestershire? What were some of your early influences, and what was your first Stephen King book and film?

Hendrik Harms: Worcestershire is a gorgeous city in the center of England. It's rich with history and culture and has excellent transport links, so travelling to wherever you need to go is a breeze. This has given me a real love for my hometown, especially trying to build a creative career as I've never had a problem reaching sets or locations. My early influences are probably whodunnit dramas. I love a good mystery series especially with a twist. I always remember the first time I watched *Se7en* and was amazed at the twists in that. My first King film was *The Shining* when I was very young (probably younger than I should have been!). My first book, I'm embarrassed to say was actually the *All That You Love Will Be Carried Away*. I've been more of a casual King lover, which was part of the reason I wanted to make a film of one of his stories, as I had an almost outside objectiveness rather than trying to live up to a favorite author.

AN: How is it that you went from Criminology to filmmaking? Looking back, do you think you would've done well in that field?

HH: I went back and forth really because I couldn't decide. Like I said before, I'd grown up on whodunnit and mysteries, and I wasn't sure if I wanted to write them or live them! I think I would have loved a job in it, but I'd have missed the freedom that a creative job gives me.

AN: You wear many hats: Writer, Producer, Editor, Actor, Marketer, and Director: what is the most challenging for you out of all of these?

HH: That's a hard one to answer because they each carry different challenges. I wouldn't say I find any challenging in the sense I struggle, but I definitely prefer writing and directing if I'm given a choice!

AN: You said you began making films for fun at the age of 16 when you got your first camera. What type of films did you want to make back then?

HH: When I was very young it was doing adaptations/reboots of tv shows I'd loved. There was one in particular that I loved around that time which was *Due South*. I was gutted when it was cancelled, and started writing how it could be remade. As I got older I honed these ideas and skills into more original stories and characters. I started writing prose, as that's a lot easier (as it's a solo task), but I've always preferred the format of screenplays, so when I started making films I was glad to be able to move back into this medium.

AN: How did you first hear about the Stephen King Dollar Baby film program?

HH: I heard about it on a news program and researched it. I almost made one a number of years ago based on *The Doctor's Case* story. I briefly considered that again when I took on this new project, but ultimately I felt that the Sherlock Holmes market was over-saturated and wanted to try a more original, lesser known story.

AN: Out of all of the Stephen King short stories, what attracted you most to *All That You Love Will Be Carried Away*?

HH: Stephen King has a lot of identifiable stories and characters, carrying through a very distinctive style. However, when I read *All That You Love*, I was surprised as it was strangely very grounded and real, and dealt with some truly prevalent issues in a heartbreaking way. That, coupled with the graffiti, made me feel there was a great template to build my story on top of.

AN: What changes did you make, to make this your own version as opposed to King's original text?

HH: The original followed just a single character, and I'd researched other versions of the adaptation online and saw that they were very faithful. My first film had actually been about a solo character, so I didn't really want to do that again, I wanted to try something new. Also, due to the nature of the story, most adaptations tell it through narration and voice overs. Although these were fantastic, I wanted to make my version a bit more dynamic, so I decided that I'd bring the graffiti to life as almost fractured personalities of Alfie who's "lives/stories" are moved forward by the different graffiti's he finds and attributes to them.

AN: So many Stephen King fans want adaptations to be as close to the book as possible. How do you handle the pressure to keep the fans happy?

HH: I didn't really feel the pressure to be honest. The Dollar Baby scheme has been running for like 40 years and there's been so many faithful adaptations of the stories, I thought I'd try something new, where fans of the story could find something unique to take away, and newcomers could also enjoy the narrative. I also felt that it was a lesser known story to the more casual of King fans, as people who watch it don't realize that I've changed anything, and think it has the King feel to it. That's a massive compliment in a way because it meant I was able to capture his signature style of storytelling.

AN: What was the main goal you wanted to achieve with this film?

HH: I wanted to do something fresh. Really amply Alfie's spiraling mental health and give it a distinct style and feel. When we had our premiere of the film we raised money for Mind (a mental health charity), so I think we not only achieved our main goal, but went above and beyond!

AN: Where was the movie filmed specifically, and were there any obstacles you had to overcome while filming there?

HH: We tried to keep filming locally as much as possible, so it was mainly filmed in Worcestershire. I am trying very hard to grow this area for creativity and filmmaking, so it's important to me that people who attend university here see that they don't need to move away to have jobs in this field. Some obstacles however, well, where to start!? We filmed in a hotel who were absolutely wonderful people but it was the height of summer in a hotel room with 8 cast members, the crew and bright neon lights… It was HOT! One actress almost fainted in one take. We also had neighbors in the hotel rooms so there would be tv's and showers going especially in the morning. Luckily they were very accommodating for us. Then we had to film in a working lobby, which means we kept having to pause to allow people to check in. The best memory of that was our Clerk actor stood behind the desk with a real customer in front of him, and him looking around for help.

AN: How long was the film shoot and process from start to finish?

HH: We shot for 5 days but pre and post production took a little longer. The whole thing was probably a year of work, which is crazy to think that it culminated in just 5 days of filming with a 45 minute film.

AN: You have an amazing cast ensemble, share with us your casting choices and the auditions for the film?

HH: We wanted to try an interesting approach for this film. We had over 100 applications and I didn't want to give away the twist that these characters were fictitious, as I thought it might affect the way they auditioned them. So, instead of giving them script pages, I gave those who auditioned just 3 words that summed up the character, and sent them off to either find a monologue, or write a monologue that they thought fit those traits. It was such a successful exercise because you could immediately see these characters coming to life. We had an absolutely stellar cast, what a line up. I do have to make special mention to the ones who were unsuccessful though, as it was so hard to choose and we were dumbfounded at how lucky we were to have such exceptional talent apply.

AN: What is your greatest achievement so far with the success of *All That You Love Will Be Carried Away*?

HH: Aside from winning awards, I'd say the relationships. I really wanted the actors to get to know each other, so we had a day of beer and pizza, and a WhatsApp group on the go. Since they were all playing, effectively, the same person, they needed to be totally comfortable with one another. Their chemistry was electric, and then after being in a hotel room like sardines, I think the crew came together in the same way. It's kind of a little family, and we're all still in touch. I'd say those friendships were worth more than the awards.

AN: What Stephen King story would you like to adapt on a larger scale?

HH: I would have said *11/22/63*, but James Franco beat me to it! I'm a sucker for time travel and alternate realities.

AN: Where and When can fans see this film? Will it be playing at film fests around the world?

HH: It will be in film festivals all over the world, if you follow Harm's Way Studios on our social media, we'll be doing announcements of when showings will be on. Hell, if you want one, get in touch and we can see if we can arrange something!

AN: Lastly, what's next for Hendrik Harms?

HH: On the film front, I am gearing up for my first feature. I have a solid story that I think will translate very well to screen. Aside from that, I have just opened up a film studio in Worcester and am working with local businesses, the university, the council to bring a city wide international film festival to my city next year. Like I said before, I am very determined to bring filmmaking to this area, for all the fantastic talent we have in this area. So, watch this space there is lots more to come!

AN: And watch we certainly will!

Thank you Hendrik, for taking time with me today, and sharing your thoughts and experience with the making of your Stephen King Dollar Baby film, *All That You Love Will Be Carried Away*.

In the Deathroom

Nicole Jones-Dion
March 1, 2020

AFTER OVER 40 YEARS of Stephen King Dollar Baby adaptations, it is refreshing to see the list of women Dollar Baby directors growing more and more each year. Their visions are unique and entertaining and my latest Dollar Baby interview filmmaker is no exception. Nicole Jones-Dion, brings here writing talents and fandom to the big screen.

Nicole Jone-Dion was born at an Army Base in Fort Belvoir, Virginia and traveled everywhere from Hawaii to Germany. She grew up in Wilmington, North Carolina (a place many of Stephen King full-length feature films were filmed years ago). She attended New Hanover High School in Wilmington and later continued her education by winning a North Carolina writer's award which got her a full scholarship to Duke University. She is studying Creative Writing, history, and theology while at Duke University. Nicole later on went into the military. Nicole has a growing fandom for video games, comic books, writing, and filmmaking. Because of that fandom, it led her to films which she made a horror/comedy called, Roadkill Zoo. It was nominated for an Eisner Award. She has won many awards and nominations for Best Director and Best Female Director.

Nicole got into film after she got out of the Army, she moved to LA to work in video games. At the time, video games were basically choose-your-own-adventure movies (remember Wing Commander)? She started writing spec scripts for games, and a friend read one of my scripts and said it would make a good movie. So she started taking screenwriting classes at UCLA Extension and ScreenwritingU. She was also in the WGA's Veteran's Writing Project, which is a yearlong mentorship program with WGA writers. Nicole doesn't remember how she first heard about it years ago. At the time, she didn't find it that appealing because there's no way to monetize the films and recoup your investment. After she did a few non-DB shorts, she realized they weren't making money anyway, so she might as well do a DB. Currently, Nicole lives with her husband, Glenn and her pet dogs in Los Angeles, California while working at PraxScope and 9 Pie Productions as screenwriter and director. Here is my film review of Nicole's adaptation of Stephen King's *In The Deathroom*.

In The Deathroom was first an audio book story in November 1999 for the audio set, *Blood & Smoke*. In 2000, it was first published in written form in *Secret Windows* and in 2002, it was published in the short story collection, *Everything's Eventual*.

The story is about a New York Times reporter by the name of Fletcher, who is captured in South America. He is brought to "the deathroom" where he is interrogated for supposedly knowing or connected to a communist insurgency of the killing of a group of nuns and one of them was his sister. Fletcher knows he will not leave that deathroom alive, so he makes a drastic decision to escape. Does Fletcher escape to tell his tell? Read this gripping tale and see what Fletchers fate just might be.

Nicole Jones-Dion did an amazing job adapting this intense story. This story is very different from Stephen King's normal tales of gore and horror. Yet, Nicole's version shows the horrors of real life and the nightmare of being captured in a deadly territory. I was entertained by the interesting story and the very enjoyable acting by its cast. A story and film worth checking out.

Here is my exclusive interview with director, Nicole Jones-Dion...

Anthony Northrup: Your parents were in the Army and you traveled many places growing up. What was it like traveling so many times at such a young age and where did you like living most?

Nicole Jones-Dion: There are pros and cons to moving around constantly as a kid... you get to live in a lot of interesting places and immerse yourself in different cultures... but you also don't have a lasting circle of friends that you grow up with. In some ways, it's similar to working on a film set — you spend 12-14 hours a day together, everyone bonds and becomes best friends, then you all move on to the next project. My favorite place to live was probably Germany (my father was stationed there the longest). It came in handy on 9/11 — I was in Europe on a business trip. When the flights were cancelled, I was able to reach out to some old friends in Germany and stay with them until I was able to return home.

In The Deathroom by Nicole Jones-Dion

AN: Later on, you got into video games and comic books as part of your writing experience. What was your favorite video game and comic book growing up and why?

NJD: I think the comic that left the biggest impression on me was the *Savage Sword of Conan*. I was probably way too young when I read it (LOL) and I've been a huge fan of sword and sorcery ever since. The video game I lost the most sleep playing was *Diablo III*.

AN: When did you first discover Stephen King and what is your favorite book by him and why?

NJD: It seemed like everyone was reading SK when I was in high school. At the time, I was living in Wilmington, NC where a bunch of SK's movies were being filmed (*Firestarter, Silver Bullet, Maximum Overdrive*). Because I know the director of the movie, I'm kind of partial to *Firestarter*… although *The Dead Zone* is pretty awesome, too.

AN: How did you first hear about the Stephen King Dollar Baby program?

NJD: I forget how I first learned about it… it was like one of those urban legends that sounded too good to be true. But then I saw on FaceBook that a few of my filmmaking friends were actually making their own Dollar Babies, so I decided to check it out.

AN: Share with us the audition process of *In The Deathroom* and what was it specifically your three actors brought to the table to land their roles?

NJD: We probably looked at dozens of audition tapes for the role of "Fletcher." Scott Bailey instantly stood out from the pack because of the vulnerability he brought to the role. Many of the other actors were playing him as a hardcore bad-ass, but the character is really a just an everyman, a reporter who gets in over his head. Scott is a veteran actor and was able to really bring a level of depth and sensitivity to Fletcher that shows on the screen. Even though Fletcher is technically the hero, we knew that the success of the film was going to depend on the actor who played "Escobar." We had originally hired Mario Rocha to just be our stunt coordinator but our 1st AD really pushed to let Mario audition for the part. His tape blew us all away. We knew immediately that he was our Escobar. It was a really good reminder that stunt performers are also actors and not to underestimate the value that they bring. I'd worked with Andrew Bering before in my sci-fi feature *Stasis,* so he was always my first choice to play "Heinz." He's Swiss and fluent in English, French, and German. He's a real sweetheart in real life, I don't know why I always cast him as the villain, LOL.

AN: Out of all the Stephen King short stories, what attracted you most to this one?

NJD: Honestly, I was originally drawn to it because I had just shot some actor reel scenes on an interrogation set so I was thinking "Oh! We can just reuse that set and shoot this really cheap!" That turned out to not be the case at all. It's a deceptive story in that it seems simple until you start breaking it down. It has numerous flashbacks and multiple locations… with stunts and VFX… it turned out to be a very ambitious shoot.

AN: What changes did you make to your film as opposed to King's original text?

NJD: In SK's original story, the character of "The Woman" was a member of Escobar's corrupt regime. I changed her to a CIA agent because the CIA was very active in meddling with Central American politics in the 1990s (when the story is set). I tied the Tomas subplot in more closely with Fletcher's search for his missing sister. And to make Fletcher's confrontation with Escobar even more personal, I made Escobar the one who killed the nuns (spoiler alert!). I also added the battle at the end… so that during the entire duration of the film, Fletcher is really just stalling, waiting for Pedro Nunez's revolutionaries to arrive.

AN: So many fans want adaptations to be as close to the book as possible. How do you handle the pressure to keep the fans happy?

NJD: I tried to stay true to the spirit of SK's story. I think (hope) the changes that I made helped tighten up some of the loose ends that were unanswered in the original.

AN: What was your main goal you wanted to achieve about this film?

NJD: I wanted to stretch the boundaries of what constitutes horror. This is a film with horror elements but is also a tense thriller with tension and action and meaty roles for all of the actors.

AN: Where was the movie filmed specifically and were there any obstacles you had to overcome while filming there?

NJD: The actual deathroom was filmed inside an authentic WW2 quonset hut, which looks amazing on screen but was a total echo-chamber when it came to sound. We tried to dampen it as much as possible on set but it still needed a lot of tweaking in post. Luckily we didn't have to go back to ADR. The river sequence (in addition to being haunted) was also in a GPS & cell reception dead zone so we were literally cut off from the outside world. We had to convoy everyone in or else no one would have found the place. Plus, it had the world's largest mosquitoes (and I lived in Louisiana before moving to California). I'd never even seen mosquitoes in Los Angeles before but these guys were able to bite through jeans. Our poor soldiers were covered in welts by the end of the day.

AN: How long was the filming process from start to finish?

NJD: The actual shoot was 4 days — 2 days in the quonset hut, 1 day in the river, and 1 day filming the Tomas flashbacks. We ended up cutting out all the flashbacks with Tomas's wife and child because they didn't test well with preview audiences. That really made me sad because we used the actor Ron Sequeira's actual 6-year old son who was adorable, and one of my favorite actresses, Crystal Mantecon, played his wife. But like they say, sometimes you have to kill your darlings.

AN: What is your greatest moment so far with the success of *In The Deathroom*?

NJD: We literally just locked pictures right now, I'm just enjoying that. We'll see what the future holds.

AN: What Stephen King story would you like to adapt on a full-length scale?

NJD: Since Blumhouse is already remaking *Firestarter*, I'd actually love to do a feature version of *In The Deathroom* where we see more of Fletcher's journey to find his missing sister... maybe he could even end up with Tomas' widow at the end?

AN: Where can fans see the film? Will it be in any film fests any time soon?

NJD: We've only just started our festival run but our NYC premiere will be at the Hell's Kitchen Film Festival on Jan 18th, the LA premiere will be during the Hollywood Reel Independent Film Festival in February, and we're also screening in Idyllwild, CA in March.

AN: Lastly, What is next for Nicole Jones-Dion?

NJD: On the writing side, I've got several feature and TV scripts in various stages of development... hopefully some of those will actually go into production this year. I'm also trying to raise money for another feature film to direct. In the meanwhile, I'll keep shooting shorts to play around with some different techniques.

Nicole was kind enough to share a little extra behind-the-scenes stories with me I'd like to share with you.

NJD: For the river scenes, we shot in a secluded little canyon outside of Los Angeles. Back in the 1800's, that area had been a thriving settlement... until a heavy rainstorm caused the river to flood, sending a wall of water rushing through the narrow canyon, killing everyone who lived there: men, women, and children. As a result, the canyon is now incredibly haunted, with most of the activity centered around the river.

Originally, I'd intended to get a shot of the nuns walking across the river on a small plank bridge. We had to cut it from the film because one of the nuns fell off the bridge. She insisted that someone had grabbed her leg and pulled her into the water.

Our 1st AD is very sensitive to ghosts. During the sequence where the nuns are being ambushed by soldiers, he could feel little hands tugging on his clothes and hear children screaming. "Make the bad men stop! Make the bad men stop!" Sometimes truth really is stranger than fiction.

AN: I would like to thank Nicole for taking the time to speak with us today.

NJD: Thank you very much!

Rest Stop by Mark Zimmerman

Rest Stop

Mark Zimmerman
March 14, 2020

I HAVE ENJOYED INTERVIEWING Dollar Baby filmmakers for years, but I always find it extra interesting when I get the opportunity to interview a Dollar Baby in another country. My latest interview is with a filmmaker from the land down under… Australia!

Director Mark Zimmerman was born in 1980 in Newcastle, NSW Australia. Years later when he was 9 years old, he moved down south and went to Camden high school between the years of 1993 to 1998. In 1999 Mark studied scriptwriting at the college of journalism in Bondi, NSW as his passion for writing led him into film making. Since 2000, Mark has made several short films. He took a break from the industry for 5 years and only recently returned with his new short film, Charlotte's Requiem in 2018 and recently the Stephen King Dollar Baby short, *Rest Stop* 2019. He continues to write and has a planned feature for 2020.

Here is my review of Mark Zimmerman's Dollar Baby film, *Rest Stop*!

The Stephen King short story, *Rest Stop*, was first published in *Esquire* magazine in the December 2003 issue. In 2004, it won the National Magazine Award for Fiction. In 2008, it was published in the short story collection, *Just After Sunset*. The story is about an author named, John Dykstra who wrote under the pen name, Rick Hardin. While John is on a road trip, he stops at a bar and has way too much to drink. Later, while he stops at a rest stop, he hears a fight between a couple nearby. He comes to the defense of the woman and beats the abusive man. As he drives down the road afterwards, he begins to get paranoid thinking the beaten man is following him.

Mark Zimmerman's version of this film was done very well. He captured King's text from page to screen very well. He made it have a very eerie feel with just enough suspense to keep the viewer interested. A very well adaptation to add to the long list of Dollar Babies.

Here is my Exclusive Interview with Dollar Baby filmmaker, Mark Zimmerman.

Anthony Northrup: What was it like growing up in New South Wales, Australia in the 1980's?

Mark Zimmerman: Growing up in Newcastle was something I can't really remember as I was just a small kid, I remember bits and pieces. My family moved to a small country town called Oakdale when I was 10 years old, from there that's where I did my real growing up, I would get in trouble all the time as I was the family's Dennis the Menace. High School you could say was where the real action was, my main talent was singing, acting and writing. So my artistic talent was what got me over the line and kept me busy.

AN: When did you first discover Stephen King? What was your first King book and movie?

MZ: I discovered Stephen King when I was 12 the first book given to me was a second hand copy of *The Shining*. It was a Christmas present from my Nana. I didn't quite understand it at first as I was a bit young to tackle such a book, but the older I got the more I read. I think *The Shining* or *Pet Sematary* were the first SK movies I saw, SUPER SCARY!!!

AN: What was it like studying at New York Film Academy and what did you learn most there that has helped you with your films later in life?

MZ: NYFA was an eye opener, it was the first time I ever traveled overseas and for NY being the first place was really exciting and nerve wracking at the same time as it was 2 years after 9/11. I left at the end of 2003 so that whole year I applied to the school and saved all year round, the best decision I ever made. The school has amazing great teachers and students from all over the country and world. I learned from other people and have stayed in contact with them all thanks to facebook. I made my first ever short on film which was a learning curve as previously I used digital tape. But as a whole what I really learned was that the industry is highly competitive and it makes no difference if you went to film school or not, if you've got it, you've got it. For me I just kept going, writing scripts and meeting the RIGHT PEOPLE, that is the key!

AN: How did you learn about the Stephen King Dollar Baby Program?

MZ: Funny enough I read it on facebook, googled it and voila there it was, so I applied and 3 days later got my contract. Very exciting.

AN: Out of all of the Stephen King short stories, what attracted you most to this one?

MZ: What attracted me to *Rest Stop,* was the getting out of your comfort zone/split personality theme. It's about a regular boring guy whose normal life hasn't gotten him anywhere until he creates his pseudonym RICK HARDIN and that's where the fun really begins. So I felt I would give it a shot and see if I could pull it off.

AN: What changes did you make to make this your own as opposed to Stephen King's original text?

MZ: Changes I made was the opening scene to set up character and the ending to raise questions about what we witnessed.

AN: So many Stephen King fans want adaptations to be as close to the book as possible, how do you handle the pressure to keep the fans happy?

MZ: Mort Rainey in *Secret Window* said "All that matters is the ending". The ending can either win over an audience or kill it for them. In the story it ends abruptly where as with mine I wanted to give a glimpse of did it or didn't it, what if and leave some satisfaction with the audience.

AN: What was your main goal you wanted to achieve about this film?

MZ: My main goal was to tell the story written and to put my spin on it while staying true to the themes Stephen King had in his book. And I hope I pulled it off.

AN: Where was the movie filmed specifically and were there any obstacles you had to overcome while filming there?

MZ: The movie was filmed in Menangle 20 minutes from where I live, the bar and Rest Stop area were close together so we didn't have to do much traveling which was good. The main obstacles where weather, freezing high winds and power outages were very frustrating.

AN: How long was the filming process from start to finish?

MZ: The filming process was over one and half months, mainly cast and crew availability and location.

AN: Share with us the audition process and what did your lead actor bring to the table that won him the role?

MZ: I don't usually audition if actors have a showreel with some impressive stuff. I will go off that and organize a meeting and see what they can bring to the role and go from there. The main actor was brought in by the actor who played Lee, he introduced me to Brad we met and judging by his personality knew he was John/Rick.

AN: What is your greatest moment so far with the success of *Rest Stop*?

MZ: The greatest moment would be everybody excited that I got to film a Stephen King story of my own, it is something I've always dreamed of and here it is. Completing it is a success on it's own, I had a great cast and crew, what more could you ask for?

AN: What Stephen King story would you want to adapt on a full scale?

MZ: The film I would like to put my spin on and Direct would be *Rose Madder*, the supernatural fantasy side of it got me intrigued when I first read it, this was not his most popular work, but for me I enjoyed It.

AN: What is the Stephen King fan base like in Australia and do you normally have to wait for his new book releases?

MZ: The Stephen King fan base here in Australia is HUGE. We get his books usually a day before the US. His film's and T.V shows get streamed here all the time, he is a big deal here in Australia. The remake of *Salem's Lot* and the series *Nightmares & Dreamscape* were both filmed here in Melbourne, Victoria.

AN: Where and When can fans see this film? Will it be playing at film fests?

MZ: My Dollar baby film *Rest Stop* can be seen on my private page on Vimeo (by Request) and I will be screening it in a few film festivals throughout the year.

AN: Lastly, What is next for Mark Zimmerman?

MZ: Last year was very busy making *Rest Stop* and also producing and acting in a web series called *Atomic Kingdom* which took almost 6 months of my time. So next for me I have a few scripts that I am writing, a feature and a short film and that will take most of 2020 to get done. So I think 2021 will be the year to keep an eye out for me. Thank you so much Anthony for this interview, it has been an absolute pleasure to chat again soon.

I want to thank Mark for taking the time to speak with us today.

Graduation Afternoon

Marie D. Jones
March 15, 2020

I HAVE INTERVIEWED SEVERAL FEMALE Dollar Baby filmmakers, but Marie D. Jones is one of the most unique directors I've had the opportunity to interview with an amazing passion and enthusiasm. Not only is she a wonderful filmmaker, but a best-selling author as well. And not just any author, she covers a very unique and controversial wide spectrum of interesting topics: UFO'S! But before we get to that. Let's find out a little more about this new Dollar Baby director.

Marie D. Jones is the best-selling author of 20 non-fiction books on disaster preparedness, the paranormal, ancient knowledge, unknown mysteries, UFOs and alien technology, surveillance and technology, conspiracy theories, metaphysics, spirituality, and cutting-edge science, including *PSIence, Destiny VS. Choice, The Déjà vu Enigma, 11:11 – The Time Prompt Phenomenon, Mind Wars,* and *The Power of Archetypes.* She wrote *Supervolcano: The Catastrophic Event that Changed the Course of Human History* with her father, geophysicist Dr. John Savino. She is also a novelist, with a middle grade novel series, *EKHO- Evil Kid Hunting Organization* written with her son, Max; and a modern fantasy novel, *Black Wolf, White Swan*, which has been optioned for film. Her horror novel, *13* will be released by Vesuvian Books in 2021.

She has written for dozens of magazines and publications. She has appeared on the History Channel's *Nostradamus Effect* and *Ancient Aliens* television series, and on over two thousand radio shows worldwide. She is also a screenwriter with projects in various stages of development and has her own company, "Where's Lucy? Productions." An indie filmmaker, she has written and co-produced two short films, *Kings Boulevard* for

Graduation Afternoon by Marie D. Jones

RockChalk Pictures and *Graduation Afternoon,* her Stephen King Dollar Baby for IronTree Films, with a feature film in the works.

She is also a fully-trained CERT disaster responder, an avid horse racing enthusiast, and mom to one amazing son. She lives in San Marcos, California.

Her websites are www.mariedjones.com and www.whereslucyproduction.com. Here is my review of Marie's film, the Stephen King adaptation of *Graduation Afternoon.*

Graduation Afternoon was first published in 2007 Postscripts magazine and in 2008 it was published in Stephen King's *Just After Sunset.* The story is a simple one: a young girl is at her boyfriend's graduation party. Everyone is having a good time, talking, laughing, and talking about future plans, but all along there are hints of something big happening in the news. The party goers are into their fun time to notice the breaking news and importance of it… before it is too late. This story is a "short but sweet" tale and basically covers the horrors of war or the end of the world, depending on how you look at it. Some say it is a semi-prequel to Stephen King's The Stand, but that's debatable. Marie's adaptation was done very well. Her location shoot was quite impressive and the ending leaves you wanting more. Enjoyable film to watch.

Here is my exclusive interview with Dollar Baby filmmaker, Marie D. Jones!

Anthony Northrup: What was your life like growing up in New York? When did you first show interest in filmmaking?

Marie D. Jones: I grew up in a suburb north of the city with woods and a lake behind my house, so I spent a lot of time in nature exploring. I also read voraciously and loved to write and tell stories, mainly ghost stories. It was a great childhood before cell phones and the Internet when kids were outside all the time playing, day and night, and nobody worried about child predators. I had, like most kids of that time, a Super 8 camera I would make dumb movies with, but it was always evident that I was meant to be a writer and storyteller. I didn't have the patience to direct!

But I loved going to the movies and the drive-in and I knew even as a child the power of storytelling and using the written word and the visual image to move people and change lives.

AN: What was your first Stephen King book and film?

MJ: I read *Carrie* when it was released and loved it. I think that was also the first of his movies I saw, the original with Sissy Spacek. But that was a long time ago! The one book of his that really made me become a superfan was *The Stand*, which I ran out and purchased the day it was released. This was long before Amazon where you had to buy a book in a bookstore! After reading *The Stand*, I was hooked and made sure I got every book he wrote, and watched all the movie adaptations as they came out. But *The Stand* is my all-time favorite novel and represents a time in my life when I was really coming to realize I was meant to be a writer, so it had extra special importance.

AN: You have written a lot of books about UFOs, paranormal, conspiracy theories, and the supernatural. What attracted you to these topics to start your writing career and do YOU believe in UFOs?

MJ: I've written over 15 books on those subjects, and written for several magazines and publications on the subject matter. I've been on television and on radio all over the world talking about the paranormal and UFOs, and associated subjects. I was interested in this stuff since toddler-hood, when I insisted Bigfoot was walking through the woods behind our house. I was obsessed as a child with UFOs, and could often be found telling ghost stories to my stuffed animals because they were a captive audience. My father was a scientist, but he was also into the paranormal, so I grew up with the understanding that it was perfectly acceptable to revere science, which I did and still do, and believe in the unseen realities, which I did and still do. My mom was the creative one who loved telling us kids stories, so I got the storytelling bug from her!

Yes, I believe in the existence of UFOs and aliens, having been involved in the field extensively, with the Mutual UFO Network, Fund for UFO Research, and Center for UFO Studies back in the 1970s-1990s, and then writing non-fiction books and magazine articles on UFO topics. My father was a big UFO believer, too, and as a geophysicist, he is the one who first turned me on to the links between quantum mechanics and the paranormal. I later wrote a book called *PSIence: How New Discoveries in Quantum Physics and New Science May Explain the Existence of Paranormal Phenomena* about those links and many others, which is considered by many in the field a ground breaking book in paranormal research.

I saw something once, in the late 1980s, over the hills of La Costa, California that I could not explain by any other means. It was definitely an UNIDENTIFIED flying object! But that doesn't mean it was alien in origin!

AN: What is your short film, *Kings Boulevard* about?

MJ: *Kings Boulevard,* which I wrote and co-produced for director Neil Payne of RockChalk Pictures, is a satirical poke at the whole "equality and diversity" movement in Hollywood and how much of it is more talk than action. It's gotten a great reception at film festivals and I am really proud of that. Neil and I have a follow-up called *Red, White and You,* which satirizes the political process, we are hoping to make soon. We enjoy doing controversial films. After that, we plan to write a feature together, although that one won't be satire!

AN: Out of all the Stephen King short stories, what attracted you most to this one?

MJ: I liked *Graduation Afternoon* because it was challenging. The story, which appears in his *Just After Sunset* collection, is told through the thoughts of the lead character and I knew it would really be fun and a good challenge as a writer to literally create a larger story with other characters that fleshed out the existing short story's foundation. We as a group chose the story because it was a one-location shoot and fit into our resources, and we loved the shocking ending. We had chosen maybe three of four possible stories, and we passed them around to the key core group of producers, including myself and director Rob Padilla, and realized we wanted to take this adaptation on. Luke Pensabene, our lead producer, agreed it was something we had all the right resources to make, including the perfect location and the crew and equipment needed, and we were off to the races! It also was exciting because there weren't a ton of other *Graduation Afternoon* films out there, so we felt like it was the perfect fit for us.

AN: What changes did you make to make this your own as opposed to King's original text?

MJ: Mainly what I said above, having to take a story set almost entirely in the head and thoughts of one character and getting that on the page in a way that expands it and makes it visually interesting, too. We also took a few liberties with changing key characters around to make it more our own adaptation, and of course we wrote it to the location we had, which required some creativity. We changed the ages of the key characters, too, and made them a bit older, and the location itself, but really the story is a universal one about class differences and prejudices, so that was the framework we stuck to. King's original story was pretty short, so we had to work hard to develop it out into a larger scope, which I think we succeeded at. Hopefully he would agree!

AN: So many Stephen King fans want adaptations to be as close to the original book as possible, how do you handle the pressure to keep the fans happy?

MJ: Oh, I am one of those fans. I actually hate it when the production companies change genders and races, or make big alterations in the stories I've come to know and love… but as a writer and now a filmmaker, I get why. Everyone has their own interpretation and vision of a story that exists on paper, in book form. Yes, I'm still a believer in keeping the most important elements intact, but how you get there is up for grabs and open to the filmmaker's interpretation. It's like knowing you need to get to Hawaii, but not knowing exactly how you will get there – boat, plane, submarine, on the back of a whale, and also what route you will take. So I now understand the anger fans feel from that angle, but also how everyone interprets a story differently within the realms of the imagination.

AN: What was your main goal you wanted to achieve about this film?

MJ: We wanted to make an entertaining and emotionally powerful adaptation with the resources we had available to us and the talent we gathered. We all wanted to come away with a great short film that was not just an adaptation, but a showcase of our work as well. This project also served as a way to bring together a team of people to see how well they worked together for future projects, too. So that was especially exciting to see how quickly our team bonded and gave our all for the film.

AN: Where was the movie filmed specifically and were there any obstacles to overcome while filming there?

MJ: We filmed the movie at the gorgeous hilltop home of our lead actor's parents not too far from all of us who lived in San Diego. It was a mansion perfect for the story, complete with an outdoor patio with an incredible sweeping view for our instrumental final scenes. The obstacles were basically trying not to break or harm anything in the house, including the floors and furniture, and to try and be packed up and out in time for the parents to enjoy their home in peace! We shot late on a weekend and did some pick-up dates, so we were intruding on someone's actual home and we really had to be aware of that and have respect for keeping things clean and staying out of private areas. We were so blessed to be able to shoot there, though, and really appreciated the parents accommodating us. There was a small scene shot in a studio as well, but again it was something one of the producers had easy access to. We really had no major hitches in terms of locations.

AN: How long was the film shoot and the process from start to finish?

MJ: The first main weekend shoot was two very full sixteen-hour days, followed by another two weekends of shorter pick-up scenes, and then the TV news reporting scenes were added last in one afternoon. The process was about a year from the time we decided to do this, picked the right story, got the contract sent off and agreed to with King's people, then got our cast and crew all locked in, our location and a shooting schedule, contracts sent out, catering, table read, then did the actual shooting, then editing, sound, music, etc. A lot of people put in a lot of hard work and effort to get to the end result and I am so grateful to each and every one of them.

This was the first time I got to be involved and on set for a film and wow, it was a lot of work and meticulous planning, and the whole team really worked together so well to make that happen. We had some setbacks and glitches, as any film would, but we came back and got through and everyone made themselves available for whatever was needed, even up to the final preparing of the film for festival submissions.

AN: What was your greatest moment so far with the success of *Graduation Afternoon*?

MJ: Just seeing the whole thing for the first time was the greatest moment. We are just sending it out to festivals and got accepted into the first one we approached, and I know there will be many more, but nothing tops that feeling of seeing it done with your name in the credits!

AN: What Stephen King story would you like to adapt on a larger scale?

MJ: I would KILL to adapt *The Regulators, Insomnia,* or *Black House*! I've read *Black House* so many times I know the story like the back of my hand. Since *The Dark Tower* series and *The Stand* are spoken for, those three would be my absolute dream projects. Mr. King, give me a shot at writing!!!

AN: When and Where can fans see this film? Will it be playing at film fests?

MJ: We are now sending it out to festivals and plan to play it for about a year before we make it open for public viewing. We're excited to see how people who have read the story respond, too! We have a *Graduation Afternoon* Facebook, Twitter, and Instagram account so people will be able to follow us and keep track of where the film is showing and what else we have planned.

AN: Lastly, What is next for Marie D. Jones?

MJ: I have three non-fiction books to write before the end of 2021, two releasing in 2020 alone which I'll be promoting, a novel coming out at the end of 2020 written with my son and part of a series, a horror novel coming out in 2021 that is now in editing, screenplays to write, radio shows to do, and preparation for hopefully one or two features I'll be writing and producing with the team over the next two years, so I'm always busy with work. I write full-time and have a million things going on at once! Oh, and I'll be at some of those festivals, too, with the cast and crew, so that will be fun. Maybe a vacation somewhere in the next year or so? You can keep up on my antics at www.mariedjones.com or on social media.

I want to thank Marie for taking the time to speak with us today and wish her the very best in her future projects.

The Man Who Loved Flowers

Mark Hensley
April 1, 2020

THERE ARE LIMITED CHOICES when it comes to deciding which Dollar Baby film a director wants to adapt into a short film. Sometimes, some Dollar Baby films have many versions. The latest version of *The Man Who Loved Flower* comes from a very talented filmmaker, Mark Hensley.

Mark Hensley was born on July 8th, 1963, in Streator, Illinois but moved to the Netherlands when he was 6 years old with his family. From a young age Mark displayed an affinity for music. As a teenager, Mark played in several bands and began his career in the music industry. At twenty three, he moved back to the United states and enrolled in a one year program at the College for Recording Arts in San Francisco. Upon graduation, he started interning at the world renowned Plant Studios in Sausalito, where he soon was hired as a staff assistant engineer. Mark also started producing local bands, which resulted in a platinum record for engineering the 4 Non Blondes hit single, *What's up*.

During a trip to Vancouver, BC, Mark met his wife Peggy resulting in his decision to relocate there. It was in Vancouver where he was introduced to audio post production for film and TV which sparked a new interest. Within a few years he was hired as staff Re-Recording mixer at one of the top studios in Vancouver "Post Modern Sound". His work there resulted in 8 Canadian sound Award Nominations and 3 wins. In 2008 Mark decided to push his career further, and moved to Los Angeles. Since his move to LA he has been nominated for 3 CAS awards and 3

Emmys. He won an Emmy in 2018 for his work as Lead Re-Recording Mixer on Genius: Picasso.

Film Making In 2016 Mark produced a short film written by his wife Peggy. Unhappy with the final product, the project was shelved. Two years later, Mark had an idea for another short film which his wife then turned into a script. Mark made the decision to direct it himself. Enjoying the process, Mark also taught himself to edit the film which went on to be accepted in various festivals around the world which resulted in a distribution deal from a European distributor. Building on his new career path, Mark then went back and tackled the previously shelved short, completing a well received re-edit. At the same time Peggy and Mark had been busy producing a musical that they created together called, *London Calling* inspired by the music of The Clash. With no previous theater experience at all, Mark set out producing the musical with a twelve person cast, four dancers and nineteen songs that had to be re-recorded. It premiered at the Hollywood Fringe festival in 2017, and was an instant hit.

In 2018 Mark shared the script with the owner of Origin Theatrical in Australia who immediately offered an option agreement catapulting the musical to the big stage. Continuing the momentum, Mark was asked to produce a run of the stage play *A Christmas Present*. The writer requested he tape one of the performances, and after thinking about it, Mark suggested to simply turn it into a movie. To prepare for the task

The Man Who Loved Flowers by Mark Hensley

of making a movie, Mark sourced cameras and equipment and directed another couple of short films. Before the end of the year, other projects include directing a music video, a short called *The Last Hit* and a short based on the Stephen King story *The Man Who Loved Flowers*. He starts directing *The Christmas Present* in January. Mark is also committed in the new year to produce another stage production of a new musical written by Peggy Lewis called *Irena Palm*. It is an adaptation of the movie of the same name that starred Marianne Faithfull and was written by Philip Blasband. Here is my review of The Man Who Loved Flowers.

This Stephen King short story first appeared in the August 1977 issue of *Gallery* magazine. It was later printed in the Stephen King short story collection book, *Night Shift* in 1978.

The story is simple: A man walks down the Springtime streets of New York and stops to buy some flowers for his beloved, Norma. He has a smile on his face, a spring in his step, and can't wait to find his "Norma". He follows a woman down an alley calling her name, "NORMA!" but she is not "his" Norma and falls victim to a very gory and horrible death by a hammer. The man goes on and on trying to find his Norma.

Mark Hensley's version of this short story, brings the pages to life, yet has his own unique twist to the story that brings gore and intense scenes that are sure to please any Stephen King fan. I think Mark's version was done very well and his lead actor brought just enough creepiness to the story that gave the viewer a fulfilling experience.

Here is my exclusive interview with Dollar Baby filmmaker, Mark Hensley.

Anthony Northrup: Tell us what it was like growing up in the Netherlands?

Mark Hensley: Growing up in The Netherlands was awesome. There was a lot of freedom. I could go out to clubs and bars when I was a teenager, and nobody cared.

AN: What was your first Stephen King book and film? When were you first introduced into his works?

MH: *Carrie* and *Christine* stand out to me from those days, long long ago.

AN: You have quite the impressive music career. Share with us what it was like working with 90's hit band, 4 Non Blondes and who else have you worked with?

MH: Working with the 4 Non Blondes was a pretty short affair. I knew their manager, and they needed a favor. They had spent their entire budget recording their album in LA, but weren't happy with the recording of *What's Up*. So, they asked if I could get them a cheap rate at The Plant Studios in Sausalito. For $500 a day, 2 days. It usually went for $2k per day. The owner said ok. They came in with their producer. Set up, and we recorded the music on day one. Day 2 we recorded Linda's vocals and mixed the song. I was also assisted on record by Santana, John Lee Hooker and Celine Dion. I also worked on demo's with Stephan Jenkins of Third eye blind. And introduced him to guitar player Kevin Cadogan and Bass player Arion Salazar.

AN: What is more challenging: working in the music industry or film industry and Why?

MH: Music industry is way more challenging, because of the frail ego's that constantly need reaffirming. Funny thing is, my whole reason to move back to the USA from the Netherlands was to have a career in music engineering and producing. It was my whole life. Until I fell into audio-post production out of necessity. Now, I couldn't imagine doing music production for a living.

AN: Please share with us about your musical, *London Calling,* inspired by music from The Clash?

MH: I came up with the idea about 12 years. I had a little "road map" with 9 songs and a bit of a story idea. When my wife and I went for our first vacation in 10 years to Greece, we sat down and fleshed out the story, then my wife sat down with some gin and tonic and wrote the first draft. We worked on it on and off over the next 7 years and it evolved into a full blown musical with 18 songs by The Clash, and a 12 member cast with 4 dancers. After 9 years of rewrites, table reads and false starts, I finally decided it was time to put on a performance. My friend Vince Jones, who is Sarah McLachlan's band leader and keyboard player, and ridiculously talented, put together a small band with the bass player from Porno for Pyros and several other top musicians who have played with everyone from Bob Dylan to Avril Lavigne. And we recorded 18 songs in 2 days for playback during the performance. It debuted at the Hollywood Film Festival and we had 7 sold out performances. It was an amazing experience. And last year we optioned it to a large theatrical company in Australia, who is working on getting all the rights secured so we can get it to the big stage.

AN: What is it like working with your wife, Peggy on musicals, projects, and your Dollar Baby film?

MH: It's actually amazing. She's an awesome writer, and we can be totally honest with each other. We're both very self critical, and we complement each other very well. She'll write something, I'll read it. Tell her what I think is wrong or needs improvement. She'll get mad, stomp around, then sit down and fix it.

AN: When and How did you first hear about the Dollar Baby program?

MH: I had actually heard about the Dollar Baby program a few years ago. Long before I even thought of being a filmmaker. I read about it in an interview, if my memory serves me well.

AN: Out of all the Stephen King short stories, what attracted you most to this one?

MH: Well, I was looking for something that had a small cast, very few locations, and would need no visual effects.. But one that I felt could be adapted without following the original exactly.

AN: What changes did you make to make this your own as opposed to King's original text?

MH: I felt there were things in the original story that work well in the written version, but get lost in the filmed version. I also wanted to try and put a little bit more in the "why" he's doing what he's doing. And try and show his descent descended from being lean to being a psychopath killing women.

AN: So many Stephen King fans want adaptations to be as close to the book as possible, how do you handle the pressure to keep the fans happy?

MH: I think as long as you try to stay true to the intent, and actual meaning behind the story, it's easy. And with *"Flowers"* I personally found it to be about him being a psychopath.

AN: What was your main goal you wanted to achieve about this film?

MH: I wanted to direct 2 more short films in preparation for a feature I am going to direct. I had directed my first one the year before. And had about 3 months to shoot 2 more. And I wanted to have a great script. I remembered the Dollar Baby program. And started going through the list of available short stories.

AN: Where was the movie filmed specifically and were there any obstacles to overcome while filming there?

MH: The film was shot at our house, and at my work. The place I work for is very, very supportive of my filmmaking. The main obstacle was time.

AN: How long was the film shoot and the process from start to finish?

MH: The shoot took 2 days. I spent about another week or 2 on and off on the edit. I also had to teach myself how to add some fake blood.

AN: Share with us the casting of the film and that process?

MH: I mostly used actors I knew from when we did the musical. So, casting was pretty easy. Sam, the lead, is amazing. All the actors are experienced. Phil Iddrissi was in one of our table reads, but wasn't available for the Fringe Festival run. He and Guy Picot made a great cop duo.

AN: What is your greatest moment so far with the success of *The Man Who Loved Flowers*?

MH: Nothing yet, as I'm just about to send it out into the world.

AN: What Stephen King story would you like to adapt on a much larger scale?

MH: *Mile 81*.

AN: Where can fans see the film? Will it be playing at any film fests across the country?

MH: I've already submitted it to festivals around the world. But I'm hoping there will be an avenue to show it to King fans. I would love to get their feedback, good and bad.

AN: Lastly, What is next for Mark Hensley?

MH: Next up will be the feature. A black comedy called, *The Christmas Present*. And I just started filming a Vlog called, *Henchman's F-Bomb*. A commentary on current issues.

I want to thank Mark for taking the time from his busy schedule to talk with us today and wish him the very best in all his future projects.

The Jaunt by Nick Smith

The Jaunt

Nick Smith
April 1, 2020

STEPHEN KING HAS WRITTEN a wide variety of different genres, mostly known for horror, or course, but once in a while he dips his toe into the science fiction genre. There have been hits and some misses (*The Running Man*, *Tommyknockers*, *The Long Walk*, and *Under the Dome*, just to name a few). However, one of his best science fiction stories and certainly a fan favorite among Stephen King fans, is his short story, *The Jaunt*. This fan favorite has been adapted into a Dollar
Baby film by Nick Smith who wrote the screenplay for the film, and during filming served as Unit Production Manager, Second Unit Director and VFX Supervisor.

Nick Smith was born on August 5th, 1978 and originally from Advance, North Carolina. He attended Davie County High in Mocksville, North Carolina. He continued his studies at the University of North Carolina at Wilmington. He has two degrees, a Bachelor of Arts in English from the University of North Carolina at Charlotte and a Bachelor of Film Studios from the University of North Carolina at Wilmington. Nick studied Production and English. Although Nick Smith had a variety of jobs, it was as Artistic Director at The Browncoat Pub & Theatre that he really showed interest in the world of entertainment and later worked at Tobbot Films where his talents turned to filmmaking.

The beginning of his film was shot at the Watson College of Education building at UNC Wilmington, a massive building (brand new at the time) on campus that was often referred to as the "Palace of Education." *The Jaunt w*as made as part of the FST 492 16mm Film Class; the entire semester was spent making the film. It has had limited release since it was originally finished in 2008. He first heard of the Dollar Baby program completely by accident; the summer before the class he was watching TV and there was a story about Stephen King on. As is his habit they mentioned something he hadn't heard of so he looked it up on Wikipedia, then fell down a rabbit hole reading about different things in King's works and his shared universe and what-not. In the process, he discovered the Dollar Baby program, and since Nick knew he was taking the 16mm class in the fall started to research it, find out what short stories were available, and got his classmates on board.

Nick was kind enough to share this Fun fact: 'We sent our dollar to Stephen King in a skull piggy bank full of pennies.' Nick Smith currently lives in Wilmington with his wife, Andi Angel. Here is my review of *The Jaunt*.

This classic science fiction Stephen King tale was first published in *The Twilight Zone* magazine in 1981. It was reprinted in the 1985 Stephen King short story collection, *Skeleton Crew*. The story takes place in the 24th Century, when a father tells his wife and children the history of teleportation known as "jaunting". As the family prepares to "jaunt" to Mars, a terrible horror changes everything and the truth about "jaunting" is revealed. The Dollar Baby adaptation of *The Jaunt* was directed by Tod Gorman, in 2009. He initiated the project (discovered the Dollar Baby program, found a story and did the deal with King's people), and he wrote the screenplay. During shooting Nick served as 2nd Unit Director and UPM, also oversaw SFX.

This Dollar Baby adaptation was quite impressive. The special effects were quite impressive and eye catching considering it is a low budget independent film. I found the acting of *The Jaunt* was very well done and the director stuck to the story to its original text. But it was the special effects that brought this Dollar Baby as one of the entertaining of the Dollar Baby adaptations.

Here is my exclusive interview with Nick Smith.

Anthony Northrup: Tell us what it was like growing up in North Carolina?

Nick Smith: I lived in the prototypical small Southern town; when I was a kid we had one stoplight and three gas stations. The joke was that you knew you were from my area when you mentioned being from a county, not a town – I technically lived in Advance, but all of us referred to ourselves as from Davie County. There wasn't anything particularly special about growing up there, though I've always been grateful I lived in an area where, as kids, we could run around the neighborhoods on our own safely, and explore our surroundings. I think it helped develop my imagination, going on all of these "adventures" through the neighborhood streets or the woods that surrounded the development. Another perk of where I lived was we had an amazing drama teacher at the high school, Freda Ramsey. Even though I only got to take it my senior year, she still had a huge influence on me and really helped me out of my shell. I definitely credit her with getting me interested and engaged with the arts in a way I'd never really been prior to her class.

AN: What was your first introduction to Stephen King, book and film?

NS: The first film I can remember seeing related to Stephen King was the TV-Movie version of *IT*. They'd done a huge write up on it in T.V. Guide and I was fascinated by the fact that John Ritter and Harry Anderson, who I knew as comedic actors from *Three's Company* and *Night Court*, respectively, were now doing this horror miniseries. Of course, it wound up freaking me right out and I actually started to actively avoid King related things after that. I was never that big on horror, anyway (which is funny when you consider where my creative career went). The first book of King's I read was *The Green Mile*, at the urging of my college roommate. He said he wouldn't allow me to go see the film version until I'd read the original novellas. So I did, and I thoroughly enjoyed it. I've dipped into some of King's other non-horror tales (*Different Seasons* is a favorite), but again, I'm not huge on horror as a genre in general so my experience with his stuff is somewhat limited. Which I know isn't the most exciting thing for this book, but it's true. All that being said, I consider *The Shawshank Redemption* to be the best film ever made.

AN: Share with us your experience in the Browncoat Pub & Theatre

NS: I had taken drama in junior high and high school, and had gotten interested in directing while at UNC-Charlotte, which is what led me to UNC Wilmington's film studies program (where *The Jaunt* was made). After graduation the film industry in Wilmington sort of fell to pieces because the state rescinded the tax incentives that had been in place so I wasn't able to get a job there, so I wound up having to get a typical 9-5 and my creative options were limited. Then I got drunk at the Browncoat one night. I'd discovered the Browncoat by accident; a buddy of mine mentioned going to a *Firefly* themed bar and I just had to investigate. I had no idea it was also a theater. I quickly became a regular, and one night, after I'd had quite a few, the owner, Richard Davis, came up to me and said "Hey, we're doing *Night of the Living Dead* on stage this fall; I know you're usually a film guy, but you wanna direct it?" I took a shot, said "Sure!", and promptly forgot all about it. Months later Richard calls me. "Hey man, I've got your cast together, you should probably start rehearsals next week." I'm like… rehearsals for what??? So that was my first theatrical directing gig. I literally walked into the first rehearsal and asked the cast – which thankfully included many people I knew –"Alright… So what do we do?" Even though I'd directed two short films at UNCW, this was a whole different beast. But I fell in love with doing it. *Night of the Living Dead* (see, here I am with horror again) was a success, so Richard offered me some other projects (a modernization of *Dangerous Liaisons*, and a locally written original called *Frankenstein is Dead*) and I also started bringing projects to him. One of the fun things about the Browncoat – though sometimes it was also stressful – was that Richard had a very "seat of his pants" managerial style which meant if he had a hole in the schedule and you had a project, chances are you could make it happen. All told, I would go on to direct 13 shows at the Browncoat before it's untimely demise in 2016, and for the last two years I served as artistic director. I sort of became known for doing things people said couldn't be done on a 16x16 black box stage like the Browncoats: Piece of My Heart not only recreated the Tet Offensive but also brought the Vietnam memorial wall to life; nobody thought a musical like *Little Shop of Horrors* could happen there but we did it, with all the plants, and won the encore magazine "Best Theatrical Production" that year; *No Exit* had an hour long light cue as red lights slowly came up over the course of the entire show as the character's resignation to their life in hell became more pronounced; *She Kills Monsters* featured a gelatinous cube that actually ate people and a final battle with a five-headed dragon. We were always trying to push the boundaries of what was possible; Needless to say, we had a lot of fun in the process.

AN: Out of all the Stephen King short stories, what attracted you most to this one?

NS: I was taking a 16mm film class, which spends the entire semester making a short film. When I discovered the Dollar Baby program, it seemed like a given that the class should undertake that as our project, so I started doing research into what short stories were available. I initially contacted King's people with an interest in doing *Breathing Lessons* from *Different Seasons*, but was told it had been optioned for a big screen treatment and so wasn't available. I was also told, at the time (this was around 2007) that they didn't have a definitive list of what short stories WERE available, which made the process a little dicey. So I compiled a list of every short story King had written, then searched online to see if I could find any trace of them having been produced under the Dollar Baby program, and marked them off the list if I could. Then, I took what was left over and started reading synopses of the stories to see if they not only sounded interesting, but also doable to a film studies class that would have access to plenty of film equipment but a very limited budget for anything else. When I came across *The Jaunt* I knew I had the right one. While the story has a lot of scope (with flashbacks to the creation of the technology, and the testing on live subjects), and deals with a family on an interplanetary trip, that scope is still contained within the family's interactions. So it gave us a real human drama to play with, and wouldn't have massive needs in terms of makeup or other practical effects. What effects were needed I knew could be accomplished digitally. And while it certainly has a horror movie twist, it plays more like straight sci-fi, which appealed more to my sensibilities. Plus, that question that's at the heart of the story… what happens, what do you experience, when you go through… and how that human curiosity transcends all sense of safety and self-preservation… It was just a great hook for a story. I fell for it pretty immediately.

AN: What changes did you make to make this your own as opposed to King's original text?

NS: The biggest issue with adapting the story for the screen is the fact that a lot of the most important information either takes place in flashback or in Mark Oates' mind. But that information has to get out to the audience. We can't have our lead actor just look like he's thinking about what happened to Rudy Foggia; we have to see what happened to Rudy Foggia. Which led to the creation of *The Stranger*. With *The Stranger,* we could have someone slip in when Mark isn't looking to tell Ricky the real story of the Jaunt, and really pique that curiosity in the young man. To what end, who knows? That's what made the character so useful; he could give us the expository dump and lead-in to the Rudy flashback we needed, but we didn't have to deal with his motivations in any way except "oh, he just overheard this and wanted to set the record straight." So while we tried to be as close to King's work as possible (who'd want to change what a master had written?) the Stranger did put our own stamp on the story. I remember the first time Tod Gorman, our director, read my first draft of the script. He hadn't yet read the short story. He says to me "You know who I really like? This Stranger character. He's so creepy. That is just such a Stephen King kind of character." That made my day and then some. Still my proudest moment as a writer, knowing I'd created something that could be mistaken for King's own work. We also had some fun toying with the idea that the Stranger actually WAS Rudy Foggia, and unlike most sane people who went crazy if they experienced the Jaunt, it actually sort of "fixed" Rudy (after the initial shock had worn off, of course).

AN: So many Stephen King fans want adaptations to be as close as possible to the book, how do you handle the pressure to keep fans happy?

NS: I think the first key, any time you're adapting something, is just to make sure you understand the heart and soul of the story, and work from there. *The Jaunt* is ultimately about a kid's curiosity getting the better of him, so as long as we stayed focused on building up that story I knew we'd be fine. Too many times adaptations wind up turning into things that have almost nothing to do with the source material except the name (*Lawnmower Man,* anyone?) but it's pretty easy to avoid that if you just understand what draws people to the story in the first place. *The Jaunt* was never going to be a high-octane thrill ride, nor a terrifying horror film; it's a story about a family trip gone wrong, if you really boil it down. So play to that, and let everything else fall around it, and you wind up golden. If you do have to change something (like introducing the Stranger), have a purpose behind it that serves that core story.

AN: What was your main goal you wanted to achieve with this film?

NS: To prove it could be done, and that we could do it. You see, in North Carolina, the UNC Wilmington Film Studies program is a bit of a black sheep. On the one hand, it's fairly new. On the other, it has to compete with the much more well-known North Carolina School of the Arts Film program, which has produced people like David Gordon Green. Not much was expected of our program, but the head of the program, Dr. Lou Buttino, came into one of my first classes and challenged us to rethink what was possible in terms of our student films. Prior to *The Jaunt,* 95% of what was being done at UNC Wilmington was the "typical" student film; 2-3 actors, in a room with white walls, talking about life or relationships or what have you. I don't want to say there was no ambition… people were doing the best that they could… but I think a lot of students just accepted that we had to work in a pretty small scale and limited scope. With *The Jaunt* we wanted to change that thinking; and it worked. Along with some similarly-ambitious shorts that came out of that time period, like *The Red Cape* and *Parabola* I think *The Jaunt* helped usher in a new era for UNC Wilmington's film program and showed students that you could think big and make it happen if you just committed yourself. I remember it felt like there was a buzz around the program while we were making it; that's the benefit you get of having a name as luminous as Stephen King's attached to what you're doing.

AN: What were your experiences working with the director of the film?

NS: Tod and I are very good friends, and we both fell in love with this project from the beginning. There was a selection/voting process to determine who would direct it, and he edged me out by one vote. So it was very hard for me to go from being the person who conceived the project and wrote the adaptation to tumbling all the way down to UPM for the actual shoot (which, on a student film, really meant I brought the coffee.) We agreed for the most part on what shape the film should take and as pre-production went on I got better about getting out of the way and letting him craft his vision, even in places where it changed drastically from what I'd imagined when I wrote it. The biggest tension that erupted between us had to do with the special effects. He'd put me in charge of making them happen, but pushed back every time I talked about doing something digitally. To me, digital effects are just another tool in the box. You use it when it solves the problem. In my eyes, we would only enhance the film by doing the teleportation effects digitally, because to do it in-camera… and, because of our resources, in a kind of cheesy way… would just reinforce that we were a student film. I had a professor who filmed a shot of me walking through a building on campus, and within an hour he'd built a 3D portal, and had me vanish through it, with no rotoscoping or compositing or anything. Why wouldn't we want to take advantage of that? But Tod is a very old-school film, and wants to try and do everything on camera and in a very naturalistic way. And I think for 95% of the film, it works really well. But I kept pushing and eventually he agreed to let the effects happen digitally, and I think the film works better as a result. Tod really brought some beautiful touches to the movie though, and ultimately I'm glad he got to direct it. I think I might have had a better grasp on the big picture, but I learned through subsequent projects that I didn't at that time know what I needed to know to get the best out of my actors, whereas that was one of Tod's biggest strengths. He had an infectious energy when he was dealing with Timmy and Jared and everyone, and I think that all came through on the screen. I also have to mention our producer, Luke Bruehlman. Many of us knew each other already prior to this class, but we met Luke during this process, and he was fantastic. No matter how stressful things got he always had a cheery, optimistic attitude; he just knew we were going to make this happen. He was a solid anchor for us when things got crazy, and in the time since he's become one of my best friends.

AN: Where was the movie filmed and were there any obstacles you had to overcome while filming there?

NS: Filming was split mostly through three different locations. The UNCW Watson College of Education building (jokingly referred to as the "Palace of Education") served as the main "Jauntport" lobby area, for most of the beginning of the film. The lobby of the UNCW Computer Information Sciences building served as the "waiting room" where Mark tells his children about the Jaunt, and also where Ricky encounters the Stranger. A friend had an old, abandoned shed building behind the house they were renting, so we dressed it up and used it to film Victor Carune's lab and his flashback; most everything else was shot in a long-closed bank downtown (including the Rudy Foggia flashback and people entering the Jaunt vault). The biggest issue we faced while filming was getting the conclusion right. Our production designer attempted to build us a set in the lobby of the old bank building for the actual Jaunt process and Ricky's crazed emergence, but again, we had very limited funds to do it up right, so the actual footage came back looking really bad, and not at all on the level of the other things we had shot. I don't blame him, because it was a nearly impossible task for him on such a strict budget; you can tell from how excellent Carune's lab looked that he could dress a set like nobody's business when you only had to worry about scrounging parts. So this led to filming being left unfinished. The semester ended, and most of us went on to a senior seminar class, but we always intended to come back and reshoot the ending to The Jaunt when that class was over. While shooting my directorial debut, Blue Skies, we had a scene that was set in a dance club. We filmed at a place called Club Vida here in Wilmington, and it had a very interesting, kitschy-sci-fi kind of vibe inside. One of our sound guys off-handedly mentioned how cool a location it would be for a sci-fi movie, and then we realized "Yes! This is it!" So we got the cast and most of the crew back together for a two-day shoot at Club Vida to redo the ending. We had to tweak some things to make it work smoothly (we added everyone getting into the "Jaunt robes" because we didn't have all the original costumes and people's hair had lengthened – plus it gave it a very cool cult kind of feel), but ultimately it gave us what we needed, and we could finish the film.

AN: How long was the film shoot and process from start to finish?

NS: We started filming in early November of 2007, and I think we initially shot a total of 10 days over 3 weeks. Then we had to take a break because of the end of the semester, and came back in early May of 2008 to do the reshoots of the ending, which I think was a two-day shoot. The "UNCW" cut of the film, which I edited, was completed in fall of 2008 and we screened at the Student Film Festival at the end of that semester. Tod played around with his director's cut for years, but never did finish it, and I'm not sure the last time he even took a look at it.

AN: What is the greatest moment so far with the success of *The Jaunt*?

NS: I'm not going to lie. A part of me is very disappointed at how it all played out; that we never officially got it out to festivals or in front of a wider audience. There's a certain momentum that develops with student projects that can very quickly die when the semester is over and there's no longer a grade hanging in the balance. For me personally, I just wanted to be in a big crowd and see that credit come up: "Based on the short story by Stephen King, written for the screen by Nick Smith." That was a big deal for me. But at least a finished version of the film exists, and people can see it if they want to hunt me down. But honestly, the biggest moment of success is the fact that we did it at all. A lot of people thought the project was too big. Even our professor, Glenn Pack, who wound up one of our biggest cheerleaders, was initially concerned we were biting off more than we could chew. Even with the relatively small scale of this story compared to a lot of King's works, this was a gigantic project for a group of mostly first-time student filmmakers, and I think that being the case it came out extraordinarily well. There's some amazing stuff happening in there, if I do say so myself. I will always be proud of what we accomplished. I also want to mention; I mean, we were a small production, but we broke some barriers that you'd typically find on film sets at the time. For instance, we had a female camera operator in Meghann Sumner. I feel like she caught a lot of resistance to the idea of her working in the camera department as it traditionally was such a boy's club, but she handled herself admirably. She went on to be my director of photography on Blue Skies, and has even worked with Terence Malick! A fun side story. Our 1st AD, Rachel Gallman, moved to L.A. after school was over and was interviewing for a job on a senior thesis project by a student at USC's distinguished film program. While going over her resume, the producer stopped, stared at her, and said "You were on The Jaunt?" She was a little shocked that he said it in such a knowing way, but she answered "Yes." The guy shook his head, laughed, and said "Man, our director HATES you guys..." Turns out he'd wanted to do the Dollar Baby program and his favorite short story was "The Jaunt," and we'd secured the rights just before he did. I thought it was a cool sort of "butterfly effect" moment. I hope the guy got to do a Dollar Baby eventually.

AN: Stephen King is best known for his horror stories, but how do you feel about his take on science fiction and stories like *The Jaunt*?

NS: I think King is something really special when he steps away from the pure horror genre. Whether it's science fiction or something else. I mean, there certainly "horror" elements in things like *The Body* or *Apt Pupil* or *Shawshank,* but they're much more straightforward stories and they're hugely enjoyable. I think *The Green Mile* is another good example. Horror elements, but a very human and very touching story that goes way beyond scares. So while horror has definitely been his bread and butter, I think he's at his best when he moves beyond that genre and tries something different. I think it's funny when people celebrate him as such a great horror writer. He's a great writer, period.

AN: What Stephen King story would you like to adapt on a larger scale?

NS: Put away your knives and pitchforks... but I'd never read any of *The Dark Tower* series before a buddy of mine dragged me to the film adaptation that came out a couple of years ago. But though by most accounts that movie was not a good adaptation/reboot/whatever you want to call it of the novels, it did make me interested enough to want to learn more about them. So while I still haven't read them all, I know enough about them to know in these days of mega-franchises and prestige television and huge streaming miniseries type things... you absolutely could do an amazing adaptation of the entire *The Dark Tower* series and furthermore, someone SHOULD do it. So, give me a big enough budget to do it right and I'd love to take that on. But then, who wouldn't? Incidentally, I still think

Breathing Lessons would make a great short film. I don't know who it was that optioned it for the big screen, but that was 13 years ago, so I'm pretty sure it's still available at this point.

AN: Where can fans see the film? Will it play at film fests across the country?

NS: The director's cut of the film was never completed; the only existing cut is the one I put together for an editing class that screened in public once – at the UNCW Film Studies Student Showcase at the end of that semester. I never sent it to any festivals because I didn't feel it was my place to do so as it was a cut Tod hadn't fully signed off on. So sadly, that's all that was ever done with it. That being said, I would like to see it show up at an upcoming Dollar Baby film festival, and I'm going to work with Tod to see if that can happen. And if there are any fans who really want to see it, they are welcome to contact me and I'd be happy to provide a link. I can't post it in its entirety online but I don't mind sending it directly to someone (I'm a bit of a feedback nut, and there's not been nearly enough from this project).

AN: Share with us your "...sending King the money in a piggy bank" story?

NS: We thought we were being so cheeky. When we secured the rights to *The Jaunt* we had to send King the dollar for the Dollar Baby, right? But it was right before Halloween, so instead of just sending him a check or a crisp dollar bill, we thought it would be fun, and play into his sensibilities, to send it in a fun way. So we went to one of those pop-up Halloween stores and brought a little plastic skull; we took a knife and dug out a slot in the top, and inside we placed exactly 100 pennies. Put it in a box and shipped it up to Maine. That was how we paid for our Dollar Baby.

AN: What is next for Nick Smith?

NS: Well, my wife and I have an amazing three-year-old that takes up the majority of my time right now, and parenthood is quite an adventure. My stage output has been reduced quite a bit by the Browncoats closing (which is a whole other story), but long term my goal would be to find a new space to reopen the Browncoat and recommit to its mission of showing original and challenging work on stage. I have a real love for the theater life and hope I can make it a big part of my world again at some point. I'm also in the very early stages of putting together a story for what might be my first novel. It's a daunting thing, but making art is one of my great joys, and I'm always looking for a way to be creative. So we'll see. There's always a new adventure on the horizon.

I want to thank Nick Smith for taking time out of his busy schedule to talk with us today and wish him the very best with future projects.

My Pretty Pony

Maciej Barczewski
April 6, 2020

THE STEPHEN KING DOLLAR BABIES come not just across the country, but from around the world! This Dollar Baby film comes all the from Poland by filmmaker, Maciej Barczewski.

Maciej Barczewski is a Polish film director, producer and screenwriter. He graduated from Gdynia Film School. His directorial debut was the short feature adaptation of a story by Stephen King *My Pretty Pony* (2017). His feature-length film debut: *The Champion* (2020), a story of the first transport of prisoners who arrive at the concentration camp Auschwitz, will be in theaters in the Fall of 2020. He is also a professor of intellectual property and media law in Gdansk and Chicago.

Here is my review of *My Pretty Pony*.

My Pretty Pony was the 6th publication in the Museum of American Art of artists and writers. It was a limited edition over-sized book with steel cover and a built-in digital clock of only 250 copies made in September 1989. There were a limited 15,000 copies printed for a Trade Edition. Later, in 1993, it was published in Stephen King's short story collection, *Nightmares & Dreamscapes*.

The story of *My Pretty Pony* is about an elderly man who has a long talk with his grandson about "time" and how fast it goes by and how precious it is. He gives his grandson a pocket watch while explaining the importance of time. This was a very short story and difficult to bring to the screen, but Maciej did an outstanding job. He captured the beautiful relationship of a grandfather and his grandson and at the same time brought the heartfelt, yet bittersweet core of the story through beauty. The beauty is the amazing and breathtaking cinematography which is, without question, the best I have ever seen in a Dollar Baby film. The

My Pretty Pony by Maciej Barczewski

beautiful countryside of the small town in Poland where it was filmed, the fields, flowers, and sunlight all are captured in stunning visuals that make this Dollar Baby films one of the very best on many levels.

Here is my exclusive interview with Maciej Barczewski.

Anthony Northrup: Share with us what it was like growing up in Poland?

Maciej Barczewski: I was born and raised in Gdansk, the city where World War II began and which was the cradle of the Solidarity movement that led to the fall of communism. From the perspective of years, growing up in such a place, and then observing the process of Poland's accession to the community of democratic European countries was an accelerated and invaluable history lesson. The reality around us was gray, but the people were cheerful. With difficult access to the media, everyone loved to read books.

AN: When did you first discover the works of Stephen King and what was your first Stephen King book and film?

MB: In the nineties, countless books of previously unavailable authors hit the Polish book market. Interestingly, among the most popular literary genres was the horror of which Stephen King was already the unquestioned king. Over the space of just a few months, several of his works went to Polish bookstores. The first that I read and which also made an unforgettable impression was 'Salem's Lot'.

AN: Is it hard to find Stephen King books there and does he have a big fan base in your country?

MB: King's huge popularity in Poland was strengthened by countless films based on his works available on the VHS market. The first of them, which scared me to the bone, was the television adaptation of 'Salem's Lot' by the late Tobe Hooper. Although horror as a literary genre has clearly lost popularity, King remains one of the most-liked writers in Poland. In every bookstore you can find at least one shelf dedicated to his works.

AN: Before we get into discussing your Dollar Baby film, tell us about your new film, *The Champion*?

MB: *The Champion* is my full-length feature film debut. It is set in 1940 and tells the true story of the first transport of prisoners, who came to the newly established Nazi death camp Auschwitz. Among them is pre-war Warsaw boxing champion Teddy Pietrzykowski. Forced by the Nazis to engage in boxing fights, he restores the hope of other prisoners that their captors are not invincible. Alas, this is also noticed by the camp authorities…

AN: What are some of your fondest memories of attending film school?

MB: I will not be extremely original – most pleasant memories are of the people whom I had the opportunity to meet. Moreover, as I started studies at the film school in my late thirties, it was nice to feel like a student again.

AN: Out of all the Stephen King short films, what attracted you most to this one?

MB: I recall that when I read it for the first time in 1993 in the collection of *Nightmares & Dreamscapes* I did not enjoy it as much as other stories. As a young reader I was disappointed that there were no supernatural elements, no twist or even a distinct ending to the story. At that time it seemed to be just a long exposition of a grandfather talking to his grandson. Many years later, when I thought about making a film about time as a main theme, and I revisited this story, it struck me as a deep and multilayered reflection on both the nature of time and family relationships. Then everything just clicked and I knew I had to make my version of *My Pretty Pony*. It is about time and it took some time to grow up.

AN: What changes did you make to make this your own as opposed to King's original text?

MB: The most difficult task was to tell this challenging, almost impressionistic text, as an audiovisual story, which would have its beginning, development and conclusion. Therefore, I had to make some shortcuts and simplifications that would bring the heart of this story to the surface. In a way, I also had to add its finale, because in the literary original it remained poetically undefined. And while this formula works in literature, the film has its own rules and requires at least a symbolic completion to the story presented. It also allowed me to enter the subtle element of the supernatural, which would not weaken the original story, but would strengthen its significance.

AN: So many Stephen King fans want adaptations to be as close to the book as possible, how do you handle the pressure to keep the fans happy?

MB: It seems to me that the most important thing is not so much to stick to the chronology of facts and events as to keep and emphasize what constitutes the heart of a given story. As long as the emotions remain unchanged, even die-hard fans will be willing to forgive a lot.

AN: What was your main goal you wanted to achieve about this film?

MB: Stephen King is one of my favorite writers. Commonly associated with horror stories, Stephen King is one of my favorite writers. Commonly associated with horror stories, he is also an outstanding creator of more traditional prose: *Rita Hayworth and Shawshank Redemption, The Body* or *The Green Mile* are his works, which transferred to the screen are now classified as cinema classics and do not have much in common with horror. In a similar vein, I also tried to adapt *My Pretty Pony*: as a timeless story about family and passing, which is supposed to touch, encourage to reflect, but also give the audience some emotional light that they can take home. It was also important for me to show that despite a symbolic budget, thanks to commitment and hard work, it is possible to make a short film, which you do not have to be ashamed of even putting it next to professional Hollywood productions.

AN: Share with us the casting process. What did your two lead actors bring to the table that won them the role?

MB: Marian Dziędziel, who played the role of grandfather, is one of the most respected Polish actors. His eyes and voice were able to convey the warmth of emotions and sadness of life experience that make up the essence of his character. Mateusz Broda, who played his grandson, was the embodiment of the innocent world of childhood, but also of hope that we can see in his eyes.

AN: Where was the movie filmed specifically and were there any obstacles to overcome while filming there?

MB: The film was shot in a rural region of northern Poland called Pomerania, spread around several dozen kilometers from my home. Fortunately, we didn't have to face any obstacles. Both local authorities and residents were very friendly towards the crew of young filmmakers, who sometimes stopped traffic on nearby roads for several hours.

AN: For me personally, this is without question, the most beautifully filmed Dollar Baby film I have ever seen. Tell us about the cinematography and who did you use for this film?

MB: Despite its intimate nature, or perhaps in spite of it, my general assumption was that *My Pretty Pony* should not differ visually from professional productions that we see in theaters. This assumption resulted in the choice of the widescreen format, the use of a crane, Steadicam or selection of lenses. Storyboards of key shots have also been helpful. In terms of choosing the light and color palette, I wanted to obtain the mood of memories of the end of summer. Achieving these goals would not have been possible without the involvement of Krzysztof Kujawski and Małgorzata Popinigis, a professional and private couple of creators of excellent commercials and music videos, whose commitment and imagination brought the picture to such a quality that they were awarded for it at several international festivals.

AN: How long was the film shoot and the process from start to finish?

MB: The shooting period lasted relatively long: 11 days. This was primarily due to care for the visual quality of the image, but also to the struggles with capricious weather. The whole process of creating the film from the beginning of work on the script to the closure of post-production lasted almost a year.

AN: What is your greatest moment, so far, with the success of *My Pretty Pony*?

MB: I think it was the reception at film festivals. Primarily in the US but also in Europe. *My Pretty Pony* has won over 30 awards around the world and has also become the most-awarded Polish short film. I especially remember winning the Special Jury Award at the WorldFest Houston International Film Festival at which George Lucas, Ridley Scott and Brian de Palma used to take their first steps. Another valuable distinction was the award at the Bridges International Film Festival in Greece, chaired by Bill Butler, cinematographer for the *Rocky* series, *One Flew Over the Cuckoo's Nest*, and Steven Spielberg's *Jaws*. Spielberg himself, as well as Francis Ford Coppola, congratulated the winners of the festival by videoconference. I also received one of the awards at the historic Raleigh Studios in Hollywood. In retrospect, one can say that this film's success opened my way to cinema screens and enabled me to make my large scale feature debut.

AN: What Stephen King story would you like to adapt on a much larger scale?

MB: I always dreamed of plunging into *The Dark Tower* universe and *Wizard and Glass* is my favorite book and a masterpiece of magical storytelling. I would have squeezed every smile and every tear from it. It would also be fun to revisit the little town of *Salem's Lot.*

AN: Where and When can fans see this film? Will it be playing at any film fests around the world?

MB: Unfortunately, its festival cycle is basically over. If, however, there will be more festivals that would like to show it, then I'm for it. Who knows, maybe someday sai King will allow the release of an anthology of short films based on his works or their one-time online presentation. I think that would make many fans and creators of Dollar Babies very happy.

AN: What is next for Maciej Barczewski?

MB: We talk at a rather specific moment, the cinemas are closed, film production is suspended due to a pandemic. Fortunately, we were able to complete the shooting for *The Champion,* so my next film is almost ready. I would like it to hit cinemas in the fall of 2020. However, when this actually becomes possible, it remains to be seen.

I want to thank Maciej for taking the time to speak with us today and wish him success in his future projects.

The Boogeyman by Mando Franco

The Boogeyman

Mando Franco
April 14, 2020

SOMETIMES, THERE ARE MULTIPLE versions of the same Stephen King short story. All are different and unique in their own special way. It makes it interesting to the viewer to see the various versions of the same basic story. Such is the case with my next Dollar Baby interview. This time it is with filmmaker Mando Franco and his Stephen King Dollar Baby film, *The Boogeyman*.

Armando (Mando) Franco, of Mexican, Spanish and French descent, is a Los Angeles native who has slowly made his mark on the LA independent horror scene. Mando grew up in the suburb of Monterey Park, CA, just outside East LA. Mando loved making movies at an early age and began as a theater actor, he went on to filmmaking in high school. Best known for his award winning short film, LUNAR and Award winning web series, 8.13, Mando focuses on bringing you chills and psychological suspense through the use of performance and camera work. Mando said this about filmmaking: 'It's not about what you see, but what you feel.'

Here is my review of Mando Franco's Dollar Baby, The Boogeyman!

The Boogeyman short story has been adapted many times since the very beginning of the Dollar Baby program. The very first version (and debatable as the first Dollar Baby film ever) came from filmmaker, Jeff Schiro. I have personally seen many versions of *The Boogeyman*, including Jeff's, and even though they are all entertaining, I have to say Mando Franco's version scared the heck outta me!

The short story, *The Boogeyman*, was first published in the March 1973 issue of *Cavalier* magazine. In 1978, it was published in the Stephen King short story collection, *Night Shift*. The story is about a man, Lester

Billings, who talks with a Dr. Harper, Lesters psychiatrist, about the murder of his three children. Lester tries to explain to the doctor that the police think he was the murderer, but tries to convince everyone that it was the "boogeyman". "Boogeyman" was the last word each murdered child screamed out. However, in typical Stephen King form, there is a twist at the end which leaves the reader wondering: Was Lester the killer or was it someone (or something) else? This is a very gripping, scary, and intense story and Mando nailed it with his adaptation. With a "grindhouse style" directing and filmmaking and a very impressive cast (actress, Miriam Korn blew me away as the mother and truly one of the best Dollar Baby performances I've seen by a lead Dollar Baby actress). It takes a lot to scare me or make me jump at the movies and Mando Franco's adaptation of *The Boogeyman* accomplished what he set out to do: scare the heck out of you!

Here is my exclusive interview with Dollar Baby filmmaker, Mando Franco.

Anthony Northrup: Tell us what it was like growing up in sunny Los Angeles, California?

Mando Franco: I grew up in a small suburb just 15 minutes from downtown Los Angeles. I'm from a family of movie watchers and movie lovers. They weren't movie buffs, but for our lower/middle class family movies at home or a blockbuster night we're our favorite forms of entertainment. We did frequent Universal Studios Hollywood, the theme park and movie studio. The tram tour set my imagination on fire. Being in an environment that was close to Hollywood was a blast for a movie lover.

AN: You studied theatre at Pasadena College, what were your experiences there like and how did that lead into directing?

MF: I grew up loving movies, so as a kid into high school I wanted to be an Actor. I took theater and performing in general very seriously and it was my passion and my dream. My Junior year in high school (11th grade) I was in a creative writing class, as a final we had to write a script and make a movie or perform in front of class. Making a movie sounded fun. I ended up being behind the camera directing it and I feel in love with the process. I sort of kept my finger in the acting pool. In college I wanted to hone the craft of acting, so I continued doing plays, got into sketch comedy , improv and stand up. All great for performing but adding to my ability as an actors director. I began dedicating all my spare time to making short films, even made a few features. They were definitely a learning curve and a blast to make, but never made anything outside of their premieres.

AN: What was your zombie web series called and about? How long did it run for?

MF: A while back, through mutual friends, I met up with a producer they wanted to create and shoot a zombie web series. I went in with my pitch and became a writer on the show. I co-wrote all of the 23 episodes and directed 9 of them. 8.13 was something I featured in all of my films/scripts. The date August 13th is Hitchcock's , who is also my favorite director, birthday , which plays a significant role in all my projects. 8.13 has many meanings in the show, but it is an ensemble piece about a zombie outbreak and where these characters are and how their stories collide. It did two seasons and was released by Machinima and still gets hits.

AN: When did you first discover the works of Stephen King? What was your first Stephen King book and film?

MF: As a kid I remember seeing Misery, which is one I have a lot of fond memories of. I also had nightmares from a small scene in *Salem's Lot*, with the kid floating outside the window. It totally destroyed my childhood. I didn't really get interested in King until I was in High School. I read a lot of his short stories included skimmed through *The Boogeyman* in the *Night Shift* collection, but didn't make an impact at the time. I'd heard of *IT* and *The Shining* as books but was more aware of the movies and TV miniseries.

AN: How did you first learn about the Stephen King Dollar Baby program?

MF: I'm a big Frank Darabont fan, and I had caught a glimpse of something he had said about adapting a King story for a dollar, so out of curiosity I thought I'd look into it. After doing some research I decided that it might be a good move for my filmmaking career.

AN: The Dollar Baby film, Boogeyman has been adapted many times and this version scared even me! Share with us some of the more memorable moments on-set of *The Boogeyman*?

MF: We shot for 7 days and had a limited time on our locations so it requires a metric ton of planning. This was the first film I made that actually had an FX budget, so doing blood and FX gags in camera was a blast. One shot I remember getting was Lester finding his house ransacked and he sees slime dripping off a doorknob. Setting up that shot and getting the timing right for a light to hit the knob and catch the drip was a victory. Such a small feat but mega exciting for me.

A question I'm often asked is, how did me make the kid cry? Little Andy has to cry in the movie, and his parents, who were on set told us he was scared of Dora the Explorer, and oddly, someone had a Dora giant head in their car. Don't know how or why, haha, but they had one. At the parents' influence, we had someone put on the mask, which scares the shit out of this kid. I felt awful, but the dad offered. It's authentic and heartbreaking to watch in the movie.

AN: Your two main leading actors in the film were amazing. Share with us the casting process and what did your two lead actors bring to the table that won them the role?

MF: The casting process was not fun. I added in some friends and professional actors that I knew, but we did a casting call for the two leads. Unfortunately, agents got involved with the casting of Rita, so we went with Miriam Korn, who was a friend of the producer , who was great. She committed hardcore to this. Her delivery of finding Denny's body was heartbreaking and intense. We did a few tales, and I guided her the best I could, but she brought it home.

We just could not find Lester. One guy we liked didn't want to do a horror movie, but we ended up going with another friend of the producer, Jason. Who was also a filmmaker. As a filmmaker he understood what we were trying to do, and he had done some acting and was just a great collaborator.

We almost had Peter Jason, he of several John Carpenter films and playing parts in *Mortal Kombat, The Karate Kid* and *Arachnophobia*. He was signed on to play Dr. Harper but had to drop out 3 days before shooting due to a project rolling over. Gregory came on board very last minute and saved the movie. He gave a very still calculated performance which captures exactly what I wanted. We also have a cameo from indie horror actress Maria Olsen. We had a very awesome and stacked cast.

AN: You make a cameo in this film. How much fun was it to direct… yourself?

MF: I don't like acting in my own films. I'll do it for anyone else but not myself. But our diner scene needed another body, so I'm just sitting in a corner in the diner. Our First AD and my friend Billy and Shannon, our FX artist were also in the diner scene. It was just like making a movie with friends.

AN: Out of all the Stephen King short stories, what attracted you most to this one?

MF: Something about a grounded take on the entity just sounded intriguing. Kind of like how The Exorcist is a very grounded story/movie. King's story was a unique take on the universal entity the Boogeyman. And I'm drawn to character driven claustrophobic stories and films. It just felt right.

AN: What changes did you make to make this your own as opposed to King's original text?

MF: The story consists of Lester and Dr. Harper. I'm in a therapy session. The whole thing is Lester describing the deaths of his kids at the hands of the boogeyman. I used flashbacks to show some of the scarier more traumatic events. My biggest contributions were the beginning and ending. I open the film like a crime thriller, with Lester getting arrested and the police finding Andy's body. The ending is very simple in the book. It's Dr. Harper coming out of the closet as the boogeyman, holding a human face mask. I spiced it up a bit. Made a portal from Lester's closest to Harper's closet showing the boogeyman can go anywhere. I also made the reveal more creature feature like from an 80s horror flick. I kept a lot of the dialogue from the book and based scenes on Lester's descriptions in the story.

AN: So many Stephen King fans want adaptations to be as close to the book as possible, how do you handle the pressure to keep the fans happy?

MF: I kept the essentials and key elements of the story, and I modernized it. It was written a long time ago so a lot of bits wouldn't fly. Lester isn't really a good person in the story. He's kinda an asshole really. But I tried to keep some jerk traits that he had but make him a better father. I think I honored the material pretty well.

AN: What was your main goal you wanted to achieve about this film?

MF: To see if I could pull it off, really. Haha. I'd never adapted anything before and for this to be my first was a high honor. So I wanted to make it grounded, scary and get solid performances. You jumped and we're blown away by the performances, then mission accomplished.

AN: Where was the movie filmed specifically and were there any obstacles to overcome while filming there?

MF: We had a wicked great art director. The biggest thing honestly was Harpers office. It's the main setting for the film. Every time I see a student film or indie micro budget film, they use their uncles accounting office. I've been to a therapist before, and there wasn't a big desk between us. It needed some atmosphere, had to be comfortable and stress free and open. With a box of tissues.

Harpers office was actually shot in my producers bedroom in her apartment. We took out her bed and furniture and moved living room furniture into the bedroom. Put some wall art and lamps up and boom. Therapy room.

We made the living room the lobby for Harper's office as well. A guest room in my producer's parents was Denny's room. Same thing, we cleared out the furniture, got an old crib and toys and our Art director made the room what it was. All of this was shot around, North Hollywood and Pasadena, CA.

AN: How long was the film shoot and the process from start to finish?

MF: We shot in March for seven days and then wrapped post in late May, June.

AN: What is your greatest moment so far with the success of *The Boogeyman*?

MF: Screening with full theaters of people who got scared. It's a triumph for a filmmaker to see audiences reacting to the film. That and being part of a Q&A panel moderated by Joe Bob Briggs.

AN: What Stephen King story would you like to adapt on a much larger scale?

MF: There is a small story that no one talks about in the *Night Shift* Collection, it's called *I Know What You Need*. It's a haunting little story about a crush. It's pretty insane and I'd love to have a crack at that one. It's a mystery/thriller type story.

AN: Where and When can fans see this film? Will it be playing at any film fests across the country?

MF: It hasn't played in a long time, as rules state, we can't put the whole film online, publicly. But the trailer can be viewed online on my YouTube channel.

AN: Lastly, What is next for Mando Franco?

MF: I'm in post on a couple new shorts and doing a lot of writing. Next up, my fifth feature film. I hope to shoot sometime in 2021.

I want to thank Mando for taking the time to talk with us today and wish him great success in the future.

The Lawnmower Man

James Gonis
April 15, 2020

LONG TIME AGO, when the Dollar Baby program was young, there were only just a handful of filmmakers who took Stephen King up on his offer to make a film for one dollar and a signed contract to adapt one of his short stories. One of those very early filmmakers, the "OG of Dollar Babies" so to speak, was director James Gonis. James was born April 12th, 1965 and grew up in the Big Apple: New York City. He studied film at NYU. In 1987, he made his Dollar Baby film, *The Lawnmower Man*. James later went on to work for Playboy Enterprises, Inc.

Here is my film review of *The Lawnmower Man*.

Stephen King's short story, *The Lawnmower Man*, was first published in the May 1975 issue of *Cavalier* magazine. In 1978, it was published in the Stephen King short story collection, *Night Shift*. There was a film in 1992 called, *The Lawnmower Man* starring Jeff Fahey, but it has no connection to King's short story except for the title. Stephen King won in court and had his name taken off the movie poster and no connections at all to the film.

The story is a very bizarre one. Harold Parkette decides to hire someone to mow his lawn after a terrible accident happens with a cat getting run over by a lawnmower. The "Pastoral Greenway" lawn service pulls up in his driveway and one of the workers begins mowing his lawn. When Harold checks up on the man's progress, he sees him naked on all fours eating the grass and even eating a mole! When Harold questions the man's actions, the man explains to Harold the "special way" their service mows lawns and if anyone has any complaints they become a sacrifice.

This very bizarre tale is one of King's very strange tales that is so bizarre it is hard to explain and you can't help but wonder: What was

The Lawnmower Man by James Gonis

Stephen King thinking when he wrote this? James Gonis adaptation is very cooky, yet has a "grindhouse" feel and look to it. And adaptation one has to see to believe.

Here is my exclusive interview with Dollar Baby filmmaker, James Gonis.

Anthony Northrup: Share with us what it was like growing up in the 1960's and 70's in New York City?

James Gonis: NYC was a great place to grow up in because it was so immense, dense and always moving, it had a sense of vitality you can only compare to other major cities. I grew up in Queens; Manhattan was especially imposing to me as a kid. It's funny, I took *All in the Family, Welcome Back Kotter, Do the Right Thing* and *Saturday Night Fever* for granted as portraying everyday life in my neighborhood. It's not until after living in L.A. for some time that I look back on those shows and think "Wow that's so… the boroughs!"

AN: When did you first discover the works of Stephen King? What was your first Stephen King book and film?

JG: Stephen King first entered my radar with the movie *Carrie*, which my kid sister was excited about, so I dismissed it at the time as "uncool." The *Salem's Lot* TV adaptation came after that and it was OK but didn't inspire me to pick up the novel. Then, as I became interested in studying film, I saw the teaser trailer for Kubrick's *The Shining*, with the blood flowing out of the elevators, and I was compelled to start reading King. *The Stand* had just come out in paperback so that was my first. Even the original, abridged edition was ambitious for me at 15, I'd never tackled a novel that long. I loved it, I was hooked. It's still my favorite novel.

AN: You attended NYU studying film. Who were some of your inspirations and were there any films you were a big fan of while attending college?

JG: At NYU Film in the 80's, Martin Scorsese's earlier and current films were very much in the zeitgeist; they reflected our "mean streets," and after all, he was an alumnus who broke through. I also discovered Brian DePalma by this time and finally saw and appreciated *Carrie*. The Cinema Studies program was great fun, screening and analyzing great films as art; the Production side was more of a challenge because we had to come up with short film ideas and I could only imagine telling stories that were feature length. So my classmates and I started writing spec screenplays. I didn't sell any, but *The Lawnmower Man's* cinematographer, Ethan Reiff, co-wrote *Tales From the Crypt: Demon Knight* and would go on to co-create *Kung-Fu Panda*. Mike DeLuca was working on *In the Mouth of Madness* (later to be directed by John Carpenter) and would go on to become a major Hollywood player.

AN: You left New York for another coast: California. You got a job at Playboy Enterprises. How did that come about and what exactly did you do there?

JG: L.A. was a bit of a culture shock, but it was easy to find temp work in the industry. It was also a good way to learn my way around the city, working in a different place every week. After doing that for three years, a temp-to-full-time opportunity came up in Playboy's Playmate Promotions Department, handling model booking requests and castings. It was extremely fast paced and consuming -- I had to hang up the writing -- but for 21 years I was blessed to work with a vast variety of interesting, talented people (employees and clients alike), travel the world, and be part of an environment that I looked forward to going to every day. There were always challenges, but I was inspired enough to push beyond my insecurities, which made the results especially rewarding. One instance comes to mind, when Roger Corman booked two Playmates for lead roles on a month-long movie shoot in St. Petersburg, Russia. I accompanied them to help them get situated for the first few days, but that turned into two weeks. This was ultra low-budget (Corman, after all) and a long way from Hollywood. When the models told me they were ready to break their contracts and take the next flight home, I found myself negotiating on their behalf for basics like drinking water, phone access and space heaters. It was part of my job, but not a role I ever pictured myself in. After that, they finished the shoot... so I like to think I single-handedly saved a Roger Corman movie! (The picture was called *The Arena,* and the director, Timur Bekmambetov, soon made it to Hollywood with *Wanted* and *Abraham Lincoln: Vampire Hunter.*)

AN: Do you have any fond memories of the late, great Hugh Hefner?

JG: Hef was brilliant and very quick-witted. One day, security and staff walked him into a convention selling Playboy merchandise and he quipped "I'll take the money now." I spoke to him directly a handful of times when there were issues with Playmates or he wanted to discuss Playmate of the Year candidates. He was very passionate about the content of the magazine, and the company did feel very much like a family while he was running it. One day I drew Snoopy in Hef's robe and Lucy as a Playboy Bunny with Charlie Brown staring at them going "Good grief!" Someone faxed it to Hef's office and he liked it enough to ask for the original (he started out as a cartoonist himself). So somewhere in his vast scrapbook collection there's a doodle of mine. Hef was also a "Monster Kid," he was especially into Lon Chaney Sr. I once met *Famous Monsters* editor Forrest J. Ackerman at a Playboy Mansion party and told him how much I loved the magazine growing up. "You weren't supposed to grow up!" he replied. Years later when Forry was terminally ill, I informed Hef's office and was told that Hef sent him a note. I like to think that cheered Forry up.

AN: Let's talk about your Stephen King Dollar Baby, *The Lawnmower Man.* Out of all the Stephen King short stories, what attracted you most to this one?

JG: The first book I picked up after *The Stand* was *Night Shift,* a remarkable story collection. *The Lawnmower Man* got under my skin, it was so random and perverse, and the downbeat ending freaked me out. A few months later I read in *Famous Monsters* magazine that British horror producer Milton Subotsky was planning an anthology movie of King stories called *Terror By Daylight,* to include *The Lawnmower Man,* and that excited me. Well, *Terror By Daylight* never saw daylight (despite the slew of King adaptations in the years to follow), and that disappointed me. By 1985, I was part of a small group of students in an NYU class where the assignment was to make a color, synch-sound 16mm short. Everyone in my group had original script ideas, including me, but nothing got us excited. So I randomly suggested we adapt *The Lawnmower Man.* Everyone in my group knew the story, liked the idea, and the adventure began. None of us knew about the Dollar Deal at the time and the question of rights never came up. We were students and this was just a film school exercise, not for public or commercial consumption.

AN: What changes did you make to make this your own as opposed to King's original text?

JG: The script was taken almost verbatim from Walt Simonson's 1981 comic adaptation in *Bizarre Adventures* magazine. Bit of a cop-out maybe, but the delay in settling on a story put us behind schedule and there wasn't much time for pre-production. Besides, my inclination at the time would've been to treat it more seriously, and in hindsight I think the lighter tone was the right way to go, more *Creepshow.*

AN: So many Stephen King fans want adaptations to be as close to the book as possible, how do handle the pressure to keep the fans happy?

JG: As a fan, faithful adaptations are important to me, so there was no question of that... Although there are examples of how a streamlined adaptation like Cronenberg's *The Dead Zone* can work out perfectly, while an extremely faithful take like Lester's *Firestarter* can miss the mark.

AN: What was your main goal you wanted to achieve about this film?

JG: The goal was to create the kind of movie that we would want to see. We might have been studying Godard and Antonioni, but we wanted to be Spielberg, Scorsese, Romero. Knowing it was an ambitious story to adapt, I think the challenge stoked our youthful bravado, yet meeting every obstacle along the way with incredible good fortune was humbling and educational. As far as the story's subtext, I never gave it much thought,

I guess the idea is "suburbanites, don't be complacent, mow your own damn lawns!" There could be more to it of course...

AN: Where was the movie filmed specifically and were there any obstacles to overcome while filming there?

JG: We found a perfect location in Dix Hills, Long Island. Kind of a tract housing development, we called it Poltergeist Village. Not far from Amityville. We knocked on the owner's door and he said sure, we could film on the property, just not inside. So the interiors were shot at my dad's house in Flushing. (The owner appears in the film as the neighbor, we wanted to give him a shot at stardom.) The location's lawn was always perfectly cut, so there was the issue of how to make the grass look unwieldy. Fortunately there was an unmowed patch nearby for the first shot of Karras crawling naked through the weeds. There were other challenges that had nothing to do with the location, like trying to convince the actor playing Karras to remove his jock strap for the big "shock" shot (he wouldn't, and I don't blame him)... and getting a good line read from the little girl hiding in the grass... and finding ways to shoot the animals to look like the dog was chasing the cat. One regret I'll always have is not getting an imposing, big-ass power mower. The one *The Lawnmower Man* uses is the same dinky one Parkette trades in. But time and resources were limited, and at that age I don't think I knew mowers could be rented.

AN: How long was the film shoot and the process from start to finish?

JG: The shoot began in spring 1985; we didn't get all the footage in the can but enough to get graded on. We went back in the summer to film the remaining shots, and a few months later did the insert shots of the cloven hoofs, and the title cards. Graduation came and went, the negative was sitting in my fridge, but I had to finish the thing! So much work went into it, the footage looked great... And the cast was awesome. Andy Clark, who played the title role, was in Woody Allen's *Radio Days* as the guy who gets spooked by the *War of the Worlds* broadcast; Helen Hanft, who played Mrs. Parkette, was well known off-Broadway and was in a slew of movies including *Manhattan*, *Stardust Memories* and *Arthur* ("my husband has a gun!"). And we couldn't have asked for a better Parkette than E.D. Phillips; sadly he passed away before we finished and never got to see it. I worked for months on a rough cut that would've been a 30 minute movie, so I paid another student, whose specialty was editing, to pare it down with a fresh perspective. He did an amazing job. So this little 12 minute student film took 2 years to make, longer than most features.

AN: In the film, the lead character eats grass and a mole. What did you use for that effect?

JG: The "mole" was actually a guinea pig we borrowed from a pet store (where does one rent a mole in NYC?); its mangled carcass was made of cooked tripe, liver, food coloring, and rabbit pelt. Andy Clark chowed down on it like he loved it, what a champ.

JG: Frank Darabont, Jeff Schiro, James Cole, and you are the "original" Dollar Babies. Share with us your thoughts of how easy (or difficult) it was to make a DB back then as opposed to now? And can share any thoughts about your fellow Dollar Baby directors from back then?

JG: I wasn't aware of the Dollar Baby program until 1987 when the film was being completed. I sent a VHS copy to King, along with a letter and a dollar bill -- I kick myself for not sending a check, I could've gotten his autograph on the back, but I was young & stupid! So there was no formal blessing to make the film, no contract, it was already done. When I met King at a book signing a couple of years later I asked him what he thought and he said he got a kick out of it, which of course I appreciated. It's funny to think that I'm among the first of the Dollar Babies, it didn't feel that way at the time -- it felt like riding the wave of the flood of King movies of the period. It was a thrill to find the Darabont and Schiro films on VHS when they came out, I had no idea. I finally had the opportunity to meet Frank Darabont in L.A. around 2010 and asked him about plans for *The Long Walk*, another favorite of mine which I heard he had optioned. "That's next," he said, and that was a great little moment for me because yes, he's a renowned director but he's also a fellow DB, and a fellow fan! Jim Cole and I were introduced in the late 1980's by Craig Goden, a book vendor who specialized in King that knew we each did short film adaptations. Since my film and his *Last Run on the Ladder* were made more or less concurrently and shared a lot of the same exposure, I like to think of them as a double feature that represent two very different sides of King's storytelling. Both were written up by Tyson Blue in the *Castle Rock* newsletter too. Jim made the big move to Hollywood before I did and was extremely helpful and supportive after I arrived; to this day he's one of my best friends. I did end up getting a letter from Milton Subotsky cautioning me that he still held the rights to *The Lawnmower Man*, which I thought was pretty cool. Was it easier or more difficult at the time? I don't know what kind of technology young filmmakers or students have at their disposal these days but 16mm was a bitch. Rickety, heavy equipment, sound recorded separately, negative cutting, mixing, color correction... As far as getting permission, the internet makes that part easier now. I haven't seen *The Lawnmower Man* as available for adaptation on the site, maybe the rights are still spoken for or tied up in old litigation from the feature. I'm surprised there've been no other faithful adaptations.

AN: What is your greatest moment so far with the success of *The Lawnmower Man*?

JG: The greatest initial moment of success I experienced was when a former NYU professor invited me to screen the answer print for her class. This was the same sophomore class I had taken where we made 3-minute black & white silent films, so this represented a quantum leap forward of sorts, and the reception was crazy enthusiastic! It felt wonderful. Since then, being included in film festivals and books, and being in the community of DB's and King filmmakers as a whole, has made my film the gift that keeps on giving. Countless superior student films were made that year -- and every year -- that deserve attention, so it's a miracle to have made one that has an audience after all this time, even as a curiosity. (The fallout from the 1992 feature has also probably helped to boost mine as being the faithful one.) It helps balance out the fact that it's an ultra low-budget student film (undergrad, at that) that is, at times, painful for me to watch. It's also a reminder that though I didn't keep making films, that I am capable of the kind of tenacity that would've enabled me to pursue that career, or tackle any goal for that matter.

AN: What Stephen King story would you like to make on a much larger scale?

JG: My reply to that question has always been *Salem's Lot,* but anticipating the next remake could do it justice I'd have to say *Thinner*. Though I liked the 1996 version, the fat suit didn't work, and now with CGI and the right lead actor it'd be worth revisiting. I might want to bring back Joe Mantegna as Ginelli though!

AN: The Dollar Baby program has been around for over 40yrs. Did you ever think it would still be around today and the scale it has grown to?

JG: I've grown to appreciate King's shorter works more these days, so I think it's great that they've inspired other Dollar Babies and kept the program going! Short stories and films don't get enough exposure so this is a neat little avenue to explore and celebrate them, and of course to share our collective inspiration from King's work.

AN: Where can fans see the film and which film fest did it play at?

JG: *The Lawnmower Man*'s first festival screening was at Horrorfest in the late 1980's, held at the Stanley Hotel in Colorado which inspired *The Shining*. The film was also part of the Dollar Baby festival in Bangor several years ago, which Jim Cole and I attended, along with Jay Holben and many other DB's we had the pleasure of meeting for the first time. There was a festival in L.A. attended by Mick Garris, Jeff Schiro and John Woodward, among others. There've been several others since then, in Texas, New York, Argentina, etc. Most recently, I was interviewed on the "Chat Sematary" podcast. The film should be available to watch on YouTube.

AN: Lastly, What is next for James Gonis?

JG: For the past six years I've co-hosted a podcast called "Monster Party," where three friends and I discuss and debate all things horror, sci-fi and fantasy. We've been lucky to have some terrific guests on, such as Jeffrey Combs, Walter Koenig, *Thinner* director Tom Holland, and *Pet Sematary's* Denise Crosby. For our episode on Stephen King, our guest was writer/documentarian Constantine Nasr, who did supplemental features on *IT* and the Darabont adaptations. The podcast sprung out of booze-fueled conversations we'd have in hotel rooms after comic conventions. The four of us are close friends but we have very distinct personalities and opinions, and good chemistry. The show has developed a healthy following, and it's been truly amazing to reach and correspond with genre fans all over the world. After six years you'd think we'd run out of things to talk about, but there's always something new, plenty of vintage stuff to discover, and no shortage of special guests we look forward to having on it.

AN: I want to thank James for taking the time to talk to us today.

JG -Thanks so much for your questions, and congratulations on your book! I can't wait to read it!

Uncle Otto's Truck

Brian Johnson
April 16, 2020

STEPHEN KING HAS CERTAINLY scared us over the years with vehicles that are either haunted or "come alive"! Films like *Maximum Overdrive* (based on the short story, *Trucks*), *Mile 81*, *Road Rage* (based on the short story, *Throttle*), *From A Buick 8*, and of course, the queen of haunted cars herself: *Christine*. However, there is another "haunted car" tale that really makes your skin crawl: *Uncle Otto's Truck*. Filmmaker, Brian Johnson brings this creepy tale to like in his Dollar Baby adaptation of the same name. However, Brian has been around awhile and certainly knows all about directing films and the film industry.

Brian Johnson was born on August 22nd, 1962. Although little is known about Brian's early life, in 1985, he received his Radio and Television Broadcasting Degree. His career began as an NBC affiliate in South Carolina. In 1987, he moved to Los Angeles where he attended the Movie Group Institute. He also studied Cinematography, Editing, and Directing. Brian continued his studying under the late Actor, Ross Hagen (*Gunsmoke, Mission Impossible, The Fall Guy*). Not long after that, Brian would go on to direct Hollywood celebrities such as Donald O'Connor (*Singing In The Rain*), Sarah Jessica Parker (*Sex In The City*) just to name a few. Brian is currently living in Wilmington, North Carolina and married to his wife, Tresha. Brian's love and passion for film has grown leaps and bounds with many future projects on the horizon.

Here is my film review of Brian Johnson's adaptation of Stephen King's Uncle Otto's Truck.

The short story, Uncle Otto's Truck was first published in *Yankee* magazine in 1983. It was later published in the short story collection, *Skeleton Crew* in 1985. The story is told by Otto's nephew about his

Uncle Otto's Truck by Brian Johnson

wealthy uncle and his business partner, George McCutcheon of Castle Rock. Their partnership falls to the wayside and Otto kills George by crushing him with his truck. Otto is uncertain if the truck did it or if he was possessed and the truck made him do it, but Otto begins to slowly fall into a state of insanity. He decides to live in the middle of nowhere on his own and insists that the truck is coming after him now to kill him!

Is it Otto's imagination or has he completely gone over the edge? Only the talents of Stephen King can answer that question.

I really, really enjoyed this adaptation of *Uncle Otto's Truck*. The locations were amazingly beautiful. The cast was impressive, but it was actor Peter Holland as 'Otto' that blew me away! Without question, one of the best performances I've ever seen in a Dollar Baby film, let alone a Stephen King adaptation in general. Peter really got into the character and at times, became very believable and scary! *Uncle Otto's Truck* by Brian Johnson is one of the best Dollar Baby adaptations I've ever seen and is worthy of a full-length big screen version. This is one you don't want to miss!

Here is my exclusive interview with Dollar Baby filmmaker, Brian Johnson.

Anthony Northrup: Tell us what it was like growing up in North Carolina? Have you always lived there your whole life?

Brian Johnson: I grew up on a farm in the piedmont triad region of North Carolina. I was the only child in sort of an isolated area so I often entertained myself by inventing characters to whom I would talk to and create a world with. It was truly my introduction into the world of filmmaking as I know it today. At the age of 15 I moved away with my parents due to my dad's business and over a course of my lifetime have moved 30 plus times attending many different schools. Looking back I'm thankful as it made me strong and resilient and easily adaptable to anything and anywhere.

AN: Where did you study and when did you first get into film?

BJ: I went to Tri-County Technical College next to the Clemson University campus where I received a Radio and Television broadcasting degree. It was shortly thereafter that I realized my burning desire to be in film. So after graduating, myself and three friends headed to LA where I would attend school once again receiving a degree in Motion Picture production. It was there I would shoot my first film. It wasn't long after that I began getting jobs in the industry.

AN: When did you first discover Stephen King's works and what was your first Stephen King book?

BJ: It would have been *Christine*.

AN: How did you first hear about the Stephen King Dollar Baby Program?

BJ: Oddly enough I was asked by someone in the industry to shoot their Dollar Baby project. Up until then I had never heard of the program.

AN: What other films have you worked on?

BJ: In 1996 I was in the visual effects department for the TV Series Seven Days. I have worked on many independent films in many positions. I was cinematographer on the highly rated CBS TV movieDocudrama *The Life and Times Of Pistol Pete*. The show won three Emmys. I have shot a lot of national commercials including Coke, GTX Castrol and others.

AN: Out of all of the Stephen King short stories, what attracted you most to this one?

BJ: Well probably because of my early attraction to *Christine*.

AN: What changes did you make to make this your own as opposed to King's original text?

BJ: Mainly a few character additions and the telling of the story from Quinten as a kid.

AN: So many King fans want adaptations to be as close to the book as possible. How did you handle the pressure to keep the fans happy?

BJ: I suppose as long as you keep the chill factor most will respond favorably.

AN: What was your main goal you wanted to achieve about this film?

BJ: To have a moral to the story.

AN: Share with us the casting process for the film and what did lead actor, Peter Holland (who plays Otto), bring to the table that won him the lead at the audition?

BJ: Most of the characters I already knew from other projects, except for Peter. I can't say enough good things about him as a human and as a character. When casting Peter he suddenly went off script and began to ad-lib. Most directors would frown on that but I like to leave it open as it gives you a chance to see the actor bring his own interpretation to the story. And in this case it paid off. He was fabulous.

AN: The use of antiques in some of the scenes were very creepy and old. What inspired you to use them and where did you find such treasures?

BJ: Living in the south you don't have to go far to find a wide array of antiques. Most folks keep things for generations just waiting for you to come along and use them as props for films.

AN: Where did you find the truck used in the film of Uncle Otto's and where is that truck now?

BJ: Once again, I love living in the South. Here not only can you find antiques rusting away in barns and various hideaways, you will also find vehicles still being used on farms and the like. So someone I knew had said he new someone who had a truck we may want to use. Well the rest is history. The owner drives it daily as a work truck.

AN: Where was the movie filmed and were there any obstacles you had to overcome while you filmed there?

BJ: We filmed in Ararat Virginia, Hillsville VA and Supply NC. We were fortunate not to run into any obstacles.

AN: How long was the film process from start to finish?

BJ: Around 6 Months.

AN: What is your greatest moment so far with your success of *Uncle Otto's Truck*?

BJ: Winning Finalist as Cinematographer in Canada Festival, Semi-Finalist in the LA Cine Fest, Semi Finalist as Cinematographer in a Europe festival, and Finalist in a Rome Festival.

AN: What Stephen King story would you like to adapt on a much larger scale?

BJ: Actually the Uncle Otto story. So if you or anyone has a direct line to Mr. King let him know.

AN: Lastly, Where can fans see the film and What is next for Brian Johnson?

BJ: I am trying to secure permission to show online. In the meantime I can send a private link if someone wants to see a film. I'm currently busy filming a few commercials and working on a few ideas of my own for producing.

I would like to thank Brian for his time to sit down with us to discuss his Dollar Baby film, *Uncle Otto's Truck*.

Mute

Rob Darren Newberger
April 16, 2020

EAST COAST, WEST COAST... Dollar Baby filmmakers come from all over the country. My latest interview comes from a filmmaker from the South and a Dollar Baby film based on a Stephen King short story you don't hear too much about. This time, my interview is with Rob Darren Newberger and his Dollar Baby film, *Mute*.

Rob Darren Newberger is from Virginia Beach, Virginia. He attended First Colonial High school in Virginia Beach and graduated in 1983. He continued his studies at TCC in Virginia Beach studying Business Administration until 1990. His education continued at the Old Dominion University studying Marketing, Finance and Economics, graduating in 1996. Rob then entered the world of filmmaking and his adaptation of the Stephen King short story, MUTE. Rob is currently in a relationship and lives in Raleigh, North Carolina.

Mute by Rob Darren Newberger

Here is my review of the Dollar Baby *Mute*.

The short story, *Mute* was first published in the December 2007 issue of *Playboy* magazine and in 2008 it was published in the Stephen King short story collection, *Just After Sunset*. The story is about a traveling salesman who goes to a priest to give his confession. While doing so, he tells the priest his story about his wife cheating on him and he found out. But the story takes a turn when he also tells the priest about when he picked up a hitchhiker who was deaf and mute. Since he couldn't speak or hear, the traveling salesman shares his story about his cheating wife to the hitchhiker and how much he hates her and wishes bad things for her and her lover. Assuming the hitchhiker can't hear him or understand, the traveling salesman thinks he's safe sharing his tale.

Events take a very strange and dangerous turn as the priest hears more than just a confession. Did the hitchhiker kill the salesman's wife and lover? Did God place the hitchhiker in the salesman's car for a reason? Only Stephen King can share that secret.

Mute adaptation by Rob Darren Newberger was filmed very well, very professionally. The cast did a very fine job and it leaves the viewer guessing just who was this mysterious hitchhiker and did he really help this sad and angry salesman? I was very pleased with this Dollar Baby adaptation and enjoyed all the hidden "easter eggs" (nods) the director slipped in there that only a true die hard Stephen King fan would recognize.

Here is my Exclusive Interview with Dollar Baby filmmaker, Rob Darren Newberger.

Anthony Northrup: Tell us what it was like growing up in Virginia?

Rob Darren Newberger: I was a navy brat and moved around a lot but landed in Virginia Beach and graduated high school and college there.

AN: When did you first discover the works of Stephen King and what was your first Stephen King book and film?

RDN: My first SK book was Salem's Lot and the movie with the most impact on me was *The Shining*.

AN: While attending college, you studied business and marketing. What was it specifically that changed your course to filmmaking?

RDN: I worked in the corporate world and was never truly satisfied. Moved to Vegas in 2007 went to acting school but figured out quickly I'm better behind the camera.

AN: When did you first learn about the Stephen King Dollar Baby program?

RDN: By accident I was surfing the internet and stumbled upon it.

AN: Out of all the Stephen King short stories, what attracted you most to this one?

RDN: The story was intriguing and loved the characters.

AN: What changes did you make to make this your own as opposed to King's original text?

RDN: The story took place in the desert which had a mysterious element to it.

AN: So many Stephen King fans want adaptations to be as close to the book as possible, how do you handle the pressure to keep the fans happy?

RDN: Kept small details but added my own twist to it.. made the story ride like a rollercoaster and develop the characters as the story moved along.

AN: What was your main goal you wanted to achieve about this film?

RDN: My main goal is to have SK see the potential enough to make a feature film and kickstart a great filmmaking career.

AN: Where was the movie filmed specifically and were there any obstacles to overcome while filming there?

RDN: Scouting the Vegas locations from North Carolina was a challenge but I had a plan B C and D for everything.

AN: How long was the film shoot and the process from start to finish?

RDN: 4 months preproduction… 6 days Scouting 3 days shooting and a 1yr editing. And had to go back and ADR the bar scene.

AN: What is your greatest moment so far with the success of *Mute*?

RDN: TBD.

AN: What Stephen King story would you like to film on a much larger scale?

RDN: I would love to film *Salem's Lot*.

AN: Where can fans see this film? Will it be playing at any film fests across the country?

RDN: *Mute* is currently being submitted to multiple film festivals.

AN: Share with us the casting process and what was it specifically your lead actor brought to the table that won him the role?

RDN: All my actors brought their A game. Rob Marrocco did a short film where he cried and laughed in the same scene. Decided he was the right actor for the character. I wrote the screenplay for the actors in mind .

AN: Lastly, What's next for Rob Darren Newberger?

RDN: I want to do a documentary on the Prescription business and one on Antarctica. Also a *Blazing Saddles* type comedy. I have a feature done before *Mute* titled, *White Paint: A Clown Story* and a script that was accepted by CAA. It's a Laurel and Hardy modern buddy story that was endorsed by Stan Laurel's daughter herself.

    I want to thank Rob for talking with us today and wish him great success in the future.

Gray Matter

Red Clark
May 12, 2020

To adapt a Stephen King story to the big or small screen is a challenge. To bring that story to life and make it as scary as King wrote it… that's an even bigger challenge. However, I can safely say that Red Clark's Dollar Baby adaptation of Stephen King's , *Gray Matter* has certainly achieved that challenge with flying colors.

Red Clark was born in Massachusetts, but lived most of his life in Chicago and Michigan. He has worked on making movies since his youth and hasn't stopped since. He has worked at Stephen King Short Movies since October 2011. Red was married in June of 2018 to Rebekah Lieto.

Here is my review of Red Clark's Dollar Baby film, *Gray Matter*.

Gray Matter was first published in the October 1973 issue of *Cavalier* magazine and was published again in the 1978 Stephen King short story collection, *Night Shift*. The story takes place during a snowstorm in Bangor, Maine. A young boy rushes into a convenience store with fear in his eyes and is there to pick up beer for his father. His father, Richie Grenadine, was injured at work years ago and has been living on workers comp ever since. However, sitting at home collecting state money, Richie has developed a serious drinking problem. He sends his son to the story everyday, all day to buy the cheapest beer they have. What Richie doesn't know is, having a drinking problem will soon be the least of his problems after a "defective" bottle of beer is consumed and the terror begins in the quiet town of Bangor.

Gray Matter is one of the creepiest, grossest, and disturbing stories of King's early works. It tackles the serious subject of alcoholism, yet in traditional Stephen King fashion makes a horror story out of it with

Gray Matter by Red Clark

death and very horrific outcomes. Red Clark's version of this story was absolutely perfectly adapted from page to screen. He kept the story close to King's original text and his talents as a director clearly shined as he brought terror, impressive special effects, and a talented cast all to the screen. And I will personally admit, this film actually scared me! I jumped several times and it is safe to say this is one of the top best Stephen King adaptations I have personally ever seen. A film that was enjoyable and scary to watch.

Here is my exclusive interview with Dollar Baby filmmaker, Red Clark!

Anthony Northrup: Although originally from the east coast, you grew up in Chicago. Share with us what it was like growing up there?

Red Clark: I started making movies when I was a little kid in the early '90s. I was one of the only kids at our school who had a camera, so I would put everyone in my films. It was a lot bigger of a deal at the time, pre-cell phone, pre-internet. I put teachers in movies, and they would hang out with me outside of class. There was a bully who didn't like me, so I asked him to come and get eaten by monsters. Jocks, nerds, and goth kids ran around with me. I got my first real date with a projectionist at my first film festival and won a $100 movie prize the same night (I took everyone out for milkshakes). So movies were a way for me to tell stories and break down walls during High School. I remember playing my movie trailer in the school lunchroom. Stop motion critters scamper around, and the school explodes Rock and Roll High School style at the end. Everyone went nuts. I decided to skip class for the rest of the day (which I never did before) and play the trailer for every lunch period. So I'd say at a very early age I fell in love with film and storytelling and knew I'd do it for the rest of my life.

AN: When did you first discover the works of Stephen King (your first King book and first King movie)?

RC: In our creepy basement, the same place I'd make one person haunted houses for my little brother and sister, a faded red book collected dust on the shelf. There was no slipcover, just the ominous title on the binding *Night Shift* next to King's name. So one windy night, I cracked it open to discover *The Boogeyman* and *Gray Matter*, stories that scared my little kiddie socks off.

It was Stephen King and Ray Bradbury who turned me on to reading outside of school, and I became a nut for books and making movies. I checked out every book on King and film-making at all the libraries in my area. After I was finished with those, I traveled out to faraway towns getting library cards so I could read all of their film books. I did the same thing with video stores. Of course, as a kid without a car, it was harder for me to get back to some of these places that were an hour or two away, so I'd get a ride as a favor and check out the maximum amount I could. The eventual price for this was an enormous amount of late fees and marks on my credit, which only decades later would I recover from… I now have good credit and always return on time, I promise! *The Library Policeman* is real, and they don't like teenage me.

One of these VHS rentals as a kid was *Maximum Overdrive*, which was probably my first Stephen King movie experience. I thought it was awesome. I remember loving the music (which I recorded on a tape cassette), and my friends and I flipping out when the little leaguer got flattened by a steam roller.

I have many early iconic King memories. Standing in an old movie theater staring at the poster for *Sleepwalkers* in wonder as I munched popcorn. Witnessing *The Stand* while bedridden with the flu. The smell of the ancient *Different Seasons* paperback at our family cottage. In the early '90s, one of my Catholic School classmates brought a copy of *Thinner* to school and decided to share a "sex scene" with us in the hallway between classes. I just remember his giggles transforming into a choking sound as his collar lifted up, and the livid nun appeared. He went directly to the principal's office and detention. The book was locked away in one of those bottomless Catholic School desks never to be seen again.

Another classmate once regaled us with tales of sneaking in to see *Misery* at a movie theater (we were shocked since it was rated R). After we cross-examined him for details, he told us the ending. "They are in a room with a single candle. The crazy lady creeps up with an ax and blows the flame out. It goes dark… kind of scary, not to me" This is pre-internet, so kids would B.S. like this all day long at school, and there was no way to know for sure. Anyway, months later, I was at home, and Misery came on right near the end. Even though I wasn't allowed to watch R movies, I wanted to check out this spooky candle cliffhanger. My dad strolls into the room, right in time for Jimmy Caan to start bashing in Kathy Bates head with his typewriter. My dad screamed, "WHAT IS THIS!?" unplugged the TV and totally flipped out. I desperately explained what I was told about the candle. I'm sure you can imagine how that sounded. Our school buddy obviously never saw one minute of *Misery*, and I got in big trouble for it.

A frightening King moment took place at my grandmother's around the holidays. Her house was very like the one in King's *Gramma* story. She was a wonderful woman, but the house had a dark side. Those creaking slanted floors, stray cats with missing tails, and beams of sun dust peeking into shadowed rooms had my imagination buzzing. I was in a back room alone with the old cathode ray TV when a trailer for the *IT* miniseries crept on. The circus music blasted, and Tim Curry crackled joyously to horrible screams. I tried to shut off the TV, but the dial jammed, so I just fell to the floor and covered my ears, humming to hide the monster sounds as my neck hair crackled. I still remember the chills scratching up my back in waves. Even though the movie is admittedly dated, the 1990's *IT* will always summon that powerful memory. Ironically, King favorite and Dollar Baby veteran Mick Garris similarly traumatized me with a moment in *Psycho IV,* but that's another story.

AN: You did another Stephen King related project?

RC: I also did a book trailer for King's publisher *Hodder & Stoughton,* for *Just After Sunset.* It was a contest King was judging that I won. They said Stephen King was quick to choose it and liked it a lot. Probably one of my all-time favorite emails. I later received a signed and dedicated book from King, and they used the video to promote the book on Amazon and elsewhere.

AN: Let's talk about your Stephen King Dollar Baby adaptation, *Gray Matter.* Out of all the Stephen King short stories, what attracted you most to this one?

RC: *Night Shift* left a mark on me as a kid. The specific moment in *Gray Matter* describing the spider spooling a litter of kittens was something I always remembered. I wanted to do a straight forward, practical effects monster movie and it seemed like the perfect fit for me. I just loved the story.

AN: What changes did you make to make this your own as opposed to King's original text?

RC: For Better or Worse, I made a few changes. I fleshed out some bits from the story, specifically with Carl and how he behaves. I added a moment with Richie's teeth and hair starting to fall out as well as him pulling down an eyelid to shoot out some "gray stuff" onto the mirror. It slithers away to Richie's amazement. The actual story has a quick finish, so I dragged out the confrontation with Richie before he begins to divide. A smaller stop motion Richie clone falls from the ceiling on top of Bertie. Carl unsuccessfully hides in a bathtub, and we finally get a look at what Richies became before he tears off Carl's jaw. These were all added gags. The spider is also only mentioned once in the story as an aside. I decided to bring the spider back a final time to bring it full circle. Just as things seemed over, I wanted to end with a sense of dread. The Gray Matter has spread into town, a worse and more dangerous blizzard darkens the horizon, and the spider has emerged from the sewer looking for snacks. It finds a baby, who giggles as the creature descends from the ceiling, opening its eight legs like a flower.

AN: So many Stephen King fans want adaptations to be as close to the book as possible, how do you handle the pressure to keep the fans happy?

RC: Since I'm also a constant reader, I adore King, so doing this was important to me. In the end, I was really just trying to follow the themes in the text, have fun, and make a movie that King might get a kick out of if he ever had time to check it out.

AN: What was the main goal you wanted to achieve with this film?

RC: My main goal was to do all practical special effects. From enlisting Thomas Hodge to do his stunning hand-painted poster, to the monsters, to the animation, all physical stuff you can hold in your hands, and as much in-camera as possible. I went to some pretty ridiculous lengths to do this, like blowing my whole budget on robotic animatronics, foam latex, and silicone creatures. We made matte paintings and miniatures and stained walls, clothes, and skin red with fake blood. The stop motion I did was for the pure joy of it. I knew that specifically looked hokey, but I didn't care. I'm a Ray Harryhausen kid.

AN: Where was the movie filmed, and were there any obstacles to overcome while shooting there?

RC: The movie was shot primarily in Michigan and Chicago, with a little in New York, where Larry Fessenden (Richie) lives. The biggest obstacle was the lack of snow. 99% of the blizzard with the actors is fake. It's hard to describe the hell I went through to disguise this and do it with practical fx, even things like clouds of breath had to be fabricated to mimic bitter cold. From using flour to blanketing the ground with foam and leaning on soft focus, faking a snowstorm was a huge ordeal. It just didn't snow the year we decided to film with the actors, and when it did, people were not available. Luckily I had some additional blizzard footage I'd shot the year earlier and got some great second unit help for much of the landscape stuff. Nobody notices it, so I guess we did ok with that.

AN: How long was the film shoot and process from start to finish?

RC: I started the film back in 2013, and it went on a couple years. Even though I typically work extremely fast, this was a passion project, so we let things spread around our real jobs. Actor availability and fabrication of the makeup effects put significant gaps between shoots. In the beginning, it was just myself and my good friend Ross, along with amazing Mike Bove on camera, just filming actors whenever they were free. I had someone come in toward the end of filming (super talented Katherin Mraz) to assist me and organize people. Like probably every volunteer, she ended up doing lots of random stuff like being a stand-in or throwing slime. Everyone helped a lot when they could, I was lucky to have a fantastic cast and crew who gave their all when time allowed.

At a certain point, it was just about getting the movie done, so I began filming myself as stand-ins for different characters. I think me and Ross played every role at some point. One night, I was stuck alone puppeteering a decayed kitten hand puppet. I threw together the cocoon last minute with coffee grounds, cotton swabs, and Elmer's glue. So I was puppeteering with one hand covered in glop, and waving a flashlight in the other for lighting. I had to use my foot to run the fog machine and press record on the camera with my tooth. Another time I just hit record, sat, dumped slime and fake blood on myself, and writhed around thinking, "I deserve this."

An eerie experience happened late at night at our empty studio. I was alone, editing and composing scary music with a waterphone and piano, already on edge from lack of sleep. I'd had to use a lifecast of myself as a stand-in corpse, and it was resting in a body bag in a room in the dimly lit studio. Kind of surreal to have something with your likeness around, especially in the dark. It was after midnight, and whenever I needed to use the bathroom or get water, I would have to sneak past this body bag. I would imagine my "corpse" in it, and that dead-looking version of my face. It started to really creep me out, and I was getting those *"Shining"* women in the bathtub vibes… I began counting down to when I'd have to walk past my body. It was freezing outside with a howling wind, so when the heat would pump back on, the bag would breathe a little like one of those half-formed things from *Invasion of the Body Snatchers*. Gave me the willies.

AN: What was it like working with a child actor, and what did he and your lead actor bring to the table that won them their roles?

RC: My main concern for working with a child actor was to follow all the SAG rules for filming with kids. So that meant limited time, lots of breaks, and a lot of money invested in "hot" catering, so everyone was fed and happy. I kept the shoots to a minimum, I think it was 3 days total with Kenneth(Timmy), and shorter days so I'd stay well under the time limit. Those were probably our most structured days of the project. I feel like all the actors did a great job, especially considering the weird circumstances for some of our shoots. William Johnson helped me cast Kenneth. The rest of the actors I sought out and were the first people chosen. They remained dedicated and professional 100% of the way. Great people.

Larry Fessenden was the biggest name on the project as an established horror icon in acting, producing, and directing. Larry has also recently been celebrated for his scripts and stories in various highly successful horror video games. I was already a massive fan of his from early on, his work inspired me a lot when I was coming up making movies. I contacted him to play Richie, and he was immediately like, "dude, how can I help?" One of the coolest, most generous people I have ever come across. I'll never forget breaking from filming and watching him perform the entire Jaws monologue in his kitchen, just for me. He can do a Robert Shaw impersonation like no other.

AN: There are a lot of "nods" to Stephen King, how fun it was to hide "easter eggs" and I noticed the song from Jaws right away. Are you a big fan of that film?

RC: I'm an enormous *Jaws* fan, and so is Larry Fessenden. We still email each other *Jaws* stuff from time to time. Our mutual love is probably why a lot of it snuck its way in. To torment the tapped heroes, Richie whistles from a darkened hallway to the tune of "Farewell and adieu to you fair Spanish ladies… ". The drunken lyrics sung in *Jaws*: *"show me the way to go home, I'm tired, and I wanna go to bed, I had a little drink about an hour ago, and it's gone right to my head"* seemed relevant. I used the 1926 version of that song in the end credits.

As far as what's become known as "easter eggs," I had put as many little references as I could into *Gray Matter*. Since it was a non-commercial passion project, I did so for myself just as much as anyone watching. It was done with love. A hand-drawn animation (by Michael Danielsen) of the cookie commercial mentioned in *Cujo* plays in the background. A red Plymouth Fury appears twice in the movie, along with a handmade Mr. Barlow (*Salems Lot*) toy made by my good friend Charlie. Harrows Supreme, Golden Light, and the beer from *Cycle of the Werewolf* appear as well as the jingle. My friend Kevin helped me fly by a Castle Rock-type Lighthouse. A cartoon clown riddled with dozens of spider-like eyes pops up on Richies TV (this was before the *IT* remake was in motion). In the *Gray Matter* story, the giant sewer spider always felt like a loose connection to Pennywise to me, if only in a visual sense. There are a lot more tie-ins. Stephen King's stories all crossover like crazy, which everyone adapting his recent work has figured out and is now incorporating. King was and continues to be ahead of his time. He'd already created a marvel universe of horror before it was "cool." I also tried to put some shout outs to real-life King achievements, with mentions of the Haven Foundation and King's old radio station WZON pop up, as well as books penned by each of the talented King family members, Tabitha, Owen, and Joe.

AN: Let's talk about the special effects in the film. I have to say they were very impressive. Share with us who your F/X team was and how some of those bigger F/X scenes were filmed?

RC: Thank you so much! The crew was small and wildly talented. As far as how it all worked: The spider was animatronic. Richie was also, but he went in stages, the first was really mostly Larry doing a great job at faking like he's falling apart. Then we see a small tendril covered in slime under his blanket, which I ended up throwing together by laser cutting a wooden armature rig with Ross. Next is a half-Richie half-melted creature puppet that eats a fake cat. Finally, Richie appears as a fully deformed animatronic creature. I wanted that so he'd look very inhuman at the end. It was all hands-on stuff. I contacted someone in Colorado, Kevon Ward, to help build the mechanics of the spider, which was the most elaborate piece. He eventually flew out to assist during the scenes. He is a massive talent. Kevon and the insanely amazing Dina Cimarusti were vital to getting all the practical effects done. Dina sculpted some stuff just from reference pictures. Rebekah Lieto and Cyle Williamson came in to help finish things during the home stretch and killed it there. We added some tentacles, fake heads, the stop motion mini-Richie, and various body parts. All the makeup people that helped on the project worked on TV shows or went on to win TV makeup show competitions. I love them all.

Since I really wanted the look of backlit hand-animation, the title card was patiently hand-etched frame by frame by Jessica Plummer. There are some miniatures. Ross Gerbasi and Jennifer Beese helped make the Night Owl location. Jim Terry, who is one of my favorite comic artists, provided some Creepshow ESC comic pages for one scene. Ironically, he went on to do the wraparound comic art for the *Gray Matter* episode of the new *Creepshow* series!

AN: Spiders.. sewer… Is this story connected to King's other novel, *IT*?

RC: King has never confirmed that. It may not be the same spider, but I was definitely thinking about it. I do believe *Gray Matter* was the genesis of the idea for Pennywise's final form though, King wrote the story very early on.

AN: What is your greatest moment so far with the success of *Gray Matter*?

RC: Playing it at the Drive-in was really fun. *Gray Matter* also played in a film festival at a historic single-screen theater near my old High School. The alleyway of this theater was the location for a werewolf attack in one of my first feature films. So it felt like coming home. It won some awards. Joe Bob Briggs presented the trailer for it at a comic-con and called it amazing. My hero, Larry Cohen, who I was graced to work with, said he loved it. My other hero, Larry Fessenden, dug the final result. What more could I ask for? Since it's non-commercial, just playing it around in festivals and giving it away for free, knowing it was made for the fun of it was the best reward.

AN: There are many versions of *Gray Matter*, what do you feel makes your version a step different than the others?

RC: First off, one of the other Dollar Baby film-makers James B. Cox (*Grey Matter*) was super supportive of my version. He and Billy Hanson were the reason my stuff played at Comicon. There are a few versions now, including the new *Creepshow* series. As far as how mine is different, I guess probably the creature effects are the standout. The *Creepshow* version does a pretty dang good job, though, but how can you compete with Greg Nicotero? They had some CGI, we didn't do any of that. They also made their adaptation way faster. I don't think Greg was filming during scattered weekends like me. I think they did it in like, one weekend, haha. To me, what elevated the newest one above any others was having Adrienne Barbeau. She is way underused and one of my favorite performers.

AN: What Stephen King story would you like to adapt on a much larger scale?

RC: My dream story would probably be *The Long Walk*, or a proper adaptation of *The Running Man*. But I say "dream" because at the rate King is becoming even more popular, it's unlikely anything will be up for grabs anytime soon. That's what makes the Dollar Baby thing so insanely generous. And King has never stopped giving and helping artists his entire career. This is with plugs on social media for authors or artists starting out, and all his financial and charity work such as the Haven Foundation. So I'd like to say thanks to "Uncle Steve" from a constant reader and from all the Dollar Baby kids.

AN: Did *Gray Matter* play at film fests? If so when and where and did you win any awards for it?
(See greatest success question)

AN: Lastly, What is next for Red Clark?

RC: Lately, I've been co-writing and directing interactive shows in partnership with Twitch with my old pal Ross, including an interactive Halloween show and a Science Fiction show. We drew in millions of viewers for those and were nominated for a midwest Emmy. We may do some more of these interactive programs. I plan to direct an original film or series, many of which I've been developing. I'd love to do something for Shudder, home of the new *Creepshow* series. I really dig what they are doing for the horror community and want to be part of it. I would say I'm still in the horror/fantasy realm for all of these, so it's friendly territory for me. I love this stuff.

I want to thank Red Clark for taking the time out of his busy schedule to talk with us today. And I wish him great success in his future projects.

Sneakers by Gino Alfonso

Sneakers

Gina Alfonso
May 26, 2020

STEPHEN KING IS NO STRANGER to the state of Colorado. Over the years, his stories have taken place there such as *The Stand* and *The Shining*. Our next Dollar Baby interview comes from a Colorado native who has worked his way up the independent film ladder to Dollar Baby status. I'm speaking of young filmmaker, Gino Alfonso.

Gino Alfonso is a filmmaker who is a proud member of the lgbt community living in Denver Colorado. He specializes in horror and lgbt films. Born November 2, 1983, Gino graduated from Overland High School in 2002 in Aurora, Colorado. Gino is a completely self taught filmmaker. Getting his roots in theater as an actor his true passion has always been writing and directing. During theatrical productions he'd watch the directors closely on blocking and character development. In high school, he would make short films for his school assignments instead of writing papers or essays.

Having made over 30 short films, Gino sold his first feature film script back in 2015 which is currently in development and back in December 2019 his first feature as a writer/director *Compatible* a horror/thriller was successfully funded on Kickstarter and stars Joseph Kelly (*Clown Motel, A Star is Born, Bumblebee*) Eileen Dietz (*The Exorcist*) Ari Lehman (*Friday the 13th*) G. Larry Butler (*Call of the Wild, American Flyers*) and Elissa Dowling (*Girl on the 3rd Floor*) and new comer Bergen Reese. *Compatible* was mentioned in an interview with Ari Lehman in a recent issue of *Fangoria* magazine. The film is in the tradition of *Unfriended, Searching* and *Unfollow*. Gino also worked as an actor and associate producer on the latest Richard Grieco, Robert LaSardo and Tara Reid film *Attack of the Unknown*, set for release August 28th on VOD. Gino has several projects in different stages of development. His latest short film just so happens to be a Stephen King Dollar Baby called, *Sneakers*. Currently, Gino works at Ginome Films and lives in Denver with his partner.

Here is my film review of Gino Alfonso's Stephen King Dollar Baby adaptation of… *Sneakers*!

The story, *Sneakers*, first appeared in a compilation called, Dark Visions in August 1988. It later was published in the short story collection, *Nightmares & Dreamscapes* in September 1993.

Sneakers is about a recording studio executive, John Tell. John finds an old, dirty, and not very presentable pair of sneakers in one of the stales in the men's restroom. He assumes they belonged to a janitor or someone. Later, while using the restroom again, he meets a ghost who tells him they were once owned by a drug dealer who was killed in that very restroom because of the head of the recording studios drug addiction debt he was in. John confronts Jennings and tells him he quits and how horrible he is. John Tell goes back to his normal life again and looks for a new job.

Gino's adaptation of this film stayed true to King's original text, adding his own flare of humor and horror. The actors did a good job and the story keeps you guessing until the very end. Gino's talents shine as a filmmaker and shows his love and respect for King's work.

Here is my exclusive interview with Dollar Baby filmmaker, Gino Alfonso.

Anthony Northrup: Your home state is Colorado. Share with us what it was like growing up in Aurora?

Gino Alfonso: It's been a great area for filmmaking, there's so much we have access too and we don't have to worry about permits and all that like California and New York.

AN: When did you first discover the works of Stephen King (first book your read & first movie you saw of his)?

GA: I was about 11 years old when I first saw *Stand By Me*, but I didn't know it was Stephen King, I just loved the movie, when I was in middle school a couple years later my friend introduced me to his books, my first two were *Cujo* and *Needful Things*.

AN: You are a self-taught filmmaker. Who were some of your inspirations and films that inspired you growing up?

GA: Steven Spielberg, James Cameron, Robert Rodriguez, Tim Burton

AN: You made five short films when you first started out, which one was your favorite and why?

GA: Hmm. *Shoes* has been my most personal about a gender confused boy and how his mother deals with finding out, that film pretty much moved me to being a professional filmmaker, my credits are actually more like 30 shorts though at this moment.

AN: You had the pleasure of working with one of horror genres icons: Ari Lehman ('Jason' in the first *Friday the 13th* film from 1980), in your film, *Compatible*. What was it like to work with him and how did that come about?

GA: He was great, very relaxed and generous and easy to direct, we shared tacos and vodka together after shooting, great experience.

AN: Let's talk about your Stephen King Dollar Baby film, *Sneakers*. Out of all the Stephen King short stories, what attracted you most to this one?

GA: It just has the King flavor of his short stories plus the humor element.

AN: What changes did you make to make this your own as opposed to King's original text?

GA: I have the main character actually talking to the ghosts instead of just seeing it's feet with the dead flies.

AN: So many Stephen King fans want adaptations to be as close to the book as possible, how do you handle the pressure to keep them happy?

GA: Well being a huge King fan myself it's easier than you might think, I just look at it objectively as a fan and know what I'd like to see in the adaptation as a fan myself.

AN: What was your main goal you wanted to achieve about this film?

GA: This is about as high as I could expect… but ideally I'd like to do what Frank Darabont accomplished with *The Woman in the Room* and start making full length King movies

AN: Where was the movie filmed specifically and were there any obstacles to overcome while filming there?

GA: It was shot entirely in Denver/Aurora Colorado in 1 day the biggest challenge was shooting in 6 locations plus heavy make up.

AN: How long was the film shoot and the process from start to finish?

GA: Took about a week to adapt, a week to cast and hire crew and about a week to scout locations- post took a bit longer

AN: Share with us the audition process and what your lead actor brought to the table that won him the role?

GA: I usually post on a Facebook Casting page called *Galina's Casting* it's a local Colorado page

AN: You have many titles: actor, writer, producer, and director, which do you personally find to be the most challenging?

GA: Producing by far, I hate coming up with money lol

AN: Tell us a little bit about special effects you used in the film and the "flies out of the mouth" scene in particular?

GA: My FXs artist is a local talent goes by Evil John Mays he is fantastic- the flies I'd asked of my editor not thinking it could be done, a big Hollywood movie that would have been a million dollar shot he called me up 3 days later said check this out… that was another addition I made to the story, it just felt very King.

AN: What is your greatest moment so far with the success of *Sneakers*?

GA: This, to be honest.

AN: I'm honored, thank you.

AN: What Stephen King story would you like to direct on a much larger scale and why?

GA: I would love to reboot *Needful Things* or *The Langoliers*, and I'd love to do *Rose Madder, Cujo*, a darker version of *Sometimes They Come Back*, or *Insomnia*.

AN: What do you think makes the Dollar Baby films so special to adapt as compared to big budget/full scale King adaptations?

GA: The fact that Sai King allows his fans the freedom to be creative.

AN: Where and When can fans see this film? Will it be playing at any film fests?

GA: It had its run a few years ago but it is available on YouTube.

AN: Lastly, What is next for Gino Alfonso?

GA: I have a lot of projects coming up on my slate for 2020/21 and a lot of opportunities coming as well after my first feature *Compatible* which is looking at a late Summer release.

AN: Thank you Gino for taking the time to speak with us today.

The Boogeyman

Jenny Januszewski
July 11, 2020

AS THE STEPHEN KING Dollar Baby Program has gone on and on through the years since its beginning in the late 1970's, there have been more and more women directors to step into the Dollar Baby ring and share their visions of King's works on the big screen. They have been most impressive with their takes of Stephen King's short stories and filmmaker, Jenny Januszewski is no exception. Jenny's adaptation of Stephen King's *The Boogeyman* has been adapted many times, including Jeff Schiro's version in 1982 which is considered the very first Stephen King Dollar Baby film.

Jenny Januszeski grew up in the state of Michigan. She traveled around in her younger years living in New York and Chicago as well. Jenny attended DePaul University studying film and television in Chicago, Illinois. She also attended Columbia College also in Chicago. Later on, she attended UCLA studying an Extension Writers Program and also at Moviola Learning in Burbank, California. She is happily married and currently lives in Los Angeles, California.

Here is my film review of Jenny Januszewski's Stephen King adaptation of, *The Boogeyman!*

Stephen King's short story, *The Boogeyman*, was first published in the March 1973 issue of *Cavalier* magazine. It was republished in Stephen King's short story collection, *Night Shift* in 1978. The story is about a father by the name of Lester Billings, who has three children and is married. However, the story mostly takes place in a psychiatrist office where Lester "thinks" he murdered his children, but believes it was really "the boogeyman" because that was the last word his children said before

The Boogeyman by Jenny Januszewski

they died. The story takes an interesting twist as "the boogeyman" reveals himself... or itself?

There have been many versions of this film in the Stephen King Dollar Baby Program, but Jenny's version I felt was very creepy, suspenseful, yet had strong performances by its adult cast members. A more... realistic version than others I have seen.

Here is my exclusive interview with Dollar Baby filmmaker, Jenny Januszewski.

Anthony Northrup: Share with us what it was like growing up in Michigan?

Jenny Januszewski: I grew up in Michigan in a very small town similar in size to Brownsville, Oregon (where *Stand By Me* or "*The Body*" was filmed). That particular story was extremely relatable to me not only because of the setting but also the desire to have adventure and danger when you're growing up in a small town. I actually flew the DP and one of the actors back to my home town in Michigan so that I could include it in the opening.

AN: When did you first discover the works of Stephen King (first book and first movie you saw of his)?

JJ: The first exposure I had to his writings was actually the short story *The Boogeyman*. Surprised? The first film I recall seeing was *IT* as a child. My older siblings tricked me into watching it. To this day, there is nothing more terrifying than Eddie's shower scene. I think it's when something happens in an unavoidable place (such as the shower) that should be safe and familiar, it's especially terrifying.

AN: What lesson did you take with you the most while studying film at DePaul University that has helped you with your film career?

JJ: At DePaul, I earned my degree in International Business and Media Coordination focusing on Film and TV Producing. I fulfilled over 90 credit hours within a year and a half. So, I learned how to deal with a lot of paperwork at the same time. It sounds silly. But a huge part of filming is the paperwork and having it all in order so that you don't get shut down during production. The most valuable on-set lessons I took were actually from a community college (or, as we call them here in Los Angeles, "city college"). I think classes were $45 or so per credit but well worth it. I took a basic film production class just to make some friends when I was new in town. The most important practical lesson I learned was to plan my shots and filming as though I were shooting on film (as opposed to digital). During our parent's time, a roll of still photo film might have 24 exposures on it. Nowadays, it's pretty endless if you're shooting photos on a camera phone. Imagine how carefully you'd manage your time and your film if you could only shoot 24 images total. As an exercise, get on ebay and find a MiniDV camera and a few tapes. The tapes are 60 minutes. Try to film your Dollar Baby using only 60 minutes of tape before you shoot the real deal in digital. You'll start to cherish the angles and limit how many takes you do for each shot. Speaking of mounds of paperwork… Since we're located in Los Angeles, I had to film our Dollar Baby pretty legit using a payroll company, SAG signatory paperwork, and city permits. If you're in a city that requires permits, be creative. Most people won't need all of this but we knew we'd be doing exterior shots and didn't want our equipment confiscated. In Los Angeles, a day permit can cost over $700. I didn't have that kind of extra money. I found out that it was less expensive to enroll in two elective externship credits at the local community college and use a letter from my instructor to qualify for all kinds of discounts--- My city permits were $50 each instead of $700+, I received 15%-20% discounts on equipment rental, and even insurance became less expensive. Being creative with the paperwork can add just as much to your film as being creative with the setup of your shots.

AN: You later attended UCLA in California. UCLA has had some of the biggest filmmakers of all-time study there. Who were your influences growing up and while studying film?

JJ: I really wish I could sound cool and list all of Kieslowski or Kubrick's films--- I actually had to just google the spelling. But I wasn't that much into movies and film as I was into collaborating and storytelling. So, I was never a huge fan of a particular director. I was just a fan of the process. BTW, I did enjoy the *Three Colours* trilogy and *A Clockwork Orange*.

AN: Let's talk about your Dollar Baby, *The Boogeyman*. How and When did you first hear about the Dollar Baby Program?

JJ: I think I heard of the Dollar Baby Program when I took the class at the community college—maybe 2011. Our professor mentioned it and *The Shawshank Redemption* and I thought, "why not me?" BTW, that should always be your response… "why not me?"

AN: Out of all the Stephen King short stories, what attracted you most to this one?

JJ: It was the first one I ever read. I loved that the story could be taken head on and literally – that there was a boogeyman that came after them. Or, it could be interpreted that the boogeyman could be within Lester Billings' psychosis. It's a seemingly simple story with extremely complex characters. Plus, if I screwed up the other shots, I could just use the office footage for the entire film.

AN: What changes did you make to make this your own as opposed to King's original text?

JJ: Most of the office scenes were taken straight from the book. I added scenes from Lester's life to flesh out his emotional journey--- how happy they were down to his low point. There were actually about four or five scenes that we filmed and left on the cutting room floor. It was filmed to be a shorter feature length film but we cut it down. Oh, and I left the end open to the idea of Lester killing Dr. Harper. Look at Lester's hand at the end of the film.

AN: So many Stephen King fans want adaptations to be as close to the book as possible, how do you handle the pressure to keep the fans happy?

JJ: I probably should have considered that while filming. There's another *Boogeyman* Dollar Baby that is probably more fulfilling to the fans as they kept it closer to horror. Their trailer looks great. I just decided to keep mine more as a narrative of how a normal guy from a small town could be driven to become the boogeyman.

AN: What was your main goal you wanted to achieve about this film?

JJ: I wanted Lester and his wife to have a relationship and make them more human. My interpretation wasn't about the boogeyman that could be in the closet. Mine was more about the boogeyman that could be drawn out of any of us if put in the right circumstances. There's B-roll in the beginning of Lester in a field doing football exercises--- remembering his past and what he used to have in life. It's those things that I wanted to fulfill.

AN: Where was the movie filmed specifically and were there any obstacles to overcome while filming there?

JJ: The interior office was filmed in Los Angeles. The interiors of Lester's house where his wife was in the scenes were filmed in Encino, CA. The picnic was at El Matador Beach in Malibu—really great seafood out that way.

The field, the children, first house (exterior), second house (interior and exterior), and car scene were all filmed in various towns in Michigan (e.g. Springport, Lansing, Ann Arbor, and Jackson).

The biggest obstacle was filming in one of the houses in Michigan. Two people had recently passed away from unnatural causes. We needed to film and do our job. Yet, we also wanted to be respectful of the space and the lives that had been there. It was a big emotional moment for the owner of the home to see one of the rooms turned into Andy Billings' nursery for the film. So, there was a bit of juggling to be sure the actor and DP felt in an emotionally safe space to do their work while also checking in with the homeowner to make sure they were comfortable as well.

AN: How long was the film shoot and process from start to finish?

JJ: It took FOREVER. Our composer was in a bad motorcycle accident and we didn't feel right replacing him. He's a good friend and former neighbor of mine. He's fine --- perhaps an inch shorter after the accident. But he now works on huge films doing music and sound design--- *Ready Player One, Onward, A Quiet Place II, Mulan,* etc.

AN: Share with us the casting process and what specifically the lead actors brought to the table to win their role?

JJ: I regret casting each and every one of them--- just kidding. I really lucked out with a few of the actors here. I wrote the role of Rita Billings for Virginia Newcomb. She had auditioned for another film of mine and I could not get her read out of my head. She's just delightful to work with and I'm so grateful she was available. Sam Brilhart (Lester) was referred to me by a bigger film casting director here in LA. Akie Kotabe (Dr Harper) was a friend of a friend and had been in a good amount of films and on TV. In fact, I think he just played opposite Salma Hayek in an action/thriller.

AN: What is the greatest moment so far with the success of *The Boogeyman*?

JJ: Finishing it. I think any film project that you actually finish is a successful one. The film has shown in a few festivals. But, just creating with friends and finishing it was the greatest moment of success.

AN: Tell us a little bit about some of the special effects used in the film? Were there any difficulties?

JJ: We had casts done of each actors' face and a skin-toned mask created from each one so that it looked like their face was hanging in Harper's closet at the end. Just to give the impression that Lester might be imagining that each person in his life was really the Boogeyman in disguise. But the faces were too translucent and it didn't read well. I let the actors keep them as souvenirs. I think I had Akie's for a while and would get creeped out every time I opened my desk because I'd forget it's in there.

AN: What Stephen King story would you like to adapt on a larger scale?

JJ: Any of them. They're all interesting and there's so much to dive into in each one.

AN: Where and When can fans see the film? Has it played at any film fests?

JJ: My contract with Stephen King's office ended years ago. So, it can no longer play at festivals. I think we have a 2yr limit.

AN: Lastly, What is next for Jenny Januszewski?

JJ: After filming, I went on to work at Technicolor in Hollywood for a few years. Now, I'm writing a few pilots that I hope to shop around town. Fingers crossed!

AN: Fingers crossed, indeed! I want to thank Jenny for taking the time to speak with us today and wish her great success in her career.

One For the Road

Joseph Horning
July 11, 2020

THERE'S NOT TOO MANY SEQUELS to Stephen King's works, but one of them is *One For the Road*, a short story sequel to *'Salem's Lot*. Before we get into Joseph's adaptation of King's story, let's get to know a little bit more about Joseph Horning.

Joseph Horning is the owner of Quarterly Entertainment, LLC based out of Montgomery County, Pennsylvania. He is a graduate of the Art Institute of Philadelphia's Video Production program. Joe began writing scripts when he was in junior high. After graduating from high school in 1997 he took several correspondence courses through the Hollywood Scriptwriting Program to help perfect and hone his craft. In 2001 he was accepted into the Art Institute of Philadelphia's Video Production program. He graduated in 2005 with honors, having won several academic achievements and a Best of Quarter Award for lighting. Upon graduating, Joe worked with several small independent projects including *False Face* which he helped to co-write and produce. The movie is currently on Netflix as part of their DVD plan.

In 2009, Joe completed his first short movie that he wrote and directed called *Masterpiece*, a psychological thriller about a deranged artist and a young woman desperate to make a quick buck. Later that same year, Joe competed in the Twenty-Four-Hour Philadelphia Film Race along with his friend Jon Robertson of Prolific Entertainment. Together they formed the partnership of P's & Q's Entertainment and shot two short movies together – *No Turning Back* (2009) and *Roads Not Taken* (2010).

In 2012, Joe's screenplay *Darkness on the Edge of Town* won the Regional Award for the Shoot in Philadelphia Screenwriting Competition. In 2016 *Darkness on the Edge of Town* received Honorable Mention at the

One For the Road by Joseph Horning

LA Screenplay Festival as well as coming in as a Top 10 Finalist in the Thriller Screenplay Festival in Delaware. The screenplay also ranked 6th Place in the national Abbott Press Screenplay Replay Competition.

In 2016, Joe partnered with Curtis K. Case to produce the feature film *Where is My Golden Arm*. They later produced the web series *Siblings the Series* in 2017 which is currently available on YouTube.

Here is my review of Joseph Horning's Stephen King adaptation of *One For the Road*!

Stephen King has written sequels to his stories before, but *'Salem's Lot* is the first King story that has both a prequel AND a sequel. *Jerusalem's Lot* is the prequel and *One For the Road* is the sequel to one of Stephen King's classic novels, *'Salem's Lot*. *One For the Road* takes place 3 years after the events of *'Salem's Lot*. On a cold winter's night, a man and his wife and daughter get stranded on a dark road outside of Jerusalem's Lot. When he goes back to the closet town and stops by a local bar for help, the locals hear where his car is stranded at and fear and a long forgotten nightmare returns for a night of terror!

Joseph Hornings adaptation of *One For the Road,* is without question, one of the most professionally filmed and horrific Dollar Babies I have ever seen. It is beautifully filmed, very high quality cinematography, the actors were not just professional, but they nailed a Maine accent perfectly. There is plenty of suspense and thrills that are sure to terrify any film goer and sure to satisfy all Stephen King fans.

Here is my exclusive interview with Dollar Baby filmmaker, Joseph Horning!

Anthony Northrup: Tell us what was it like growing up in Pennsylvania?

Joseph Horning: Not that different than growing up anywhere else, I imagine. I grew up in Norristown, a small suburban city outside of Philadelphia, a place with roots in America's history from the Revolutionary and Civil Wars through the Underground Railroad to Presidential elections. I had a very normal childhood and never really got into much trouble. It wasn't until I got much older that I learned Pennsylvania was a creepy place to live. There are a lot of strange and bizarre places around Pennsylvania that make it ripe for tales of horror and the supernatural. I won't bore you with details, but you should check out the history surrounding the Cult House and Skull Tree on Cossart Road. It's interesting. A good friend of mine and I love going on road trips and exploring places we discover. That's where a lot of my ideas for horror stories come from.

AN: When did you first discover the works of Stephen King (your first book, first King movie you saw)?

JH: The first time I can ever remember watching a Stephen King film was probably *Creepshow* after it came out on cable. At the time I was maybe 4 or 5 and didn't know anything about Stephen King, just that what I saw scared the hell out of me. It wasn't until years later when I was a teenager and I watched *Creepshow* that I remembered seeing it as a kid. The first time I became fully aware of Stephen King and his work though, was when the *IT* mini-series debuted back in 1990. It was a huge event that was advertised everywhere. TV Guide had a cover story about it, kids in school were talking about it. I *had* to watch it and I loved every minute of it! From that moment on I was determined to read the book, however back then I wasn't as big of a reader as I am now so when I told my mom I wanted to read the book she told me that I would never do it. It was too long, and she was right. I struggled to get through the first few chapters and put it down. I opted to start light and picked up *Cujo* instead which I loved but haven't read since. After that I wanted to read anything and everything by Stephen King. And yes, I finally did finish *IT*, which was the novel that inspired me to make films.

AN: You began writing scripts in Jr. High (impressive), who were your inspirations back then and what genre were your scripts?

JH: My inspirations back then were of course Stephen King and *Star Trek*. A strange combination I know, but I believe Mr. King is a Trekkie as well so not too strange. As I stated, *IT* inspired me to make films, but it wasn't the only thing that influenced me. I had a teacher, John Doyle, who taught photography at a summer arts consortium at my high school in the early '90's. The first year I went he told us that besides photography we would also be making a short film. So, I guess you could say that was the start of my fascination with films.

Anyway, When I finished the novel for the first time in the summer of 1993, I was disappointed – not in the book but the movie. I felt that the mini-series did a great job at emphasizing the friendship and nostalgia of being a kid and having a group of friends that you played with daily, and the struggle to rekindle those feelings you had after you've grown up and grown apart. Had the mini-series been about that I think it would've been an outstanding drama. But the elements of horror, the stripped-down rawness of what Pennywise was wasn't there. That's not to say Tim Curry's performance wasn't outstanding, it was but I felt like there was so much more that could've been done, even for regular TV. So that set me down a path of wanting to rewrite and remake *IT* as a full-blown horror film. Without any clue as to what I was doing I sat down and started working on a screenplay adapting the whole novel. Not just bits of it, the WHOLE novel. I didn't know how to pick and choose sections of the book to focus on, so I just put it all in there.

My script was more massive than the actual book. Over time as I learned the craft of screenwriting, I began to whittle down what I wrote. As we all know I didn't get the chance to remake *IT*, sadly. That was left to Hollywood.

As for *Star Trek*, I grew up watching the original series on reruns and watched all the spinoffs and movies up until just recently. I won't go into my feelings for the direction *Trek* is going in just that I feel like it's strayed from Gene Roddenberry's vision. Anyway, when I was in High School, I began to develop story ideas for *Star Trek* and wrote over a dozen scripts for *Voyager*, only one of which I submitted to Paramount through their open script submission program. My dream was to become a staff writer for the show. It's still a dream of mine to this day.

So yeah, I love writing horror and sci-fi, though I have dabbled in comedies and dramas over the years with screenplays for the films *A Time in Philadelphia* and *The Trainer*, two films yet to be produced with my business partner Jonathan Cross of New Galaxy Pictures.

AN: You have quite the impressive list of credits of films and short films. Share with us a few thoughts on your films, *False Face, Masterpiece, Darkness on the Edge of Town* and your web series: *Siblings the Series*? Which was more enjoyable to work and which was challenging?

JH: *False Face* was a project that I was brought onto early on by the two writers/directors of the film. I came in and polished up the script, came up with an intriguing ending and then started helping with the casting. I pretty much did everything a producer would do, much as I did on *One for the Road*. I was excited to work on this film because it was going to be a feature and it was the first project I worked on after graduating from the Art Institute of Philadelphia. However, when we got into production there were some disagreements with a lot of things and the ending was changed for something more subdued so I decided to leave the project over creative differences.

Shortly there after I began working on *Masterpiece*, a short film about a deranged artist and a young woman who is down on her luck and desperate for a change. For me, *Masterpiece* is one of the best projects I worked on personally and one of the best times I had making a film. I loved the whole process of coming up with new angles because of the limited space we were shooting in and overcoming obstacles to production design. For example, the script required our lead actress to call her mother from a payphone; well the shopping center we were shooting in had just taken down all the payphones and we were up you know where without a paddle! So, I went on eBay and bought an actual payphone to use in the film! The whole casting process was a blast as well. When our lead actor Gary Gustin came in to audition for the role, he brought with him these ideas for the character that I hadn't even thought of before. When I write I have an idea of who the character is; what their personality will be, and I can sort of have tunnel vision in that respect. This is my character. This is who he is, how he walks and talks and what his mannerisms should be. Casting someone to fit your vision is difficult. But then along comes an actor who breathes life into that character and their personality takes shape. Gary had developed these subtle nuances that made his character of Reginald Dearborn even more frightening than I had anticipated. I loved working on this film and would love to remake it one day, fleshing out the story and shooting it as a feature.

Siblings the Series is an idea developed by my partner in CKC Quarterly Productions, Curtis K. Case a few years back. It's a web series focusing on an African American family living in Washington D.C. who are gathering for the first time after being apart for years. It's a comedy drama that takes place over the course of one night in this family's life where they must deal with racism and diversity. It also deals with the false perceptions we might have of who our family was versus who they are now. David the main character of the series must cope with the fact that his family isn't exactly quite how he remembers them, which leads to some funny moments. *Siblings* was a fun project to work on. I wrote all the scripts with story ideas shared by Curtis and myself, but I wasn't involved directly in the filming of the series. That was done out in L.A. while I stayed here in Pennsylvania.

AN: Let's talk about your Stephen King Dollar Baby film, *One for the Road*. When and How did you first hear about the Dollar Baby program?

JH: The first time I ever heard about the Dollar Baby program was in Stephen Spignesi's *The Complete Stephen King Encyclopedia*. I had gotten it one year for Christmas sometime around 1993 or 1994 and I had read about James Cole's adaption of *The Last Rung of the Ladder* and thinking how cool it would be to make one of my own, but at the time I didn't feel like I had the right skills or equipment to take on the task. Over time I had forgotten about the Dollar Baby program until I came across an article a few years back about a group of filmmakers producing *One for The Road*. I don't think their adaptation was ever completed, but it got my wheels turning that maybe this would be the right time to make a Dollar Baby film of my own.

AN: Out of all the Stephen King short stories, what attracted you most to this one?

JH: Well for one, I read the story so long ago that I had forgotten about it until I saw the article I just mentioned. I went back and re-read the story and was hooked by it. There was something about the isolation of 'Salem's Lot in the middle of a snowstorm that made it feel like a classic gothic tale and that intrigued me. Plus, I love a good vampire film. If you've ever read *Dracula's Guest* the omitted chapter of Bram Stoker's novel, the main character wanders into an abandoned village after being warned not to and encounters supernatural forces that threaten his life. That's *One for the Road*.

AN: What changes did you make to make this your own as opposed to King's original text?

JH: The original story for *One for the Road* starts with Tookey and Booth about ready to close the bar for the night when Gerard comes bursting through the door. As the story progresses, he tells Tookey and Booth about their journey up to Maine. None of the other adaptations I've seen had actually shown the family on their trip, getting lost and leading to them being stranded in 'Salem's Lot. That was something I wanted to show, mainly because it would give the audience a chance to connect with the characters of Gerard, Janey and Francie more so when we come to this tragic ending you feel heartbroken for what happens to them.

One other thing I wanted to do was to make this a direct sequel to the 1979 mini-series directed by Tobe Hooper. So, I had my prop maker Bud Bullens create a replica of the 'Salem's Lot population sign that we see David Soul's character Ben Mears drive past at the start of the film. There are also little Easter eggs in the film calling back to the mini-series as well as connecting it to an RV on the municipal side of the bridge so that all of our actors had a warm place to change, get their makeup done and have dinner without freezing their butts off!

AN: Where was the movie filmed specifically and were there any obstacles to overcome while filming there?

JH: There weren't any real obstacles for us to overcome at the locations, in fact everyone we worked with welcomed us without hesitation and were more than happy to be a part of this experience. However, obstacles in getting this film made from start to finish. That I could write an entire novel on!

AN: How long was the film shoot and process from start to finish?

JH: Longer than I anticipated! I received my first contract from Stephen King's office in February 2017 with the hopes of shooting sometime in November of that year. Things didn't work out as planned due to rescheduling casting calls, people dropping out at the last minute, to getting all the merchandise ready for our crowdfunding contributors. Principle photography started in January 2018 and was only supposed to last a week, however like pre-production, things didn't work out as planned. Pennsylvania is a very temperamental state. One day it can be sunny and sixty degrees and the next it's rainy and temperatures near freezing. When we began it was reported that we would have a mild winter. It was anything but that. There were nights when it was hovering around nine degrees, days when it snowed – which helped with some shots – and then other days where it was close to fifty and all the snow we needed was melting away. I had to schedule several reshoots for scenes all the way up until February of 2019, which included shooting winter scenes in the middle of summer the previous year! There was extensive post production work adding in special effects to make digital snow scenes and creating more haunting atmospheres for the shots in *'Salem's Lot*. All the while I was getting extension after extension to finish the film. There was no way I was going to call it quits though. Every few months I would tell everyone that the light at the end of the tunnel was getting closer, though I must admit I thought I would never see it! So, from start to finish it took three and a half years!

AN: In the film, it takes place during winter. What time of the year did you film this and was it difficult to create snow?

JH: We shot the film in the middle of winter, though at the time there were no snow storms reported in our neck of the woods. That all changed though as a storm was scheduled to come in on our fourth day of shooting. Everything we had planned were night shots on a bridge with all our main cast and extras. Considering the distance a lot of people had to travel and how treacherous the snowstorms can get, my producer Chris and I decided to call the shoot and reschedule what we had planned for the following night. I mentioned how temperamental the weather can be here, right? Well the snowstorm never came, so we wasted a night of film. It did however hit us the following night when we rescheduled our scenes we had scrapped the night before. Which led to the creepy atmosphere we were hoping for. I should add that I had written the script without any snow in mind. Not knowing when we would get snow to schedule our scenes around, I devised an idea that allowed us to still strand the family in '*Salem's Lot* without it. It's still in the film though now there is snow thanks to the storm. They get caught in a ditch as they are backing up to turn around. Originally, I was going to have them hit a huge pothole that would cause the tire to bend but that wasn't feasible on our budget.

Once principle photography was finished and we had to schedule reshoots it came down to me figuring out various ways of creating fake snow to add to scenes. There is a mixture of practical and digital effects in the film. The physical fake snow we used – which is hard to see in the film due to a lot of quick cuts – was a fine powdery mix that expands when water is added to it. That was used in the shoots we did during the summer on the bridge. The digital snow appears in various shots from the roof of Tookey's Tavern to an entire landscape of snow near the end of the film. Creating the digital effects wasn't too challenging as I purchased pre-made snow effects that I could use and manipulate with 3D lights and shadows in post-production, though it is something I never want to have to go through again unless I'm paying someone to do it!

AN: Share with us a few special effects secrets such as the glowing eyes and the vampire teeth. Was it a challenge to the actors to wear these effects features?

JH: When we were still in pre-production, I decided that I wanted the vampire's eyes to glow red, so I ordered these red contacts that were supposed to glow on camera. When it came time to shoot the scenes with Sandy Lawler and Veronica Garrubbo (Janey and Francie Lumley) the contacts didn't show up very well on camera and I didn't think I would be able get the effect I was looking for. I ended up compositing the red eyes in post, blending the red with the original video footage and adding glow effects to them. It helped to enhance what was already there and comes across well in the finished film.

I remember when I was sent a photo of Veronica with the final teeth and make up effects that Beverly Hegmon did while we were setting up our shots. I was overwhelmed with how amazing she looked. When she and Sandy got on set, that's when I knew everything was coming together!

None of our actors really complained about having to wear the contacts or vampire teeth except for one person – Wade Kownatsky. Wade is one of my Executive Producers and was dying to play a vampire in the film. When I was making this movie, I wanted a connection to the mini-series, and I thought about who Wade could play. I watched the movie repeatedly and saw a resemblance to Wade and the character of Ned Tebbits, so that became his character. When it came time to get him into makeup to play the part, you could've heard him cry over putting those contacts in and taking them out from here to Australia. And then when he learned that I was enhancing the eyes in post and that contacts weren't necessary, the rovers on Mars probably picked him up. I'm kidding of course. Wade loves to rub it in how much of a pain it was to wear them and told me that he will continue to complain to anyone who will listen to him until the day he dies.

AN: Speaking of the cast, share with us the audition process. What did your lead actors bring to the table that won them the role?

JH: We had a lot of fun with the casting process. It started off with me putting up a casting notice on Backstage and we were just inundated with headshots and resumes. I think when people saw it was a film for Stephen King they just leaped at the opportunity. We even had some interests from actress Francesca Scorsese – yes that Scorsese – who auditioned for the role of Francie! She was one of two actresses in the running for the role, the other being Veronica Garrubbo. However, due to scheduling conflicts and our film shoot revolving around the time she was going to start college, she had to bow out before we could perform chemistry matches between her and our other candidates for Gerard and Janey.

Speaking of Veronica, she was amazing. When she came into the room to audition, she asked me if I wanted her to do the hiss and the scream as it was written and I said "Sure, go for it."

When she did, the three of us (myself, Chris Wagler and Gus Garfield, our production designer) jumped three feet out of our seats and anticipated her mother to come charging through the door demanding what we were doing to her daughter! But she didn't, which is funny because the reverse almost happened during the ADR sessions when

Veronica's father brought her. Anyway, Veronica was the right age for the part, exhibited a little bit of that teen angst in her audition and just won us over with her personality. I don't think *One for the Road* would be the film it is without her.

Eric Slodysko, Sandy Lawler and Roger Middleton all submitted video auditions for their roles as Gerard and Janey Lumley and Tookey. Come to think of it, half of our cast showed up in person for the auditions and the other half submitted videos. Gus and I had worked with Sandy before on a short horror film that never got finished called *Midnight Coffee* so we knew how dedicated and talented she was. It was down to her and another actress for the role of Janey but when we did chemistry matches, she seemed to be more natural for the role, especially with Veronica. They paired together so well I wish I had more scenes between the two of them.

Eric was a friend of Chris' who he had known through a small film group out of the Lehigh Valley. He had an interesting take on the character of Gerard than most of the other actors we auditioned. He presented this level of frustration at the Lumley family's situation that no one else had given during the auditions that I liked. When we paired him, Sandy and Veronica together you could see the dynamic of the Lumley family come together and the irritation that Gerard felt in the script just manifested itself naturally.

The other good thing to come out of the auditions besides our cast was that I got to meet Scott Surochak, one of Chris' friends who ended up being an executive producer on the film. Scott showed up to help on one of the two days we were holding auditions and showed a real interest in working on the film. Thanks to him we had merchandise for a stint we did at Horror Con in New Jersey, got Beverly Hegmon to fly up from Atlanta to do makeup and had the RV for all of our actors to stay warm in while the rest of us froze our tuchus' off in the middle of winter!

AN: Your supporting actors pulled off a pretty good Maine accent. Did you give them any pointers or film recommendations for them to perfect that accent? **JH:** I didn't have to give them any real directions on how to speak with a Maine accent. Lou DiPilla III who plays the gas station attendant was the only actor we cast before he left the room during the auditions. When he came in, he was the only person to read for the part of the attendant. When I asked him if he could speak with a Maine accent he said "No, but I'll give it a try." I think he was pulling my leg because he hit a home run his first try at bat by nailing a Maine accent without a hint of hesitation. I think the three of us—myself, Chris Wagler and C. Augustus

Garfield—were all grinning ear to ear when Lou left the room. We all agreed that he had the part without needing to see anyone else.

Roger Middleton who plays Tookey is from New York and isn't using an accent at all. He just naturally looks and sounds like he's an old timer from Maine. However, Wayne Shearer who plays Booth traveled from Philadelphia to New York in his spare time to meet with a dialogue coach to get the inflections down. He did that on his own without any encouragement from me. When I called and offered him the part he said he wanted to be as true to the character as possible and had already contacted someone to help him with his speech if he should happen to get the part. That is true dedication.

Sadly, Wayne passed away in early April 2019 due to complications with lung cancer. I didn't know Wayne for very long but in the time I did know him, I got to know a man who has lived many phases of life. During our ADR sessions he would regale us with stories of his time in Vietnam to coming home and starting a computer business long before computers were a common everyday household item. He worked in the music industry for a brief time and even found time to be a teacher. Acting was a spontaneous decision in his life, and it was something that he thoroughly enjoyed. He was the embodiment of what it means to never give up on your dreams, no matter how long it takes. That is why this film is dedicated to him.

AN: I know this was a very long and hard process to make this film. Were there any moments you felt overly challenged?

JH: I constantly felt overwhelmed, especially once principal photography had wrapped. If I had hair, I would've gone bald trying to figure out and schedule re-shoots. There were more than a few nights when I lost sleep wondering I was ever going to finish this film on time. Not having enough free time personally to focus on the film like I wanted to was probably the hardest part about this whole process. Between work and life getting in the way, it took far longer than I anticipated. I was fortunate enough to be granted more extension to complete the film.

AN: The music in the film is very eerie, tell us more about that process and the "singing lady" part of the soundtrack?

JH: My musical taste is eclectic to say the least. I can listen to pretty much anything from big band to rap to heavy metal to classic rock all in one sitting depending on my mood. One genre of music I love more than anything though, is classical. It's what I listen to when I read and write, especially when I write. A good piece of classical music can speak volumes to you without saying a word. It's the emotions it evokes. During the writing process of the screenplay I had listened to a lot of Ralph Vaughan Williams and had been going through all his symphonies when I came upon his 7th Symphony, the Sinfonia Antartica. It is probably the closest thing I've heard by him that resembles a horror score. It's dark and foreboding and at the start of the second movement there is a soprano section of a woman singing this haunting melody that conjured up images of vampires gliding out of the dark. I thought to myself this is what the movie needs, a legitimate score. Normally I would write the music myself or pay for royalty free content, but since classical music is public domain and this piece fit into the film I decided to use it and another classical piece by Gustav Mahler at the start of the film. When my director of photography Robert Neil heard the Vaughan Williams section at the end, he said it reminded him of an old Universal horror film which is exactly the feeling I was trying to create.

AN: You wore many hats for this film: writer, music, editor, producer, director, casting, and more – What is the most challenging title for you?

JH: That's tough. Working on the music, casting and editing isn't that hard to do, at least for me. I find that part fun. Producing was a matter of gathering the pieces that would make up the team that led to making the film. Although it can be daunting at times, it still wasn't the hardest job I had to do on this or any other project. Directing was probably the most challenging aspect of making *One for the Road*. I'm naturally a writer and feel more comfortable at my desk creating worlds in my head and on paper than I am in front of a group of people shouting orders. I'm also not your typical director who feels that it's my way or the highway. I like to collaborate with everyone on set, from the actors to the PA's. sometimes someone might see something I don't that would enhance the scene and make the film better. If they do, I listen to their ideas, film the scene two different ways and see which one works better. To me filmmaking is supposed to be fun and collaborative. Yes, there are rules to follow but it shouldn't be so regimented where everyone feels like they're robots on an assembly line and not enjoying themselves.

AN: What is your greatest moment so far with the success of *One for the Road*?

JH: That everyone who has seen it so far has had nothing but positive things to say. There have been a few nitpicks here and there but overall, it's turned into a wonderful film and the support and praise I've received has been heartfelt.

AN: What Stephen King story would you like to adapt on a much larger scale?

JH: That's another tough one. I said earlier that I always wanted to remake *IT*. Who knows, maybe in 5 years I will, that seems to be the growing trend in Hollywood these days! I would also love a shot at a true adaptation of *The Gunslinger*. About 15 years ago I adapted the novel, incorporating elements from the other books in the series that would allow for a cohesive thread throughout the remaining movies, if they happened to be produced. Longshot dream I know but stranger things have happened. If I had to choose though, I would say *Insomnia*. I love the concept of the little bald doctors and the Crimson King. Plus, it takes place in Derry and is a part of the *Dark Tower* saga!

AN: Lastly, where and when can fans see the film and what is next for Joseph Horning?

JH: Well as of this writing I am working on a few minor fixes to effects but once that's done we're going to have a digital premiere for our cast, crew and all our crowdfunding backers. After that I'll be submitting it to various film festivals so everyone will just have to keep an eye open to see if *One for the Road* gets accepted into festivals near by so they can check it out!

What's next for me? No rest for the weary. I'm in the early stages of developing a feature length horror film based on an original screenplay as well as setting up a few other shorter projects. I've also been writing several short horror stories I'd like to publish as a collection as well as a horror novel that I began just before finishing editing on *One for the Road*. So there's more to come, and who knows, I might just shoot another Dollar Baby again sometime in the future!

AN: And we will certainly be waiting for Joseph. I'd like to thank Joseph Horning for taking the time to speak with us today and wish him well and success.

Morning Deliveries

William Roberts
July 19, 2020

ONE OF THE THINGS I absolutely love about the Stephen King Dollar Baby program is, there are so many filmmakers that come from not just the United States, but from all around the world. My latest Dollar Baby interview comes from across the pond from the United Kingdom. This time it is Stephen King's story, *Morning Deliveries* from director, William Roberts.

William Roberts, is 37 years old. He was born and lives in Llandudno, North Wales, UK. He studied art and media in Llandrillo College, Wales (1999-2002) and Creative Studies at Bangor University, Wales.(2007-2010). He continues to work in freelance media. He has worked as an actor, extra, runner, editor, writer and crew assistant on several film and television productions. William has worked and trained with companies such as Shepperton Studios, Universal Studios, Channel 4 and BBC. He has worked on several feature films including *King Arthur* (GuyRitchie), *Spike Island, Apocalypse* and *Outpost:Black Sun*. *Morning Deliveries* is Williams first short film.

Here is my review of William Roberts adaptation of Stephen King's *Morning Deliveries*.

Stephen King's short story, *Morning Deliveries*, was first published in the short story collection, *Skeleton Crew* in 1985 under the full title: *Morning Deliveries (Milkman #1)*. The story is about a Milkman named Spike Milligan who leaves special "surprises" in the milk bottles left on the door steps of his milk delivery route. Spike leaves these "special gifts" to people he believes deserves them. Bad people or people who have done wrong. And the "surprises" well, that's just part of the gory details of King's very creepy tale.

Morning Deliveries by Will Roberts

Will Roberts did an amazing job adapting King's story. He filmed his Dollar Baby film like an old 1970's or 80's grindhouse horror film, complete with a gritty, grungy, low budget look even with scratches on the film to make it look even more like a grindhouse movie. I loved this adaptation! It was creepy, scary, and the grindhouse look gave the film the perfect feel only a talented director like Will Roberts could pull off. There are gross-out scenes and "nods" to other Stephen King tales hidden throughout the film. This is certainly one of the best Dollar Baby films I've seen.

Here is my exclusive interview with Dollar Baby filmmaker, Will Roberts.

Anthony Northrup: Share with us what it was like growing up in North Wales, UK?

Will Roberts: I grew up in Llandudno, North Wales in the UK. Our town is known as the 'Queen of Resorts' and as kids we were spoiled with the surrounding mountains, two beaches and a Victoria Pier full of arcades. In the summer the town was vibrant and busy but in the autumn and winter it became a ghost town. Empty, quiet and dark.

AN: When did you first discover the works of Stephen King (first book your read/film you saw)?

WR: I was reading from an early age – *Tom Sawyer, A Kestrel For A Knave, Nightmare on Elm Street* tie-in novels- and soon found Stephen King. I remember asking the local library for a Stephen King book and being told I was too young as it was in the adult section. That just threw wood on the fire. The first Stephen King book I read was *The Talisman* when I was 12 years old and I remember the journey into that book vividly. I haven't read it since and can still remember the characters, locations and scenes from 25 years ago.

AN: When you went to college, you studied art and media. Who were some of your film inspirations growing up?

WR: Me and my brother Danny were film buffs and loved our trips to the local video shop – Jubilee Video. They had a terrifying backroom that contained all the cult, horror and adult films and it was like Stelling into a horror dimension. Artwork from the massive VHS boxes such as *The Stuff, The Hidden, From Beyond* and *Scanners* were etched into our minds.

AN: You have had many titles in your career: actor, extra, runner, editor, writer, crew, and director. Which one do you find more challenging and Why?

WR: I think the most challenging aspect of working in freelance media is finding the work and persevering after countless moments of uncertainty or disappointments and maintaining that focus and drive. My friend, the late author Alan Eltron Barrell, sent me a message before he passed 'Keep chasing. Nothing will ever be more worth it'. That has stayed with me.

AN: You have worked on various films during your career including *King Arthur* by director Guy Ritchie. Share with us what that experience was like? Were you one of the actors or did you work behind-the-scenes? And what is it like to work with the very talented Guy Ritchie?

WR: I was very lucky to work on the *King Arthur* film Guy Ritchie. It was the first huge budget film I had worked in for Universal Studios. I had a non-speaking extra role as a Dan Clan Traveller and was excited to see my name on a sign on set and have my own costume and weapons. I was selected to work on a scene with Charlie Hunham and Djimon Hounsou. It was surreal, being directed by Guy Ritchie, as *Lock, Stock and Two Smoking Barrells* was such a significant film from my youth.

AN: Let's talk about your Stephen King Dollar Baby film, *Morning Deliveries*. How and when did you first hear about the Dollar Baby program?

WR: I first heard about Dollar Baby films through an interview with Frank Darabont. I had no idea you could apply independently , I thought you would have to at least have some sort of contact. My favorite Dollar Baby is *The Boogeyman* from 1982. I love the vintage aesthetics and low budget vibe. I have seen a lot of Dollar Baby films and enjoyed them all. I love that these opportunities are readily available to independent filmmakers.

AN: Out of all the Stephen King short films, what attracted you most to this one?

WR: I knew I wouldn't have a budget so I tried to choose one that I knew would be inexpensive to produce based on the Synopsis. After reading the story over and over, and despite it being a fraction of an unfinished story and with no beginning middle or end, I fell in love with the main character 'Spike Milligan' and knew this had to be the one.

AN: What changes did you make to make this your own as opposed to King's original text?

WR: The original story has a lot of internal monologue, a lot of descriptive sentences about the local nature and neighborhood and a lot of Americanisms that I knew would be difficult to translate to a North Wales setting. I read some Edgar Allen Poe stories and real letters from serial killers and started to develop a confessional narrative that is not in the original story. I tried to be as faithful to the source material as possible, using the same characters, locations and events but using a new story.

AN: So many Stephen King fans want adaptations to be as close to the book as possible, how do handle the pressure to keep the fans happy?

WR: I put as much of the original story in as possible. Spike, Rocky, Leo, tarantulas, the milk float, the dairy and even the old radio on a meat hook. I knew hard core Stephen King fans would be watching so I wanted to have as many recognizable moments as possible within an original take on the story.

AN: What was your main goal you wanted to achieve about this film?

WR: I sent the email without expecting a response and can not describe my excitement when I saw an email 'From the office of Stephen King'. I knew by hook or crook I had to make this short film. I took inspiration from many other films including *Henry: Portrait of a Serial Killer, Benny's Video, Trash Humpers*. Anything with that distorted VHS aesthetic. I was most inspired by the early Dollar Baby films like *The Boogeyman, Disciples of The Crow* (1982), *Strawberry Spring* and *The Man Who Loved Flowers*.

AN: Where was the movie filmed specifically and were there any obstacles to overcome while filming there?

WR: The film was shot around my hometown in Llandudno. It was shot mostly on Builder Street, an eerie industrial estate. The exterior of the dairy was an old slaughterhouse and I was told blood would spill from its pipes out into the street. I knew the shots we needed with the milk float, the dairy and the tarantula would be the most difficult so they were organized early on in the production. We were stopped twice by the police at night filming on an industrial estate , I'm not sure if they believed our story that we were making a horror film but they gave us a suspicious stare down and let us carry on

AN: How long was the film shoot and process from start to finish?

WR: The first few months after getting the greenlight were spent planning and raising a small budget of £600 on Kickstarter to buy some props and pay the main cast and crew. It took six months to plan, shoot and edit the film which went through many incarnations and edits before settling on the confessional version.

AN: Let's talk about your lead actor in the film, Landon Sweeney. What was his audition like and what did he bring to the table that won him the role?

WR: Landon Sweeney is a trained theatre and television actor from Cardiff and based in North Wales. Landon was the first actor I auditioned in person for the role of Spike and I knew instantly. Landon has a great physical presence on camera and he can make himself imposing and menacing but also very funny which was important for the role of Spike. There is a wry, dark humor to the character in the story and I think Landon made his own brilliant version. We did very few takes for each shot as Landon instinctively knew how dark or light to play it. Landon was very invested in the role and willing to try anything as well as contributing a lot of ideas that were used in the final film.

AN: The film is shot in an old 1980's VHS/grindhouse style. Are you a big fan of the 1980's and/or horror films from that decade particularly and that's why you filmed it that style?

WR: I am a massive fan of VHS, especially the vintage, grainy, damaged kind, and I tried to recreate the tone and aesthetic of several Dollar Baby films including Frank Darabont's *The Woman in The Room*. I tried shooting on a VHS camcorder but the test was too clean so we shot on an expensive camera and a smart phone with a mix of layers of preset after effects. After trying many variations in the end the best VHS effect was from a free phone app.

AN: You put lots of "nods" and easter eggs from other King's works. Did you do this because you wanted the viewers to have fun while watching the film?

WR: The Stephen king references were added as another layer to the film. I knew there would be Stephen King fans watching this so I wanted to place some obvious and obscure references to Stephen King films. I counted ten the last time I watched it but there may very well be others I added during filming that I have forgotten about.

AN: What is your greatest moment so far with the success of *Morning Deliveries*?

WR: The greatest feeling was starting a short film and seeing it to completion. There were obstacles and disappointments and the film we came back with was not the film we set out to make but somewhere along the way, thanks to a combined effort from everyone involved the film developed a personality of its own. I was so lucky to have a great poster by Chris Barnes from Brutal Posters, a soundtrack by Paul Duffy from The Coral (UK band) and a stellar performance from Landon. The feeling of posting the DVD to the office of Stephen King and knowing he may have seen it (I am told he watches them all) is still surreal to me.

AN: What Stephen King film would you like to adapt on a much larger scale?

WR: My favorite Stephen King story is a little known short story called *The Man in The Black Suit*. A macabre tale about a devilish man and a young boy. I would love to have the budget to turn that into a folk horror film.

AN: Where can fans see the film? Did it play at any film fest around the world?

WR: I am happy to share the film with anyone that would like to see it and have had people contact me wanting to see it. Unfortunately, just before COVID19, the film was set to screen before a public screening of Stephen King's *Creepshow* which I hope still happens.

AN: Lastly, What is next for Will Roberts?

WR: I am currently seeking funding for another adaptation – a version of the *Great God Pan* by welsh horror author Arthur Machen. It's only a short film script at the moment but my goal is to produce a couple more short films and maybe one day even attempt a feature.

AN: We will be looking forward to it Will.

I want to thank Will Roberts for taking the time to speak with us today and wish him great success in his future projects.

Rainy Season by Patrick Haischberger

Rainy Season

Patrick Haischberger
July 23, 2020

THERE ARE MANY STEPHEN KING short stories that are really scary and get right under your skin. Some of these have been adapted as Dollar Baby films. And some of these adaptations have been many versions of that particular story. One of those is the Dollar Baby, *Rainy Season*. Filmmaker Patrick Haischberger can be added to that list with his very creepy adaptation of *Rainy Season*. But first, let's learn a little bit about this Dollar Baby filmmaker.

Patrick Haischberger was born November 23rd, 1984. He is an Austrian award winning director, screenwriter and producer. Patrick graduated from film school in Austria and made horror short films. He won international awards. Patrick is a big Stephen King fan and knows all of his books inside out. Patrick really wanted to make a story of Stephen King's works. However, he didn't have the money for film rights. Patrick simply asked Stephen King's assistant. He didn't know anything about the Dollar Babies at that point. She told Patrick there was a way to get a story from Stephen King for a dollar. The contract was signed a day later. And from there, Patrick was on his way to being part of Stephen King filmmaking history. Patrick has won film awards in Los Angeles, New York, Las Vegas, Florence, and Kosic. His other films include, *Wonderland* (2016), *Damnation* (2018), and *Rainy Season* (2019). Patrick currently lives in Horsching, Oberosterreich, Austria.

Here is my review of Patrick Haischberger's Stephen King's *Rainy Season!*

The short story, *Rainy Season*, was first published in Midnight Graffiti magazine in the Spring of 1993 issue. It was the answer Stephen King's writer's block had at that time. It was republished in the short story collection, *Nightmares & Dreamscapes* which was also published in 1993.

The story is about a married couple who travel to Willow, Maine for some summertime rest and relaxation at a summer home. The locals warn the couple they should turn back, that something very dark is coming if they stay. Every seven years, a curse comes over the town of Willow. The locals are spared but only if there is a sacrifice made. The curse is an evil not from below, but from above that "rains" death down on every town of Willow. An evil of the "reptilian" form.

Director Patrick Haischberger's version of *Rainy Season* is very creepy and dark in the sense of an *"Insidious/The Conjuring"*-type generation of horror films. It has beautiful scenery and locations that lead to a terrifying ending. Out of all the various adaptations of Dollar Baby versions of *Rainy Season*, this version is a sure beat to scare you and lives up to King's horrifying work.

Here is my Exclusive Interview with Dollar Baby filmmaker, Patrick Haischberger!

Anthony Northrup: Can you share with us what it was like growing up in Vienna, Austria?

Patrick Haischberger: Growing up in Austria is very idyllic and quiet. We have many mountains and forests, where often a dark fog hangs. So perfect for a horror lover.

AN: When did you first discover the works of Stephen King (your first book you read, the first Stephen King movie you saw)?

PH: I discovered the books of Stephen King for myself when I was 16. My first book I read was *Misery*. The first movie *The Shining*.

AN: When you studied film, who were some of your inspirations?

PH: Definitely John Carpenter, Wes Craven and James Wan.

AN: You also worked on two other films: *Wonderland* and *Damnation*. Can you tell us what these two films are about?

PH: *Wonderland* is a thriller. It's about a rock star who wants to get out of the business. But of course the record company has something against it. *Damnation* is a science fiction horror movie about the end of the world. An alien threat makes us experience our worst fears.

AN: Let's talk about your Stephen King Dollar Baby movie *Rainy Season*. How did you first learn about the Dollar Baby Program?

PH: I am a big Stephen King fan and know all of his books inside out. I really wanted to make a story of him. But didn't have the money for film rights. I simply asked Stephen King's assistant. I didn't know anything about the Dollar Babies at that point. She told me there was a way to get a story from Stephen King for one dollar. The contract was signed a day later.

AN: Of all the Stephen King short stories, what attracted you most to this film?

PH: That the realization is a challenge. And *Rainy Season* was the first short story I read about Stephen King.

AN: What changes did you make to make it your own, as opposed to King's original text?

PH: I'm having the whole story set in Austria, of course. Then I introduced a cult, which fits the story well. And the ending is a different one.

AN: So many Stephen King fans want adaptations that come as close as possible to the book. How do you deal with the pressure to keep the fans happy?

PH: I make films with the eyes of a fan. And as a fan you naturally wish for a good adaptation. As a Stephen King or horror fan, you naturally make the film you would like to see yourself. And I hope the result pleases the people.

AN: What was your main goal you wanted to achieve with this film?

PH: To finally have a Stephen King story played in Austria. To bring him to my home.

AN: Where exactly was the movie filmed, and were there any obstacles to overcome during the shooting there?

PH: In Upper and Lower Austria. Thank God everything went well during the shooting.

AN: How long did the filming and the process take from start to finish?

PH: I wrote the script in two days in Lombok, Indonesia. The shooting took three days. Altogether with the planning and postproduction about three months.

AN: Share with us about the auditions of your leading actors. What did they bring with them that earned them the role?

PH: I always had Thomas Stipsits and Sabrina Reiter in mind when writing the screenplay. Both are very well known in Austria. They liked my screenplay very much and were immediately on board. Thomas Stipsits is actually known from comedies. I really wanted to see him in a horror movie. He mastered it incredibly well.

AN: Can you tell us a little bit about the F/X you used and how you found so many frogs!

PH: The FX company made a lifelike toad that you could crush. They make animals for cinema and TV. For the real toads we had our own breeder for toads. We had up to 50 frogs.

AN: What was your greatest moment with the success of *Rainy Season?*

PH: The biggest moment is certainly that we will have the premiere in October 2020 at the TLC Chinese Theatre in Hollywood. Also that we won the Film Award in the category Best Horror Film in Los Angeles, New York, Las Vegas, Florence.

AN: Which story of Stephen King would you like to tell on a larger scale?

PH: *Salem's Lot* and *The Stand.* These stories are long overdue.

AN: Where and When can fans see this film? Was it shown at any film festival?

PH: Yes, at the film festivals in L.A., New York, Las Vegas and many more… In October you can see it at the world premiere in Hollywood.

AN: What's next for Patrick Haischberger?

PH: I am writing a screenplay for an American production company for a feature film. And an Austrian drama is in the making.

I want to thank Patrick for speaking with us today and wish him great success in his future projects.

That Feeling, You Can Only Say What It Is In French

Nathan Gathergood
July 25, 2020

IT IS SAFE TO SAY, this is the longest title of any Stephen King story he has ever written. It would take a talent director and an impressive vision to bring this story to the big screen. That talented filmmaker is Nathan Gathergood. Lets learn a little more about Nathan.

Nathan Gathergood grew up on the south coast of England. He studied film after attending college. From there, he got a job at his local TV station, which soon got scaled back massively, due to budget cuts. Nathan moved on to the news department. Having read many of Stephen King's short stories, Nathan went online to try to find out how many there were and stumbled upon the Dollar Baby program. Feeling creatively moribund in the news department, the idea of making a short appealed to Nathan, so he re-read the short stories—this time with a view to filming one. In 2011, he adapted the Stephen King short story, *That Feeling, You Can Only Say What It Is In French*. Nathan turned to acting in 2013 in the film, *Tales of the Troll*. He currently still lives in England.

Here is my review of *That Feeling, You Can Only Say What It Is In French*.

That Feeling, You Can Only Say What It Is In French was first published in *The New Yorker* magazine in the June 22, 1998 issue. In 2002, it was part of the short story collection, *Everything's Eventual*. This horrifying tale is about a married couple on their second honeymoon. While in the car, the wife gets the strange feeling of I over and over and over with the same terrifying ending repeating itself. Is the married couple in some sort of *"Twilight Zone"* episode or are they in Purgatory or worse… HELL!

Nathan's vision of King's tale was very entertaining, professional, and really grabs the viewer into the story. The lead actors did a very impressive job and the special effects were quite impressive for a short independent film such as this. Quite enjoyable with a creepy twisted ending.

Here is my exclusive interview with Dollar Baby filmmaker, Nathan Gathergood.

Anthony Northrup: Share with us what it was like growing up in London, UK?

Nathan Gathergood: I grew up in the suburbs, so long Summers at the park playing football and longer Winters hanging out with friends, watching films or messing about.

AN: Did you study film in college? If so, Where and what helped you the most later in your career?

NG: I went to a south coast university and did a foundation year in art. We had various units on fine art, fashion, photography, 3D, graphics and film, if I remember correctly. I always really enjoyed the film history lessons and went on to do my degree in Moving Image, as it was called. This gave me the tools I needed to make films and television.

AN: When did you first discover the works of Stephen King? Your first Stephen King book & King movie?

NG: Gosh, now that's a tough question! My first Stephen King book might have been *Misery*. It's certainly the first one that I remember the cover of and being completely absorbed by. In terms of film, it might have been *Misery* as well. I also remember seeing *The Lawnmower Man* (possibly at the cinema) and my cousins had the video game on the SNES. I also would have seen *Stand By Me* in the early nineties and I vividly remember watching the Tim Curry *It* two-parter, again with my cousins. We absolutely lost our shit over that one.

AN: Did you find it challenging working at the BBC? Did your experience there help with your film career later on?

NG: From university, I managed to get a job working for ITV in the UK, working in a multi-skilled department, making regional TV programs.

That Feeling, You Can Only Say What It Is In French by Nathan Gathergood

This department was disbanded due to budget cuts, a few years after I started and I was welcomed into the news department. Working in news is very draining, so in that respect, it didn't help my film career. It can also be quite dull creatively, so that probably helped my film career (although my output is so low, I am not sure if I could call it a career, exactly!).

AN: Tell us a little about your film, *Tales of the Troll*. What is that about?

NG: Jane Glennie (who was one of the leads in my Dollar Baby), was at the school gates talking to Nicola O'Neill, one of the other mums. Nicola said that she was casting a short she had written called *Tales of the Troll* and Jane said that she should consider me. I played a bad guy and absolutely loved it, chewing the scenery as I went!

AN: When and How did you first hear about the Stephen King Dollar Baby program?

NG: I think that I was trawling the internet for a decent short script or story that I could make. I don't know why I didn't write one myself. Maybe I was blocked or short on time, I can't remember. But I came across the Dollar Baby program and was blown away! I read every synopsis and read or re-read most of the stories, searching for the best fit for my budget and ambition.

AN: Let's talk about your Dollar Baby film, *That Feeling, you can say what it is in French*. That's a long title, but out of all the Stephen King short stories, what attracted you most to adapt this story?

NG: It's a very long title – I dread to think how much time I have spent saying, typing or writing it over the years! When selecting my story to adapt, I set myself some criteria. It needed to have a low number of characters and locations, I think there were about four or five of each. It needed to be a sensible length – I think it was about 18 pages, maybe, so that was good. It needed to be filmable, but also be quite challenging, which it definitely was – It's quite conceptual, so I liked that I could be a little bit playful and surreal with it. Finally, I wanted to try to shoot one that no one else had done at that stage. So *That Feeling, You Can Only Say What It Is In French* was the perfect choice.

AN: What changes did you make to make this your own as opposed to King's original text?

NG: I obviously had to Anglicise some of the language and make the places relevant, but I tried to change as little as I could. I had to change some of the smaller details, like the girl and her dolly, for practical, filming reasons.

AN: So many Stephen King fans want adaptations to be as close to the book as possible, how do you handle the pressure to keep the fans happy?

NG: I suppose I didn't really consider the fans, as I didn't really expect anyone to see it. The tragedy about the Dollar Baby program is that you can't leave the film lying around in the public domain – it's a condition of the contract you sign. I think that I was relatively faithful to the text, for my own sense of satisfaction, but the geographical references were southern England instead of Florida. That said, I threw some extra King references into the script, some Easter eggs, if you will!

AN: What was your main goal you wanted to achieve about this film?

NG: I just wanted to have a laugh making something with my friends that I could use as a calling card for Hollywood's inevitable interest!!

AN: When was the movie filmed specifically and were there any obstacles to overcome while filming there?

NG: We filmed the short in 2011 (I think!), over a few days in the Summer. Each scene had its own obstacles, but the hardest were the bluescreen driving shots and the plane sequences. We filmed in a training plane at a college and a fire alarm was going off on the campus, but because it was the weekend, there was no one around to turn it off. I spent about an hour sprinting around an empty college trying to find someone to turn it off.

AN: How long was the film shoot and the process from start to finish?

NG: I think the filming itself was four short days over a few weeks. I edited, graded and sound mixed everything myself, so post production took a few months. Even looking at it now, there are slight tweaks and changes that I would make. It's the old adage of a film never being completed, merely abandoned!

AN: Lets talks about your cast. What were the auditions like and what did your two lead actors bring to the table that won them the role?

NG: My two lead actors were/are married and friends I saw regularly. Jane (Glennie) is an actor and Andrew (Pate) a news correspondent who has a hidden talent for thesping. Jane was very upset when one reviewer compared Andrew to Robert de Niro, but didn't offer a comparison for her – especially as she is clearly like a young Meryl Streep! Richard Jones was also a correspondent and I thought he had a good piloty voice. We rushed his recording a bit, so a tweak I would make now would be to do that again. Bill's love interest was another colleague, Lucy Adams. We grabbed a couple of photos of her and Andrew for the opening montage after work one day. I had to put a rather embarrassing ad onto a casting website, looking for someone with "nice legs". Luckily Kari (Frette) applied and didn't think that I was some sort of pervert! Actually, maybe I approached her, based on her height – I can't remember now. However I got her onboard though, she was a pleasure to work with.

AN: Share with us some behind-the-scenes secrets of your special effects used in the film. Were any difficult or challenging?

NG: As the post production department was pretty much just me, I found a lot of the effects very challenging and time consuming. I had some great camera and sound crew in Dan (George), Mick (Hopley) and Amanda (Piper), but as we had to film the in-car scenes outside, the only blue screen I could get was a curtain, which blew around in the wind. The final effect isn't great, but, like the empty plane, I thought it lent an eerie air to things.

AN: What is your greatest moment so far with the success of *That Feeling, you can only say what it is in French*?

NG: I think the greatest achievement was finishing/abandoning it! After that, the bronze award it got at Vegas Independent Film Festival and the silver it got at the Isle of Wight Film Festival.

AN: What Stephen King story would you like to adapt on a much larger scale?

NG: *The Dark Tower*. I've read the books several times. I've cycled through the audio books. When the film/films/series were announced, I bounced off the walls with excitement. I counted down the days to release. I speculated with my cousins which characters would be in it and what elements they might include. Then I saw it. There are so many ways in which that story, that opus could be told and I would love to have a crack at it. It would be a life's work, but by gosh, it would be fun!

AN: Where and When can fans see this film? Did it play at film fests?

NG: I think that the nature of the Dollar Baby program means that it is almost impossible to see these films, except at festivals. It debuted at Cannes and as I said earlier, it played at VIFF! And the IOWFF, but also at a couple of Dollar Baby festivals. Sadly I couldn't make it to any, so I've never seen it on a big screen!

AN: Lastly, What is next for Nathan Gathergood?

NG: I really should get off my arse and make another film!

AN: Well, we certainly look forward to that Nathan.

I want to thank Nathan Gathergood for taking the time to speak with us today and wish him well in his future projects.

The Woman In the Room
Frank Darabont

The First Dollar Baby... or is it?
Anthony Northrup

FOR THIS BOOK, I felt that the artistically appropriate thing to do was to review the first Dollar Baby film ever made. But what is the first? The subject is debatable. I have been honored to interview 55 Stephen King Dollar Baby filmmakers for this book, but there was one filmmaker who I did not get to interview: director Frank Darabont.

I have met Frank, though, and before my review, let's take a look at my first encounter with him. When I worked at a Laser Disc Video store in the San Fernando Valley in California in the early 1990's, a lot of celebrities came into the store to shop. Some came in every day. Many were big name celebrities, one of whom was Frank Darabont. Frank did a lot for that store. He was close friends with the owners and he didn't mind doing in-store signings and meet and greets. Frank was, and still is, a very kind and generous man. But bear in mind that when I met Frank, it was before he had done his flawless trilogy of Stephen King films: *The Shawshank Redemption*, *The Green Mile*, and *The Mist*. He had, though, done a short Stephen King film years before all of them, *The Woman In the Room*.

I didn't know Frank's film credits prior to meeting him. He had written scripts for *A Nightmare on Elm St. Part 3*, *The Blob*, *The Fly 2*, and other films. I knew him from the short-lived television show, *The Young Indiana Jones Chronicles*. In fact, that's how we first met. He came into the store one day and started talking about Indiana Jones. We talked and laughed and had a good conversation. Then I mentioned my *Indiana Jones* comic book collection and how I was missing issue #1 of the new *Indiana Jones* comic that had been "rebooted" by Darkhorse Comics at that time (MARVEL

The Woman In the Room
by Frank Darabont

did a run of *Indiana Jones* comics from 1981-1985). The next time Frank came in, he said he had something for me, and he put the *Indiana Jones* comic #1 on the counter. I was so happy and very surprised, and I still have it today. That's the kind of guy Frank is.

As to the "First Dollar Baby" debate, I have asked Dollar Baby director, Jeff Schiro; Stephen King expert Stephen Spignesi; and others just which was the first Dollar Baby: *The Woman In the Room* or Jeff Schiro's *The Boogeyman*? In 1980, after Stephen King announced his Dollar Baby program for young filmmakers, Frank asked if he could have the rights to adapt King's short story, "The Woman in the Room." However, Frank wouldn't be able to actually film the movie until 1983. Before Frank could get the cameras rolling, though, director Jeff Schiro adapted Stephen King's short story, "The Boogeyman" in 1982. So, Jeff's movie was filmed first, but Frank got the rights for his film before Jeff's. So, I like to think they both deserve equal first rights credit. With that explanation out of the way, here is my review of the Frank Darabont Dollar Baby adaptation *The Woman in Room*.

Stephen King's short story, "The Woman in the Room," was first published in King's short story collection, Night Shift in 1978. Frank Darabont adapted the film in 1983. His film was on the semi-finalist list for an Academy Award that year. It was made with a budget of approximately $30,000. Frank was only 20 years old when he made the film. The story is about a young lawyer whose terminally ill mother is in the hospital. There is nothing the doctors can do for her but ...

Many people with fatal illnesses have often expressed a desire to "move on," rather than wait and linger through an unbearable hell of suffering. Thus, the son, a troubled lawyer facing personal demons of his own, must make a horrifying decision as to what to do. After visiting one of his clients in prison, the son looks at his mother's situation in a different light.

I think this adaptation is not only one of the better Dollar Baby films, but also certainly one of the biggest tear-jerkers of all of Stephen King's stories. It ranks right up there with King's story, "*Last Rung On the Ladder*" (another Dollar Baby adapted beautifully by James Cole). The casting was well done, but surprisingly, it was actor Brian Libby (the aforementioned Prisoner) who impressed me the most. Brian went on to be in Darabont's other Stephen King films: *The Shawshank Redemption, The Green Mile,* and *The Mist*. And even though those were bigger films, it is his performance in this short film that really made me sit up and take notice.

Frank has admitted that he wasn't 100 percent happy with *The Woman in the Room,* but I feel it was emotionally moving and entertaining. Even though I have now seen a wide variety of Dollar Baby films, and various other interpretations of King's stories—and many boast some of the most amazing filmmakers in the world—it was the fearsome four: Jeff Schiro, Frank Darabont, James Cole, and James Gonis— who paved the road in the early 80's for hundreds of Dollar Babies to come.

Dollar Baby filmmakers often move on to other films and projects, and Frank is no exception: He adapted some of Stephen King's biggest and best films, especially the aforementioned memorable classics. He also did other films, including his biggest project, a TV series called *The Walking Dead,* which has since become one of the most popular shows of all-time. And that shows that short films can lead to a long future. Just ask Frank Darabont!

PART THREE

"The Dollar Babies Have Left the Building!"

WHEN I WAS A KID going to the movies, I always got excited when the final scenes were about to roll and always hoped for a little extra before the credits would run. However, most of the time, there were no "little extras" and the film left you wondering: What happened next? I would wonder: what happened to the characters? Did they live? Die? Get Married? Will they come back? What about a sequel?

These days, I still wonder about these things when I watch a film, however, modern cinema most of the time have added scenes during or after the credits which answer some of your questions you might have like I do. The same can be said for books too. You read a really interesting or entertaining book and you can't get the book out of your head for hours, days even and you begin to wonder: What happened next?

So, I felt the same way about the Dollar Babies I interviewed. I wondered as I started this book: What happened to them after they finished filming their Dollar Baby? Did they have success? Failure? Stay in the movie business or go to a regular job? Did it make their career or break their career? And many other questions. 'Curiosity killed the cat…' as they say '..but satisfaction brought him back.'! So, I contacted as many Dollar Babies as I could that I interviewed to find out what happened after they made their Dollar Baby film. This next chapter will reunite us with most (not all) of them and answer our question and a whole lot more.

So, get ready because here comes the Dollar Babies... Where Are They Now?

Where Are They Now?

Bryan Higby – *Here There Be Tygers*

The film was selected for the 2020 Snowtown Film festival in Watertown NY. I hosted my 1st Dollar Baby fest in Lowville NY back on 10/19/19. King almost attended but was called away for his production of *Lisey's Story*. *Here There Be Tygers* also played at Hudson Valley Community College during their Fall Arts Festival 2019. The film also opened Halloween Dollar Baby fest at the George Eastman Museum in Rochester NY. Also it was selected to play at a festival in the Netherlands but missed out on the fest dates. My film allowed me to be invited to the Northern NY Film lab in Albany NY Nov 2019, where I met and now have an entertainment lawyer Paul Rapp. Paul and I are now submitting projects to actor Danny McBride's Rough House Pictures. The DenMark Chronicles IP's are up for sale with Rough House. Please see the link to my author page here:_https://www.amazon.com/-/e/B00CWEFNVS I also have a professional cinematographer Steve Ciferelli, and we're in pre production for my first feature film to be shot this summer 2020 titled: PUBLIC ACCESS TO THE COSMOS, a horror/science fiction.

James Douglas – *The Doctor's Case*

Once I had sent off our hopeful Blu-ray copy of *The Doctor's Case* to Stephen King, our team immediately began prepping for what turned out to be a rather successful film festival run. Our world premiere was held at the Julien Dubuque International Film Festival in April of 2018, and since then we've screened at nearly 40 festivals in about eight different countries. We've won a total of 15 awards in a variety of categories including Best Feature, Best Period Film, Best Production Design, Best Costumes, Best

Editing, and Best Performance, and we've met some incredibly talented people along the way (some of whom have become life-long friends and collaborators). The first person I ran into at the Julien Dubuque festival, for example, was a filmmaker named Skye Borgman. Skye was there with a documentary she wrote and directed called *Forever B*, which went on to win Best of Fest.

Nine months later her film—now called *Abducted In Plain Sight*—premiered on Netflix with a massive amount of buzz attached to it and has become one of the Top 10 true-crime documentaries ever presented by the streaming service. Fast forward a couple of years and Skye, Norm Coyne, Len Pearl, Denise Crosby and I are currently shopping around a documentary/scripted reality series called *Hollywood Forever* that we are all pretty excited about. Through our company Barker Street Cinema, Norm and I have just produced the pilot episode of a 30-minute supernatural/history show called *Wicked Ways: History Is Haunted*, co-hosted by cosplay superstar and paranormal investigator LeeAnna Vamp, and Canadian actor/comedian Mark Meer (perhaps best known as the voice of Commander Shepard in the *Mass Effect* video game series). We're also about to start production on my directorial follow-up to *The Doctor's Case*, a short science-fiction film written by our good friend Chris Dias, called *Ariel Alpha*. Shot entirely in the Prince George region of British Columbia, *Ariel Alpha* stars Madison Smith (*Riverdale, Narcoleap*) and Becca Scott (*Greg & Becca, South Park*) and is in some ways the spiritual successor to films like *Blade Runner, Ex Machina,* and *My Dinner With Andre* (yes, you read that right). As well, Barker Street Cinema is producing a documentary series about the burgeoning film industry in our region called NORTHERN LIGHTS, CAMERA, ACTION!, featuring extensive interviews with visiting industry professionals like actor Edward James Olmos (*Blade Runner, Miami Vice*), producer Michael Uslan (*Batman, Joker*), cinematographer Skye Borgman (*Abducted In Plain Sight, We Are Galapagos*), director Rachel Talalay (*Doctor Who, Tank Girl*), and writer Marc Bernardin (*Castle Rock, Treadstone*).

In addition, I have been working with my TDC co-director Len Pearl on two of his upcoming projects: part one of the now complete documentary mini-series *Search the Land: The Story of the Jewish Canadians*, to be broadcast this summer, and an as-yet-to-be-named, but incredibly true historical drama about the Canadian woman who ultimately saved countless American lives from the horrors of Thalidomide in the early-1960s. If that weren't enough, horror-writer and Stephen King collaborator Bev Vincent and I have started the very early process of adapting his short story, *Zombies on a Plane*, into a low-budget-but-totally-fun, feature-length horror movie. All in all, it's been a very satisfying couple of years.

Jeff Schiro – *The Boogeyman*

I was a film student at New York University when I directed *The Boogeyman*. Just a kid with stars in his eyes. In 1985 it was released on home video, and I went on to direct a music video for The Ramones, along with an episode of *Tales From The Darkside (The Grave Robber)*. I soon decided Los Angeles is where I had to be. Shortly after moving to LA, I found an amazing thing was happening in the world of post production. It was called "non-linear editing," the ability to cut a film on a desktop computer, and I was soon seduced. With that in mind, I've been a working editor in Hollywood ever since. My work has been fairly eclectic. I started off cutting commercials (FORD, NISSAN, ORACLE), promos for Disney, an award winning sports film called *Organ Donors*, and a feature called *Malaika*. From there I cut dozens of docu-dramas and documentaries for the major cable networks, shows like *The Deadliest Warrior, Amelia Earhart: Lost Evidence, Monster In My Family, Gettysburg: The War That Changed America, Hell On the Highway*, and the list goes on. It's a changing industry with the likes of streaming video, so who knows what'll be coming down the pike next.

Shawn S. Lealos – *I Know What You Need*

After making my Dollar Baby, I worked with several other Dollar Baby filmmakers to write my own book on mine and their experiences making the films as well as what it led to in later careers – called *Dollar Deal*. After writing the book, I was brought to Houston to run a Dollar Baby Film Festival at Comicpalooza, which was also attended by James Cox (*Grey Matter*) and Rodney Altman (*Umney's Last Case*). I was then flown to Seattle to run another Dollar Baby Film Festival at Galacticon. Since that time, I worked on several short films as well as a YouTube series that lasted one season called *The Starving Dogs Show*. After that, I moved back to writing, working as a film critic who is a voting member of the Oklahoma Film Critics Circle as well as a writer for Comic Book Resources (CBR), *ScreenRant*, and as an editor for *Monsters & Critics*. I am currently working on my first fiction novel called *Fallen Star*. It follows a police officer who deals with crime in a world where superheroes are real and is planned as the first in a series.

Right now I am writing a fiction novel called Fallen Star. "Superheroes are real. However, while they are there to save the world from superhuman threats, someone has to solve mysteries and protect people from the still dangerous human threats. That is where Detective Steve Samson enters the picture. An old homeless man is killed in a dark alley and then hung up and crucified for the world to see. Steve Samson knows that this has something to do with a group of religious fanatics who protest superheroes actions and want them deemed illegal. When more deaths start to pile up, it is up to Samson to find out who is killing these people and stop them before it threatens to bring down the heroes who protect the world.

Mando Franco – *The Boogeyman*

After the festival run, Mando took a brief hiatus from film and relocated to the Midwest. He is married with 1 child and has recently returned to the directors chair. He is currently submitting a Christmas slasher film to festivals and is currently writing a supernatural horror feature and looking to shoot in 2021.

Brian Johnson – *Uncle Otto's Truck*

Uncle Otto's Truck to date has been awarded the following: FINALIST / Canadian Cinematography Awards SEMI-FINALIST / NEW YORK Cinematography Awards SEMI-FINALIST / Los Angeles Cinefest SEMI-FINALIST / European Cinematography Awards SEMI-FINALIST / Los Angeles Cinematography Awards OFFICIAL SELECTION / Rome Independent Prisma Awards In the meantime after being ask to submit an outline, I'm waiting for and answer from Stephen King's office after submitting a proposal for turning *Uncle Otto's Truck* into a feature film project. Projects I'm working on at the moment and are coming in 2020:

1. Currently in pro-production for a feature I'm shooting later this summer starring a character from *Deep Space 9*. I can't reveal details and / or names yet.

2. Also in pre-production for a country music video I'm producing and shooting in Tennessee later this summer. I just finished post production on a national commercial shot a few months ago and am preparing to begin pre-production on another national spot in a few weeks. I'm knee-deep in prepping for the future I'm shooting starting August 3 in Virginia.

Maria D. Jones – *Graduation Afternoon*

After completion of our film, we began submitting to festivals when the Coronavirus hit, so now we wait to see what plays out from that. Our IronTree Films team members are all moving on to new projects, and we hope to shoot something together later in the year, or at least start on our first feature together. I am working on the script with director Rob Padilla and we are super excited.

For me personally, I am a full-time writer so I have since completed two non-fiction books that are currently being edited for release this year from Visible Ink Press, and I am writing a third, followed by a fourth, then one early next year. My writing schedule is always full. I also have a novel coming out next summer from Vesuvian Books that is in editing, and I am finishing a couple of novel series, but those will be over the course of the year. I am working on a new horror script with my writing partner, Denise A. Agnew, and we are outlining what will be our first horror novel together.

In addition, I became the horse racing blogger for Sports As Told By a Girl, and I continue to do radio shows to promote my past books. My first short film with director Neil Payne of RockChalk Pictures, *Kings Boulevard*, is continuing to get into film festivals and I turned in a script for our next short, *Red, White, And You*.

I am also a trained disaster responder with my fire department through FEMA and the Red Cross, so I am continuing my training on an ongoing basis.

Warren Ray – *Maxwell Edison*

After *Maxwell Edison* I was involved in the project called, *Orbs they are among us*, where I played a Apollo astronaut in the flashback sequences I was also the second unit director for the interior Apollo scenes that film got best paranormal at Fright Night Film Fest in 2014 I believe then I was involved in a film called, *Kill Kill Vigilante 7* and I played a Russian hitman and then after that I was involved in a Anthology called, *Volumes of Blood Horror Stories* and I believe *Fangoria* magazine said it was the best and talk to you 2016 it also got best Anthology at Fright Night Film Fest that year and then after that I was involved in a movie called, *What Lies Ahead*. I just have a small cameo in that with a few lines but I got to work with Rumer Willis Bruce Willis's daughter so that was pretty cool. I'm continuing my recording career and songwriting career. I've got a new record coming out this year called Alberta.

Also in 2016 I was in a film called, *Der Vertrag* with Vernon Wells of the *Road Warrior* fame also played a Russian hitman in that film haha. Since my version of *The Man Who Loved Flowers* was a mash-up with The Beatles *Maxwell's Silver Hammer* idea it was pretty cool there for awhile if you Googled *Maxwell Edison* my photograph came up I grew up a huge Beatles fan so that was kind of neat to hack my way into their mythology there for a moment in time. *Maxwell Edison* played in 14 different countries around the world at various Stephen King Dollar Baby film festivals it played in Russia twice it really a created a lot of neat friendships for me and all these different countries with other directors and Film Festival organizers I was really made to feel welcome by the Stephen King fan and Dollar Baby family nothing but good things to say about the Dollar Baby program I think it's a wonderful program that mister King provides for film students and wayward filmmakers. An opportunity to work with one of the greatest writers of all time.

James Gonis – *The Lawnmower Man*

For the past six years I've co-hosted a podcast called "Monster Party," where three friends and I discuss and debate all things horror, sci-fi and fantasy. We've been lucky to have some terrific guests on.

Maxwell Heesch – *Everything's Eventual*

I'm currently rocking the world of TV Post Production in Los Angeles while I attempt a living in screenwriting.

J.P. Scott – *Everything's Eventual*

After making *Everything's Eventual*, I approached Stephen King and his agent about selling the film. I was granted rights to sell the film under pretty lofty conditions (I should have negotiated but I was a naive young filmmaker, haha). We needed $1 million dollars and a 1000 screen wide release. The film was considered by Lionsgate and others but they passed. The best offer I was able to get was around $100k and a few hundred theatres. An awesome offer but not up to the agreement so I was forced to reject it. It was really cool just to be in that situation and I am still very grateful for even the opportunity. The film ended up getting me my second feature film as a director which I likely would not have been chosen for had I not had this feature under my belt.

Corey Norman – *Suffer the Little Children*

Suffer the Little Children had a very successful festival run lasting just under a year. It had 20 award nominations and 9 award wins, including: Best Short Film (HorrorHound Film Festival), Audience Choice (Sanford International Film Festival), Best Director (Phantasmagorical Film Festival, Horror Society Awards, Los Angeles Horror Competition) and Best Actress (HorrorHound Film Festival, Phantasmagorical Film Festival). Director Corey Norman is now a professor in the Communications and New Media department at Southern Maine Community College where he inspires the next generation of filmmakers. In 2019 he was appointed to the Maine Film Commissioner where he worked to further film production in the state while building a creative economy for the youth. But fear not, he hasn't given up his passion for filmmaking. He's directed several music videos for the Indiana based progressive metal band *The Contortionist*, released several shorts on anthology collections such as: *The Invoking* 2 (Image Entertainment), *The Witching* (Synergetic),, *Charlotte* (Synergetic), *Dread Central's Monsterland* (Image Entertainment), and *Monsterland* 2 (Uncork'd Entertainment). His debut feature film, *The Hanover House*, also starring Anne Bobby (*Suffer the Little Children, Nightbreed*) was the first release from HorrorHound Films."

Dan Sellers – *Uncle Otto's Truck*

As I write this narrative, Uncle Otto's Truck is making its way around the festival circuit. We've hosted a handful of public screenings of the film around North Carolina but our main focus with the film is to get it in front of the eyes of as many folk as possible. We've launched a fairly aggressive film festival campaign, which so far includes about 40 festivals, which is a lot for our small production company.

Considering that festivals typically charge anywhere from $10 to $60 for submissions, this represents a significant investment for us. So far the film has had about a 70% success rate of getting accepted into film festivals and of the ones we've gotten into, we've won awards at about every one. The feedback I'm hearing from our audiences has been overwhelmingly positive. Immediately after our world premiere, at our own film fest, the Wreak Havoc Horror Film Festival in Greensboro, NC, I met a filmmaker who was impressed with the film.

The next week I received an email from this filmmaker asking if I'd be interested in directing one of his scripts. We had another meeting and have been hard at work on pre-production for a new horror short film. This represents the first time I've ever been hired, and paid money, to direct a film. For me, that's a big deal and I owe it to the success of Uncle Otto. Not only does this producer want me to direct, but he also wants the creative time behind Uncle Otto to help bring his vision to life. I'm so grateful to Mr. King and his associates for allowing us to make a Dollar Baby. I would encourage other filmmakers to produce one themselves.

I was recently contacted by another filmmaker in Hollywood who just got the right to produce a Dollar Baby and asked for advice. I told them to be faithful to the spirit of the source material but to not be beholden to it. It's important to make it your own while not losing what makes the story special. The cool thing about having a Dollar Baby film is that for a lot of folks, having King's name involved might get their attention. In our case, it's actually drawn by many members of our audience. But the trick is you've still got to make an entertaining and compelling film. The pressure is on with a Dollar Baby to live up to the expectations of the King name and not let audiences down.

A.J. Gribble – *Cain Rose Up*

After my Dollar Baby (*Cain Rose Up*) was finished, I had it premiere at my local movie theater and over 100 people came! It was nominated for multiple festivals and won a few of them! After 'Cain', I did a few more short films and I am now working on my first feature length film.

I graduated high school and tech school in the class of Audio Visual, top of my class I should add! Recently moved to Florida. I am now in post-production on my first feature length film which will be released soon.

Jacob Sanders – *One For the Road*

My adaptation of *One for the Road* got me into Nightmares Film Fest based in Columbus, Ohio. My short was accepted during their inaugural year and since then the festival has gone on to become a more significant festival in the horror film world. I would continue my career as a filmmaker by shooting an independently financed TV pilot about a dysfunctional community theater in the Rustbelt. I currently work for Tennessee Performing Arts Center in Nashville. My professional career is in live performance work, but I maintain a desire to produce more video content.

Selina Sondermann – *Dedication*

I assisted production on several student films, am set to act in a short film in April and am still writing the script for a feature length version of *Anthropophilie*.

Nicole Jones-Dion – *In The Deathroom*

Our film just started its festival run, but we've already won Best Horror Short at the Hollywood Reel Independent Film Festival, and we've been nominated for 6 awards at the Idyllwild International Festival of Cinema.

Jon Mann – *Popsy*

I have finished writing a horror feature called Devil's *Landing*, which is in its financing stage. I'm also an Associate Producer on a short film called North Star, starring Kevin Bacon, Laura Innes, And Corey Reynolds.

Stephen Tramontana – *A Very Tight Place*

We wrapped AVTP's run with a presentation at the George Eastman Museum, which was an absolute thrill. They programmed an entire Dollar Baby night, and I was able to be there with another filmmaker – Walter Perez – for a Q&A. As we finished AVTP's post-production, we actually started filming our next short: Grief Counseling, which we just finished today and will be going into fests this year. A lot of the equipment and techniques we used on GC we actually perfected during our time on AVTP, so I consider them kind of sister projects.

Jennifer Trudrung – *Here There Be Tygers*

Since writing and producing *Here There Be Tygers* I've gone on to focus on writing horror feature screenplays. My screenplay *The Bewailing* was picked up by Suttle Film and just wrapped production. The movie will be released in October of 2020. Another feature screenplay, *Spectrum*, is a finalist at the 2020 Women in Horror Film Festival and I'm hard at work on my third feature screenplay. *Here There Be Tygers* has won several awards in the film festival circuit including "Best North American Drama Short" at the Nevermore Film Festival. '*Tygers*' has already screened at numerous amazing film festivals around the US and world and its journey is continuing and we are excited to see where else it will be screened.

Joe Kowalski – *I Am The Doorway*

While I haven't made any huge films as of late, I did spend a few years as an editor for a morning news program and continue to produce sketches and music videos on my own time. Currently, I am a documentary film editor for Transition Studios, primarily in the true crime genre. I also have begun publishing short stories in literary journals. One that is coming soon is entitled *Bloodbrewer*, and will likely be enjoyed by fans of Mr. King! I have also started a web series with my girlfriend about the art of Disney films called *Not So Small World*.

Mark Zimmerman – *Rest Stop*

I have been involved in some acting in a web series called, *Atomic Kingdom* which will hopefully be released in the second half this year, that's all I've done.

Jackie Perez – *Beachworld*

Since completing her Dollar Baby *Beachworld*, Jackie Perez has shared her film around the world at Dragon Con, the Library of Congress, Sick Chick Flicks, Buffalo International Film Festival, Adirondack Film Festival, Ax Wound, Midwest Monster Film Fest, Dunedin International, the Netherlands, and the 45th annual Boston Sci-Fi Film Festival. Then Covid-19 hit, throwing the film festival world upside down. In a rare turn of events, she requested and received permission from Stephen King to stream her film online for a limited time during the pandemic. Jackie currently lives on the island of Oahu. She's the Director of Development for the Hawaii Filmmakers Collective and a nuclear engineer at the Pearl Harbor Shipyard. Her first book will be published in the fall of 2021, a new biography on astronaut Sally Ride. She continues to write screenplays in her free time and still loves making films.

Dean Werner – *The Reaper's Image*

After playing Dollar Baby festivals, Dean did a short film with veteran character actor Jack Kehler. He's also helped program the AFI Film Festival. And done ghost writing and script editing for various production companies and individuals. Currently Dean and his *Reaper's Image* producer Nichole are working on a feature film.

Billy Hanson – *Survivor Type*

Here's everything I've been working on since *Survivor Type*! In 2014, I wrote and directed a pilot for a music-based drama series called, *No Place to*

Fall. I directed the Funny or Die series, *Lightning Dogs*, which was released in summer of 2017 and is still available on FunnyorDie.com. I've produced two short films with writer/director Tara Price, called, *Earworm* is available to stream on Amazon Prime, and Tea Time is just about to begin its festival run in summer of 2020. I worked with London-based singer, Coach Hop, on four music videos. Currently released are *I Love You, Goodbye, La Petite Mort*, and *Everything's Fine*, with another video called, *Every Part* to be released in Spring of 2020. I wrote and published *Spider Season*, released in October of 2018. The book is available in paperback, ebook and audiobook. I've also written several issues for Zenescope Comics, including *Grimm Tales of Terror, Red Agent* and *The Bridgewater Triangle* limited series. And in 2020, I will complete my first feature film as a writer/director, called Bone *Cold*, which follows a black-ops sniper team on a doomed mission as they flee a violent militia and something inhuman and monstrous, that cannot be stopped with bullets.

James B. Cox – *Grey Matter*

In 2018, *Hacked*, written and directed by yours truly, was released worldwide. This is my first feature film about an AI experiment gone wrong in an office building and the hackers who need to stop it before it destroys the world. It's currently available to stream on Amazon Prime: tiny.cc/hackedprime. I'm currently working on my next feature film for next year but near the end of this summer I will be launching the comic series, *The Boatman*, co-created with Baruch Kaufman (producer of *Hacked*) with art by Greg Woronchak. It's a modern day heist story set in the world of black market art dealing featuring mythological gods and goddesses.

Maria Ivanova – *Beachworld*

I work as a digital artist and animator. I work on my own personal project—animated film. As always (as it was with *Beachworld*) I work alone, so it will take a lot of time to complete my film. At the same time I create digital art, illustrations and paintings. I have my site now https://www.mariaivart.com.

Rodney Altman – *Umney's Last Case*

After making *Umney's Last Case* I moved to Los Angeles and started working as a development executive. I helped develop movies like *The Mule* and *Scary Stories to Tell in the Dark*, and series such as *The Witcher* and *The Expanse*. Most recently I've been working as one of the writers for PUBG, the original battle royale video game.

Damon Vinyard – *In The Deathroom*

I'm a commercial producer and was running Domino's, American Airlines and Infiniti but now at a new agency and I make all of Dairy Queen's commercials. So lot's of Blizzards are eaten! I am working on a documentary project with a company out of China about the Hump Pilots that flew in China in WWII. I have been filming some veterans here in the US that are going into the Chinese version. Once that is finished I will get their footage and make a US version and pursue getting it picked up by History Channel or something like that. It is a passion project since my grandfather flew over 180 missions over in China during the war.

Ranjeet S. Marwa – *Cain Rose Up*

Since finishing my Stephen King movie I have been fortunate enough to direct a TV trilogy which aired worldwide to over 8 million people in India, Canada, the UK and America. I have also gone on to direct an Amazon Prime miniseries titled *Daughter Unknown*. I was also able to direct a black-and-white art house horror movie titled *The Missing* which was bought by Amazon. I directed a theatrical movie titled 'Citizen Erased' which had a limited theatrical run here in the UK. The movie is a true story about a girl who was raped and brainwashed into becoming a terrorist organization's sex slave before she was eventually caught by the police. I also directed a documentary which was executive produced by veteran Hollywood actor Bruce Payne titled 'The Boy Who Never Came Home: A True Story' which tells the story of an illegal organ trafficking situation of a 4 year old boy in India. The documentary went on to premier in downtown LA theatres and was in consideration for an Academy award. The documentary is set to be released on Amazon Prime later this year. I also directed a World War II feature film titled 'Memoirs of a Sikh Soldier' and the film also premiered in LA theatres for a limited theatrical run. Currently I am set to film an action/thriller movie in Indonesia with all of the cast from the movie 'The Raid'. The film is titled 'Blood Rush' and will debut in theatres worldwide in 2021 hopefully. I cannot say any more about it's further release but it will be on a platform that you are all very familiar with.

James Cole – *Last Rung On The Ladder*

Considering that my Dollar Baby adaptation of the Stephen King story 'The Last Rung on the Ladder' was shot in the summer of 1986 and completed in May 1987, it's only been 33 years since then. To put it in perspective, I was a twenty-year-old college student in the summer of '86, still living at home on Cape Cod when not in school. I was still a kid – which makes me all the more proud of how well my Super-8 film adaptation of "*Last Rung*" – made with partner Dan Thron – turned out. It was an important experience in my filmmaking education and a stepping stone for my eventual move to Hollywood, where I dreamed of writing movies for a living.

That journey began in 1991 when I drove across the country and moved to Los Angeles. Though I hoped "*Last Rung*" would generate some interest, it sadly did not open any doors for me, let alone get me a single meeting. (By the 1990s a film made in Super 8 – though viewable on VHS video – was deemed not professional enough.) Instead I focused on learning the craft of feature film screenwriting, penning several scripts. But even in this pre-Marvel comic book era my stories were deemed, in industry lingo, too "soft" (I wrote mainly dramatic scripts as opposed to comedy or "high concept" stories), so I had to survive with a day job as a Temp. Initially this involved being sent all over L.A. and working at non-industry secretarial jobs. Eventually I landed a recurring gig at Walt Disney Imagineering, a wonderful creative arm of Disney where they build and upgrade the Magic Kingdom and other theme parks. I worked on and off at "WDI" for almost exactly ten years, still writing and hoping for a break. Ironically my break did finally come in part because of my Dollar Baby…but not in the way I had anticipated.

In 2000 I heard about a new generation of Dollar Babies, including an adaptation of King's poem "*Paranoid: A Chant*" from *Skeleton Crew*. The film so impressed King that it was granted a brief window of availability on the internet, which was a great promotion for the film's director, Jay Holben. To put it simply, this "King Konnection" with Jay would help me fulfill my dream. Jay and I connected through our work, had several meetings, and got to know each other. But it was a chance meeting just before Christmas 2001 that would change the course of my life. Jay was among contributors to "*Creepshows*," a book about King movie adaptations by Stephen Jones. I happened to attend and did my best to chat with Jay between his signing books. Just before I left, something made me pause and ask, "Do you have any future short films planned?" Jay's face lit up. He explained that he was indeed planning to shoot a new film in March of 2002 but didn't have a script. He asked if I had one. I told him no, "But I do have a short story." When I got home I emailed Jay "Hot shots," an autobiographical story about one of many hospitalizations as a child.

I didn't have high expectations. I knew this was another "soft" story; a drama that actually featured three boys in a single room. Not many visual possibilities. I just hoped Jay would like the tale. Well, not only did Jay like it, he loved it, and announced in his email reply that he wanted my story to be the basis for his next film! Not only did this actually happen, it happened very quickly.

I spent the next two months adapting my own short story into a 22 page screenplay. Many specifics were changed but the core story remained the same. Jay put together an amazing team of crafts people, and on March 1, 2002, I drove an hour up the coast to an abandoned mental hospital in Camarillo, CA, where Jay and his crew had dressed one of the empty rooms and created the set of a hospital room. That morning as I stepped through the doorway I felt as if I'd gone back in time. More than that, I felt as though this talented team had somehow reached into my brain, into my memories, and recreated an environment from my childhood. The set was amazing, but what really made this a dream production were the young actors we had cast – especially 11 year-old Lucas Riney playing the lead "Danny" (my alter ego). For four days I rehearsed and worked with the kids in preparation for filming under Jay's direction, and I also served as an official still photographer, taking six rolls of behind the scenes photos during the four day shoot. The days were long but they flew by, and suddenly it was late Sunday afternoon and we wrapped on schedule. I drove home exhausted but thrilled. I would end up having to wait thirteen months to see the finished film. Jay and our editor worked together in their off-hours and I was involved in the final revisions, working with Lucas on some dubbed lines (as well as contributing some sound effects of my own!).

Just as the film was completed, Jay informed me that it had already won an award! It would be presented with The American Cinematographers Society Showcase Award – recognition for up-and-coming cinematographers, in this case our talented Director of Photography Christopher Probst. This meant *"The Night Before"* (our final film title) would be presented with the other winning short films in the Directors Guild of America theater right in Hollywood!

The first time I ever saw my story up on a big screen was in one of the finest and biggest theaters in the country! I was terrified but happily the film was warmly received. Just as memorable, Jay arranged an official premiere for cast, crew, and invited friends on the Warner Bros. studio lot in early June. I invited just about every friend I knew and we had a great turnout in one of the screening rooms we rented. We showed the film twice that night and even had an intermission outside on the lot with drinks and snacks. It was one of the proudest nights of my life. "*The Night Before*" may not have been a 2 hour feature film but in every other respect it was a "real" movie—my first professionally-produced script. I had finally written a movie all my own and Jay's wonderful direction brought my words to vivid life.

What I'm most proud of is that "*The Night Before*" was the first time I wrote about living with my birth condition Bladder Exstrophy, and all the corrective surgeries required to put me back together (performed between birth and age 16). As such I have presented the short film to medical conferences and gatherings for families of "BE" kids from around the world. The short has been shown in New York, Philadelphia, Milwaukee, Seattle, and even Australia! It continues to be a source of pride and education 17 years after its birth. Years after its production, "*Last Rung*" continued to gain attention. With the new modern generation of Dollar Babies (and digital productions), festivals began to appear. One of the biggest took place in Maine at the University of Maine, Orono campus, and I actually flew back east to attend with Jay, meeting other Dollar Baby directors (and meeting up with my dear friend James Gonis, the first director I ever met way back in 1988 due to his faithful and funny adaptation of King's "*The Lawnmower Man*"). King himself was originally going to attend the festival, but this was the year the Red Sox finally won so he was down in Boston watching a game.

Other festivals followed, including one in Hollywood in 2010, which Dan Thron was able to attend. Perhaps the biggest door "*Last Rung*" opened for me was my connecting and becoming friends with director Frank Darabont, whose 1983 adaptation of "*The Woman in the Room*" is perhaps the most famous of the first generation Dollar Babies. This short so impressed King that he granted Frank the rights to adapt his novella "*Rita Hayworth & Shawshank Redemption*" into the brilliant, classic film that has become beloved by audiences. I met Frank not long after he finished shooting his film and maintained a friendship for many years, long enough that I was able to watch Frank shoot his second "Stephen King Prison Movie," "*The Green Mile,*" in 1998. I spent four incredible days on set. I met almost all the actors, and watched the magic of movies being captured live.

As for my own journey, in the years that followed I continued to write and attempt to break into the business. The closest I came was through a friend who worked on the CBS drama series "*Without a Trace.*"

He pitched a story to me, and I co-wrote the teleplay. We actually received guidance from the show's star Anthony LaPaglia, who was wonderfully supportive. Sadly, internal politics prevented our making a sale. We did not give up, however. As the seasons passed Anthony gained allies and by the end of season seven we finally had enough people behind our script to overrule main producers. One of the show's directors considered it the best "spec" script he'd ever read. I was so excited. I was finally going to make a sale! Then CBS canceled the show. That was it for me.

I had actually become disabled in these later years (fallout from all the major surgeries I'd had as a child) and I didn't have any stamina left to keep pounding against that industry door. At the same time both my mom and dad were struggling with health issues (both were in their mid-80s by this time). I began looking after Dad, driving 2 hours north to the Santa Ynez valley every couple weekends to help him out, but he eventually had to be moved into a nursing home.

At that time my brother began looking at facilities on Cape Cod so we could move him back east to be with the rest of our family on

From the Dollar Baby Festival at the Silent Movie Theater in Hollywood 2010. L-R: Mick Garris, Daniel Thron, James Cole (on knee), Jeff Schiro, James Gonis, Robert Cochrane, Doveed Linder, and John Woodward (crouched – orange shirt).

Cape Cod... but Dad died days after his 86th birthday in 2013. We had a wonderful memorial for him, and I began planning to leave L.A. after 22 years. I made the move in the summer 2013, living at my Mom's little house on Cape Cod. Sadly, within six months Mom's health began to fail as well, and I became a caregiver once more. She eventually passed in December 2015, yet I have remained on Cape Cod since then. I still write and still dream of seeing one of my scripts produced independently (perhaps with Jay as director), but my time is now spent working on a book (my memoirs) and writing a weekly film column for "*The Cape Cod Chronicle*."

My life has been an adventure in the years since I made "*The Last Rung on the Ladder*," and I will always be grateful to the connections this little film provided, the friendships I have made, and most of all, meeting Jay. That fateful encounter at the "*Creepshows*" book signing changed the course of my life and allowed me to write a real movie. Maybe someday the Stephen King connection will help me get a feature script produced, too. No matter what happens, I will always be a Dollar Baby.

Pablo Macho Maysonet IV – *The Things They Left Behind*

I made 2 feature films since then, the most recent being Await the Dawn starring a few Stephen King alum's such as: Dee Wallace (*Cujo*), Courtney Gains (*Children of the Corn*), and Bruce Davison (*Apt Pupil*). The film is currently under negotiations for a release. Also returning to the film is Caitlyn Fletcher who starred in *The Things They Left Behind*. Besides that, I'm currently residing in Los Angeles working on a few projects for several major studios and prepping my next feature film.

Peter Szabo – *Love Never Dies*

Since 2015, I've written and directed another psychological-drama short called LIGHT AND SILENCE. I also produced a feature-length sci-fi/action film called DEFECTIVE, sold around the world and available on iTunes, Google Play, and Amazon Prime. Am currently working on a script for a short that's adapted from a script I wrote that I'd like to be my feature directorial debut. To be honest, making a Dollar Baby hasn't helped my career at all, mostly because I can't promote the film anywhere except at festivals, which have long since run their course. It looks good on the résumé and I had a blast making it, but without wide, public exposure, it basically sits on a shelf collecting dust.

Tony Pomfret – *Night Surf*
I went back into education, got my MA and now I'm teaching film and media rather than shaking the foundations of the film industry.

Patrick Abernethy – *Rest Stop*
We placed our Dollar Baby film "*Rest Stop*" into a few festivals since it's completion, but no awards were won. As for me, I haven't directed any other short films, but have been writing several and hope to begin filming on one of them very soon. I've mostly been focusing on my professional life since our DB film, making sure that the bills are paid, but the next film project is definitely on the short list of things I want to accomplish soon. *Rest Stop* was my first attempt at directing and was a great experience from start to finish. I hope that anyone who even slightly considers making one, or being a part of one, decides to do it! It's definitely worth it, and it's fun to know that the man himself, Stephen King, has seen something that you worked on. That's a pretty awesome deal!

Vanessa Ionta Wright – *Rainy Season*
Rainy Season was shot in August of 2016 and premiered to a sold out, private audience in March 2017. The film had a successful run on the festival circuit, screening at over 40 festivals and earning multiple awards. Since the film, I have gone on to co-found and run the Women in Horror Film Festival (www.WIHFF.com) and I was asked by Jen & Sylvia Soska (American Mary, Rabid) to direct a PSA for the 2018 Women in Horror Month Massive Blood Drive. I have also embarked upon my first film project outside of the horror genre, venturing into western territory with a proof of concept called *Goldentooth*. It is the origin story of a central character in the feature I am co-writing and directing called *The Badge, The Gun & The Hangman's Noose*.

Robert Cochrane – *Luckey Quarter*
Since making *Luckey Quarter*, Robert made the award-winning Roland Meets Brown short adaptation from *The Gunslinger* for Simon & Schuster's American Gunslinger Contest. Robert got to share the film with King personally at the publisher's office in Manhattan. They talked about many things, including meeting up for a game at Fenway as part of Robert's award-winning documentary film, *Boys of Summer*. Unfortunately, their schedules didn't align. King was nice enough to send autographed copies of all of the *Gunslinger* books, which Robert treasures. Robert has made

five more feature-length documentaries since that time, including this summer's *Boys of Summer: Short Stop*, the third film in that series. For more on that project, please visit www.bosmovie.com. He is currently pursuing his PhD in Kinesiology, studying the effect of improvisation on Parkinson's disease.

Maciej Barczewski – *My Pretty Pony*

In post production for my feature debut '*The Champion*', which is supposed to be in cinemas in October 2020.

Jay Holben – *Paranoid: A Chant*

In the 20 years since the release of *Paranoid*, Holben has maintained a consistent and active career in the motion picture industry. Until 2008, he was primarily working as a director of photography and a producer on feature films, commercials, music videos, documentary and television projects.

As a cinematographer he was involved with visual effects photography on Steven Spielberg's *Minority Report* and for director Mike Mitchell's holiday comedy *Surviving Christmas*, in addition to dozens of other projects as cinematographer including *Mothman* and *2 Million Stupid Women*—both of which he also produced. At the end of the first decade of the 2000s, Holben proverbially hung up the light meter and focused his career on producing and directing full time.

His films have screened globally to international acclaim including at the Cannes Film Festival and two of his short films, *The Night Before* (written by fellow Dollar Baby James Cole) and *Descent* are in the official Academy of Motion Picture Arts and Sciences film archives. His work is also included in three different anthology feature films *The Invoking 2*, *All Hallow's Eve 2* and *Strange Events*. He was the 2nd unit director and cinematographer on HBO's *Femme Fatales* and consultant on the first season of Showtime's *Dexter*. He was the supervising director on the gritty love story *Black Tar Road* and, recently, directed and produced the romantic drama *Before the Dawn*, which has received significant critical acclaim.

He is the creator, producer and director of *Filmmaker in a Box*, a unique, intensive, educational program on micro-budget filmmaking. In addition to his work in the production field, Holben has been a prolific technical journalist on the side and has been an active contributing editor to *American Cinematographer* magazine since 1997 with more than 300 published articles to date. He was also a technical editor for *Digital Video* and a columnist for *TV Technology* magazines as well as a contributor to the *Hollywood Reporter*, *Government Video* and *Geek* magazines. He is the author of two books on cinematography, *A Shot in the Dark: A Creative DIY Guide to Digital Video Lighting on (Almost) No Budget* and *Behind the Lens: Dispatches from the Cinematographic Trenches*.

Most recently, tapped for his expansive technical expertise and journalistic skills, Holben was hired by Lucasfilm to document the groundbreaking technology of *Star Wars: The Mandalorian* Disney+ series and he spent four months entrenched with the production to cover the state-of-the-art technology for an extensive internal white paper that will help inform future productions on the abilities, limitations and evolution of Industrial Light and Magic's (ILM) Stagecraft system. He is also an international lecturer who has traveled around the globe teaching master classes on filmmaking and cinematography including a faculty position with the Global Cinematography Institute, a program started by the late Academy Award-winning cinematographer Vilmos Zsigmond, ASC. In 2017 Holben became an associate member of the American Society of Cinematographers and he chairs two committees, and sits on several others, for the ASC's Motion Imaging Technology Council.

Rob Darren Newberger – *Mute*

In 2009, I was Asst Director in legend Ted V Mikels *Astro Zombies:M3 Cloned* and made *White Paint* (feature killer clown film) Stephen King's *Mute* Dollar Baby. Wrote a screenplay Keep Them Laughing, a Laurel and Hardy buddie cross country feature. Creative Artists Agency has accepted it which is rare. I know Tom Shadyac's people which they referred me Shadyac imdb Google him Have done small roles and extra stuff in *Evan Almighty, John Adams* and *Iron Man 3*. The story behind *White Paint* is interesting. The actor that played the clown committed suicide and other interesting stuff, i.e. Tony Curtis was suppose to play a psychic in a WP scene and passed two weeks before filming. Beverly Washburn played the role. She starred in *Spider Baby, Old Yeller*, etc., *Greatest Show on Earth*... also my Laurel and Hardy got endorsed by Stan Laurel's daughter. Good stuff!

Doveed Linder – *Strawberry Spring*

After my Dollar Baby, I became very involved with the sport of boxing and wrote the book "*Ringside: Interview with 24 Fighters and Boxing Insiders.*" I am currently in post-production on a sci-fi feature called "*The Box*" and am in pre-production on another feature.

Places Dollar Babies Filmed

States:

- California
- Colorado
- Oregon
- Texas
- Massachusetts
- Ohio
- Nevada
- Missouri
- South Dakota
- Kentucky
- Tennessee
- Maine
- Pennsylvania
- North Carolina
- South Carolina
- Illinois
- New York
- New Jersey
- Oklahoma
- Arizona
- Indiana
- West Virginia
- Georgia

Countries:

- Russia
- Germany
- France.
- Worcestershire
- Poland
- Austria
- United Kingdom
- Toronto Ontario Canada
- Netherlands
- New South Wales, Australia
- British Columbia
- Nova Scotia

Stephen King Dollar Baby Films Available to Film

Titles currently available for adaptation:

"Morning Deliveries" (Milkman #1)
"All That You Love Will Be Carried Away"
"Mute"
"Beachworld"
"Nona"
"Big Wheels: A Tale of the Laundry Game" (Milkman #2)
"One for the Road"
"Cain Rose Up"
"Rainy Season"
"Dedication"
"The Reach"
"The Doctor's Case"
"Stationary Bike"
"Graduation Afternoon"
"That Feeling, You Can Only Say What It Is In French"
"In the Deathroom"
"Uncle Otto's Truck"
"L.T.'s Theory of Pets"
"Willa"
"The Last Rung on the Ladder"
"The Woman in the Room"
"Luckey Quarter"
"The Man Who Loved Flowers"
"The Man Who Would Not Shake Hands"

"CUT! That's a Wrap!"

Dollar Babies Final Thoughts on the Dollar Baby program and Stephen King

J.P. Scott – *Everything's Eventual*

It is a really cool thing to be an A list writer and allow a program like this to exist that encourages young creatives to do what they love. I hope that King has made plans to keep this tradition alive even after he, to use his words, gets to the clearing at the end of the path. I hope that day is far ahead as I'm sure he does. I do hope that he knows that he has not only had a big impact on his readers but also a massive impact on every Dollar Baby filmmaker. He certainly has on me. Getting the opportunity to even attempt my dream and make my passion a profession is more than what many get a chance to do. I count myself lucky and will always remember *Everything's Eventual* and Stephen King's Dollar Babies. And, I think that is what King wanted. To encourage young and passionate creatives to do something that will drive them to bring to fruition their dreams and ambitions.

Nicole Jones-Dion – *In The Deathroom*

It's unprecedented for an author of Mr. King's stature to share his work with other artists. I love his "pay-it-forward" attitude to help the next generation of aspiring filmmakers. I plan to continue his spirit of giving by helping others who are coming up behind me to reach their goals as well.

Jon Mann – *Popsy*

Stephen King is my literary hero. I believe he will go down in history as the American writer with the most emotional range across his body of work. It's unbelievable that stories like *The Girl Who Loved Tom Gordon* and *Shawshank* came from the same imagination that gave us *It* and *Carrie*. People always talk about how 'prolific' he is, which is a word that is thrown around a lot in art. He's an absolute workhorse. I've always looked up to Mr. King's work ethic. I am sure that he would probably bring that all back to his love for the craft and his passion for literature and the paranormal—which is equally as inspiring.

Jennifer Trudrung – *Here There Be Tygers*

I feel that the Dollar Baby program is such a gift. We creatives normally feel so disconnected from our heroes. It can feel like they live on another plane and to be able to have the freedom to mold and work with our hero's story and to have his name attached to our project is huge. Stephen King has so heavily influenced my imagination and world and I have great respect for him and his voice.

Joe Kowalski – *I Am The Doorway*

I think one reason we all love Stephen King so much is that he puts himself entirely out there. I can't tell you how many ideas I never flesh out into writing simply because I fear that I'm going to make something bad by the end of it. Yet Stephen King doesn't let that fear stop him. He seems so open to any idea and concept. Yes, sometimes the end result is mediocre. Other times it's a story that will last for generations. Either way, he moves on to the next story and the next story after that. It's fearlessly forward-thinking, and it's something I strive to learn from.

A.J. Gribble – *Cain Rose Up*

The Dollar Baby program is the best thing for any young filmmakers or just filmmakers in general! They have the chance to adapt a King story and possibly get a career started because of it. I believe that it is so nice of Stephen King to do that for us. And if I ever get the chance to meet him, I would just like to say thank you.

Vanessa Ionta-Wright – *Rainy Season*

I think one of the great aspects of this program is that it allows aspiring and student filmmakers who have not yet established themselves in the industry, to start their careers with an established piece of material to breath life into. Even though King, himself, isn't directly involved in the productions, just having his name on the film gives instant credit to the project, which can really help elevate a new filmmaker's career. I had a lot of people from my community and the community we shot the film in, offering services and resources simply because they wanted to be attached to a King related film. For a first time filmmaker, this is invaluable. The fact that King releases his work to the general public to help aid in an artist's career, speaks volumes about his character and the type of man he is. He is constantly giving back and creating opportunities, which is inspiring. I appreciate his work, as a constant reader, and I appreciate his place in this community and very grateful to him.

"CUT! That's a Wrap!" (Part 2)
My Final Thoughts on the Dollar Babies and Stephen King

IT'S HARD TO BELIEVE that over forty years of Stephen King fandom would lead me to this point. From reading the books, watching the films, fan pages, film fests, interviews, reviews, and now this: a book. If someone told me forty years ago I would be writing a book about Dollar Babies I would've lost that bet. But here we are. I feel… complete… somehow. I feel that feeling one gets after a long journey comes to an end, but it's not the end… it's only the beginning. As long as Stephen King has ideas in his head and stories to tell (and I'm sure there's a secret vault somewhere packed full of stories just ready to be shared with the world at the right moment), there will be Dollar Babies to make.

As I've been a part of the Dollar Baby community for eight years, I have gotten to know these amazing, talented, and beautiful people. They are some of the most wonderful and interesting people I have ever met in my life. The Dollar Baby program is like the golden ticket and once you get to go inside the chocolate factory, you experience a world unlike any other. A world full of filmmaking only a true lover of film can understand. I sometimes wonder what that first feeling was like for these filmmakers the very first time they got inspired by Stephen King and grabbed their camera to bring their vision of his stories to life? Independent filmmakers and directors of short stories don't have the big budgets, the studios suits to front the money, nor the expensive equipment to make a film you'd see at your local matinee theater.

What they DO have is passion, determination, vision, excitement, respect, and the love for the written word. Some of these filmmakers went on to great things, others it was their fifteen minutes of fame, but that doesn't matter. What matters is, they became part of Stephen King history. They became part of the Stephen King Universe that very few and privileged people get to see and experience. I have been extremely lucky to be a part of that experience. I never will forget this journey that I have been on for eight years.

The beautiful and wonderful thing about the Dollar Babies is that these talented individuals did something very few people do: they took a chance. They took their dream and made it happen. All it took was a vision, a dream, a dollar, and a signed contract, and they grabbed their camera and were on their way to making Stephen King history. Stephen King himself came from nothing and looked at him today. I have been a dreamer my whole life. I read books and watched movies and hoped that one day I would make something that would bring interest and joy to those who are just as passionate as I am. I am a perfect example of dreams coming true because I never would've guessed in a million years I would have written a book, let alone about someone I admire, respect, and find inspiring like Stephen King. The Dollar Baby program has been around for over forty years and as long as there are Stephen King stories to tell, there will be Dollar Babies to make. I don't know where any of us will be forty years from now, but what I do hope is that someone, somewhere will find this book as fun, entertaining, educational, and inspiring as I did writing it. And maybe, just maybe, someone will have a dream too and grabs a camera or a typewriter and makes their dream come true too. I wrote this book as a fan for fans. It is a love letter to the Dollar Babies. A Thank You letter for eight years of writing, trust, and friendship.

Gordie LaChance in Stephen King's "*The Body*" once said: 'Friends come in and out of your life like busboys in a restaurant.' Those are the most true and honest words Stephen King has ever written. But the Dollar Babies aren't busboys in a restaurant… they're family. And that, my friends, is worth a whole lot more than… a dollar.

Dollar Baby Treasures

OVER THE 8 YEARS of doing Dollar Baby interviews, friendships develop and in that development Dollar Babies are very generous. Generous in the sense that I have received "Thank You" collectible gifts such as, signed posters, 8 x 10 glossy pictures, postcards, buttons, stickers, T – shirts, DVD's, CD's, books, and more! However, the most interesting collectible gifts I received are these two seen here: A signed sword used as the murder weapon prop used in the James Douglas Dollar Baby film, *The Doctor's Case* and a Security Guard shirt used in Jon Leo's Dollar Baby film, *Popsy*.

Dollar Baby Props Collectible Gifts.

Acknowledgements

WITH SO MANY YEARS involved in compiling everything it took to complete this book, suddenly this long journey has come to an end. I used to think if there'd even come a day when I'd get a book published, who would I thank for helping to make this possible? It's not as easy as I thought, as there are so many dear family members, and friends. However, I do know that it took more than a dream to get me here, and several very good people.

First, I'd like to thank the most important person in my life, my wife, Gena. Words can not even begin to express my love and gratitude. You have been my constant companion and best friend, movie partner, therapist, my biggest fan, the one I've had to bounce all my ideas off of first, and the love of my life. You are the light in my life each and every day. I love you, my baby doll.

I guess I'd have to say, I inherited kids, two great people who I truly love. That being said, I'd like to thank my son, Dustin. You accepted me into the family, and into your life. Although we are only a few years apart in age, over the years we've created our own bond, and that means a lot. I am very proud of all that you are, and all that you do.

To my daughter, Jessyka, who has always been my girl. You are beautiful, strong, kind and loving. You are a great mother, and I thank you for always supporting me, and calling me "Pops". I love you Jess.

Thank you to my son in-law, Ralph, daughter in-law, Elisha, and all the grandkids. My granddaughters: Sicily (and her son, my great grandson Niko), Sophya, Saydhe, and Kendyl. As well as my newest grandkids, from Dustin and Elisha's blended family, Domonique (and her baby daughter Amelia, my newest great grandgirl), Domonick, and Adam, my uber smart grandsons. Having all of you to love makes me happy, and your positive support along the way kept me going.

To my brother in-law Mark, and all three of his boys (Christopher, Markus and Nicholas), my nephews, thank you for always having confidence in the fact that you believed I would be published someday. Love you guys!

To my sister in-law Crystal, and her two children, Bryanna and Keenan (my niece and nephew), thank you for believing in me, and supporting me along the way. Love you all.

Thank you to my son in-law, Ralph, daughter in-law, Elisha, and all the grandkids. My granddaughters: Sicily (and her son, my great grandson Niko), Sophya, Saydhe, and Kendyl. As well as my newest grandkids, from Dustin and Elisha's blended family, Domonique (and her baby daughter Amelia, my newest great grandgirl), Domonick, and Adam, my uber smart grandsons. Having all of you to love makes me happy, and your positive support along the way kept me going. I'd like to acknowledge my mother, Karen. Thank you for giving me the knowledge and passion to appreciate the written word, film, and music. I know it wasn't always easy bringing Julia and I up, being a single parent, but I am happy I learned all that you could teach me. I love you both, and my niece Hannah as well. There are a few people whom I have loved dearly, and have lost along the path of my life. They always believed that I would someday be published. Firstly, thank you, Anthony W. Northrup Sr. (my beloved father), who I miss, and I know would be very proud of me, I love you dad. Second, my father in law, whom I always called 'Papa'. He became the dad I never had. He was such an avid reader of Stephen King, and loved all the books as much as I did. Not a day goes by that I don't miss him. He was truly a 'gunslinger'. Next, my mother in law, Trudy, who passed in 2018. I love you Nanza, and I know you were happy I was writing this book. I always remember when you would call Gena, and at the end of the conversation you'd tell her, 'give Tony a kick 'n' a hug'. My beloved sister in law, Judy, she was my true friend as well, and she would always encourage me with my writing, even way back when. Love you Judy, and miss you always. Lastly, a dear lady, who always supported me from the minute she read one of my very very early short stories, many years ago, and made me feel like a million bucks. Thank you Barbara Morgan, your belief in me has truly boosted me to this place I am today. I truly wish all these people were here with me still. All were family members in some capacity, and I love and miss them all.

I want to thank my brother in arms, and best friend, Stephen Spignesi. You are not just a great friend, but my mentor as well.

I want to thank my publisher Ben Ohmart, at BearManor Media, as well as the editors at BMM. A big thank you to a truly great friend, Paul Michael Kane, for his graphic art, cover, and promoting, especially for helping me compile this book (to get off to the publisher). Lastly, Andrew J. Rausch, without you this project wouldn't have been possible.

I want to thank all of the Dollar Baby filmmakers for trusting me, welcoming me into the DB community, and working with me for the past eight years. Your talents, visions, and support go above and beyond. I love you all.

Dollar Babies: James B. Cox, Dean Werner, Maria Ivanova, Rodney Altman, Damon Vinyard, Jay Holben, Ranjeet S. Marwa, James Cole, James Gonis, Pablo Macho Maysonet IV, Robert Cochrane, Doveed Linder, Jeff Schiro, Frank Darabont, Mando Franco, James Renner, J.P. Scott, Tony Pomfret, Patrick Abernethy, Drew Newman, Corey Norman, Shawn S. Lealos, Peter Szabo, Justin Zimmerman, Max Heesch, Warren Ray, Dave Brock, Jacob Sanders, Joe Kowalski, Vanessa Ionta Wright, James Douglas, Selina Sondermann, Stephen Tramontana, Jackie Perez, Bryan Higby, Jennifer Trudrung, A.J. Gribble, Jon Mann, Dan Sellers, Hendrik Harms, Mark Zimmerman, Brian Johnson, Nicole Jones-Dion, Marie D. Jones, Rob Darren Newberger, Joseph Horning, Mark Hensley, Maciej Barczewski, Nick Smith, Will Roberts, Red Clark, Jenny Janvszewski, Patrick Haischberger, Gino Alfonso, Nathan Gathergood. Thank you all for allowing me the great opportunity to view, review your films, and then interview all of you. It's been my pleasure.

Then there's Billy Hanson. Billy you gave me my start in the Dollar Baby community, lent a hand by allowing me to feature your film when I was hosting my two Dollar Baby film fests, and have been a great friend and supporter… THANK YOU!

I'd like to thank all of those who have contributed to the Dollar Baby book: Stephen Spignesi, Andrew J. Rausch, Billy Hanson, Richard Chizmar, Mick Garris, Tommy McLoughlin, David Tocher, Brooklyn Ann, Tina Rooker, Karen Steinley Beaudrie, Amber Pace, Glenn Chadbourne, Monica Wooddall, James Cole, James Douglas, Nicole Jones-Dion, Jay Holben, Lee Gambin, Hans von Wirth, Frank Lewis, Kevin Quigley, Bryan Higby, Will Roberts, Tifaine L. Lafrance, Oscar Garrido, Robin Furth, Tina Navarro, Peter Holland, Curt Destler, LaWanda Odom, Tonya Ivey, Greg Buchner, Nick Kaufman, Nathan Monsour, Sara Kinney, Terri Nielsen, Amy Baker, and Hans-Ake Lilja, and Gena Lawson-Northrup.

Thank you to some very close friends, who have been supporters, have encouraged me along the way, and who inspired me as well: John Callas, Michael Part, Gabrielle Stone, Adrienne King, Joe Quintanilla, Beverly Randolph, Linnea Quigley, Dave Hinchberger, Adam Marcus, Rutanya Alda, Mark Dawidziak, Corey Dee Williams, Carol Holm, Joe Skeen, Myrna Marsh Lohrmann, Sarah French, Joe Knetter, Giulio de Gaetano: Through the Black Hole web page, Laura Tykowski, Truman Ness and Ness Press, the Tri County Sun newspaper, Davide Melini, Don Hinrichs, Kendra Frazier, Bernd Lautenslager, and Klaus Spangenmacher.

I want to give a shout out to all the staff and crew of the Crypticon Horror Con in Minneapolis, Minnesota, especially Nick Kaufman, for letting me host two Dollar Baby film fests there. Thanks guys! I would like to give a special shout out to my ATK moderator, Stephen Spignesi, co-administrators, Amber Pace, Gena Lawson-Northrup, and lead co-ad Hans von Wirth, thanks guys. However, to all my members at my Facebook Stephen King fan page, All Things King, you guys rock! You are all amazing, and great supporters. I love you all!

Thank you to everyone who purchased this book. I hope you have enjoyed reading it as much as I enjoyed writing it. Your support means the world to me. I appreciate it sincerely.

I also thank God, for giving me the gift of gab, the enthusiasm for being such an avid reader, and the great company of very talented people of all walks in life.

Lastly, but certainly not least, I'd like to thank the man who inspired me, and many, Stephen King. You came into my life through books and film, your stories entertained and scared me. If it weren't for your masterful storytelling, none of this would be possible. I thank you for creating the Dollar Baby Program. Thank you Sai King for making a huge difference in my life. Long Days Pleasant Nights, to you, and all constant readers.

Special Dedications

This is a very special dedication to my mother in-law, Trudy "Nanza" & Bob "Papa". They were great supporters to my writing and the parents I never had. I miss them dearly. Love you both.

This is a special dedication to author Stephen Spignesi's mother, Lee Mandato Spignesi. She enjoyed reading my articles and was a great supporter. Her son, Stephen read to her and it made me so honored and proud when I first saw Lee holding one of my articles from our local newspaper, the Tri County Sun. This picture's is from March 3, 2020. Sadly, Lee passed away in 2020. You will be missed.

www.ingramcontent.com/pod-product-compliance
Lightning Source LLC
Chambersburg PA
CBHW051531230426
43669CB00015B/2569